TOBRUK
1942

TOBRUK
1942

ROMMEL AND THE BATTLES LEADING TO HIS GREATEST VICTORY

DAVID MITCHELHILL-GREEN

Cover illustrations courtesy of The National Archives and Records
Administration, United States

First published 2016
This paperback edition first published 2022

The History Press
97 St George's Place, Cheltenham,
Gloucestershire, GL50 3QB
www.thehistorypress.co.uk

British Library Cataloguing in Publication Data.
A catalogue record for this book is available from the British Library.

ISBN 978 0 7509 9892 5

Typesetting and origination by The History Press
Printed and bound in Great Britain by TJ Books Limited, Padstow, Cornwall.

Trees for LYfe

Contents

With banded backs against the wall,
Fiercely stand, or fighting fall.

The Siege of Corinth, Lord Byron, 1816

★★★

Millions of tongues record thee, and anew
Their children's lips shall echo them, and say –
'Here, where the sword united nations drew,
Our countrymen were warring on that day!'
And this is much, and all which will not pass away.

Childe Harold's Pilgrimage, Lord Byron, 1818

Acknowledgements

Work on this book has spanned several years. Many veterans, their families and relatives generously offered me a host of materials during the early stages of my research. I would like to thank (in no particular order): Richard Weston, Peter Rymer, May Green, Eric Watts, Dorothy Gibbs, A.R. Duckworth, Jack Holdsworth, Bert Thwaites, Bill Harvey, Harold E. Gibbs, Joy Ogley, Gloria Tonta, Rob Sangster, Jack Caple, Joyce and Ken James, Lloyd Tan, Betty Smith, Clare H. Walker, Roy Jardine, Olga Henwood, Margaret Donaghy, Ross Scholes, Dulcie Bowditch, Noel Shaw, Jack Caple, G.J. Tyler, Kerry Duce, John Best, T.H. Anderson, F.M. Paget, Meryll Williams, Joan Mawson, Jim Tattersall, Keith G. Secombe, Sylvia Sutcliffe, Joe Madeley, Gordon Hughes, A.C. Fletcher, M.D. Burles, Sue Lasky, H. Wilson, L.L. Barton, J.H. Flak, Janice Auburn and Murray Welton, Heinz Kilanowski, Rolf Werner Volker, Kurt Sawall, and Heinz Becker.

My heartfelt appreciation is also extended to Professor Mesut Uyar who kindly provided materials relating to the first battles for Tobruk from the Turkish perspective; to Carrie White-Parrish for critiquing the manuscript; and to Michael Leventhal and Chrissy McMorris for their enthusiasm in bringing this project to life. Errors of omission, fact or judgement are mine alone.

Finally, I would also like to acknowledge my family's long-standing support and understanding. Thank you Jennifer, Harvey and Hana.

Abbreviations

ADC	*Aide-de-Camp*
AIF	Australian Imperial Force
AWM	Australian War Memorial
BBC	British Broadcasting Corporation
BEF	British Expeditionary Force
CIGS	Chief of the Imperial General Staff
CRA	Commander of the Royal Artillery
DAK	*Deutsches Afrikakorps* (German Africa Corps)
Div	Division
GHQ	General Headquarters
GOC	General Officer Commanding
HQ	Headquarters
OKW	*Oberkommando der Wehrmacht* (High Command of the German Armed Forces)
RA	Royal Artillery
RAF	Royal Air Force
RAN	Royal Australian Navy
RASC	Royal Army Service Corps
RHA	Royal Horse Artillery
RN	Royal Navy
RTR	Royal Tank Regiment

RVNR Royal Volunteer Naval Reserve
SAAF South African Air Force
SAI   South African Infantry

Preface

Modern European interest in North Africa began with Napoleon's ill-fated expedition to Egypt in 1798. It marked the beginning of an imperial crusade that would continue over the next 150 years. France's next move was to seize Algiers in 1830. Tunisia and southern Morocco subsequently became French protectorates in 1881 and 1912 respectively. Britain followed suite, assuming control of the Suez Canal in 1875 and occupying Egypt in 1882. The Spanish occupied the Moroccan Atlantic coast (Ifni) in 1860, the Western Sahara in 1884 and northern Morocco in 1912. Our story begins around this period when Italy entered Libya. It continues on to the Italian invasion of Egypt in 1940 and the subsequent battles for control of the Middle East in the course of the world's bloodiest war in history.

Benito Mussolini's march on Egypt endangered the security of the Suez Canal and the Middle East oilfields fuelling Britain's war effort. The ensuing war in North Africa evolved in an uncharacteristic way. Arid swatches of empty desert offered no opportunity for terrain-related defence. Instead they became an ocean for Europe's mechanised armies to manoeuvre across. In naval-like engagements, a position could change rapidly, stagnation spelt danger;[1] lonely coastal ports along the northern Mediterranean became indispensable supply points. In the pages that follow, we will examine why the remote Libyan fortress and harbour town of Tobruk holds a special place in the history of the Second World War – how it became a focal point in the Desert War, the objective of Axis and Allied offensives and a battleground that has since become the stuff of legend.

First occupied by the Italians in 1911, Tobruk was over-run by the British after a brief siege in January 1941. Soon afterwards in April 1941, a mixed British Commonwealth force was forced to retire into Tobruk in the face of an Axis advance led by the daring German commander, General Erwin Rommel, who had arrived in Libya to buttress the flagging Italians. The ensuing 9-month siege – the longest in British military history after the eighteenth-century invest-ment of Gibraltar by France and Spain – catapulted Tobruk from obscurity to headlines around the world, a *cause célèbre*. It was, like the Battle of Britain, a bright note for the Allies in the aftermath of a string of defeats across Western Europe by Hitler's *Wehrmacht* and the Dunkirk evacuation. It was also the albatross that thwarted Rommel's unauthorised and auda-cious plan to seize Cairo.

In June 1942, Rommel again pressed forward and threat-ened Tobruk. However, many of the players in this desert drama had changed over the preceding months, as had the stage. Tobruk bore little resemblance to the bastion it was during the height of the second siege of 1941. Nevertheless, its reputation from that period remained – influencing the fateful decision to hold it again, despite a directive at the beginning of 1942 that forbade another siege. The upshot of this decision led to one of the worst British defeats of the war, the repercus-sions of which were felt around the globe.

In examining the Desert War I have long been intrigued by how the British defenders of Tobruk were able to stave off all attacks by Rommel's Italo-German forces during the entire year of 1941, when they succumbed to his forces in just 24 hours a year later. Could such a comparison be made? In 1944 Lieutenant General Sir John Lavarack panned an official British government publication, *The Eighth Army*, for following up the 'old policy of belittling the early operations for the defence of Cyrenaica in April, 1941, in an endeavour to gloss over the failure of 1942'.[2] According to the publication, 'No comparison can be justly be made between holding Tobruk then and losing it now,'[3] a statement Lavarack slammed as 'incorrect and unfair'. Former South African Brigadier E.P. Hartshorn later dismissed the idea of a comparative investigation as 'ludicrous'.[4] Perhaps Hartshorn was influenced by the unfortunate defeat suffered by the largely South African garrison in 1942, a sore point in South Africa that is now largely forgotten.[5] Yet by directly comparing and contrasting the individual battles for Tobruk today, I trust we can better understand its strategic and political prominence, as well as the myriad of intertwining factors that culminated in its surrender – Rommel's greatest conquest.

★★★

A few notes on vocabulary and geography: Although it may be offensive to some today, the term 'British' will be used in its contemporary context to denote Commonwealth and Empire troops – who actually outnumbered the British for much of the North African Campaign – drawn from the Antipodes, India and South Africa. Specific formations have been identified by their country of origin.

For the purpose of this book, the exact geographical meaning of North Africa will coincide with present-day Morocco, Algeria, Tunisia, Libya and Egypt. During the war, Tobruk was spelt in several ways, including Marsa Tobruk, Tobruq and the Italian form *Tobruch*. In terms of pronunciation, the Italians stressed the first syllable, the British the last. I will use the word 'Tobruk'. Inconsistencies in spelling and grammar have been retained in quotations. In keeping with the period, imperial measurements will be used.

David Mitchelhill-Green, 2022

1

'Supremacy of the Mediterranean'

'Rivers of blood were poured out over miserable strips of land which, in normal times, not even the poorest Arab would have bothered his head about.'

– Erwin Rommel

War is no stranger to the ancient Libyan landscape. Over millennia, the arid expanse that became Libya – a name bestowed by Italy in 1934 – was passed in bloody combat from the Greeks to the Ptolemies to the Romans to the Arabs, and toward the end of the sixteenth century, to the Ottoman Turks. Centuries later in 1937, the German Military Attaché in London, General Baron Leo Geyr von Schweppenburg, a future tank commander in Adolf Hitler's Polish, French and Russian campaigns, inspected British troops stationed in Egypt. Thousands of years of conflict between the East and West over Mediterranean dominance had already taught two key lessons: firstly, that possession of the Nile Delta is crucial. Secondly, Egypt, which is shielded by the Western Desert, has been conquered from the east, from the sea, but never from the west.

Egypt's strategic significance, now, was obvious, particularly when escalating tension between London and Rome was the hottest topic in Middle East politics. Schweppenburg noted the dichotomy between the two nations preparing for a possible war – how the British were quietly undertaking defensive measures; how the Italians were doing exactly the opposite; and how no one could envisage that Germany would enter the threatening North African fray. It was clear the Italians would face enormous challenges should they invade Egypt. Schweppenburg was impressed with British preparations for combat along the Libyan frontier. He noted the simple desert compasses used for navigation across the featureless desert, a generous provision for hauling water and the importance placed on robust, wheeled transport. At the sea, he foresaw the Royal Navy mauling Italian supply lines across the Mediterranean. And, as Schweppenburg concluded, 'From the British point of view, the situation in Egypt must seem assured. *Any attack from the West would, at the very worst, be halted at the Nile.*'[1]

Tobruk: the Key to Mediterranean Supremacy

Most of the fighting in North Africa during the Second World War was centred around Libya, the fourth largest country on the African continent, and the backdrop to our story. From a historical perspective, Libya is divided into two provinces: Tripolitania in the west and Cyrenaica in the east, although the Germans and Italians referred to the area east of Gazala as 'Marmarica'. The capital, Tripoli, abuts the northern Mediterranean coastline. While the Middle East – in 1940, Libya, Egypt, Turkey, Syria, Lebanon, Palestine, Transjordan, Arabia, Iraq and Iran – is the meeting point of three continents, the Mediterranean is the intercontinental sea separating them. More than 970,000 square miles in area, the widest point of the sea between Europe to Africa is 850 miles; the narrowest is a mere 8 miles, across the Strait of Gibraltar at the western entrance to the Atlantic Ocean.

Tobruk has a long and colourful history as an important deepwater harbour and fortress on this sea. In ancient times, it flourished as an important Greek agricultural colony known as Antipyrgos – a haven for pilgrims travelling to the Egyptian Oasis of Siwa. The Roman Emperor Justinian later built a fort above the harbour, Antipyrgon, to guard the Cyrenaican frontier. Centuries later, the Saracens (or Muslims) built a castle on the north side of the harbour, known as Marsa Tobruk – the Bay of Tobruk. It later changed ownership when the Ottoman Turks took control to defend against any attack by warring states across the Mediterranean.

The importance of the port continued into the so-called modern world. In July 1798, a number of French corvettes, frigates, triple-deckers and transports from General Napoleon Bonaparte's fleet under Vice Admiral Francois-Paul Brueys d'Aigalliers sheltered in Tobruk's harbour, to escape British attention. They were en route to Egypt, and eventual defeat at the hands of Admiral Horatio Nelson in the Battle of the Nile.

Tobruk's strategic value began to soar during the late nineteenth century, when Europe's Great Powers began to look with interest at neighbouring Northern Africa. After visiting the harbour in 1883, the German explorer Georg Schweinfurth reported that Tobruk would assure no less than the 'supremacy of the Mediterranean'.[2] Heightened Italian sentiment in the months leading up to the Italo-Turkish war led one nationalist – foreshadowing what the Allies would come to realise and fight for in the Second World War – to protest that his homeland could never be free if Tobruk, 'the Bizerte of the eastern Mediterranean', remained occupied by another power.

An article published in a 1911 geographical journal reported how 'all visitors agree as to the excellent qualities of the harbour'. Italian interest was chronicled the same year in the *Encyclopaedia Britannica*, which foresaw Tobruk as a future 'man-of-war harbour'. The harbour's allure – the largest port between Ras el

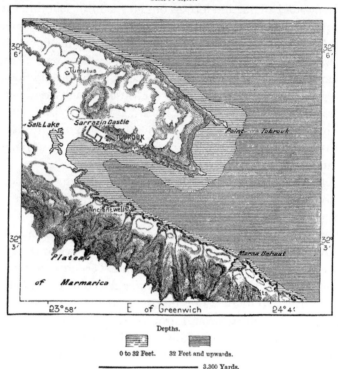

A nineteenth-century map of Tobruk. Note the Saracen castle, site of the future harbour city.

Tin, the British naval base near Alexandria in Egypt, and Tripoli – even encouraged Lord Kitchener to annex it for neighbouring Egypt, until that action was barred by the British Foreign Office.[3] Keenly eyed, it would not be long before Tobruk was more permanently seized by a European power.

The Rise of German and Italian Nationalism

'We do not intend to remain eternally as prisoners in the Mediterranean.'

– Mussolini, March 1939

Over the past 200 years, the map of continental Europe – and consequently much of the rest of the world – has changed dramatically as nations emerged, empires withered and territories passed from vanquished to victor. We turn now to the mid-nineteenth century to examine the events that preceded and precipitated the battles for Tobruk; in particular, the demise of the Ottoman Empire, the precarious European political climate of the late nineteenth and early twentieth century, Germany's jockeying for position, Italy's quest for power and prestige, and the various incidents that drew Europe irrevocably into the maelstrom of two world wars.

Germany and Italy: Birth of the Future Belligerents

For centuries, the Italian peninsula remained a fragmented collection of independent states. A final push for Italian unification began after the 1859 defeat of the Austrians by the French. State elections held in northern Italy were followed by the convening of a national parliament in March 1861 and the proclamation of the Kingdom of Italy under King Vittorio Emanuele II – a united Italy for the first time since the Roman Empire. The new government introduced three measures to unify the country: a national railroad system, a national education system and a national army to carry out its policies.

The first attempt to unify the German states analogously occurred in 1848, the most widespread revolutionary year in European history. Revolutionaries in the German states called for a national militia and parliament as well as a fairer taxation system and freedom of religion. By late 1848, however, the movement had dissolved. The next endeavour to unify Germany was undertaken through force by Prussia's prime minister, Otto von Bismarck – the so-called Iron Chancellor. The 1862 Danish War, the first war of German unification, was followed by the 1866 Austro-Prussian war, the second war of unification. Italy joined Bismarck in the seven weeks' campaign that annexed many southern states that had sided with Vienna. Having formed the North German Confederation in 1867, Bismarck's territorial ambitions were further realised after the defeat of Napoleon III in the Franco-Prussian war of 1870–71, the final act of unification.

Bismarck became the chancellor of a new German Empire, which he termed the Second German Reich, its 1,000-year predecessor having been destroyed by Napoleon in 1806. The Empire was proclaimed in the former French royal palace of Versailles – a site where victor and vanquished would again meet in 1919. It was here that William I of Prussia was crowned Kaiser, or emperor – the first Head of State of a united Germany. On top of their defeat, the French suffered further embarrassment in the Treaty of Frankfurt, which ceded territory and huge sums to the Germans in reparations. Within Germany, a new wave of Prussian militarism emerged

– a menace to Europe that receded only after the collapse of the Third Reich in May 1945.

Bismarck next turned his attention to establishing a series of alliances across Europe. Aimed at securing Germany's position, his manoeuvring fuelled a growing sense of rivalry and apprehension between the European powers. From the turn of the century until 1912, European politics would be dominated by nationalism and colonialism. This was a period when a country's international status – its power – was measured by the size of its foreign empire. Germany's imperialist taste, within this expansionist environment, was sated with new colonies spread across Africa, New Guinea, China and the Pacific.

Italy, too, was eager to assert itself on the world stage, although its late sitting at the imperialist table left few scraps in the 'scramble for Africa' worthy of consideration. Rome's African affair, however, would prove to be a costly undertaking that reached its zenith – and undoing – during the Second World War. The 17,000-man Italian expedition that seized present day Somalia and Eritrea was overwhelmed humiliatingly by Ethiopian fighters in March 1896, at the Battle of Adowa – one of the finest victories ever by an African army over a European power. In the wake of the disastrous massacre, Rome looked for a new colony, one closer to home. For many years prior to unification, Italian statesmen had eyed Ottoman-held North Africa with keen interest. Now tension arose between Constantinople, the Ottoman capital, and Rome, as the latter's expansionist aspirations became apparent.

Benito Mussolini

Italian sentiment at the time was divided. On the one hand, nationalists and newspapers were rousing the public's support for a new war to erase the painful memory of Adowa. Socialists and Republicans, on the other hand, were staunchly opposed to any conflict. Still, it seemed only a matter of time before Italy invaded Ottoman-held Libya.

Socialist and one-time schoolmaster Benito Mussolini was particularly hostile toward any Italian intervention in North Africa. 'Every honest Socialist must disapprove of this Libyan adventure. It means only useless and stupid bloodshed,' he avowed.[1] Born in northern Italy near Forli on 29 July 1883, Mussolini was the son of a blacksmith and part-time socialist journalist, and schoolteacher mother. Incensed by his country's military involvement in Libya, the future fascist leader/would-be empire builder was, paradoxically, arrested for attempting to block the passage of troop trains bound for Tripoli. Although he would one day order their mass subjugation, he boasted, in his youth, that he was on the side of the Libyans.

However, Libya was attractive to Italy. Despite the obvious historical ties and proximity to southern Europe, it was one of the few African territories not to have fallen under European rule. This was, in part, due to its limited strategic and economic value (oil would not be discovered until after 1945), and also because it remained part of the sickly Ottoman Empire. With neighbouring Tunisia already under French control, and Egypt, Malta and Cyprus under British occupation, Libya could provide Italy with a 'fourth shore' on which to underpin strategic security in the Mediterranean.[2] It would offer emigration and economic benefits and, if managed properly, once again become a food bowl for Rome.

In Germany, an anxious Kaiser William II monitored events closely. He pondered whether Italian expansion into Libya would lead to new unrest in the Balkans. Would it push the British to occupy Arabia? Or would it trigger another European war?

Anxiety intensified in Rome that another European power might occupy Tripoli (especially after a dispute between Germany and France in July 1911, when a German gunboat arrived at the Moroccan port of Agadir, which France had already claimed) or Tobruk. Eventually, after years of hesitation, Italy staged a confrontation with Turkey. An ultimatum was issued on 28 September 1911 to the Ottoman Grand Vizier Hakkı Pasha, calling for the occupation of the Libyan provinces of Cyrenaica and Tripolitania. Having read the document, Pasha is said to have exclaimed, '*C'est donc la guerre!*' Snubbing the Turkish response, Italy's Prime Minister Giovanni Giolitti declared war.

The Italo-Turkish War

Reports in the Italian press suggested an Arab population indifferent to, or even anticipating, a new occupation. Giolitti's government had taken no stock for possible Ottoman resistance. The kingdom's military confidently predicted a short campaign, little more than a 'military promenade'; a 'walk in the park' among a populace waiting with open arms. The Italian General Staff even felt that the seizure of key ports would be enough to drive the Turks to the bargaining table.

The Italian expeditionary force comprised 34,000 men, 6,300 horses and mules, 1,050 wagons, forty-eight field guns and twenty-four mountain guns. For the first time, aircraft and airships – the latest weaponry – would be used in combat. Rome bullishly anticipated that the 7,000-man Turkish garrison would crumble, while the indigenous population would rush to greet the invaders as liberators, ending centuries of oppressive Ottoman rule. Following two days of naval bombardment, Italian marines stormed the Libyan capital of Tripoli on 5 October 1911. The landing, however, was endangered by the hasty diversion of a large Italian naval force, comprising six battleships, destroyers and torpedo boats to support operations at another priority target: Tobruk.

Vice Admiral Augusto Aubry's substantial fleet entered Tobruk's harbour on 4 October, and the Italian flagship *Vittorio*

Emanuele opened fire at close range, forcing the recalcitrant Turkish commander to surrender. A landing party of 400 men swiftly occupied the town, reinforced by an Italian expeditionary corps the next day.[3] Overwhelmed, the small Ottoman defending force – an infantry company lacking heavy arms – withdrew south, while the Italians, now at a regimental level, secured the town and surrounding desert on 5 November 1911. The Italian press rejoiced over the victory. Yet London's *The Times* questioned 'of what practical utility Marsa Tobruk will be to Italy, even if it is eventually converted into a naval base and adequately defended'. According to *The Times*, the 'Italian Navy must either use Marsa Tobruk in war or not use it. If it is not used it is only an unprofitable expense'.[4] It was an astute observation; Rome would pour enormous resources into turning the port into a fortress, though as we will learn, for only a modest return.

Tripoli, Benghazi and Derna also succumbed to the Italian expeditionary force while opposition grew the further the invaders pushed inland from the beachheads. The ranks of the retreating Turks quickly began to swell with thousands of Sanusi and Berber volunteers opposed to the 'liberating' infidels. The Turks issued modern rifles and schooled them in digging trenches and using grenades. Rome, consequently, now faced the prospect of a lengthy guerrilla conflict in the poorly mapped Libyan interior – a harsh desert environment without water or the infrastructure needed to transport and support the substantial body of men and horses required to overwhelm the resistance.

The Italians, however, held the upper hand in terms of heavy artillery, 100,000 troops, mechanised transport and the earliest military aircraft. History was made when the Italian 1st Aeroplane Flotilla conducted a pioneering aerial reconnaissance and bombing raid, using hand grenades. Civilian pilots, keen to join the new war, also flew their primitive craft from Italy to the new airstrips at Derna and Tobruk. According to a 1914 Italian account of the conflict: 'The dropping of bombs, while they did no material damage, had a wonderful moral effect. Our troops were the first in the world to use this method of offense.'[5]

Notwithstanding their superiority in men and firepower, the Italians did little more than slowly extend the fortified perimeters of their Libyan coastal positions. Caught in a deadlock, Italy had misjudged the enemy's capabilities, and thrust an unsuited conscript army into a protracted desert war. It was a situation not unlike Mussolini's forthcoming Egyptian campaign.

The First Battle of Tobruk

On the Turkish side, one officer who rushed to join the fighting in Libya was Ismail Enver Bey (later Enver Pasha). A member of the Young Turks (the name given to a band of Turkish army officers who started a nationalist reform party, seized power from Sultan Abdul Hamid II and ruled the Ottoman Empire from 1908 until the end of the First World War), Pasha left his post as Turkish military attaché in Berlin to lead the resistance around Benghazi. As a *Kolagasi* (a rank between captain and major), Pasha assumed command of the Tobruk region on 20 November 1911.

Another Turkish officer and Young Turk who hurried to Libya was 30-year-old Mustafa Kemal – a man destined to become one of the great leaders of the twentieth century. Arriving in neutral Egypt in civilian guise, Kemal helped recruit native Sanusi Arab volunteers to join the Islamic Holy War, or *Jihad*, in Libya. Dressed in Arab dress, he then crossed into Cyrenaica, where he joined the small Turkish force encamped west of Tobruk. Kemal soon discovered that the Italians had already bolstered their presence and begun fortifying the town against a landward attack. A reinforced enemy infantry company equipped with heavy machine guns on a hill south of the harbour presented an easy target, but given the size of his meagre force, Kemal could do little more than encircle Tobruk and compel the Italians to divert additional resources and men there by sea.

To strengthen his ranks, Kemal persuaded a local sheikh and his Sanusi tribesmen to join him in an attack on Tobruk. After several weeks of training his men in how to use their newly acquired rifles, Kemal decided to strike at dawn on the morning of 22 December. Leading a native force of 200 against the Italian hill position, Kemal quickly trounced the enemy company and captured their weapons; the Italian defending troops, as obliging as their 1940 counterparts, threw down their arms and surrendered.[6] The Italian reinforcements rushing to Tobruk to aid their fellows were caught in a series of ambushes and forced to retire with heavy casualties[7]

The Ottoman Empire's defence of Libya ultimately proved futile. A renewed Italian offensive in July 1912, plus the ever-worsening political situation along the Balkan Peninsula, moved the Turks to seek an armistice. The fighting concluded with the signing of the Treaty of Lausanne on 18 October 1912. For the Italians, however, victory was bittersweet. While Tripolitania and Cyrenaica were formally transferred to Italy, the Machiavellian surrender document stipulated Turkey's continued control over Libya's religious affairs. Because Islamic law did not differentiate between civil and religious rule, the Sultan of Turkey – in the position of *caliph* (leader of Islam) – still retained considerable influence. Soon thereafter, his Libyan subjects took up arms and began a lengthy colonial war – resistance that Benito Mussolini would eventually quell some twenty years later.

Yet another dark page in the Kingdom of Italy's nascent military record, the Libyan campaign had seriously drained Rome's military resources, and challenged Prime Minister Giolitti to rethink his countrymen's fighting abilities.[8] All on the eve of a new European war.

The First World War

The ink was still drying on the peace settlement between Turkey and Italy when an anti-Turkish uprising in Albania and Macedonia encouraged the Balkan Alliance – Montenegro, Serbia, Greece and Bulgaria – to declare war on the Ottoman Empire. Soundly beaten in what became known as the First Balkan War (October 1912 to May 1913), the Turks relinquished control of nearly all their European territories – a historic end to 400 years of Turkish rule in Europe.

Barely four weeks passed before the victors began squabbling among themselves over recent spoils and newly drawn borders. This led Bulgaria to attack the new Serbian–Greek alliance in Macedonia, and the advent of the Second Balkan War (29 June to 10 August 1913). This time, however, the Bulgarians were the vanquished, and forced to cede much of what they had acquired in the First Balkan War. Simultaneously, Greece secured Crete and southern Macedonia, Serbia received northern Macedonia and Kosovo, and Albania became an independent state.

Although it maintained a delicate façade of peace, the region then became a political powder keg poised to explode. The Serbians, forced by Vienna to yield their conquests, harboured a deep resentment toward Austria. Conversely, Bulgaria now looked toward Vienna for support. Elsewhere in Europe, relations between Austria–Hungary and Russia had soured, as had those between Germany and Britain. In the midst of this pan-continental mistrust, a web of alliances was drawn up in the event of war between the Central Powers of Austria–Hungary and Germany – and the Triple Entente partners of Britain, France and Russia.

The European tinderbox exploded on 28 June 1914, when a Serbian teenage terrorist assassinated the Austrian heir-apparent, Archduke Franz Ferdinand, and his wife in Sarajevo, Bosnia. Austria–Hungary immediately declared

war on Serbia. This third Balkan war, however, quickly esca-
lated into something much larger, and by the beginning of
August 1914, Europe had plunged headlong into a new
conflict. One with enormous ramifications. Germany ambi-
tiously declared war on Russia and France at the beginning
of August, before launching a flanking offensive against the
French through neutral Belgium. Bound by treaty obligation,
Great Britain (followed by its Dominions) declared war on
Germany on 4 August. A series of domino-like events ensued:
Austria–Hungary declared war on Russia; France and Britain
declared war against Austria–Hungary; and Montenegro
and Serbia joined the Allies in declaring war on the Central
Powers. Romania, however, failed to its honour its treaty obligations with Austria, and chose to remain neutral. Italy also
chose to disregard its Triple Alliance obligations to Germany
and Austria–Hungary, and instead sat on the fence, awaiting an
opportune moment to enter the war.

The withering Ottoman Empire was a latecomer to the
table. Formerly dependent upon Britain, on 14 November
1914 Constantinople entered the war as an ally of Germany
and launched a *jihad* against Britain, Russia, France, Serbia
and Montenegro.

The Western Front soon became mired in a bloody stale-
mate of trench warfare, and Whitehall (site of Britain's
Ministry of Defence) developed a grandiose idea to overcome the impasse. Besides, after five months of war, the Allies
needed a victory, anywhere. Rather than open a new front
against Germany directly, the operation would support the
hard-pressed Russians and strike at the Central Powers by hit-
ting the comparatively weak Turkish forces in the Dardanelles
(the narrow stretch of water straddling Europe and Asia, which
joins the Aegean Sea to the Sea of Marmara). The concept of
a purely naval assault against the Dardanelles was particularly
appealing to the young British first lord of the Admiralty at
the time, Winston Churchill.

Winston Churchill

The son of British Tory politician Lord Randolph and American heiress Jeanette Jerome, Winston Leonard Spencer Churchill was born at Blenheim Palace, Oxfordshire, on 30 November 1874. Through his mother's connections, Churchill was accepted into a cavalry regiment, the 4th Hussars, in 1895. Shortly afterwards, he was posted to India, where the young cavalry subaltern also served as a war correspondent – a second and far more lucrative profession. Longing for battle, which would both fascinate and serve him well in his imminent shift into politics, Churchill first saw action in September 1897, along India's North West Frontier. The following year he joined the 21st Lancers in Cairo, Egypt's capital, and rode in the cavalry charge during the battle of Omdurman in the Sudan – a victory that established British dominance in the region.

Resigning his commission in 1899, Churchill followed his father's vocation and entered politics. After losing in an election as Conservative candidate at the Lancashire town of Oldham, he sailed to South Africa to cover the Second Boer War as a reporter for London's *Morning Post*. Shortly after his arrival, during the siege of Ladysmith, Churchill was taken prisoner when the armoured train he was travelling in was ambushed. He escaped from a prisoner of war (POW) camp in Pretoria, earning himself acclaim throughout the Empire, and joined the South African Light Horse. He saw further action before returning home to fame, victory in the Oldham election of 1900 and a seat in the House of Commons.

Building upon his recent experience in South Africa, Churchill imagined that any future European war would be a bloody, protracted affair. Accordingly, he lobbied for Britain's defence spending to be directed toward building up the Royal Navy (RN). As First Lord of the Admiralty, Churchill worked tirelessly to hasten the RN's combat readiness and championed the largest naval expansion in British history. Firmly convinced of the benefits of oil over coal, he was instrumental in commissioning the new *Queen Elizabeth* class battleships – powerful and fast vessels powered by oil. By 1914, Britain had the largest navy in the world. With great foresight, Churchill also presented a bill to Parliament to purchase a 51 per cent stake in the Anglo-Iranian Company – the future British Petroleum (BP) – which further cemented Whitehall's strategic interests in the Middle East.

An ardent proponent of the above mentioned 1915 Dardanelles operation, Churchill believed that it might, if successful, induce neutral Greece and other Balkan states to join the war on the Allied side. On 25 April 1915, the Mediterranean Expeditionary Force, a mixed British, Australian, New Zealand and French group, under the command of General Sir Ian Hamilton, landed on the Gallipoli peninsula. Opposing the invasion – the largest amphibious assault to date – was the Turkish Fifth Army under German General Otto Liman von Sanders, head of the German Military Mission to Turkey. Leading one of the two Turkish divisions already stationed on the peninsula was Lieutenant Colonel Mustafa Kemal – a man already familiar with the area from the earlier Balkan wars. It has been suggested that Kemal's experience at Tobruk was a lesson on how warships would support an amphibious landing and protect those troops being ferried ashore.

Hence, on hearing the distant thunder of naval gunfire, which heralded the Allied invasion, Kemal exceeded his command authority and, compass and map in hand, rushed the men of his 57th Regiment forward to repel the first waves of assaulting infantry.

The Australian and New Zealand Army Corps (ANZAC), meanwhile, had unintentionally landed at the wrong beach – later to become known as Anzac Cove – and now faced stiff resistance, steep cliffs and a morass of tortuous ridges and gullies. Bitter fighting broke out; the ANZACs desperate to retain their toehold, the Turks determined to drive them back into the water. A proposal to evacuate the beachhead later the same day was vetoed. Digging in, the Australian soldiers earned the enduring soubriquet 'Digger'.

Leslie Morshead

One of the junior Australian officers who waded ashore at Gallipoli was Leslie Morshead, a former schoolteacher born on 18 September 1889. Morshead was commissioned as a lieutenant in in the 2nd Infantry Battalion of the 1st Australian Imperial Force (AIF) in September 1914. Promoted to captain on 8 January 1915, he landed at Anzac Cove on 25 April 1915, where and his battalion made the best progress of any Australian unit. Under heavy fire from the Turks, who dominated the high ground, Morshead was quick to assess the situation and reassure his men, who were shaken by determined Turkish counter-attacks and the horrors of war. Charles Bean, Australia's then-official historian, later described him as a 'commander marked beyond most others as a fighting leader in whom the traditions of the British Army has been bottled from his childhood like tight-corked champagne'.[9]

Further along the Gallipoli peninsula, British and French troops had also made little headway from the beachhead. Reinforcements and a new offensive led to further bloody fighting in August, but without a decisive result. Paradoxically, both sides were soon ensconced in trenches, behind barbed wire stretched across a chaotic battlefield that resembled the Western Front. Territorial gains were correspondingly measured in yards, with small pockets of land captured in bloody hand-to-hand combat. Morshead's bravery during intelligence-gathering patrols across no-man's-land and repelling Turkish counter-attacks merited special mention in dispatches.[10] This early experience in stealthily probing enemy positions would prove invaluable for Morshead in France, and later at Tobruk, where his troops would similarly venture out beyond the perimeter wire during the hours of darkness.

Dissatisfied with the progress in the Dardanelles, Churchill sacked his commanding officer, General Hamilton. His successor, Lieutenant General Sir Charles Monro, saw little point in continuing the costly campaign, and recommended an evacuation. Under the very noses of the Turkish defenders, the combined Allied force was stealthily withdrawn, without loss, through December and early January 1916. For the Turks, Gallipoli represented a major triumph. Their hero, Kemal, was promoted to general, and today he is celebrated as Atatürk, the father of modern Turkey.

For Churchill, the Gallipoli enterprise proved catastrophic. 'Let me stand or fall by the Dardanelles,' he proclaimed.[11] Prime Minister Herbert Asquith's response was to demote Churchill from the Admiralty. Subsequently blamed for the whole debacle, Churchill resigned from the War Cabinet on 11 November 1915, his political career seemingly over. A week later, he was back in France on active service. Relishing a return to the battlefield, he declined the command of a brigade and instead joined the 2nd Battalion Grenadier Guards, where he was appointed battalion commander in the 6th Royal Scots Fusiliers. After six eventful months on the front lines, and several lucky escapes from death or serious injury, Churchill returned home to resurrect his flagging political career. Hounded by continued taunts over his responsibility for the Dardanelles operation – a claim overturned by an independent review in March 1917 – Churchill was appointed minister of munitions in June 1917. Importantly, one of the projects Churchill threw his characteristic energy into in this position was the development of what he termed a 'land ship'. Since his Admiralty days, Churchill had enthusiastically supported this novel project to overcome the gridlock of trench warfare, and now he had the chance to bring it to life. It was an armoured, caterpillar-tracked weapon that would revolutionise warfare – what we know today as the tank.

The Siege of Kut

Shortly after Gallipoli, while Churchill was serving on the front lines of Europe, the British Army endured another humiliating defeat at the hands of the Turks in Mesopotamia. This time the lesson was in siege warfare. After occupying Basra (in modern day Iraq) in November 1914, to safeguard their Persian oil facilities, and protect India from the threat posed by the Turkish Sixth Army, the British pushed onward towards the capital, Baghdad. Reaching the town of Ctesiphon, Major General Charles Townsend's largely Indian force was held up by Ottoman troops under the command of the elderly German Field Marshal Colmar von der Goltz. Falling back to the ancient town of Kut-el-Amara, Townsend decided, hesitantly, to stand his ground. He predicted that his garrison would be isolated for up to two months before there was any hope of relief, but was gravely misguided in the belief that he could emulate an earlier British feat: The defence of Chitral on India's North West Frontier in 1895 in which a besieged force of 400 British men was successfully relieved after six weeks.

The siege of Kut began on 7 December 1915. After 143 days and several valiant but futile relief attempts, Townsend surrendered his long-suffering garrison of 13,000 men on 29 April 1916, thus ending the longest unrelieved siege in British history. A further 23,000 men had been lost during an unsuccessful relief attempt. Kut was a brutal reminder of the folly of allowing a sizable force, with flagging morale, inadequate defences and insufficient means of supply, to become besieged for a protracted period. A costly misjudgement, Kut yielded an enormous propaganda windfall for Germany and its then ally, Turkey.

Italy Enters the War

Despite Italy's apparent neutrality and reluctance to enter the war in Europe, Prime Minister Antonio Salandra was nevertheless keen to use the conflict as a lever to elevate his country to Great Power status. On 26 April 1915, Rome became an opportunistic signatory to the secretive Treaty of London. It promised Italy, in victory, the Italian-speaking territories of Trentino, South Tyrol, Trieste and northern Dalmatia, plus colonial compensation in Africa and Asia Minor. For this reason, after nine months of uncertainty, and with the promise of more generous concessions than what the Central Powers offered, Italy entered the war alongside Britain and France.

In Milan, Mussolini remained vehemently opposed to war. One of Italy's most prominent young socialists, he had earlier founded the newspaper *La Lotta di Classe* (*The Class Struggle*). The paper's success led to his appointment as editor of the official socialist broadsheet: *Avanti!* (*Forward!*). It was at the helm of this anti-militarist, anti-nationalist paper that Mussolini vented his anger over Italy's decision to join the war. 'Down with the War. We remain neutral,' he wrote in an August 1914 article.[12] Inspired by the Marxist principle that social revolution is usually a consequence of war, Mussolini's ardent stance shifted in an abrupt about-face, and to such a degree that he turned to actively supporting Italian belligerence. Predictably, such a radical change of thinking led to Mussolini's expulsion from the Socialist Party, which in turn drove him to establish a new pro-war newspaper, *Il popolo d'Italia*, which was to become a driving force behind Italy's widespread support of the war.

Notwithstanding its own unpreparedness to wage a land war in Europe, Rome declared war on Austria–Hungary on 23 May 1915 (Italian rivalry against Austria dated back to the period after the Napoleonic Wars, when several large Italian cities were ceded to Austria). The first surprise assault, however, quickly floundered. What followed was a series of ineffective and costly offensives against the Austro-Hungarian forces along the Isonzo River (in what today is Slovenia), in one of the most difficult fronts of the entire war.

Italian aggression also hauled the ongoing Libyan conflict into the First World War. This prompted the Sanusi to renew their Turkish alliance and, with idealistic abandon, join the war against Britain and France. To fight the 60,000-odd Italian troops stationed in Libya, Sanusi insurgents were supplied with arms and military advisors from both Germany and Turkey. The Italians, who had declared war against the Germans on 28 August, now found themselves fighting German guns in Libya as well. The Sanusi, under Turkish leadership, also launched a campaign into neighbouring Egypt in October 1915, with the objective of tying down British and Italian forces in North Africa. They advanced across the Western Desert to within miles of Mersa Matruh before being beaten back by a composite British column.

The Italians, realising that the Sanusi might attack Tobruk as well – an area surrounded by open desert and devoid of natural protection – began fortifying the harbour and constructing an extensive outer perimeter to ward off a landward attack. No assault was ever launched, however, and Tobruk later played host to the Anglo-Italo mission in January 1917, in concert with the peace negotiations during which the Sanusi leadership formally concluded the First Italo-Sanusi War.[13] Meanwhile, Italian losses continued to mount in the inconclusive battles along the Italian Front. A combined German–Austrian push through the Isonzo front in October 1917 led to the disastrous fall of Caporetto, in which the demoralised *Regio Esercito* (Royal [Italian] Army) lost some 600,000 troops – mostly as prisoners of war or through widespread desertion. The war had not played into Italy's hands as originally hoped. Prime Minister Antonio Salandra's government fell after a victorious 1916 Austrian offensive. His successor, Paolo Boselli, was similarly ousted from office after the Italian defeat at Caporetto. Vittorio Emanuele Orlando became the next prime minister in 1917. A strong supporter of Italy's entry into the war, he would also back Mussolini when he seized power in 1922.

For the moment, however, Mussolini was fighting as a corporal in the *Bersaglieri* (or 'sharpshooters') along the Isonzo River. Wounded in action by a grenade blast in February 1917, he was discharged from a military hospital in Milan and returned to his newspaper. There, the future dictator began challenging what he saw as the feebleness of Italian internal politics, in what he called upholding the cause of the common soldier. At that time, there was a real possibility that the Italian military, beset by strikes and anti-war demonstrations, would also collapse. Revolution could foreseeably follow, leading to a political watershed similar to the one unfolding in Russia. (The riots in Petrograd in March 1917 had prompted the abdication of the Tsar, followed in November by the Bolshevik Revolution. Shortly afterwards, Moscow signed an armistice with the Central Powers.)

Erwin Rommel

Among the German officers serving on the Italian Front in 1917 was a young professional soldier from an elite mountain battalion. He would later become one of the most well-known German generals of the Second World War. His name: Erwin Rommel. Born at Heidenheim, Württemberg in 1891, a youthful Rommel broke with the family tradition of teaching to become an officer cadet in the 124th Württemberg Infantry Regiment in 1910. The following year he met Lucia Maria 'Lucie' Mollin, whom he married in 1916. He saw action in France, Romania, and Italy, and became renowned for his leadership at the front, calculated risk taking, tactical prowess and ability to deftly exploit a situation. One of his greatest successes was the capture of Monte Matajur on 26 October 1917 – a bold thrust that netted more than 150 Italian officers, 9,000 troops and eighty-one artillery pieces. Shortly afterwards, his unit entered Longarone and captured a further 10,000 enemy troops. Promoted to captain, he successfully lobbied his superiors to receive the *Pour le Mérite* – Germany's highest decoration at the time, and the equivalent of Britain's Victoria Cross or the United States' Medal of Honor.

It was during the course of the fighting in Italy and Romania that Rommel honed his practice of outmanoeuvring the enemy and attacking their rear via daring flanking actions. These first lessons in combat would influence the future practitioner of mobile armoured warfare. In this way, he was ahead of some of his future Allied opponents, including Leslie Morshead and Bernard Montgomery, whose early influences in battle were shaped by the bloody quagmire of positional trench warfare rather than rapid manoeuvring.

The German High Command now concentrated on winning the war in the West, though time was running out for the Central Powers. The last nation to join the war on Germany's side – Bulgaria, in October 1915 – was also the first to seek an armistice in September 1918. The Turks followed suit shortly afterwards. Uprisings in Vienna and Budapest after a major victory by the Italians (reinforced with British and French troops) forced Austria–Hungary to withdraw from the war as well. Faced with mounting starvation and civil unrest, the failure of its March 1918 offensive, and a successful new Allied counteroffensive in July 1918 (with the American Expeditionary Force), Germany signed an armistice on 11 November 1918. The 'Great War' was now over. It was, however, not the 'war to end all wars', since the framework for an even larger conflict had already begun to take shape.

The Interwar Period and the Rise of Fascism

On 28 June 1919, within the Hall of Mirrors in the palace of Versailles, German representatives signed the Treaty of

Versailles, a peace accord designed to permanently quash any German military threat to France. In contrast to 1871, it was now the Germans who were humiliated, their fatherland stripped of its Great Power status. Germany's post-war discontent rivalled the resentment festering in victorious Italy. Having joined the Entente nations for a share in the spoils, Rome was indignant over the terms of the 1919 treaty of Saint Germain, which failed to honour the Allies' secret 1915 promise. Former Austrian territories on the Adriatic Sea were given to the newly created Kingdom of Yugoslavia, while Britain and France helped themselves to the former Ottoman territories and Germany's African colonies – a slap across the face that only hastened Italy's political upheaval. Italy's meagre pickings amounted to only an oasis on the Egyptian–Libyan frontier (ceded from Britain) and a trifling change (by France) to the Libyan-Tunisian frontier. Eventually, after much haggling, Britain also conceded part of her East African colony, the province of Jubaland, in 1925.

Political feebleness, crippling inflation, chronic food shortages, strikes and civil turmoil gave rise to a new paramilitary, black-shirted brigade of mostly right-wing veterans and students – the first Fascists. Their charismatic and outspoken leader, Benito Mussolini, dubbed his followers the *Fasci di Combattimento*, after an ancient Roman symbol of authority. After his historic 'March on Rome' in October 1922, Mussolini became prime minister of a fascist-dominated Italian coalition government. Three years later, he assumed dictatorial powers. As *Il Duce* – the leader – Mussolini became known as the man who made 'the trains run on time'. A gifted diplomat, he obtained generous concessions in the settlement of Italy's war debt, both from an admiring Chancellor of the Exchequer, Winston Churchill, and the United States. A visionary, he dreamed of a new Italian Empire and a time when his military would avenge the lingering humiliation of Adowa and Caporetto.

Adolf Hitler

In Germany, a man named Adolf Hitler was closely watching the Duce's ascent to power. Born on 20 April 1889 at Braunau am Inn in northern Austria, Hitler had left school early with a poor academic record and spent most of his early life in Linz and Vienna as a part-time decorator and aspiring artist. Despite having been declared unfit for Austrian service earlier in his life, Hitler was accepted into the German Army and assigned to the 16th Bavarian Reserve Infantry Regiment as a *Meldegänger*, or dispatch runner. Serving on the bloody Western Front, he was twice decorated for bravery, receiving the Iron Cross First and Second Class. For Hitler – like Winston Churchill and Benito Mussolini – fate had intervened on the battlefield on several occasions, shielding him from death while many of his comrades fell. He was hospitalised for injuries in 1918, and discharged after the armistice, amidst the innumerable problems troubling inter-war Germany. By that time, Adolf Hitler had become embittered.

After a botched coup in 1923, and a period in prison, where he dictated the first volume of his political manifesto *Mein Kampf* (*My Struggle*), Hitler emerged to once again take control of the Nazi Party. In January 1933, Hitler became chancellor of Germany, grandly proclaiming a new 1,000-year empire – the Third Reich – that was to (ultimately) last twelve years and three months. Withdrawing Germany from the League of Nations in 1934, Hitler revealed his secret rearmament programme the next year and reintroduced conscription. Then, in complete defiance of the Versailles treaty, he reoccupied the Rhineland in 1936. Nazi Germany's armed forces – the *Wehrmacht* – were now on a war footing, and Hitler's expansionist intentions became all too clear in 1938, with the bloodless annexation of Austria and Czechoslovakia.

Mussolini's imperialistic ambitions also came to light during this turbulent period, beginning with the second Italo-Sanusi war in 1923. By this time, Italian jurisdiction over Libya had been formally recognised under the Treaty of Lausanne. And, whereas Mussolini had once sided with the Libyans' cause, he now unleashed a campaign to brutally suppress them. Although the odds overwhelmingly favoured the well-armed Italians, small Sanusi bands were still able to a wage a successful guerrilla war against the slow and unwieldy Italian columns. Realising that stronger measures were needed to crush the resistance, Mussolini issued a proclamation calling for the Arabs to surrender unconditionally or face extermination. It cost the native population dearly. With the outside world largely oblivious to their plight, some 60,000 Libyans perished in concentration camps, public hangings, shootings, large-scale deportations and mass starvation.[14]

Sanusi resistance was finally worn down by Marshals Pietro Badoglio and Rodolfo Graziani by the end of 1931. In the final twelve months of the fighting, the Italians slaughtered an estimated 1,605 Sanusi (and captured 600 camels) for the price of 132 killed and 257 wounded. Having pitilessly quelled native resistance, large sums were invested in the development of a modern strategic infrastructure, including railways, roads and aerodromes. Colonisation was encouraged, and by 1936, the resident Italian population in Libya had swelled to 110,000. Tobruk also gained prominence as an important stop on Britain's new air service to India. Imperial Airways' Short Calcutta aircraft would leave Greece, arrive in Tobruk in the afternoon for a night's accommodation, and set off for the next stop, Alexandria, early in the morning. Dutch KLM aircraft en route to Batavia (today Jakarta) also flew via Tobruk, as had Antipodean aviator, Bert Hinkler, on his record-breaking 1928 solo flight from London to Australia.

Presage to War

Mussolini no doubt monitored Japan's 1931 invasion of Manchuria (north-east China) with strong interest, watching the League of Nations' impotence at first-hand. Having smashed Sanusi resistance in Libya, in October 1935 he thumbed his nose at the League and, ignoring the 1928 Kellogg–Briand Pact, which prohibited the use of war to achieve national policy, invaded Abyssinia (today Ethiopia). He entered the capital, Addis Ababa, in May 1936, strengthening his influence over the Red Sea and presenting a new danger to the British at Suez.

London and Cairo became anxious about future Fascist moves inside Africa, though Mussolini's first gambit was, in the long run, to backfire. This new menace to Britain's African interests encouraged Whitehall to modernise and boost its military presence in Egypt, then still chiefly dependent upon foot soldiers and cavalry. The newly mechanised Mobile Force created from the existing Cairo Cavalry Brigade became a formation whose expertise in desert driving and navigation – as General von Schweppenburg had witnessed first-hand – would prove invaluable in any future fighting in the Western Desert.

Mussolini's Abyssinian campaign may have avenged the memory of Adowa, but it had come at a considerable cost in terms of men and materiel. Moreover, this dusty new colony was devoid of the untapped mineral wealth that the Italian industry so badly needed; precious natural resources at home had been further depleted when the Fascist and Nazi parties supported General Francisco Franco's Nationalist forces in the Spanish Civil War (July 1936 to April 1939) – a proving ground for Europe's newest weaponry. In yet another geo-strategic disappointment for Mussolini, his involvement in the Spanish conflict failed to deliver the rewards of Majorca and Ceuta (in Spanish North Africa), opposite Gibraltar.

British naval bases at Gibraltar and Egypt had long rankled the Italians as maritime manacles 'imprisoning' them within the confines of the Mediterranean. Rome yearned for the ancient ideal – *mare nostrum* ('our sea') – rather than an Italian lake constricted by small British-controlled outlets at either end. Thus, in order to gain 'free access to the oceans', Mussolini planned to conquer Egypt – part of a grander vision for a new Roman Empire stretching from the Mediterranean to the Indian Ocean. Such flamboyant dreaming would, of course, require a large, well-equipped military. But as a consequence of his early expansionist policies, a poor industrial base and a dearth of raw materials, Italy's rearmament programme was lagging well behind those of Britain, France and Germany. Italy was also weakened by the recent fighting against Ethiopia and the Spanish Republic and it would be many years before the country was ready fight a major war, and then only with considerable economic and military assistance.

With his French and British relations deteriorating, Mussolini turned to Germany for support – the foundation of a new Rome–Berlin Axis. In October 1936, it was agreed that Rome would have political – but not economic – influence over the Mediterranean, a position that would cause future tension within the Axis camp. On 22 May 1939, Italy signed the Pact of Steel with Nazi Germany: an agreement that one country would come to the other's aid if attacked. While Mussolini clarified to Hitler that his country was unprepared to wage war against a European power before 1943 at the earliest, and even then only with the assistance of considerable amounts of German military aid, Hitler expressed his wish not to become involved in any future Mediterranean conflict, as this would be an Italian theatre of war.

Aligned for political purposes, the tempestuous relationship between Rome and Berlin began to sour in the turbulent days preceding the German invasion of Poland, fuelled by mistrust and lies amid the political uncertainty of a continent headed for war. Mussolini's position shilly-shallied. One minute he favoured neutrality, the next moment he envisaged a sense of honour in marching alongside Germany. He dithered though fear of Hitler's angst and a possible denunciation of the pact between the two countries. An Italian request for materiel was delivered to Germany in an attempt to demonstrate the current inability of Italy to enter into conflict without receiving vast supplies of additional provisions. Hitler's reply brought the promise of iron, wood, and coal together with the acknowledgement of his proposed single-handed onslaught aimed at Poland, France, and England.[15]

Mussolini's son-in-law and foreign minister, Count Galeazzo Ciano, staunchly opposed his homeland being swept into a new war, especially in an alliance with Germany. In this, he mirrored Mussolini's own 1914 stance. He urged Mussolini to appreciate his role as being placed secondary to Hitler, his diminished prestige, as well as the anti-German mood of the Italian people.[16] For the most part they felt trapped by the Pact of Steel, fearing and mistrusting Hitler. The acrimonious Axis partnership, as we will discover, was already unravelling.

Europe was nearing crisis point. Hitler played his next hand on 1 September 1939 when nearly 1½ million German troops invaded Poland – a gamble that plunged the world into war again.

Blitzkrieg in the West

'The twentieth century will be known in history as the
Century of Fascism.'

— Benito Mussolini

Twenty-one years after the signing of the Armistice, the major
protagonists of the First World War — Germany, France and
Britain — were again at war. Mussolini, meanwhile, monitored
this new conflict closely, displaying what Ciano described as
'intermittent belligerent flashes' while he watched what was
dubbed the German *Blitzkrieg* (literally, 'lightning war') drive
deeper into Poland.[1] Though he was excited to learn of the
fall of Warsaw, Mussolini was loath to intervene and declare
war, just yet. There would be a more opportune moment.
Instead, it was the Soviet dictator, Joseph Stalin, who joined
Hitler in annihilating the Poles. His Red Army invaded Poland
from the east on 17 September 1939 — the result of a 10-year
German–Soviet Non-Aggression Pact signed only weeks earlier in Moscow.

The war in Poland was a jolt to Britain's strategic thinking. While Italy was viewed as the primary threat in the
Mediterranean and the Middle East, it looked as though Russia

too was now another possible enemy. Would Stalin, who in accordance with the Nazi–Soviet Pact had begun to exercise his military muscle across Eastern Europe, move into Persia (Iran) and threaten Britain's oil supplies, or, alternatively, annex Afghanistan and endanger India? While the world waited to see where Hitler would strike next, Stalin invaded Finland. Meanwhile, a voice was speaking up in Whitehall, pressing for a more aggressive response to be taken against German belligerence – Winston Churchill.

Churchill's Return to Power

History had turned full circle for one of Hitler's staunchest critics. Ironically, on the first day of the war, Chamberlain appointed Churchill as First Lord of the Admiralty – the same post he had held at the outbreak of the First World War. As in 1915, Churchill strove to circumvent bloodshed on the Western Front by exploiting Britain's naval superiority and opening a decisive second front on land. He also championed the disruption of Swedish iron ore through northern Norway as a means of crippling Germany's steel production. However, Hitler acted before that plan could go into action, invading neutral Norway and Denmark on 9 April 1941 – a move designed to safeguard both his northern flank and precious Swedish ore supplies. Caught off guard by the bold German operation – the first joint air, land and sea campaign in history – Britain hurriedly dispatched a new Allied expeditionary force to Norway.

Midway through the ensuing campaign, the commander of the Allied land forces in Norway, Major General Pierse J. Mackesy, was removed and replaced by Lieutenant General Sir Claude Auchinleck, the former deputy chief of the general staff in India. Now acting as the newly appointed commander of the Anglo-French forces in Norway, he was advised on

25 May to abandon the campaign and evacuate on the grounds of strong opposition and the deteriorating situation in France. The cause in Norway was lost. Britain needed her soldiers at home, preparing for further battles.

The Scandinavian campaign was a costly affair for both sides. And the failure and subsequent evacuation of the Franco-British expeditionary force from Norway – what Churchill described as a 'ramshackle campaign' – led to a sharp decline in public support for Chamberlain. Norway was a swifter and even more humiliating defeat for Britain than Gallipoli had been. In London, a fiery debate in the House of Commons, plus the refusal by the opposition Labour Party to form a coalition, rendered the prime minister's position untenable. Having changed his mind several times as to whether he should remain in office or not, on 10 May 1940 – the same day that Hitler invaded neutral Luxembourg, Holland and Belgium – Chamberlain resigned.

That evening, King George VI invited Churchill to Buckingham Palace. Although instrumental in the abortive Norwegian landings – the very sequel to the Gallipoli fiasco – Churchill was anything but disgraced. Twenty-five years since his dismissal over the Dardanelles operation, he was sworn in as Britain's new prime minister and minister of defence; a post he personally created. His first speech to the House of Commons three days later set the tone for the coming years: 'You ask what is our aim? I can answer in one word: Victory.' Amid the uncertainty of Europe's latest conflict, he was a man with a vision, one of triumph.

Fall Gelb – Hitler Strikes West

After postponing his offensive in the west nearly thirty times, Hitler announced to his senior staff members on 9 May 1940: 'Gentlemen, you are about to witness the most famous victory in history.' *Fall Gelb* ('Case Yellow') began the next morning at dawn, with the invasion of the Netherlands, Belgium and Luxemburg. The main German thrust then easily outflanked France's elaborate Maginot Line border fortifications and pushed through the supposedly impassable Ardennes Forest into France. On 13 May, German troops crossed the Meuse River, and a week later the German 'sickle' swung around to reach the English Channel, creating a pocket along the coast that entrapped the Allied forces. After an abortive armoured counter-attack at the town of Arras in north-eastern France, the British Expeditionary Force (BEF) retreated toward the coastal port of Dunkirk. Hitler's infamous order of 24 May halted his ground forces for two days, which, in combination with a depleted Luftwaffe operating from distant airfields, spared the retreating British columns from a certain *coup de grâce*.

Meanwhile, the withdrawal from Norway was also underway, with some 25,000 Allied troops evacuated by 7 June. This was a precarious moment for the Allies. In addition to the routs in France and Norway, the Dutch had capitulated on 14 May and the Belgians on 28 May. Notwithstanding pockets of gallant resistance, the French capitulated on 20 June 1940.

The six-week campaign in the West now presented Hitler with a goal that had eluded the Kaiser's army for more than four years. Germany had once again humiliated France in one of its worst defeats in history. To settle the score of 1918, the armistice was signed on 22 June in the same railway coach at Rethondes, in the Compiègne Forest, where Marshal Ferdinand Foch had received the German surrender twenty-two years before. As part of the settlement, Germany agreed to occupy only northern and western France, some 60 per cent of the country. The elderly Marshal Philippe Pétain, a national hero following his triumph at Verdun during the First World War, and his collaborationist Vichy regime would govern the remaining unoccupied area, as well as France's colonial possessions, including Tunisia, Morocco, Algeria, Syria and Lebanon.

The Armistice also specified that the powerful French fleet – the fourth largest in the world – was to be demobilised rather than be pressed into Axis service. For Churchill, this potential threat to his trade routes was too great. Could Hitler really be trusted here? An ultimatum was issued to the French calling for the ships to join the British or they would be sunk. After negotiations proved unproductive, on 3 July 1940, Admiral Sir James Somerville's RN 'Force H' was faced with the unpleasant task of shelling the French fleet at Mers el-Kebir in Algeria, killing 1,297 French sailors. It was with tears in his eyes that the premier broke the news of this attack to the House of Commons. Pétain responded by breaking off relations with London. The attack soured British and French relations for years and led to pointless bloodshed in later campaigns. But to the rest of the world, in particular the US, it was proof of Churchill's conviction to fight the Axis at all costs and to protect British interests in the Mediterranean and the Middle East.

Rommel's Dash through France

So far, the war had progressed along different lines to what many veterans of in the First World War had foreseen. Rather than a lengthy war of attrition, it was a series of short campaigns. Germany's use of concentrated airpower, in unison with a tactically superior handling of armour, overwhelmed the land forces of the Allies, who appeared impressive on paper but were hamstrung by obsolete doctrine, poor intelligence and fateful decision-making. Germany's superior battlefield doctrine had crushed the Allies' morale and led to defeatism and a common belief that the *Wehrmacht* was invincible.

The campaign in the West had cost Germany 163,213 casualties – far fewer than the enormous sacrifices in the trenches of the previous war. This success of the Nazi war machine surprised even Hitler and his generals.

One particular general, commanding of the 7th Panzer Division, nicknamed the 'Ghost Division', had sped across France to the English Channel. A dynamic 48-year-old: Erwin Rommel. During the interwar period, Rommel had served as an officer in several infantry regiments before receiving a promotion to major and command of a mountain battalion. His 1937 military textbook, *Infanterie greift an* ('The Infantry Attacks'), achieved widespread prominence, and led Rommel to the command of the Führer's personal security battalion. In 1938, he was placed in charge of the war academy at Weiner Neustadt, near Vienna. During the annexation of the Sudetenland and the Polish Campaign, he again returned to lead Hitler's escort battalion – service that certainly stood him in good stead for the Führer's favour. It was after the fall of Poland that Rommel requested and received the command of a Panzer division. (*Panzer* is the German term for tank shortened from *Panzerkampfwagen*, literally 'armoured fighting vehicle'.)

Inexperienced in armoured combat, Rommel drew upon his daring and tactical resourcefulness for this new command. Throughout the French Campaign, he pushed his men to their limits. Personally leading armoured columns, directing fire on individual targets, or observing the progress of his men from the ground or the air, Rommel would disregard personal injury to be at the forefront of his armoured thrust. His advance of more than 150 miles on 16 June alone was, according to the British military historian and pre-war advocate of mechanised warfare, Sir Basil Liddell Hart, probably the greatest in the history of warfare.[2] For his leadership and bravery during the opening stages of the campaign, Rommel was awarded the coveted *Ritterkreuz* (Knight's Cross) decoration.

During the campaign, Rommel was struck by the ability of firepower to weaken an enemy's morale: 'I have found again and again that in encounter actions, the day goes to the side that is first to plaster his opponents with fire. The man who lies low and awaits developments usually comes off second best.' Interestingly for us, Rommel's unorthodox, sometimes experimental, method of command was criticised by some of his divisional officers. His indefatigable presence in the front lines – no doubt refreshing to his junior troops – was to the frustration of his staff officers, who often had no idea of his exact position. He was, as many of his senior officers in Africa would learn, often a difficult man to serve under.

Several aspects of Rommel's character and conduct during the French campaign also merit attention for our later understanding of the Desert War. Firstly, his optimistic, almost-boyish enthusiasm for combat: 'Everything wonderful so far,' he wrote home to his wife Lucie (Lu) two days into the campaign.[3] His sanguine, perhaps naïve, appreciation of events led him to predict a quick conclusion to the fighting, in much the same way that he believed Tobruk would fall into his hands in April the following year. Secondly, after a battle, he was prone to exaggerating or downplaying elements of the fighting to suit his needs. His account of the fighting in France, for example, practically ignores the role of the Luftwaffe, while his push through the Maginot Line – which he wrote of as 'hardly conceivable' – was at a far less formidable part of the line than what he portrayed. Thirdly, it was during the British counter-attack at Arras on 21 May that Rommel first encountered the heavily armoured British Infantry Tank Mark II, known as the 'Matilda' after a comic strip duck. Immune to smaller-calibre anti-tank guns, this tank proved no match for the Germany's superb high-velocity 88mm anti-aircraft gun, when fired in a flat trajectory, anti-tank role. It was a tactic Rommel would later use with deadly effect in North Africa. Lastly, Rommel, like so many central figures in this book, possessed a 'charmed' fortune in battle, especially in light of his penchant for being in the vanguard of an attack. On several occasions, he escaped unscathed when those around him were killed. Providence would continue to look after him on his next assignment – a theatre where his characteristic drive and enterprise would earn him legendary status.

Hitler's Strategic Dilemma

With the fall of France, Britain now stood alone. Confronted by the vexing question of how to overcome his recalcitrant opponent, Hitler briefly considered two possibilities: a direct invasion of Britain, codenamed *Seelöwe* ('Sea Lion'), or a broader strategy. Either, if successful, would ultimately lead to the collapse of the British Empire. On 16 July, Hitler issued Directive No. 16, one of fifty-one such offensive commands issued between 1939 and 1943, which outlined preparations for a landing in Britain, should it prove necessary. The succeeding directive, issued a fortnight later, called for an intensification of the air war as a prelude to an attack. Reichsmarschall Hermann Göring's Luftwaffe was now pitted against Royal Air Force (RAF) Fighter Command – which Churchill had expanded in 1937 – for air supremacy over Britain. By early September 1940, however, it was clear that the Luftwaffe had (narrowly) failed to defeat the RAF and destroy its bases across southern England. Heavy aircraft losses forced Hitler to switch the focus of the campaign, from attacks on vital airfields and ground installations to the bombing of London and other cities; a respite that enabled the battered RAF to rebuild its strength.

Incapable of overwhelming Britain's valiant 'Few', on 17 September 1940 Hitler postponed Sea Lion indefinitely, though whether the undertaking was ever seriously considered is open to debate. But as German surface raiders and U-boats came perilously close to severing Churchill's merchant navy lifeline (in what was dubbed the Battle of the Atlantic), the Führer turned his attention to opening a new front in the East. On 21 July 1940, in one of the most historic decisions of the entire war, Hitler directed his army commander-in-chief, Field Marshal Walther von Brauchitsch, to prepare reports for invading his ideological enemy: the Soviet Union.

The Soviet Red Army, though still recovering from Stalin's purge of 1938, was fast becoming a significant threat to the Third Reich. A showdown between the two great powers seemed inevitable, as Stalin's shadow continued to fall across Eastern Europe; the Red Army having marched into Lithuania on 15 June 1940, followed by Latvia, Estonia and several Romanian provinces. If his forces could quickly overwhelm Russia, Hitler believed, Britain would lose all will to fight.

However, more time was needed before the *Wehrmacht* would be ready to mount its colossal campaign in the East. Britain, meanwhile, remained defiant under under its stalwart premier – one of Churchill's finest moments as leader – during the indiscriminate bombing campaign popularly known as the 'Blitz'. Churchill's decisive leadership was proof to the world of his country's determination to 'defend the world cause'.

As in the First World War, Britain's hope lay across the Atlantic Ocean, and US president Franklin D. Roosevelt was especially keen to support Britain. But post-1918 America had no desire to enter into any new foreign conflict. As a consequence of the country's isolationist stance and the Neutrality Acts of the mid-1930s, Roosevelt, for the moment, had little choice but to uphold neutrality. Shortly after the war began in 1939, he persuaded Congress to allow Britain and France to purchase arms on a cash-and-carry basis, and negotiated the 'non-neutral' exchange of fifty ageing navy destroyers for 99-year leases on eight British naval and air bases in Newfoundland and the Caribbean. While US public opinion polls supported Britain's plight, the majority of Americans still wished to remain out of the war. Roosevelt nevertheless managed to enact America's first peacetime draft, though he pledged that no troops would be shipped to 'any foreign wars' in his 1940 election campaign.

It was an empty promise. Winning his third term in office in November 1940, Roosevelt broadcast his intention to make America the 'great arsenal of democracy'. There could now be little doubt that the world's largest economic and industrial power would soon enter the war on the side of the Allies.

Britain, for the moment, was safe. The focus of the ground war shifted to a new continent. As Churchill had foreseen several months earlier, the next phase of the war would take place in the Middle East: 'If the Germans are frustrated in an invasion of Great Britain or do not choose to attempt it they will have great need to press and aid the Italians to the attack of Egypt.'[4]

Mussolini's Readiness for (a Parallel) War

Having observed Hitler's victorious march across Europe, the Duce became impatient to acquire his own share of the spoils and elevate Italy's standing. We should remember that the Second World War was not only an enormous military confrontation of differing ideologies, but also a global economic conflict. And as we saw earlier, the origin of the Second World War was heavily rooted in the ashes of the First. As a result of the Great Depression of 1929, the old imperial nations, such as Britain, France and the Netherlands, turned to their respective empires as a source of available commodities and secure markets for their exports. Alternatively, the future members of the Tripartite Pact: Germany, Japan and Italy, began to look for self-sufficiency by breaking away from their reliance upon uncertain external markets and the world economy.

A critical shortage of fuel and raw materials would also constrain Italy's offensive capabilities and limit its manufacturing base. Mussolini advised his industrialists – Italy being the smallest of the European industrialised nations – that economics had never 'halted the march of history'; the urgings from his Minster of Exchange and Currency, Raffaello Riccardi, that he stay out of the war on financial grounds had gone unheeded.[5] Still, his imperialistic aspirations would require Britain's elimination from the Mediterranean, as 80 per cent of Italian raw material and food imports normally passed through either the Straits of Gibraltar or the British-controlled Suez Canal. Economic fettering to one side, Mussolini grew progressively angrier over the seemingly unstoppable movement of the German armed forces across Europe. 'We Italians are already sufficiently dishonoured,' he declared on 13 May 1940.[6]

But could Mussolini march against Britain alone? For all its bluff, Fascist Italy had neglected to modernise its military during the interwar period. Moreover, many of the Duce's senior commanders were averse to any new war against a European foe. A chorus of criticism regarding the capability of the armed forces rang out from the highest quarters. Ciano noted privately in August 1939 that the Italian army was in a 'pitiful' state[7]; Marshal Emilio de Bono, veteran of the Italo–Turkish and First World War, and one of the founding members of the Fascist party, described the possibility as 'materially and morally disastrous'.[8] Marshal Pietro Badoglio, the Chief of the General Staff and former governor of Libya from 1928 to 1934, may have crushed the primitive opposition in Ethiopia using lightly armoured tankettes – which even natives had on occasion disabled – in concert with artillery and mustard gas, but his army in 1940 was far from ready to fight a modern European adversary.

Mussolini had boasted to the world in 1936 that his army wielded '8 million bayonets'. Reality, however, was vastly different. In mid-1940, the *Regio Esercito* comprised 1,687,950 men, though only ten of the forty-five divisions were fully equipped. (An Italian division usually contained two regiments of three battalions, whereas a British division was composed of three brigades of three battalions.) Instead of increasing the mobility and firepower of his army, Badoglio believed the key to victory lay in an overwhelming superiority infantry, even though the majority of formations were now worse off than their 1915 equivalents in terms of weaponry and basic equipment. A shortage of raw materials, fuel and machine tools had severely restricted the development of new weapons in the interwar period, with much of Italy's front-line artillery dating back to the collapse of the Austria–Hungary coalition in 1918. In the period from 1939 to 1943, some 2,500 fewer guns left Mussolini's arsenals, compared to the period 1915 to 1918. Even the quality of the projectiles was compromised. Australian troops in North Africa were astounded by how Italian 'shell fragmentation seemed poor and [that] many men blown off their feet got up again'.[9] They were also intrigued by the standard issue bolt-action Carcano rifle, which looked like a toy beside their larger Lee–Enfield .303 equivalent, and the thin-skinned Italian hand grenades, which were feeble in comparison to their far more lethal British equivalent, known as the Mills Bomb. Significantly, the basic firepower of an Italian Army division was markedly behind that of modern armies, equivalent to a quarter of a French division and a ninth of a German one.

Crucially, in this age of increasing battlefield mobility, the Italians had not anticipated the growing importance of fast-moving armoured formations, as had leading visionaries such as Germany's Heinz Guderian, Britain's Basil Liddell Hart and J.C. Fuller, and America's George S. Patton. Largely unimpressed by Hitler's new Panzer divisions, Badoglio's response to a 1940 army intelligence report on German battlefield performance was that he would 'study it when the war is over'.[10] Mussolini's light tanks were more suited to fighting a war against a northern enemy across the Alps than against the British in the desert. His small arsenal of medium-sized tanks were mechanically unreliable and far too lightly armoured – a problem stemming from a lack of funding and a corrupt, inefficient manufacturing duopoly by the Italian industrial giants Ansaldo and Fiat. Italy's main medium tank, the eleven-ton tank *Carro Armato* ('armoured vehicle') M11/39, though clearly superior to the L.3/33 and L.3/35 tankettes, was nevertheless handicapped by having its main 37mm gun mounted in the hull beside the driver with limited traverse, while the rotating turret only housed two machine guns. To rectify the problem, Badoglio unsuccessfully tried to acquire some of the 700 French tanks captured by the Germans, and for a period Italy even considered manufacturing the more reliable Panzer III under licence.

Not the least of the Italian army's problems was transport. Italy possessed only 469,000 vehicles of all kinds in 1939, compared to Germany's 1.99 million and Britain's 2.42 million. As Rommel later noted, 'the decisive disadvantage of the Italian Army *vis-à-vis* the British was that the greater part of it was non-motorised.'[11] Whereas Italy had transferred 52,000 vehicles to the Balkans, by November 1940 there were only 3,844 vehicles available to support the 100,000 troops stationed in Cyrenaica.

Mussolini's *Regia Aeronautica* (Royal [Italian] Air Force) was similarly outgunned and outperformed by British aircraft – a consequence of the pre-war fascist quest for breaking speed and altitude records in place of developing advanced, operational combat aircraft. Success against inferior opponents in the air over East Africa and Spain had also produced overly optimistic reports that overrode objective analysis. As a result, of the 3,000 aircraft available to Italy in 1940, only 900 bombers and 270 fighters could be classed as 'modern'. Italy's front line fighters included the Fiat CR.42 *Falco* ('Falcon'), an outclassed biplane, and the equally obsolete open-cockpit Fiat G.50 *Freccia* ('Arrow'). It was not until manufacturers fitted license-built German Daimler-Benz DB 605 engines in their later aircraft that they could seriously compete with contemporary Allied monoplanes such as Britain's Supermarine Spitfire and Hawker Hurricane. The main Italian bomber at the start of the war was the three-engined Savoia Marchetti SM.79 *Sparviero* ('Sparrowhawk'). Rugged and reliable, it was nevertheless poorly armed, and could carry only a tiny bomb load. The bombs themselves were generally small and ineffective. Lacking dive-bombers, the Italians employed a small number of German Junkers Ju 87 B-2 or *Stuka* (from *Sturzkampfflugzeug*, meaning 'dive bomber') aircraft, known by their new owners as the *Picchiatello* (or 'Crazy Diver').

Apart from the aforementioned shortcomings of aircraft, combat effectiveness was further restricted by a shortage of radio sets and poor aircrew training. Again, as with artillery, the Italian aircraft industry was unable to deliver sufficient numbers of machines; the average annual production between 1940 and 1943 only just above Britain's monthly average. Nonetheless, Italian airmen fought with a valour not commonly recognised.

The *Regia Marina* (Royal [Italian] Navy) was a powerful force, in theory. Built up during the 1930s under the premise that France would be Italy's primary foe, it entered the war with four operational battleships, eighteen operational cruisers and sixty-three operational submarines. Like Germany, Italy possessed no aircraft carriers. Hitler hoped the outwardly impressive fleet could shift the balance of power in the Mediterranean, but it too was beset by a variety of operational shortcomings and a chronic shortage of fuel oil. The combat effectiveness of the capital ships was further impaired by the inaccuracy of the main guns, poor training in night combat, and a lack of radar systems and submarine detection apparatus – the British ASDIC (Anti-Submarine Detection Investigation Committee) and US Sonar (SOund Navigation And Ranging). The Germans were far from generous in sharing their advanced radar technology, and by the time Italian warships were finally retrofitted, it was too late in the war. In the jaundiced opinion of the German naval attaché in Rome, the Italian fleet was skilled in fair weather manoeuvres but lacking in a propensity to engage itself in more difficult, combat-like exercises.[12]

Mussolini was especially proud of his submarine fleet, however – the largest in the world, after Russia. Though impressive in number, the Italian boats were nevertheless slow to dive, sluggish on the surface, and plagued by defective air-conditioning systems that could vent poisonous gases if damaged. Far more successful, however, were exploits of the courageous frogmen operating 'chariots', or two-man torpedoes, which sank or damaged twenty-eight ships during a number of daring raids on Allied harbours, including Alexandria and Gibraltar.

'Italian People, Rush to Arms'

When war broke out in September 1939, Mussolini declared his 'non-belligerence', despite being a signatory to the aforementioned Pact of Steel. His foot-dragging frustrated Berlin; an appeal by Hitler proved futile. Much of what followed was an indictment of the Axis alliance. The two statesmen put on public displays of unity during official visits to Berlin in 1937 and Rome the following year, but beneath this veneer of apparent accord was a disparate alliance characterised by years of uncertainty, suspicion, rivalry and political manoeuvring. The rocky path ahead of the Axis became evident in the months leading up to the war. Hitler's 'secret' annexation of Czechoslovakia in March 1939, for example, provoked uneasiness in Rome. The Italians, in turn, refrained from notifying Berlin of their invasion of Albania the following month. Hitler's non-aggression pact with the Soviet Union also displeased the Italians, as well as the Japanese, who were clashing with Russian forces in the Far East.

With growing distrust over the expanding Nazi and Soviet influence in Europe, Rome chose to throw its support behind the Finns, even dispatching a small contingent of men and aircraft to their aid. Along its northern frontier with the Greater Reich, construction of *Vallo Alpino* – Mussolini's version of the Maginot Line – continued even after Italy had entered the war against the Allies, the value of such expensive defensive lines now highly questionable. Not surprisingly, by the end of 1939, the Axis alliance had sunk to a low point.

Watching Duce's swagger and belligerent indecision, General Sir Archibald Wavell, Britain's Commander-in-Chief of forces in the Middle East, likened him to a swimmer atop a diving platform, who had bared his chest, yet was hesitant to jump. As late as 29 May, the Italian dictator had assured his Chiefs of Staff that 'on the land front we cannot undertake anything spectacular, we shall remain on the defensive'.

The rhetoric finally ended on 30 May. Mussolini informed Hitler of his decision to exploit Nazi Germany's astonishing success and open hostilities. From the balcony of his fifteenth-century Roman palace, the Palazzo Venezia, a buoyant Mussolini proclaimed – to the somewhat unenthusiastic audience gathered below – his declaration of war against France and Britain, effective midnight, 'Italian people, rush to arms and show your tenacity, your courage, your valour.' As in 1911 and 1915, the elderly King Victor Emmanuel III once again consented to a new war. 'May God help Italy!' Foreign Minister Ciano noted in his diary.[13] Ten days later, on the eve of the French surrender, Mussolini opportunistically launched an attack on France across the Alps.[14] His army's only success on the ground was the capture of the small French town of Menton. It was brief, yet costly, battle. The poorly equipped and badly led Italian force lost 631 men killed and 2,631 wounded. A further 2,151 troops were struck down with severe frostbite. Tellingly, the French Army lost only forty killed and eighty-four wounded.

Mussolini was thus holding a weak hand during the following Italo-French armistice talks on 24 June; the French under no illusion who their conquerors really were. The area awarded to Italy, including Menton and its 28,500 French inhabitants, measured a mere 320 square miles, buffered by a demilitarised zone of 31 miles. All told, it was an ignominious entry into the war.

Mussolini's Mediterranean Gamble

'If I were the English commander, I would already be in Tobruk.'

– Marshal Italo Balbo, a week after Italy joined the war

It is said that the Middle East is the most bloodstained region on the planet. As a land bridge connecting Europe, Asia and Africa, it was the crossroads of Britain's Empire – the primary thoroughfare for London's commercial, political and cultural ties. Britain had long challenged any country, including Turkey, Russia and France, who had sought to dominate the eastern Mediterranean and the Levant (which included Israel, Jordan, Lebanon, Palestine and Syria). Key naval bases were established by Britain to protect her sizeable commercial fleet at Gibraltar (taken from the Spanish in 1704), Malta (captured from the French in 1800) and Alexandria (occupied in 1882). By 1940, the Middle East was politically, economically and strategically indispensable to Britain. The 5 per cent of the world's oil produced there was more than enough to cover Britain's immediate needs, or indeed those of the Axis. Further, its geographical depth shielded India and safeguarded the Suez Canal. It also underpinned British prestige. To lose

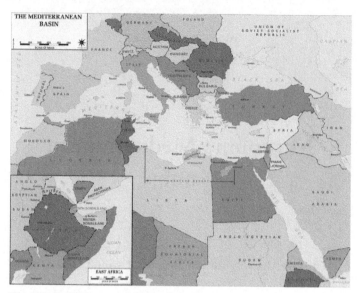

The Middle East, crossroads of the British Empire.

the Middle East, with its oil and strategic significance, to the Axis would be calamitous for Britain, her standing allies, and potentially new ones at a time when it was far from certain if America would enter the war.

Italy, as we have seen, was the first nation after 1918 to alarm Britain militarily. And after entering the war in mid-1940, it was Mussolini, not Hitler, who posed the greatest danger to British Empire lifelines through the Middle East. But while Churchill appreciated this threat, he was oblivious to the manoeuvring within the fascist partnership – an alliance, we have seen, built largely upon disparate objectives. Rather than working in close unison with Hitler, whom he was relying upon to defeat Britain via a cross-Channel invasion, the Duce intended to wage his *own* war. He even coined the term 'parallel war' to describe his intended path of conquest, independent to that of Germany and designed to further Italian, not Axis, interests. Hitler's obsession with the

Soviet Union was already taking precedence over Britain's defeat and the Axis partnership, which, tainted by years of rivalry and mistrust, now strained under the yoke of differing goals, unequal economic reserves and disparate military capabilities. In truth, Rome and Berlin were looking to opening new fronts independently.

Archibald Wavell

Responsibility for Britain's shaky control over the Middle East lay with General Sir Archibald Wavell. Born into a military family on 5 May 1883, Wavell was a gifted soldier with a flair for literature and the classics. His relationship with the Middle East began while serving as liaison officer to General Sir Edmund Allenby (Commander-in-Chief of the Mediterranean Expeditionary Force) during the 1917 to 1918 Palestine campaign. In July 1937, he returned to Palestine to assume command of the British forces during the violent Arab rebellion. With Europe edging closer to a new war, he predicted that a future conflict would be lost or won in the Mediterranean:

> The last war was won in the West, and could only have been won in the West, though a success in the Mediterranean at Gallipoli might have shortened it by a year or two. The next war, as I see it, will be won or lost in the Mediterranean; and the longer it takes us to secure effective control of the Mediterranean, the harder will the winning of the war be.[1]

Wavell was appointed commander-in-chief of the Middle East on 2 August 1939, joining Admiral Sir Andrew Cunningham, commander-in-chief of the RN in the Mediterranean, and Air Chief Marshal Sir Arthur Longmore, commander-in-chief of the RAF in the Middle East. His vast area of command, which covered two continents, encompassed Egypt, Palestine, Transjordan, Sudan and Cyprus. The outbreak of war brought the extra responsibility of British Somaliland, Aden, Iran and the coastline of the Persian Gulf, plus the role of liaising with the French military commands in Syria, North Africa and French Somaliland, the Turkish general staff and, potentially, the general staff of Greece and Romania.

A number of disturbing possible scenarios also existed within his immense area of responsibility. What if the Axis enticed Vichy France's African states to join the war against Britain? What would be the upshot of the Arab world's growing unrest and impassioned opposition to British authority, especially after successive British defeats in Europe? Would Germany intervene? As we recall, there was also the prospect of Russian expansion into the Middle East, at a time when Moscow was at least theoretically allied with Berlin. Would Stalin invade Iran and endanger British oil supplies? Alternatively, would the Soviets annex northern Afghanistan and bring northern India within range of their bombers? Or would the Red Army instead enter Turkey? Finally, would Mussolini consolidate his position in East Africa and disrupt British shipping through the Red Sea, or would the Duce, free from any threat from French-controlled Tunisia, invade Egypt? Things were going to come down to a pitched battle somewhere, and all of the Middle East – perhaps the war itself – was going to depend on the outcome.

Italo Balbo's Dilemma

Wavell's equivalent across the Libyan frontier in 1940 was the charismatic Marshal Italo Balbo. A decorated officer in the Alpine Corps during the First World War, Balbo was drawn to fascism in 1921 and joined Mussolini in his March on Rome the following year. An avid pilot, Balbo's courageous interwar transtlantic and record-breaking Schneider

Trophy flights had helped launch Fascist Italy on to the world's stage. Balbo also advocated the modernisation of the armed forces, while calling for Italy to become a major power in the Mediterranean. Before any of his reforms were realised, however, Mussolini (who was planning to invade Abyssinia) appointed, or more appropriately exiled, his ambitious and popular air minister to Libya as its new governor. Balbo arrived in Tripoli on 15 January 1934, to begin what he termed his 'political retirement'.[2] Despite his initial disappointment, Balbo soon threw his energy into the colonisation of Libya – Italy's new 'Fourth Shore'.

Italy had spent two decades dealing with internal conflict against the Sanusi and Libya remained an underdeveloped liability. The country still required modern infrastructure, education of the native population, sustained agricultural growth and an influx of immigrants. One of Balbo's first accomplishments after taking power was to unite the country's two provinces, Cyrenaica and Tripolitania, and to join them by a sealed coastal highway. Dubbed the *Via Balbia*, the coast road snaked 1,132 miles across Libya's coastal fringe country, from the Tunisian border in the east to the Egyptian one in the west. Amid much fanfare, Mussolini travelled to Libya for the inauguration of the road – an impressive engineering feat of immense strategic value – in January 1937.

Looking to the north, Balbo was appalled by the imminent prospect that Italy might enter a new war allied with Germany. After Hitler entered Poland, he predicted a repeat of 1918 – a German defeat at the hands of the Allies, with disastrous consequences. He appealed to Rome to delay Italy's entry into this new conflict so he could consolidate his resources in Libya, his communiqués complaining of poor morale and the need for reinforcements. His warnings, however, were ignored. On the day Mussolini declared war, he again expressed his apprehension over the capabilities of his Italo-Libyan army in terms of their arms, writing: 'It is not the number of men which causes me anxiety, but their weapons. With two big formations equipped with limited and very old pieces of artillery, lacking in anti-tank and anti-aircraft weapons.'[3]

Balbo was also acutely aware of the substandard level of his troops' training – a shortcoming compounded by their lowly calibre. In 1940, approximately half of Mussolini's soldiers were from peasant backgrounds, unable to differentiate their left hand from their right. In jest, a frustrated Balbo requested that his personal aircraft be brightly painted red to avoid being shot down by friendly fire – an ironic foretelling of his own death at Tobruk several months later.[4]

Despite his protestations, Balbo had, under pressure from Rome, drawn up tentative pre-war plans for what was literally a march – since his infantry divisions, as we saw, were poorly motorised – on Cairo – some 1,250 miles away, across a mostly waterless desert. Several months after the start of the war, there were still fewer than 2,000 vehicles in the whole of Libya; less than what a single German motorised division possessed. To overcome a lack of modern armour, Balbo requested fifty German tanks and fifty armoured cars. Typically loathe to accept any German assistance within 'his' sphere of influence, Mussolini agreed instead to providing seventy of the latest M11/39 medium tanks – every vehicle that the Italian Army possessed at this time.

To reach Cairo, Balbo's army would first have to cross the Western Desert. Over the centuries, the desert had witnessed the destruction of the Persian army of King Cambyses II in 525 BC, the defeat of Napoleon Bonaparte's expedition to Egypt in 1801 and, more recently, Italy's suppression of the Sanusi. An unforgiving environment for any army, Churchill described it as an adversary like 'nothing in the world'. In 1940, *Newsweek* described the desert as:

> … a strange and wonderful fighting place … it was a vast manoeuvre ground, with no civilian population to hamper

operations, plenty of gullies and hills to provide concealment, and a terrain on which tanks could operate in any direction.[5]

Most of the fighting took place along the vast and largely featureless coastal plain, where only small towns and isolated forts punctuated a sparsely populated wilderness. Rather than a sea of dunes as one might imagine, the terrain is mostly a hard limestone base, covered with fine sand and interrupted by patches of protruding hard rock. The ground was often so stony that digging trenches proved almost impossible without explosives or power tools. With experience, soldiers knew to look where desert rats had dug their holes – a sign that the ground would be softer. An Australian Army training bulletin directed that 'slit trenches will be dug on all but the shortest of halts. Even a shallow trench is better than nothing. Unwilling troops will quickly become keen to dig after their first raid.'[6] As German Lieutenant Joachim Schorm (5th Panzer Regiment) observed: 'The war in Africa is quite different from the war in Europe … Nobody and nothing can be concealed.'[7]

The few natural landmarks and small number of tracks, often appearing on maps with dubious accuracy, dictated the need for skilful driving and precise navigation by using the sun, stars, compass and speedometer. Visibility was usually around 3,000 to 4,000yd, though mirages brought false hope of nearby water to the inexperienced, while the heat haze made observation and range finding difficult and inaccurate during the hottest part of the day. The effect of light on the landscape also changed the appearance of objects over the course of a day; a sandy mound, for example, would look far more prominent in the morning than it would later in the day when the sun rose.[8]

Daytime temperatures in the interior were invariably warm to very hot. Sun-baked steel became too hot to touch and photos of eggs frying on armour plate became a popular newsreel theme. Night-time temperatures, conversely, could plummet to below freezing.

Drinking water was always scarce, and rainfall was rare. Tobruk and the surrounding areas, for example, received an average of roughly 11in of rain annually, mostly in January or early February. Sudden storms would flood the narrow desert ravines, or *wadis*, and turn the neighbouring desert into a quagmire.[9] Aside from small daily rations delivered to the front lines, water could be found at secluded points along the coastal strip, or occasionally in Roman-built wells or inland oases. The small daily ration was used not only for drinking, but also for shaving, washing and cooking. Dirty water, where possible, was reused, as radiator coolant and the like.

A much-despised curse blew northward from the Sahara. Known to the British as a *khamsin*, and to Italians as a *ghibli*, these blinding desert sandstorms were a menace to men and machinery alike. Visibility was reduced to barely a few yards, halting all movement. Flying was impossible. The driver of a car could not see beyond the bonnet before him. Maintenance would cease, weapons would clog and lungs choke. Optical instruments were ruined. Whirling sand particles generated electrical disturbances that rendered a compass useless and on one occasion, in May 1942, the destruction of an ammunition dump was attributed to an electrical discharge from such a storm. A *ghibli* could last for days, blanketing hundreds of square miles and testing the patience of all exposed severely. Under Bedouin law, it was even permissible for a man to be found innocent of killing his wife during a *khamsin* lasting five days!

When the air cleared, the lack of cover made air attacks deadly. Vehicles, accordingly, were dispersed over wide areas, to lessen the risk of becoming a target, and detract attention from dumps and headquarters. The harsh environment placed enormous strain was placed on vehicles, with engine and track life considerably shortened compared to movement on bitumen roads. The movement of vehicles across the desert floor also raised clouds of dust as fine as talcum powder, a telltale sign to friend and foe alike. Weapons and equipment were especially affected by the dust with special care needed to clean moving parts and cover them when not in use.

Since the desert itself yielded virtually nothing to support an army, every individual item necessary for living and fighting required transport from the rear supply bases to the front lines. A key logistical challenge, it was further compounded by victory – as an advancing army gained ground, so did its supply lines correspondingly lengthen. It was for this reason that coastal ports such as Tobruk and Benghazi became so valuable.

Living in the desert also brought the nuisance of scorpions (which could nest in boots), vipers and tiny sand fleas. The flies seemed countless. As a captured German report grumbled: 'Plagues of flies and danger of infection are the inevitable results of any but most scrupulous cleanliness ... The menace of flies cannot be exaggerated, as they convey the most serious diseases with which the armies in the field will have to contend.'[10] The desert took a tremendous toll on Rommel's *Afrikaner*. In the period from March to June 1941, for example, the Germans lost 12,203 men: 3,512 as battlefield casualties and the remainder through sickness, dysentery and jaundice.

The relative absence of civilians and refugees on the open Western Desert battlefield for the most part spared the opposing armies from the problem of killing or wounding innocent bystanders. While the to-and-fro movement of armies across Cyrenaica would have brought about economic devastation and social collapse in a European state, the nomadic Bedouin were barely affected, and continued grazing their animals as they had done for centuries. Those who remained by the busy coastal road watched the movement back and forth of various armies, holding up eggs for those who had the time or inclination to purchase. Unbeknownst to them, the Western Desert had been thrust on to the world stage as the British and the Axis clashed over the dominance of Egypt and beyond.

An Asymmetric Response

Italy in 1940, as we have seen, was far from prepared to wage a war against a modern European enemy such as Britain. Yet shortly after the French armistice, Mussolini found himself engaged in this very predicament. And across three separate theatres: at sea in the Mediterranean, and on land in East and North Africa.

Whereas Balbo was vehemently opposed to invading Egypt, Wavell reacted swiftly to Italy's declaration of war (on 10 June) with plans to 'dominate the Mediterranean at the earliest possible moment'. The next day the RN sailed from Alexandria toward the heel of Italy in an unsuccessful attempt to draw the *Regia Marina* into battle. A dawn attack against Tobruk by nine RAF Blenheim bombers and two RN cruisers severely damaged the elderly Italian cruiser *San Giorgio*, a veteran of the earlier Italo–Turkish and First World Wars. Concerted raids continued against the town's harbour and airfield; an attack by Swordfish aircraft from the RN aircraft carrier HMS *Eagle* on 20 July compelled the Italians to abandon Tobruk as an army supply centre and base for their light naval forces.[11] The Italians responded with a series of retaliatory bombing missions against British targets in the desert and Alexandria, though the bombing was inaccurate and the damage slight.

The British firmly held the initiative on the ground where invaluable experience in desert warfare was gained against a hesitant enemy. The men of the 11th Hussars, 7th Armoured Division easily broke through the triple lines of rusting barbed wire along the Egyptian–Libyan border – a 169-mile-long barricade known as the 'Graziani Wall' – in their ageing 1920s-model Rolls-Royce and Morris armoured cars. Italian telegraph communications were severed, convoys were ambushed and remote enemy outposts attacked in the ensuing guerrilla campaign. Among those captured during the initial skirmishes was Brigadier General Romolo Lastrucci, the engineer in chief of the Italian Tenth Army, and the first of many Italian generals to fall into British hands.

The British frontier raids had a devastating effect on Italian morale. Balbo became ever more pessimistic *vis-à-vis* Italy's desert fortunes. Lacking armoured cars, reliable tanks and adequate trucks, his troops fought back against the British armour with rifles and machine guns. He assured Rome that 'we will not give up and we will perform miracles'; more accurately, he quipped, 'If I were the English commander, I would already be in Tobruk'.[12] Tragically, Balbo died on 28 June, when the Savoia-Marchetti SM.79 aircraft he was piloting was mistakenly shot down by his own anti-aircraft batteries, shortly after a British air raid, as he approached Tobruk. Mussolini received the news impassively. The colony, rife with rumours that Balbo's death was anything but accidental, officially mourned his passing for five days. In one of the many chivalrous exchanges of the desert war, a letter of condolence from Arthur Longmore, RAF commander-in-chief, Middle East, was dropped over Tobruk, paying homage to a 'great leader and gallant aviator'.[13]

Balbo's successor was Marshal Rodolfo Graziani, Italy's foremost 'colonial' soldier. Having seen action on the Italian Front during the First World War, Graziani ended that conflict as the army's youngest colonel. From 1928 to 1934, he served in Libya, where he became known as 'the butcher' for his brutal repression of the native tribesmen. Graziani later led the invasion of Abyssinia (in October 1935) from Italian Somaliland, where he was governor. Appointed army Chief of Staff in October 1939, he returned to Libya upon Balbo's death on 30 June 1940, to assume command of the jittery Italian forces, his enthusiasm for the projected march on Cairo little better than that of his predecessor.

Mussolini, meanwhile, awaited Hitler's crossing of the English Channel before single-handedly launching his own invasion of Egypt. He boasted to Graziani via telegram that victory over Britain would not only provide an overland passage for Italian troops to Abyssinia, but also seal the fate of her Empire. Graziani begged to differ, and promptly proffered his resignation over an operation he believed would be a 'total disaster'.[14]

While Graziani sat firm, Mussolini struck elsewhere in Africa – where the British were at their weakest. On 4 July 1940, Prince Amedeo II di Savoia-Aosta, commander-in-chief of Italian forces in East Africa, invaded British Sudan. His combined army of 92,000 Italian and 250,000 native troops vastly outnumbered the 40,000 British troops, the majority also native, including the wonderfully suggestive Somaliland Camel Corps. Three weeks later, Italian General Guglielmo Nasi launched another operation to capture Berbera, the capital of the Protectorate of British Somaliland. Overwhelmed, the British were forced to retire. Although largely a sideshow, the East African fighting delivered Mussolini his first British colony – an impressive propaganda coup.

To the north at his headquarters at Tobruk, however, Graziani continued to stubbornly delay his Egyptian venture. A British air raid on the base on 31 August – his first experience of such an attack – so unnerved the veteran commander that he fled eastward to the relative subterranean security of the ancient Greek and Roman ruins at Cyrene. Citing the need for additional time, equipment and trucks, he again appealed to Rome for the date of the operation to be pushed back, this time to the end of October. But sensing Britain's downfall, Mussolini stood firm. As he had with his eleventh-hour intervention in France, the Duce needed troops fighting in Egypt to ensure his slice of the territorial cake once Churchill finally capitulated. Graziani, for that reason, received orders to launch his invasion on 9 September 1940. Resigned to conduct what would be his final offensive, he despondently inscribed in his diary: 'For whatever evil may occur, I, before God and my soldiers, am not *responsible*.'[15] Across the Mediterranean, Ciano

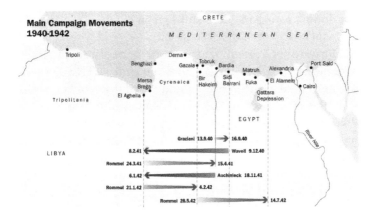

The fluctuating fortunes of the Axis and Allied armies during the North African Campaign.

portentously recorded that: 'Never has a military operation been undertaken so much against the will of the commanders.'[16] Similarly doubtful, the German military attaché In Rome, General Enno von Rintelen, predicted 'no immediate prospect of [Graziani] capturing Alexandria, the Delta, or the Canal, nor of opening up the route to East Africa.'

Graziani's 'Colonial' Offensive

As the fighting in North Africa during the First World War had demonstrated, even a small force of native tribesmen and Turkish soldiers could threaten Egyptian security and tie down enemy resources. With his Tenth Army now assembled on the Egyptian border in readiness for battle, Mussolini believed that victory beckoned. He would be responsible for bringing Britain to its knees as an imperial power. He would deliver the *coup de grâce*. But how would his troops actually perform against a well-equipped enemy well versed in desert warfare? Would the operation be a repetition of

Mussolini's less-than-successful French enterprise, or would Graziani's men reach the Nile Delta?

Outwardly, Graziani held a distinct numerical advantage over the British in infantry, armour and artillery. Five divisions of the Italian Tenth Army would participate in the invasion: the 1st Blackshirt '23 March' Division (the Blackshirt divisions were named after the anniversaries of the Fascist revolution), 62nd 'Marmarica' and 63rd 'Cirene' Division, 1st and 2nd Libyan Divisions, plus a small mobile force under General Pietro Maletti, comprised of three Libyan battalions and an artillery unit. Held in reserve at Tobruk were the 61st 'Sirte' and 4th Blackshirt '28 October' infantry divisions. Lieutenant General Valentino Babini's armoured force comprised six battalions – a mix of light tanks and seventy of the newly arrived M11/39 medium tanks. The 5th *Squadra Aerea* would provide aerial support with 336 aircraft, including 170 fighters (which, despite Italy's broad experience in Libya, still lacked crucial engine sand filters), 110 bombers, fifty ground attack aircraft and six long-range reconnaissance aircraft. Additional aircraft from Italy would arrive on the day of the attack.

Across the frontier, the RAF possessed 100 bombers, 140 fighters and 270 other machines, though a number of these aircraft were engaged in patrolling the Red Sea. While Italian intelligence erroneously estimated 100,000 British troops in Egypt, in reality, there were only 36,000, of whom only 25,500 were part of an organised formation. Under the command of Lieutenant General Sir Henry 'Jumbo' Maitland Wilson, the Army of the Nile, as it was known for propaganda purposes, comprised the 7th Armoured Division – one of only two armoured divisions that Britain possessed – the newly arrived 4th Indian Division, the Australian 6th Division and the New Zealand Division. Of this force, the Indian division lacked transport, ammunition and artillery; the Australian 6th Division was only partially trained; and the armoured division was below strength with only 4,000 men, thirty-eight armoured cars and fewer than seventy tanks.

Heavily outnumbered, the British tanks were still more than a match for Italian armour in terms of specialisation, armour and weaponry. Mobile armoured support was provided by the lightly armoured Universal Carriers (also known as the Bren Gun Carrier), which were open-topped tracked vehicles usually armed with machine guns or a Boys anti-tank rifle. While Italy was primarily reliant on light tanks and a limited number of medium tanks, British pre-war doctrine divided armour into three specialised categories according to role: the smaller and less well-protected light tanks were designed for reconnaissance duties; 'Cruiser' tanks, being fast and lightly armoured, were intended for mobile warfare; and 'Infantry' tanks were slow, heavily armoured and designed to support advancing infantrymen. British tanks in Egypt in 1940 comprised an assortment of Vickers Mark VI series Light Tanks, armed with two machine guns; medium Cruiser Mark I tanks, armed with a 2-pounder gun (Britain's standard tank and anti-tank gun of the time) or a 3.7in mortar for close support; and the heavily armoured and slower Infantry Tank Mark II or 'Matilda'. Commonly referred to as an 'I' (Infantry) tank, the Matilda was protected by a substantial 2.95in of frontal armour. While it was armed with the obsolete 2-pounder gun and a 7.92mm Besa machine gun, it was still largely invulnerable to the small Italian anti-tank weapons of the time, earning it the nickname 'Queen of the Desert'. Experience quickly led to a request for a tank more mobile than a Matilda but equally well protected, though no British tank meeting this specification would fight in the Western Desert.

Mussolini's Egyptian quest began on an inauspicious note. Even before his troops had crossed the frontier, a series of last-minute hitches dictated a revision of the original plan. Insufficient wheeled transport forced the two Libyan infantry divisions, originally scheduled to push inland with Maletti's mechanised force, to alternatively advance along the coastal road, together with the main body of the Tenth Army. Trouble struck Maletti's brigade, which become lost. Eventually located by air, short of fuel and water, the delay caused in redirecting it toward the frontier compelled Graziani to abandon his original plan of turning the inland flank of the British forces. Graziani's entire invasion force would now proceed along the coast after crossing the frontier.

Dawn on the morning of 13 September 1940 was accompanied by an impressive Italian artillery barrage, though most of the shells fell uselessly on to the recently evacuated British airfield and barracks at Sollum. Resembling more of a ceremonial military parade than an invasion, Graziani's offensive lacked enterprise, enthusiasm and tactical flair. Many junior Italian officers panicked under the accurate British return fire, and more than once the commander of the forward elements, General Annibale 'Electric Whiskers' Bergonzoli – so named because of his fiery red beard – physically coerced his artillery officers back to their guns.

On the British side, although the majority of the 7th Armoured Division had already withdrawn to Mersa Matruh, a small support group of artillery, engineers, machine gunners and cruiser tanks under Brigadier William 'Strafer' Gott had remained behind. (The soubriquet 'Strafer' was a play on the German Army's First World War slogan *Gott strafe England*, 'May God punish England'.) Skilfully retreating ahead of the Italians, Gott's small force briefly held up the Italians before withdrawing further east.

Given no specific objectives, Graziani felt vindicated by his limited incursion into Egypt. But that was the end of it. As British intelligence had correctly predicted, the reluctant Italian commander's 'colonial' offensive stopped at the town of Sidi Barrani on 16 September, after advancing just 65 miles![17] He was still some 80 miles short of the British base at Matruh, 360 miles short of Cairo. After a week of fighting,

Italian casualties stood at 530 – a lopsided indicator in comparison to the British loss of fewer than fifty men. The Italian propaganda machine, nevertheless, worked tirelessly to turn the capture of the small, dusty town into a major victory, proclaiming: 'thanks to the skill of Italian engineers, the tramcars were again running.'[18] Not that the primitive village needed or actually possessed anything resembling an electric public transport network. Graziani also deceitfully boasted that he had destroyed half of the British armour, and that his advance had 'surpassed all expectations'.

In reality, Graziani had achieved little. By capturing the British airfield at Sollum, just inside the Egyptian border, he had restricted the RAF's range and kept RN ships from bombarding Italian positions of air cover. But he had foundered by not pushing further and securing Mersa Matruh. Had he captured this important base and railhead, Italian bombers may well have driven the British fleet from Alexandria. As it stood, Italian supply lines now extended across miles of virtually worthless desert, to what was hardly a strategic prize.

Graziani, in the finest tradition of his ancient forebears, proposed the building of an aqueduct while his troops began constructing a series of independent fortified camps – similar to the 'boxes' later used by British to defend the Gazala Line in 1942 – around Sidi Barrani.[19] Despite notifying Marshal Badoglio (Chief of Staff of the *Regio Esercito*) that he was uncertain when he would resume the offensive, Ciano found Mussolini the same day 'radiant with joy'.[20] The 'invasion' had been disappointing at best, but Italian troops were firmly ensconced within Egypt, and the main British force had withdrawn east.

These modest fortunes, however, were to be short-lived. Wavell had already started planning a counter-attack against the encamped enemy. Moreover, the unpopular Egyptian operation was now jeopardised by Mussolini's independent plans to enter the Balkans by invading either Greece or

Yugoslavia – a folly that would have immense bearing upon the Axis partnership.

Mussolini's Balkan Watershed

The Balkan Peninsula, like the Western Desert, has a long history of hot-blooded violence. As we saw earlier, the region's volatility gave rise to the events that produced the First World War. On 7 April 1939, a new chapter was written when Mussolini invaded Albania. Albania's King Zog was forced into exile and the newly installed puppet government declared war on the Allies. For the nominal cost of twelve killed, the annexation of this small country gave Italy control over the Adriatic Sea and a platform from which Mussolini could attack neighbouring Greece.

Greece's leader at the time, General Ioannis Metaxas, was head of a right-wing quasi-fascist dictatorship. Although he lacked the magnetism, popularity, theatrics and trappings of his equals in Berlin and Rome, Metaxas nevertheless decreed a 'Third Hellenic Civilisation', complete with designs on Cyprus, the Dodecanese, even Constantinople. When war broke out in 1939, Metaxas adopted a neutral stance, though he was prepared to provide small-scale military assistance to Britain if necessary.

Ciano met with Hitler on 7 July 1940, to seek his endorsement of an Italian push into the Balkans. Circumspect about his ally's involvement in Greece, the Führer vetoed any advance into Yugoslavia, a move that could prompt a Hungarian invasion of Romania, or push the Soviets to occupy the Turkish straits. As an alternative, Hitler suggested the occupation of Crete and Cyprus as a means to destabilise Britain's presence in the Mediterranean.

With Greece firmly set in Mussolini's sights, Rome began escalating diplomatic pressure on Athens, while Italian newspapers ran threats. The Italian military upped the ante by blatantly attacking merchant and naval shipping in Greek waters, including the torpedoing of the elderly Greek cruiser *Elli*, at anchor during a religious celebration on 15 August. Yet despite such intense goading on the cusp of a new Italo-Balkan war, a dearth of leadership and strategic direction existed within Mussolini's *Comando Supremo*, the Italian High Command and equivalent to Germany's *Oberkommando der Wehrmacht* (OKW). On the day of the unprovoked *Elli* attack, General Quirino Armellini, Badoglio's deputy, wrote:

> We continue in the greatest disorder and complete chaos. In *Comando Supremo*, everyone commands. The last man to speak is always right. Strategic conceptions are regularly reversed with an astonishing lack of logic … The Duce hasn't the least idea of the differences between preparing for war on flat terrain or in mountains, in summer or in winter. Still less does he worry about the fact that we lack weapons, ammunition, equipment, animals, [and] raw materials.

On the eve of Mussolini's Balkan (mis)adventure, Berlin again called on Rome to avoid any provocation in the Balkans that could trigger British and Soviet intervention. For the moment, however, Mussolini returned to his Egyptian undertaking, which as we have seen, had halted at Sidi Barrani. But even as he pressured Graziani to press onward to Mersa Matruh, clandestine preparations continued for the invasion of Greece – independent of Hitler's victory over Britain, or even his support.

Germany's Peripheral Strategy

Representatives of Germany, Italy and Japan gathered in Berlin on 27 September 1940 to sign the Tripartite Pact, an agreement to provide mutual assistance should any of the signatories suffer attack by any nation not already involved in the war. It was, as Ciano penned in his diary, a disheartening sign that the war would be a long one.[21]

Aside from propaganda milage, the Pact revealed the overall inadequacy of Axis co-operation and strategy, particularly in comparison to the Allied Grand Alliance. Rather than cementing collaboration, the treaty was little more than a superficial show of unity. With Sea Lion effectively shelved, Hitler hoped that an alliance with Japan would continue to keep America neutral, at least for the short term, and prevent Roosevelt from coming to Britain's aid. The Pact also threatened Russia with war on two fronts. But as one historian termed it, the Japanese–German alliance was a 'hollow' one.[22] By mid-1940, its Italo-German equivalent was also fast becoming a major liability – one that was about to drag Hitler away from his strategic focus on the Soviet Union, and into a series of new and unwanted campaigns.

This was seminal point in the war for the Axis. Having already observed the lack of direction inside Comando Supremo, we find a parallel situation within Hitler's headquarters. General Walther Warlimont, Deputy Chief of OKW Operations staff, for one, deplored the lack of strategic direction, what he called a 'morass'.[23] Hitler still needed to eliminate British resistance (before the US entered the war), while also preparing for a campaign in the East. In lieu of a cross-Channel landing (since the Luftwaffe in the skies over Britain), the Führer could take only 'peripheral' action against Britain. With winter approaching, his senior army and naval commanders turned to alternative means of crippling Britain by intervening in the Mediterranean and Middle East.

For the second half of 1940, OKW contemplated whether to support an Italian invasion of Egypt, although the proposed scope and commitment fluctuated in line with Rome's recalcitrant agenda. A powerful voice in Hitler's ear, Grand Admiral Erich Raeder – the commander-in-chief of the *Kriegsmarine*

(German Navy) – fully supported the idea of driving the British from the Mediterranean, 'the pivot of their world empire'.[24] He also argued that Italy would soon become an Allied target, and pushed for the capture of Gibraltar, the Suez Canal, Syria and Palestine. In addition, he predicted that Britain, in partnership with Gaullist France and possibly the United States, would eventually use North West Africa as a base from which to attack and eventually defeat Italy. In early September 1940, Raeder highlighted to Hitler the importance of maintaining the current treaty with Russia and to avoid war on two fronts. Stressing the value of Suez (Egypt) and Gibraltar to Churchill, and the need to conquer Britain before the United States entered the war, Raeder deemed the Mediterranean 'decisive'.

While OKW evaluated deploying troops in North Africa, Hitler was only too aware that Mussolini viewed Egypt exclusively as an Italian domain. The Duce was already indignant over Germany's presence in Romania – again within *his* Balkan sphere of influence. The Kingdom of Romania, under Prime Minister Marshal Ion Antonescu, was now dependent upon Germany, both economically and militarily, especially after the ill fortunes of Bucharest's primary guarantors of territorial integrity: Britain and France. Strongly pro-German, Antonescu was a signatory to the Tripartite Pact, and his troops would later march alongside Germany's in the invasion of the Soviet Union. In October 1940, he welcomed a German military mission – a vital win for Hitler – to protect the vital Ploesti oilfields, which supplied the bulk of Germany's oil imports, and which were now placed in jeopardy by the Red Army, fewer than 100 miles away.

Stalin initially displayed no outward reaction to the German military presence in Romania, though Mussolini was furious. When he learned of Hitler's latest manoeuvre, primarily through newspapers, he telephoned Ciano, requesting corresponding action be taken to 'elicit a [Romanian] request for

Italian troops'. Outraged by a German infiltration once again undertaken with neither his consultation nor collaboration, the Duce made one of his most catastrophic decisions. 'Hitler always faces me with a *fait accompli*,' he declared. 'This time I am going to pay him back in his own coin. He will find out from the papers that I have occupied Greece.'[25] Ciano concurred, believing it would 'useful and easy'.[26]

To the outside world, Mussolini projected the image of a self-assured warlord, proudly jutting his chin as he reviewed his modern day Roman legions. However, behind this cocksure façade was a military incompetent about to commit some of his gravest blunders. On 15 October, he gathered his generals together to outline his plans for the occupation of Greece. To circumvent British intervention, he called for Graziani to push ahead and seize Mersa Matruh. At the same time, General Sebastiano Visconti Prasca, commanding officer of the XXVI Corps in Albania, was to cross the border into Greece. Neither decision was well received. Graziani's response that he needed two months for preparation further enraged Mussolini, while his increasingly pessimistic army Chief of Staff, Badoglio, threatened to resign behind his back should the Greek venture proceed.

In keeping with his private parallel war, the Duce dispatched a letter to the Reich Chancellery on 23 October, in which he categorically rejected any offer of German assistance across the Mediterranean and North Africa. He argued his case for invading Greece on the pretext of possible British collaboration with Athens. He also stated his refusal to co-operate with Vichy France and Spain. He was moving forward, whether Germany liked it or not.

Hitler Woos Spain and Vichy France

Mussolini's fateful communiqué, however, did not reach Hitler for several days, as the Führer had left Berlin on 20 October aboard his armoured command train (named *Amerika*) to meet separately with Vichy France's Marshal Pétain and Spain's fascist dictator General Francisco Franco (who had emerged victorious from the Spanish Civil War). Hitler sought closer co-operation with Pétain and Franco in forming what would be a continental bloc against Britain. What ensued, though, was an unproductive series of bargaining sessions in the midst of a remarkable week.

Hitler first met with the French deputy premier, Pierre Laval, on 22 October. Their discussion proved inconclusive; his talks with Franco the next day were equally fruitless. Spain was important to Hitler; its geo-strategic domination over the Western Approaches and the British base at Gibraltar had the potential to tip the balance against the Allies in both the Mediterranean and the Atlantic if Franco sided with the Axis. But would the cautious *Caudillo* (leader) join forces with Hitler? Although a signatory to a Treaty of Friendship with Germany on 1 September 1939, Franco continued to affirm Spain's neutrality. He later changed his position to one of non-belligerency after Italy's declaration of war, and occupied the international city of Tangier in Morocco. Later the same month, Franco advised Hitler that once he had won over public support, he would be willing to bring Spain into the war in return for French West Africa, French Morocco and Gibraltar, plus considerable supplies of food and arms – lavish demands that Hitler considered unrealistic.

Despite his sympathy for the Axis cause, Franco's willingness to enter the war amounted to little more than words. Three years of civil war had left Spain impoverished, and it was only though considerable British economic assistance and influence that Madrid was able to stave off economic collapse in mid-1940. Until the fall of France, Britain's naval blockade had severely curtailed Spain's trade with Germany. Even with overland transportation restored post-Armistice, Franco's primary trading partners remained Britain, the United States and

Argentina. Given Spain's substantial reliance upon imports, especially US oil, Britain's promise of continued credit and supplies of wheat, and the inability of the Axis to meet its own raw material requirements, we can appreciate Franco's hesitation in declaring war against the Allies. Furthermore, the Spanish army was both unprepared and ill equipped to fight a new war, lacking sufficient artillery, ammunition, spare parts, officers and fuel reserves.

In his next round of talks, Hitler met with Marshal Pétain on 24 October to broach Vichy France joining the war against Britain. Coming shortly after the defeat of the Anglo-Free French (the Free French Government exiled in London and led by Charles de Gaulle had rejected Pétain's armistice) expedition to the Vichy-held African port of Dakar, and Vichy's retaliatory air raid on Gibraltar, Hitler's conference with Pétain ended on a promising note. But while co-operation with the Third Reich was agreed to in principle, Pétain's intended collaboration, like that of Franco, carried little credence.

News of Mussolini's Greek enterprise, revealed in a translated copy of the aforementioned letter, finally reached Hitler the next day, 25 October. Infuriated, Hitler learned of the actual invasion – what he later dubbed an 'idiotic campaign' – en route to a meeting with Mussolini in Florence, where he had hoped to forestall it. Composing himself in time for the reception at the train station several hours later, he was greeted by a buoyant Mussolini boasting how 'early this morning [28 October], in the dawn twilight, victorious Italian troops crossed the Greco-Albanian border'.[27]

Mussolini's 'Idiotic Campaign'

The Italian invasion of Greece followed Metaxas' single word response – 'no' – to a 3.00 a.m. ultimatum demanding the right to occupy certain strategic territory in light of Athens' alignment with Britain. In what proved to be yet another embarrassing failure for Mussolini, any hopes for an Italian *Blitzkrieg*-style conquest were soon dashed. Through a combination valiant resistance, unfamiliar mountainous terrain and icy weather, the invasion soon stalled. Italian General Ubaldo Soddu replaced a disgraced Visconti Prasca on 10 November. Four days later, Soddu was fighting off a Greek counteroffensive and, humiliatingly, forced to retreat back across the border. By December, the Greeks had liberated one-third of Albania – the first Allied triumph on land since the beginning of hostilities two years earlier.

In yet another fundamental setback for Italy, aircraft from the carrier HMS *Illustrious* severely crippled the Italian fleet at Taranto on the night of 11 November. The two waves of elderly and cumbersome Swordfish aircraft delivered a courageous and hefty blow – later credited as the attack that brought the era of the battleship to an end. The Stringbags, as they were affectionately known, permanently disabled the battleship *Cavour* and put two more, *Littorio* and *Duilio*, out of action for six months. For the price of two planes and their crews, this forerunner to the Japanese attack on Pearl Harbor immediately swung the balance of naval power in the Mediterranean toward Britain. Elsewhere in the Mediterranean that night, British cruisers sank a convoy of four merchant ships, totalling nearly 17,000 tons, headed for the Italian port of Brindisi.

It was now five months since the Italian declaration of war; the Duce's 'private' campaigns in Egypt and Greece were a humiliating failure. Mussolini's Chief of Staff, Badoglio, became the scapegoat, labelled an 'enemy of the regime' and a 'traitor'. A malicious editorial attack in the fascist paper *Regime Fascista* prompted his resignation on 26 November 1940. His replacement, General Ugo Cavallero, was considered by many to be the Duce's greatest military commander. A brigadier general in the First World War, Cavallero assumed personal command of the Albanian Front in December. Mussolini had just relieved Soddu, having been dissatisfied for some time by his inconsistent behaviour, the final straw being the discovery that his commander in the field was spending his evenings in Albania composing film scores!

Shortly before his resignation, Badoglio had refused an offer by Field Marshal Wilhelm Keitel, Chief of the OKW, for two Panzer divisions on the absurd grounds that the tanks would be 'ineffective' and unable to operate in a sandy desert environment. Despite Italy's ongoing aversion to receiving much-needed modern armoured reinforcements, Germany continued to study sending armour and troops to North Africa, as well as intervening in Mussolini's Greek debacle. But as Hitler complained:

> The lunacy about it all is that on the one hand the Italians are screaming blue murder and painting their shortages of arms and equipment in the blackest terms, and on the other hand they are so jealous and infantile that they find the using of using German soldiers and German materials quite repugnant.[28]

To alleviate Italian misfortune, on 4 November 1940 Hitler ordered preliminary plans drawn up for an offensive against Greece the following spring. This unfortunate and unforeseen intervention was necessary to counter the Italian rout, to safeguard Germany's southern flank in the lead up to the invasion of the Soviet Union, and to protect Germany's economic interests in the Balkans. Aside from Romanian oil, Greece and Yugoslavia also supplied 45 per cent of the Third Reich's bauxite. Yugoslavia alone supplied 90 per cent of Germany's tin and 40 per cent of its lead. It was vital that those areas be protected.

With winter fast approaching, the Führer also returned to the Spanish question. Notwithstanding El Caudillo's obstinacy, on 12 November 1940 he issued Directive No. 18, detailing *Unternehmen Felix* ('Operation Felix'): the capture of Gibraltar and the need to bring Spain into the war. The document also called for the safeguarding of France's colonial possessions against British and Free French forces, and the possible invasion of Portugal should Britain land troops there. A month later, on 8 December, Franco confirmed that he would not repeat Mussolini's folly and enter the war. Hitler now abandoned his strategic vision for the Western Mediterranean, as well as the mooted occupation of the Azores, Madeira, Canary and Cape Verde Islands. With Felix shelved, Hitler switched his attention to the opposite end of the Mediterranean. On 13 December, he issued Directive No. 20, specifying *Unternehmen Marita*, the invasion of Greece. In the meantime, however, a new crisis in the Western Desert was deepening for the Axis.

'One of the Decisive Events of the War'

'Seldom has a victory over such a large area been more swiftly won.'

The Times, 24 January 1941, on the fall of Tobruk

Wavell, the Quiet General

Even before Graziani had grudgingly crossed the frontier into Egypt, Wavell had requested an appraisal for an operation in the opposite direction, terminating at Tobruk. In it, he underscored the need to 'avoid the slow ponderosity which is apt to characterise British operations',[1] and advised that the march be undertaken by late 1940 or early 1941. Churchill was naturally also eager to strike, but was Wavell the right man for the job? At this early phase in the desert campaign, Churchill was already critical of Wavell's deployments, and unconvinced of his suitability as commander-in-chief, especially after the recent setbacks in East Africa. Wavell was summoned to London in early August 1940, to meet with the premier and his Chiefs of Staff and discuss the situation first-hand. He arrived at a desperate hour. At that point, a mere 21 miles of water at the narrowest point of the English Channel separated Britain from Hitler's legions in France. The tortuous contrails above southern England were testament to Britain's heroic struggle against the Luftwaffe, Hitler's Directive No. 17 calling for the Luftwaffe to destroy the RAF. Would invasion follow?

An inauspicious series of discussions followed, beginning 8 August. The atmosphere was tense, especially given the prime minister's unremitting questioning and Wavell's close-to-pathological reluctance to speak out. His taciturnity was particularly irritating to Churchill, who judged it as symptomatic of a man lacking in 'mental vigour and [the] resolve to overcome obstacles'.[2] Aside from a clash of character, neither individual fully understood the challenges the other faced. Yet despite Churchill's reservations, he chose – for the time being – not to dismiss Wavell.[3] The commander-in-chief departed London on 15 August, the same day a huge armada of 1,120 Luftwaffe aircraft crossed the Channel to entice the beleaguered RAF into the air. He had just finished briefing Churchill on the current withdrawal from British Somaliland. When the premier heard of the relatively light casualties sustained in an evacuation, he demanded that Wavell suspend his commander, Major General Alfred R. Godwin-Austen, and open a court of inquiry into his suspected cowardly conduct. Wavell, however, stood defiant in defending Godwin-Austen, and refused to carry out such an investigation. His inflammatory retort that, 'a big butcher's bill was not necessarily evidence of good tactics'[4] enraged Churchill; the intractable relationship between the two was now beyond resolution.

Churchill, in turn, wasted little time in dispatching his General Directive for Commander-in-Chief Middle East: a highly detailed document that was essentially an order to Wavell, with tactical instructions down to a battalion level. Such a directive from a minister to a commander in the field was not only highly unusual, but a merciless indictment of his leadership. Yet Churchill, the amateur strategist, was both inexperienced and ill-qualified to offer such absolute direction from abroad. Wavell described the premier's need for absolute control and a proclivity for meddling in every aspect of Britain's military endeavour as his penchant for 'at least one finger in any military pie'.[5] While Churchill's own military experience may have been broad, he nevertheless lacked the insight and experience of his commander on the battlefield, casting doubt, for example, on Wavell's report that an armoured group could traverse the desert as easily as it could a sealed road.

To better appreciate the precarious situation in Africa, Churchill dispatched his Secretary of State for war, Anthony Eden, to Egypt. Arriving on 15 October, Eden inspected the British garrison and Egyptian defences. On 28 October – the day Mussolini invaded Greece and enmeshed his military in a new theatre – he flew with Wavell to Khartoum (the capital of Sudan), to meet with the prime minister of the Union of South Africa, General Jan Smuts; the exiled emperor of Ethiopia, Haile Selassie; and local senior commanders. Plans were worked out for an operation in East Africa, to begin the following month. Apart from striking back at the Italians, the new offensive would yield political payback: Eden needed a successful land offensive to ameliorate the pro-German atmosphere in the Middle East, and Smuts needed a victory to counter the pervasive anti-British sentiment within the Union.

Jan Smuts, a Boer War veteran, had fought the Germans under Paul von Lettow-Vorbeck in Africa and had been a member of the Imperial War Cabinet during the First World War. Elected prime minister for a second time in September 1939, following the resignation of General (James) Barry Hertzog over a failed attempt to keep the Union neutral, he faced the challenge of leading a country deeply divided by the war. The Black people had little interest in this new conflict. Of the white minority, the non-English speaking Afrikaners, whose defeat by the British during the Second Boer War

(1899 to 1902) was still a painful wound, were vocal opponents of what was Britain's war, not theirs. Germany, naturally, was favoured as the victor. The deep-seated Afrikaner opposition to Smuts' government saw the *Ossewabrandwag*, an organisation formed to preserve Afrikaner traditions, rapidly burgeon into a violent neo-Nazi organisation. It was in regular contact with Berlin, and committed to the removal of Smuts' government. Pro-Nazi leader Dr. Daniel Malan's 'storm troopers' incited unrest between civilians and the military, committed acts of sabotage, and assisted German internees to escape. At its height, its membership reached 400,000 in a country whose white population was only 2,230,000. Anti-British feeling was fanned by Nazi propaganda broadcasts in Afrikaans from Germany and intervention by the *Abwehr* – the German intelligence and counter-intelligence organisation.

This internal resistance notwithstanding, the Union responded swiftly to Italian aggression. South African Air Force bombers, already stationed in northern Kenya, attacked enemy positions in Italian-held Abyssinia on 11 June 1940. But it would be months before the troops of the South African Army – the 'Springboks' – would be ready for battle. Their first campaign would be to evict the Italians from East Africa before joining the battles for the Western Desert.

Operation Compass

On the morning of 9 December 1940, three months after the Italian invasion of Egypt, General Wavell announced to an unsuspecting group of war correspondents gathered in his Cairo office, 'We have attacked in the Western Desert.' Elaborating further, he cautioned that, 'this is not an offensive and I do not think you ought to describe it as an offensive as yet. You might call it an important raid.' That night, after a spectacularly successful first day of fighting, he drafted a

'Special Order of the Day', in which he speculated how the operation 'will be one of the decisive events of the war'.[6]

Leading Operation Compass – Britain's first land offensive since 1918 – was Lieutenant General (later Sir) Richard O'Connor, arguably one of Britain's finest field commanders. Born into a military family in Kashmir, India on 21 August 1889, O'Connor had graduated from the Royal Military Academy at Sandhurst in 1908. Serving on the Western Front during the First World War, he was awarded the Military Cross (MC) and Distinguished Service Order (DSO) in 1915. As a battalion commander, O'Connor's division was transferred to Italy in 1917, where it fought with great success against the Austro-Hungarians in their last offensive at the Battle of the River Piave. Ironically, he received the Italian Silver Medal for Valour, a decoration he would later wear while charting the downfall Mussolini's army in North Africa.

O'Connor's force in Egypt comprised the 4th Indian Division, under Lieutenant General William Platt; the 16th (British) Infantry Brigade; the 7th Armoured Division (soon to become known as the Desert Rats, because of the division's jerboa or desert rat insignia); the 7th Royal Tank Regiment (RTR); and the 36,000-odd men of the Mersa Matruh garrison. In preparing for Compass, originally designed to be a five-day raid, O'Connor modified Wavell's early orthodox plan of a straightforward frontal attack in favour of a far more daring strike. Aerial reconnaissance and reports from ground patrols had revealed vehicle tracks leading from the western, or rearward, side of the Italian strongholds, as well as an apparent absence of minefields and field obstacles. O'Connor planned to take advantage of this glaring defect, the large distances between Graziani's isolated camps (which prevented them from being mutually supportive), and launch a series of surprise attacks them from the rear.

A concerted RN and RAF bombardment of the Italian camps on the night before the assault helped to mask the clatter of advancing British columns. Surprise the next morning was complete. Many Italian troops emerged from their tents to the sound of gunfire, discovering armour and supporting Indian infantry storming their positions. The Matilda tank, as yet untried in desert conditions, immediately proved its worth with Italian anti-tank shells ricocheting harmlessly off the thick frontal armour. The weather also favoured the attackers, as it grounded Italian aircraft across the frontier. Despite pockets of determined resistance, the Italian camps fell in quick succession. Two Italian divisions caught in the open desert between Sidi Barrani and Mersa Matruh also surrendered.

After only three days of fighting, the first phase of Compass had utterly smashed Mussolini's immediate threat to Egypt. O'Connor next retook Sidi Barrani, with a windfall of 38,300 Italian prisoners, 237 artillery pieces and seventy-three tanks. More than 1,000 vehicles were also captured and pressed into service. British casualties stood at a relatively light 624 men killed or wounded.[7]

For the most part, the Italian soldier in North Africa fought his British opposite – an important First World War ally – with little real conviction. Even Mussolini conceded that 'the Italians of 1914 were better'. His was an army 'not flattering for the regime', and he ridiculed his people as a 'race of sheep'.[8] For the British, this lack of resolve was an unexpected logistical headache, as thousands of dejected enemy prisoners now required food and shelter. At one of the bagged enemy camps, a British officer surveyed the scene before him, estimating 'twenty acres of officers and a hundred acres of men'. Seemingly endless lines of Italian POWs and mountains of abandoned equipment would become a familiar sight as the British raid blossomed into a full-fledged campaign.

O'Connor's attack, wrote Ciano, struck 'like a thunderbolt'.[9] Not surprisingly, Rome's hostility to German ground forces quickly disappeared, and General Cavallero's request (on 18 December) for an entire Panzer division was followed by a similar appeal from Mussolini. Despite Hitler's waning enthusiasm for joint operations with Italy, the *Wehrmacht* now seemed certain to intervene in North Africa. To assist his troubled ally, Hitler suggested on 5 December 1940, as a first step, that Tobruk might be used as an intermediate landing field for Ju 87 dive-bombers based at Sicily and Apulia, to assist the Italians in harassing the British,[10] whose next objective was Bardia – the first significant Italian garrison inside Libya.

Fortress Bardia

Graziani issued orders for the fortress ports of Bardia and Tobruk to be held during a pause in O'Connor's advance at the end of 1940. Whereas Mussolini fully supported the decision, the former reassessed his position and advised Rome on 17 December that Bardia would be difficult to reinforce. Instead, he recommended that all available forces be marshalled for the defence of Tobruk. The Duce, however, was adamant that everything must be done to weaken and delay the British, including the defence of Bardia. Stopping the British as far east as possible would allow additional units to be ferried across from Italy. There was also the question of prestige in holding Cyrenaica, especially after the recent fiasco in Greece.

Mussolini had heavily fortified Bardia, though it was of dubious strategic value, as one of two key fortresses guarding Cyrenaica, the other being Tobruk. A small harbour town close to the Egyptian border, Bardia was enclosed by an 18-mile arc of outer defences, comprising an anti-tank ditch, minefields, barbed wire and eighty individual defensive posts. Impressive in scope, the defences were nevertheless flawed. The reinforced concrete perimeter positions – built flush with the ground and constructed at great cost in labour and materials – were impervious to all but the heaviest bombardment. Yet they were poor defensive positions to fight from – a crucial flaw in their design we will return to later. Within the outer perimeter lay a second inner line of defensive posts, plus a number of individual strongholds. The fortress garrison, under General Annibale Bergonzoli, was the equivalent of four full infantry divisions, with elements of the 1st and 2nd Blackshirt, 62nd 'Marmarica', 63rd 'Cirene' and 64th 'Catanzaro', plus frontier guards. There were also 130 tanks, chiefly light ones, and more than 400 artillery pieces.

Repeated sea and air bombardments hammered the besieged fortress in the hope the Italians would surrender or flee, as preparations for the main British assault continued. Although the 1941 to 1942 Western Desert Campaign was a largely mobile conflict between two modern, mostly mechanised armies, most of the fighting at Bardia, and later at Tobruk, was a form of warfare as old as war itself – the siege.

The words 'siege' and 'fortress' are emotive terms, conjuring up images of a heroic stand by a garrison against its encircling foe. The term 'siege' is derived from the French word, *sege*, a seat, and the Latin *sedere*, to sit down – in effect the 'sitting down' of an army before a fortress. The *Oxford Dictionary* defines a siege as 'a military operation in which an attacking force seeks to compel the surrender of a fortified place by surrounding it and cutting off supplies.'[11] Similarly, to 'invest' a fortress or city is to surround it and prevent passage into or out of it. From a concurrent angle, *Newsweek* in 1941 defined siegecraft as:

> The systematic organization of an attack in which the besieger aims to 'invest' the place and capture it. Starving out the garrison is always included in the plan. This necessitates cutting all supply communications … the garrison normally makes its defense behind fortifications consisting of both permanent and field works, which are temporary fortifications usually constructed just before or during the siege.[12]

Equally important as a besieged garrison's fortifications was the availability of supplies (including food, water, medical supplies and ammunition) and – as will become important for our under-standing – the morale of the defenders. It may be said that the resolve of a fortress commander is more important than his oppo-site number in the field in determining the outcome of siege. By allowing his forces to become besieged – which frequently ends in failure – a commander is denied the benefit of manoeu-vre (as at Bardia and Tobruk) and forced to await relief. His army (usually) plays only a minimal role in a broader campaign.

Blooding the Australian 6th Division

Since Wavell had transferred the victorious 4th Indian Division to the Sudan for operations against the Italians in East Africa, General Bergonzoli's Bardia garrison would face the untried Australian 6th Division. This was first formation of the 2nd Australian Imperial Force (2nd AIF) – drawing upon the traditions of the 1st AIF that had served in the First World War – to be raised and shipped abroad following the outbreak of hostilities. We should recall that a division was the primary tactical formation within an army on both sides during the war. Dominions forces were aligned with the British model: an infantry division contained three brigades, each of three battalions, made up of between 750 and 850 men. Each bat-talion was further broken down into sub-units: A company would contain 120 to 130 men, a platoon 30 to 37, and a sec-tion 9 to 11. Supporting each brigade was a 'field regiment' of artillery, a 'field company' of engineers, a 'field ambulance' and smaller service units. Altogether, a division contained approxi-mately 17,000 men, though few units in practice were ever at their 'establishment' strength.

Whereas the majority of the Australian 6th Division's men – all volunteers – had yet to see combat, their commanding officer, Major General Iven Mackay, was an experienced and decorated First World War veteran. He had rigorously and realistically trained his division in Palestine, though it was still under strength and short of equipment – not ideal for its first assignment. Missing one of its three field artillery regiments, of the two available, one was equipped with obsolete First World War-era 4.5in howitzers and 60-pounder guns. The division also lacked a machine gun battalion and anti-tank regiment. Yet what the Australians lacked in equipment was compensated for by its *esprit de corps*; if anything, there was a feeling of dread within the ranks that the division might arrive too late on the battlefield to see action against the Italians.

'The Resistance of Our Troops was Brief'

Mackay's troops prepared to storm Bardia: the 16th Australian Brigade took up the position on 19 December, followed in turn by the 17th Australian Brigade and the 16th British Brigade (less one battalion) on 27 December. Nocturnal patrols, in the proud tradition of their forebears on the Western Front, reconnoitred the enemy defences boldly at night. Compass in hand, the men would disappear into the darkness. When they reached the enemy lines, patrols would carefully record the amount of barbed wire present, the dimensions of the anti-tank ditch and the exact positions of the perimeter posts. Though quick to open fire on the intruding parties, the Italian defenders were also loath to venture out beyond their own lines. That meant no-man's-land belonged to the Australians. The information assembled on Bardia's defences convinced Mackay to begin his initial attack along a section of the western perimeter, at a site 2½ miles south of the road to Tobruk, along a gentle rise that would favour the use of the available tanks and artillery.

Two days of aerial and naval bombardment preceded the assault. As H-hour approached on the morning of 3 January 1941, the Australian infantry fixed bayonets in preparation for battle, and set out, weighed down by their steel helmets, great-coats, gas masks, ammunition, grenades and three days' rations of biscuits and tinned beef. Sleeveless leather jerkins provided some comfort against the cold, though one wonders how much. Ahead lay the enemy.

The opening barrage lit up the darkened sky as the pioneers and engineers edged forward with Bangalore torpedoes (steel tubes filled with explosive) to clear the barbed wire perimeter obstacles. Once the double-apron of barbed wire was breached, the men of the 2/1st Australian Battalion quickly crossed the anti-tank ditch and secured the bridgehead. Pinned to the back of each man was a piece of white cloth – an aid for recognition in battle, first employed at Gallipoli in August 1915. It meant the Australian troops would know who was friend and who was foe in this closely fought engagement.

Bardia, Bergonzoli had declared confidently, was 'impregnable'. Indeed, the Italians felt that the British would not assault the fortress at all, but instead rely upon the age-old siege tactic of starving it into submission. The attack, therefore, must have come as a surprise.

Less than 2 hours after an opening artillery barrage, British Matilda tanks were trundling forward to engage individual defensive posts inside the perimeter. Some fought hard, while others quickly surrendered. Italian artillery was generally accurate but inconsistent, and therefore ineffective. An Australian soldier wounded in the first day of fighting later described the capture of one of the perimeter posts:

[They] started to came up from below with their hands up and we searched them and sent then back to the rear. I found a grenade in the pocket of one of them and when I took it from his pocket he snatched it back, saying something in his own language. Thinking he was going to blow us both up, and the safety catch on the rifle being on, I was just resigned to having to use the bayonet on him when the grenade came apart, it was full of cigarettes instead of explosives much to my relief. The next [Italian] was only about 17. He was shaking with fear and white as a ghost and had been wounded on the hand. I felt sorry for him and gave him a smoke, tried to tell him that he would be alright and there would be no more war for him.[13]

Only hours into the battle, Bergonzoli described the situation as 'very critical'. As was the case at Sidi Barrani, Italian naval support was non-existent. The *Regia Aeronautica* was also largely absent, a surprise to the attacking infantry who had anticipated the kind of aerial onslaught that characterised Germany's European conquests. The much smaller British Desert Air Force thus held the initiative in patrolling, bombing forward enemy airfields and strafing strongpoints within the fortress.

The fortress fell on the third day of fighting, 6 January 1941. The 'resistance of our troops was brief', Ciano noted, 'a matter of hours'.[14] In this latest whitewash, the Italians lost more than 40,000 men, mostly captured as prisoners of war. Drawing inspiration from Churchill's famous speech about the Battle of Britain, Eden quipped, 'Never before has so much been surrendered by so many to so few.'[15] The spoils were enormous. More than 400 guns, including 216 field guns and 146 anti-tanks, were captured – more than twice the number O'Connor possessed – together with thirteen medium and 117 light tanks. The transport-poor Australians especially welcomed the haul of 708 enemy trucks. Notwithstanding the relative ease with which Bardia had fallen, Mackay's losses were proportionately higher than at Sidi Barrani. Strong isolated resistance had caused 456 casualties within the 6th Australian division: 130 killed, or who later died from their wounds, and a further 326 wounded.

Lessons from the Fall of Bardia

The fall of Bardia amply demonstrated the vulnerability of a fortress to a well-armed and determined besieging army. From the outset, the Italians confined themselves within their sequestered fortress, not daring to disrupt the besieging force. Their fixed defences were easily reconnoitred from the air or ground, with little done to stave off probing patrols. The concentrated artillery barrage at the commencement of the assault fire drove the Italian defenders deep into their concrete shelters – and away from their weapons – at a critical point, when Mackay's troops were negotiating the outer defences.

The use of the Matilda tanks in following, then leading, the advancing infantry helped to prevent many casualties. Yet although these tanks again provided invaluable support on the battlefield – Mackay later claimed that each vehicle was worth an infantry battalion – they were far from invincible. Many had been immobilised by enemy mines, and the turrets of several others had jammed after direct hits. There were also a number of mechanical breakdowns. By the last day of the fighting, only six were still operational – a disturbingly small number, had fighting continued, and an operational weakness that needed to be addressed before O'Connor pushed any farther.

The victory, of course, was not only due to Mackay's meticulous planning. Bergonzoli erred by abandoning freedom of manoeuvre in favour of passive defence. No plans were formulated for a counter-attack, should the 'pie-crust' perimeter be pierced, and no effective chain of inner defences existed. The Italian opposition was therefore rather piecemeal as it went up against the skilful co-operation practiced between the British armour, artillery and air support. In contrast, Italian air activity during the battle was practically non-existent, and only after the battle was over was the southern sector of their fallen fortress bombed ineffectually.

News of Bardia's fall alarmed Italy. Mussolini likened the blow to a load of washing needing 'at least a week' of drying time before his people could come to terms with it. Further disheartening news was then received from the Albanian front, where the Greek counteroffensive continued to gain ground.

Fortress Tobruk: 'A Very Serious Mistake'

On the day Bardia fell, Churchill pondered building up Wavell's forces for an unhurried, months-long advance along the coast to Benghazi. Tobruk soon caught the premier's eye, however, in what marked the beginning of a long and tempestuous connection. The benefits of securing the port were clear, for Tobruk had the potential to ease significantly the strain on the already overworked land transport that sustained O'Connor's westward advance. But there was also the question of prioritising theatre objectives, especially in the Balkans. On 8 January, Britain's Middle East commanders-in-chief were advised that once Tobruk was captured all subsequent operations would be directed toward assisting the Greeks.

Wavell's victorious (newly renamed) XIII Corps continued to push west along the coast. Minimal resistance was encountered. In fact, the entire undertaking was proceeding so smoothly that Mackay issued a warning to his newly blooded troops against what he described as a 'picnic spirit' attitude: 'We all wish to capture Tobruk but we shall never do it by slackness and complacency …'[16] A strict adherent to military protocol, Mackay forbade the wearing of enemy clothing and any experimenting with enemy ordnance. Yet the men's natural curiosity about captured Italian weaponry, including anti-tank guns and mortars, significantly boosted the division's firepower. Many troops had also resorted to wearing Italian army boots simply because their own had worn out. Enemy booty – a salient feature of the Desert War – was already overcoming the logistical nightmare of supply. Indeed, the use of captured enemy equipment would become common practice by both sides throughout the campaign.

With preparations under way for the assault against Tobruk, Wavell and Air Chief Marshal Longmore flew to Athens to offer assistance to the Greeks – a gesture that amounted to little more than a token force of one squadron of 'I' tanks, a regiment of cruiser tanks, ten regiments of artillery and five squadrons of aircraft. Metaxas, though, rejected the British offer outright on the grounds that it would give Hitler the excuse he needed to push through Bulgaria into Greece. Shortly before his death on 29 January 1941, Metaxas again refused an offer by Churchill to provide ground troops, and another month would pass before Athens finally accepted British military aid.

Returning to Tobruk, we find the first troops of the Australian 19th Brigade moving into position around the eastern side of the fortress late on the morning of 7 January 1941. Italian gunners promptly replied with airburst-artillery shells timed to explode in the air above the infantry. The Australian 16th Brigade arrived the following night, though at least a week was needed to bring supplies and ammunition forward, in readiness for an assault. Conditions were difficult for Mackay's men, who were encamped in the open desert at this point, and sleeping in hollows gouged out of the stony ground.

Severe sandstorms brought additional discomfort and disorder, often for days. Fine dust would penetrate anything not wrapped tightly. One convoy carrying a week's supplies for the 7th Armoured Division (positioned to the west of Tobruk, to prevent reinforcements from reaching the besieged fortress) was lost in a *khamsin* for four days during the build-up, its progress stymied far more by the elements than the enemy. Caught in a sandstorm on 15 January, Australian journalist Chester Wilmot found it to be 'thicker than the worst London fog. You could not see a man ten yards in front of you.'[17] The

ferocity of these storms, as reported by a London *Times* correspondent, uprooted telegraph poles, swept trucks off roads and
blew away tents; 'All round and in Tobruk troops lie pressed
to the ground, blinded and choking with dust ... No gun can
find direction even if the numbed and blinded crews could
stand against the wind to load and fire.'[18]

Tobruk was in many respects a larger version of Bardia.
Mussolini, as we saw, had begun fortifying the town and harbour to ward off an overland assault by the Sanusi. By 1940,
it had become Italy's primary stronghold guarding Cyrenaica.
Certainly no natural fortress, its strength lay in the lack of cover
around it – any attacking army would have to traverse large
swathes of open land before reaching the extensive perimeter
defences, also sited on a relatively flat plateau. The harbour,
some 2 miles long and a mile wide, was the heart of the citadel. The Italians had constructed a garrison town along the
northern shore of the harbour, protected by a long finger-like
promontory. Replete with hotels and a church congregated
around the Piazza Vittorio Emmanuelle, the town was dominated by the large three-storey Naval headquarters building,
which sat on a bluff above the water. The peacetime population of the garrison included roughly 10,000 Italian and native
soldiers, plus 1,000 Italian shopkeepers and civil servants. Some
9,000 Arab civilians lived in a village north of the Italian town.

An enemy approaching Tobruk overland would first
encounter a 30-mile semi-circular defensive perimeter,
carved into the desert floor. It enclosed an area of nearly
135 square miles.[19] The perimeter defences included an anti-
tank ditch, barbed wire, minefields, and two concentric rows of
mutually supporting concrete strongholds. In total, there were
128 individual and sequentially numbered posts – the odd-
numbered ones situated 600 to 800yd apart on the perimeter,
the even ones sited some 500yd behind, to cover the gap
between the forward ones.[20] Each defensive post was protected
by barbed wire, with the forward ones surrounded by a second

anti-tank ditch. The firepower of each post varied; all contained two or three machine guns, plus a light field piece or anti-tank gun. Some also contained a mortar. The main weapons in each post were mounted inside a circular concrete pit, flush with ground level, with trenches leading to subterranean ammunition storage and cramped sleeping quarters that could accommodate some twenty men. Although the posts were well positioned, with a good field of fire, they nevertheless lacked the overhead shelter of a pillbox. Yet another crucial weakness lay in the small number of men, fewer than five in each post, who were able to actually fire their weapons. When it came to a bombardment or armoured attack, the remainder were trapped below ground, as happened at Bardia, and unable to fight.

The rocky desert floor of the outer perimeter descends to sea level via three wide steps, or escarpments. The edges of the escarpments contain a number of gullies, or *wadis*, which the Italians used for hiding artillery and command centres. Inside the perimeter (to quote a 1941 Australian Army engineering report), the only defensive works were 'numerous artillery emplacements, some ineffective anti-tank ditches, and [some] shallow weapons pits' – certainly no unified barrier.[21] The most formidable obstacle was at the junction of the Bardia and El Adem roads – later known as 'King's Cross' – where the Italians had dug in thirty-seven of their tanks, spaced 50 to 100yd apart, to serve as pillboxes. Other fixed defences included individual machine gun emplacements, minefields, barbed wire and aerial bombs buried in the ground and detonated by trip wires. Four ships of the 1st Destroyer Squadron and the two squadrons of the 6th Submarine Group were based in the harbour. Also anchored for anti-aircraft defence was the battered cruiser, *San Giorgio*. Four other airstrips were situated by the small civil aerodrome situated on the promontory and were home to various squadrons of Fiat biplanes and other *Regia Aeronautica* aircraft.

Tobruk's commander, 72-year-old General Petassi Manella, was charged with defending an area twice the size of Bardia, but with just over half the men. His garrison was comprised of the 25,000 men of the 61st 'Sirte' Division, the artillery regiment of the 17th 'Pavia' Division, two other battalions, anti-aircraft, coast artillery, communication, and assorted naval personnel. Labelled by Ciano: 'king of the artillerymen',[22] Manella possessed a considerable number of artillery pieces, including 232 heavy, medium and field guns, forty-eight heavy anti-aircraft guns, and four large-calibre naval guns, sited for coastal defence. His artillery commander, General Umberto Barberis was purportedly so confident that his guns alone could thwart an attack that he refused to plan any farther than that. It was only after he received pressure from his subordinate officers that he deigned to draw up plans for counter-attack, in case the British should take over the eastern ridges within the perimeter. Manella and his troops were also 'armour-poor', with only twenty-five medium and forty-five light tanks with which to defend and counter-attack.

Back in Rome, the Italian monarch foresaw yet another disaster. On the morning of 16 January, King Victor Emmanuel cautioned Ciano against holding the fortress, believing that it was 'a very serious mistake' that would yield no practical benefits, and serve only to further weaken Graziani's limited forces.[23] His concern was justified, as events at Tobruk soon began to mirror the underpinnings of the Bardia debacle. From the outset, Manella's poorly motivated men were wary of patrolling outside their perimeter, choosing instead to remain within the safety of their concrete positions and loose salvoes at anything resembling a target. The already weakened *Regia Aeronautica*, hampered by the loss of the main Italian airfield and repair depot at El Adem, did little to intervene, save for dropping (largely unheeded) leaflets encouraging the garrison to stand firm. Mistakenly, Italian intelligence also held that a concerted assault against Tobruk could not take place before February 1941.[24]

Preparations for the British assault, however, were in full swing. Patrols along the perimeter had revealed the unpleasant discovery of a continuous line, some 6,000yd long, of booby traps in front of the outer anti-tank ditch. Activated by a trip wire 6in above the ground, these traps killed and wounded several men before their positions were mapped sufficiently. Fortunately, they proved relatively easy to disarm, or 'delouse'. The probing infantry were also exposed to scattered 'thermos bombs' – explosive devices resembling a thermos flask that detonated upon the slightest movement or contact. A 7-hour patrol by two Australian officers on the night of 15 January measured the distances the infantry would have to cover to reach the perimeter defences, and the location of the mine-fields, booby traps and, critically, a shallow section of the anti-tank ditch between Posts R55 and R57. Mackay, accord-ingly, selected a south-eastern section of the perimeter, 3 miles east of the El Adem road, as the best site for the assault. This point was also – fortuitously – the seam between two Italian unit sectors, and it was hoped that multiple incoming reports of the assault would mislead the Italian headquarters into believing that the British were attacking on a far wider front than they actually were.

Mackay's painstaking planning covered details down to the smallest level, even specifying where the dead were to be buried. The attacking forces would penetrate a small section of the perimeter, from which to 'bite deeply into the defences'.[25] After the Australian 16th Brigade had established a bridgehead, the 'I' tanks of the 7th RTR and the men of the Australian 17th Brigade would push forward and secure the eastern sector of the fortress. The Australian 19th Brigade would then drive north and capture the town and harbour. The 6th Division's artillery commander, Brigadier Edmund Herring, was given the task of silencing enemy weapons in the zone where the initial penetration would take place, before putting down a curtain of steel in front of the advancing

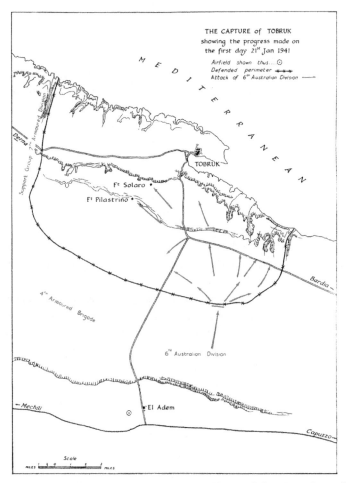

The capture of Tobruk on 21 January 1941. The assault by Major General Iven Mackay's Australian 6th Division in many ways foreshadowed Rommel's victorious assault eighteen months later.

infantry as they pushed inward. Herring's guns would also silence the enemy batteries, particularly those that could target the bridgehead.

For Mackay, the problem in assaulting Tobruk lay not in whether he could capture the fortress, but in the questions of how fast and at what cost. Once a bridgehead was established, speed would be essential, to overwhelm resistance and foil any counter-attacks, while also denying the Italians the opportunity to demolish the harbour installations and water distillation plant – key objectives of the attack.[26] D-Day, originally scheduled for 20 January, was pushed back 24 hours to allow the commander time to increase the number of operational 'I' tanks from thirteen to eighteen. Sixteen turncoat Italian M13/40 and M11/39 medium tanks would participate under new ownership. Operated by the enterprising 'A' Squadron of 6th Divisional Cavalry, the captured tanks sported uniquely Australian livery in the form of large white kangaroos – the divisional symbol – painted on the turret sides. Added fire support would come from mortars mounted on Bren Gun Carriers, the machine gunners of the 1st Royal Northumberland Fusiliers and 1st Cheshire Regiment, and the massed guns of the Royal Horse Artillery (RHA); a total of fifty-two 25-pounders, sixteen 4.5in guns, two 60-pounders and eight 6in howitzers. The British were well prepared for the attack, the Italians woefully unprepared.

H-Hour: Tobruk

The morning of 21 January was cold, the skies clear. As H-Hour approached, twin-engined Vickers Wellington bombers from the RAF's Nos 37 and 38 Squadrons blasted the fortress and nearby enemy airfields, the noise helping to drown out the din of Mackay's assault force as it formed up. Matilda tanks with their exhausts removed crawled along the perimeter to keep the Italians guessing as to where the actual attack would take place. Australian patrols had already laid out lines of tape, to guide the infantry to the point in the front lines where they would break through the perimeter wire. At sea, HMS *Terror* and several British gunboats shelled the fortress's inner defences, while destroyers lay in wait should the crippled *San Giorgio* attempt to escape.

An Australian infantryman of the 2/2nd Battalion captured his feelings in a letter to his parents:

> I am scribbling this in the half dark before we go into action … in the battle for Tobruk I am writing this last note to be sent back in case I do not come out. This will be my baptism of fire, but with the rest of the boys I am looking forward to it cheerfully. Two of my mates were killed at Bardia. Will avenge them to night. Don't fret about me. If I go [it is] in a wonderful way and for a good cause.[27]

The thunderous British artillery barrage, which began at 5.40 a.m., was the largest to date in the Western Desert. First to move off were the infantry of the 2/3rd Battalion, the troops considerably less encumbered by kit than they had been at Bardia. Advancing into battle was a welcome respite from the anxiety of waiting, where they'd been unable to smoke or talk. And the men were excited. Some literally ran into the darkness and unknowingly ventured too far to the right. A booby trap was detonated, killing three and wounding twenty. But as the battalion had learned earlier at Bardia, speed was essential. Post R57, for example, was reached before the sheltering occupants had even emerged. It surrendered without a shot being fired. Resistance in the forward line posts varied enormously, with many failing to return fire at all; comparatively little expended ammunition was later noted after the battle.[28] Post R55, however, proved more stubborn, with fighting lasting more than 30 minutes. Still, the battalion's progress was good, and within an hour five posts had fallen, yielding a bridgehead a mile wide and a mile deep.

By 9.00 a.m. twenty-one perimeter posts had fallen; any delusions regarding Tobruk's invulnerability were shattered. The remaining battalions of the 6th Division, and the British tanks, now proceeded to fan out and overcome scattered pockets of resistance, before a co-ordinated enemy counter-attack could be launched. Shadowing the creeping artillery barrage, the infantry had little patience for defenders who were slow to surrender. Bloodied at Bardia, they were quick to lob hand grenades into stubbornly defended strongholds. They did encounter some staunch resistance from the dug-in Italian tanks at the Bardia–El Adem road intersection. Positioned to meet an enemy coming from the south, and not the east, many of the crews manning the stationary armour fought courageously. Unlike the perimeter posts, however, few prisoners were captured, as the Australians stormed the tanks, each one overwhelmed separately by a combination of small arms, bayonets, grenades and anti-tank rifles.

On nearing the harbour, the infantry seized a series of concrete dugouts, and found a most welcome prize – the fortress artillery headquarters, including General Barberis and his staff. A counter-attack by nine medium tanks and several hundred troops on foot was beaten off with the assistance, and timely arrival, of two Matilda tanks and the anti-tank guns of the RHA.

As the enemy fell back, the Australians charged with 'wild yells and fixed bayonets'.[29] In one of its last confrontations before nightfall, the 2/4th Battalion was clearing the enemy from a series of tunnels when an immaculately dressed Italian major appeared, demanding the presence of a British officer. The 2/4th Battalion's commanding officer, Lieutenant John Copland, weary and dirty, was directed underground to an elderly senior officer, 'dignified and quiet, and very tired'. This was Petassi Manella. With tears in his eyes, Manella unholstered his pistol and presented it to his much younger captor.

Drawing upon his schoolboy French, Copland offered his condolences as best he could in this extraordinary situation: '*C'est la guerre.*'

'*Oui,*' Manella replied. '*C'est la guerre.*'[30]

Taken to the headquarters of the 19th Brigade, an obstinate Manella steadfastly refused to order his men to lay down their arms despite the hopeless situation. Firing from both sides continued for several hours after nightfall, by which stage the battle was essentially won. Explosions from the hurried demolition of ammunition and fuel stores in the harbour area illuminated the sky, silhouetting the profiles of the conquering infantrymen. Beyond the perimeter, the 8,000 or so prisoners taken that day were congregated together around fires – an unfortunate beacon to a squadron of Italian aircraft, whose pilots unknowingly bombed their huddling compatriots, killing up to 300 and wounding a similar number.

Minimal Italian resistance was encountered the next morning, 22 January. Two Italian officers approached the lines of the 2/8th Battalion from a *wadi* in the north western side of the fortress, advising them that Brigadier General Vincenzo della Mura, commanding officer of the 61st 'Sirte' Division, wished to surrender. Large groups of Italians appeared elsewhere under white flags as well, some presenting themselves as if they were on parade. Admiral Massimiliano Vietina and his 1,500-strong naval contingent surrendered in a ceremony observed by Brigadier Leslie Morshead, the commanding officer of the 18th Australian Brigade. Without an Australian flag to hoist in celebration, a jubilant soldier ran a slouch hat up the flagpole outside of Vietina's headquarters.

The last few remaining pockets of resistance along the western perimeter collapsed during the afternoon of 22 January. This was a shock to both the German and Italian High Commands, who had assumed that the fortress would hold out for a considerable period. Instead, Tobruk had fallen in 29 hours. '... easily wrestled from us', Ciano recorded dolefully in his diary.[31]

A British gunner recalled how:

> Thousands and thousands of prisoners came out. They looked pathetic, calling *Aqua, aqua* … In the afternoon we drove through an area we had been shelling and there were lots of Italian bodies lying there. I laughed, more hysteria than anything. You got used to the sight of the dead.[32]

Celebrating one of the swiftest reductions of a fortress of that size in history, Britain's *Times* proclaimed: 'seldom has a victory over such a large area been more swiftly won.'[33] Australian 6th Division casualties amounted to forty-nine men dead and 306 wounded. What the Italian press described as a 'national calamity' was a boon for O'Connor – a major victory that netted 25,000 prisoners, including 2,000 sailors, 208 artillery pieces (the nucleus of the Australian 'bush artillery'), 87 medium and light tanks, and 200 vehicles. The twenty 105mm and twelve 149mm guns uncovered in an ordnance store were gratefully received by the embattled Greeks, along with other captured military hardware. The harbour demolitions were modest, with a variety of small vessels abandoned without damage. The power station (with 4,000 tons of coal), bulk petrol storage, refrigeration and water distillation plants were all captured intact, as was a cache of several thousand cases of mineral water and sufficient tinned food, including the welcome dietary addition of tinned fruit and vegetables, to feed the occupying force for two months.

Admiral Andrew Cunningham noted with satisfaction how the harbour was a far more sheltered anchorage than he had anticipated, and offered 'ample room for our supply ships'. This despite the quays having been damaged and the cranes rendered unserviceable.[34] The harbour was swept for mines, and within three days was receiving supplies directly from Alexandria, in readiness for XIII Corp's march on Tripoli.

Lessons from the Fall of Tobruk

Looking back over the course of the battle, we are reminded of the inherent weaknesses of Mussolini's coastal fortresses and the crucial failure by his commanders to launch an early, co-ordinated counter-attack against a well-orchestrated assault. The Italian defenders were again averse to stopping the nightly patrols by Australian troops that collected priceless knowledge of the outer defences and the most appropriate site for punching through the outer perimeter: the anti-tank ditch, which was incomplete and easily surmounted. Once the perimeter defensive posts, upon which so much of the Italian defensive strategy hinged, were overcome, there were only various scattered sangars (small fortified positions constructed from piled stones or sandbags), weapon-pits, dug-in tanks and a number of ineffective anti-tank ditches to overcome.

General Manella was kept guessing as to the place, time and nature of the attack. He lacked sufficient manpower and obstacles to provide defence in depth and had only twenty-three operational medium tanks and a single infantry battalion available in reserve to counter-attack. On top of that, Manella's ground forces had fought alone. The *Regia Aeronautica* was (again) critically absent from the battlefield. The RAF, on the other hand, enjoyed complete mastery of the air, allowing invaluable reconnaissance and undoubtedly sapping the morale of the Italian defenders below. On the day of the assault, three squadrons of RAF Blenheim bombers had flown fifty-six sorties against the enemy defences, with only a single air engagement with an Italian aircraft recorded. The *Regia Marina* was similarly missing from action, leaving British warships free to support the assault. Mackay may have fielded fewer Matilda tanks than at Bardia, but his force was otherwise stronger in supporting arms.

O'Connor attributed the victory to Mackay's excellent plan of attack, 'executed with great dash by Australian infantry, and British tanks, supported by British and Australian artillery, British Machine Gun Units and with the co-operation of the RAF.'[35] And as Mackay later pointed out, the assault was, in many respects, a forerunner to the one General Erwin Rommel planned for November 1941, and ultimately launched in 1942.[36]

'Fox Killed in the Open'

Benghazi, the largest town in Cyrenaica, was O'Connor's next major objective. At the same time he planned to annihilate the remaining Italian ground forces in Cyrenaica: the 60th 'Sabratha' Infantry Division and General Babini's armoured brigade. Keeping the Italians on the run would also prevent them from forming a new defensive line before the Libyan capital of Tripoli.

O'Connor wasted no time in dispatching the 6th Australian Division west along the coast road, and the 7th Armoured Division inland, to seize the small inland village of Mechili. Ahead of the advance, Babini did manage to extricate his numerically superior brigade of 100 medium tanks and 200 light tanks in darkness on the night of 26 January 1941, much to O'Connor's irritation.

Graziani also slipped away from the port city of Derna, which the Australians occupied on 29 January. With his position in Cyrenaica now untenable, Graziani notified Mussolini on 1 February of his decision to retreat into adjacent Tripolitania. He was concerned not only by the British advance, but also by British Special Forces, Colonel Phillipe Leclerc's Free French forces operating in southern Libya, and suspicions over Vichy French intentions in North Africa (especially uncorroborated reports that Vichy-held Algeria might join the Allies).

RAF reconnaissance reports the next day showed the unmistakable signs of an Italian withdrawal. This prompted

O'Connor to press ahead immediately. He boldly directed his remaining armour to traverse the desert and intercept the retreating Italian columns south of Benghazi – a move British intelligence knew from intercepted signals that the Italians believed was impossible. Advancing from Mechili on 4 February 'across the unknown country in full cry',[37] the meagre British force of thirty-nine operational cruiser tanks and 3,000 troops made contact with the Italians near Beda Fomm the next morning. Simultaneously, the Australian 6th Division moved forward, reaching Benghazi before nightfall on 5 February. Over the next two days, heavily out-numbered – in tanks alone, approximately four to one – and increasingly low in ammunition and fuel, the British prevented the majority of the desperate Italians, many of whom fought courageously, from escaping into Tripolitania.

Under competent leadership, the Italians could have easily broken through the slender British defence lines. Fortune, however, favoured O'Connor's risky manoeuvre. And once again, the spoils were enormous: another 20,000 prison-ers, including the elusive 'Electric Whiskers' Bergonzoli, 120 medium tanks and 216 guns. O'Connor triumphantly cabled Wavell, declaring the 'Fox killed in the open'.[38] Compass, his original five-day raid, had evolved into a staggeringly suc-cessful campaign. With the one infantry and one armoured division available, O'Connor had adroitly won a series of bat-tles stretching from Sidi Barrani to Beda Fomm, in just ten weeks. For the relatively low loss of 500 dead, 1,373 wounded and fifty-five missing, he had utterly destroyed the Italian Tenth Army.

O'Connor, whose bold and unorthodox flanking moves would soon be emulated by the audacious German General Erwin Rommel, observed: 'I think this may be termed a com-plete victory as none of the enemy escaped.'[39] The brilliant campaign, with unwitting irony, earned Wavell the original moniker of the Western Desert 'Fox'.[40] During the course of his 650-mile advance, O'Connor captured 130,000 prisoners, 380 light and medium tanks, and 845 medium and heavy artillery pieces – a flicker of good news for the free world at a point in time when Germany's military might appeared seemingly invincible.[41]

Tripoli Spared

Never short of ideas, Churchill now championed the raising of an anti-Mussolini or Free Italian Force from the 100,000 disgruntled Italian prisoners held in Egypt, the capture of the Italian island of Pantelleria, the invasion of Sicily, a landing in the Dodecanese, an expeditionary force to Turkey, and the offer to Pétain of six British divisions to take up hostilities against Germany in France's North African colonies. More pressing, however, was the need to intervene in Greece.

On 12 February, as O'Connor prepared to push ahead into Tripolitania, Wavell therefore received a notification from London that his 'major effort must now be to aid Greece and/or Turkey'.[42] Whether O'Connor should have pushed onward to the main port and capital of Libya remains one of the most contentious issues of the campaign, if not the war. Tripoli was protected at this time by the 5th Italian army, under General Italo Garibaldi, comprising four infantry divisions: 25th 'Bologna', 55th 'Savona', 17th 'Pavia', 27th 'Brescia', and the partially deployed 'Ariete' armoured division, plus a small German detachment. In light of the weakening Italian morale and only moderate strength, O'Connor may well have banished the Axis from North Africa at this time, two years earlier than their eventual defeat in Tunisia. The fallout from such a catastrophe may well have shaken Mussolini's leadership and brought Italy's war to a premature end.

Britain's failure to sweep through to Tripoli astounded Berlin. General Warlimont (Deputy Chief of OKW Operations

Staff) could not comprehend 'why the British did not exploit the difficulties of the Italians in Cyrenaica by pushing on to Tripoli. There was nothing to check them. The few Italian troops who remained there were panic-stricken …'[43] Instead, Churchill, with Wavell's agreement and the endorsement of the other commanders-in-chief in the Middle East, opted to protect Britain's only remaining continental ally, Greece, by dispatching an expeditionary force of sixty thousand men to the Balkans. As Eden later noted, the world's public opinion was with the Greeks, and to have stood aside would have brought ignominy upon Britain as Greece slid under Axis occupation.

Postscript

In 1964, Iven Mackay protested over the building of an Australian memorial building associated with personnel who had served in Tobruk during the 1941 siege because it disregarded the efforts of his men in the Australian 6th Division, who had originally captured the fortress from the Italians in January 1941.[44] This victory is now largely forgotten, and Tobruk is remembered mostly for the 242-day siege that began three months later. We should remember that the crushing of the citadel was important because the subsequent Italian rout brought Rommel to North Africa and, as we will learn, Tobruk would be his undoing in 1941.

6

African Sunflower

> 'Probably never before in modern warfare had such a completely unprepared offensive as this raid through Cyrenaica been attempted.'
>
> – General Erwin Rommel

Closely monitoring events in North Africa in early January 1941, General Erwin Rommel noted that he wasn't 'surprised that our Allies aren't having things all their own way'.[1] A month later, he was in Tripoli directing an operation to prevent the Italians from losing Libya altogether. In the meantime, Wavell had launched a counteroffensive in East Africa, a further knockout blow to Mussolini's fading dream of an African empire.

Wavell's East African Victory

Britain's Operation Compass, as we saw, eliminated Mussolini's immediate threat to Egypt and pushed what remained of his routed army back to Tripoli. Wavell could now turn to trouncing the Italians in East Africa. Demoralised by the British fortunes in the Western Desert, the Duke of Aosta was also becoming increasingly isolated in that region. Since Britain controlled the exits at either end of the Mediterranean, Italian shipping was unable to reach him. And because no overland link existed with Libya, only a limited amount of supplies could be sent via long-distance aircraft flying over British Sudan. Faced with no alternative, he adopted a defensive stance and, with permission from Rome, withdrew his men from the Sudanese frontier. Now we come to the first time that the interception of German encoded Enigma messages – codenamed Ultra – directly shaped the outcome of a land battle. British Intelligence reports about those messages had disclosed the retreat, which encouraged Major General William Platt to begin an offensive three weeks ahead of plan. On 19 January 1941, his two Indian Infantry Divisions began advancing after the Italians. As Platt pushed into Eritrea, Lieutenant General Alan Cunningham (younger brother of Admiral Andrew Cunningham) launched a series of separate attacks from Kenya. They were aided by a small amphibious force from Aden.

British Somaliland fell in March, followed by the Ethiopian capital (Addis Ababa), which surrendered on 6 April. After only eight weeks, Cunningham had advanced more than 1,700 miles and trounced Aosta's forces for the loss of 501 men and eight aircraft. The two main British formations then closed on Aosta's mountainous retreat, from where he finally surrendered on 16 May 1941, though remnants of his army held out until the end of November in North West Ethiopia.

The campaign was another significant victory over the Italians and a welcome boost for British morale. Mussolini's greatest military triumph had been upended, and Italian colonial rule in East Africa effectively terminated. The end of the campaign not only freed British naval, land and air forces for operations elsewhere, but also allowed Roosevelt to lift a restriction on US shipping using the Gulf of Aden and the Red Sea. From 11 April 1941 on, shipments of American arms and equipment bound for Egypt were shipped directly to Suez, thus relieving the enormous strain on the struggling British Merchant Navy. Importantly for our story, the East African campaign also facilitated Alan Cunningham's debatable appointment as commander of the newly created British Eighth Army in North Africa in late 1941. The army was so-named because the Allies had fielded seven armies against Germany in the First World War, and this nomenclature retained a sense of continuity against an old enemy. The fighting in East Africa, as in Greece, also helped pave the way for an influx of German troops into Libya, and Rommel's subsequent page in history, for it is unlikely that he could have routed the British in Libya at the beginning of 1941 had the 1st South African, and 4th and 5th Indian Divisions been situated in the Western Desert in place of East Africa.

German Intervention: A Matter of 'Strategy, Politics, and Psychology'

Unlike the Kaiser's Germany, which occupied four African colonies (all of which were forfeited under the Treaty of Versailles), Hitler's Germany harboured no grand plans to forge a new Nazi African empire. Following Mussolini's urgent (post-Compass) request for aid, the Führer announced at his Bavarian alpine retreat, the Berghof, on 8 to 9 January 1941, that an armoured 'blocking force' would be sent to Libya on 22 February. Details of the operation were outlined in his Directive No. 22, dated 11 January 1941:

> *German Support for battles in the Mediterranean area*
> The situation in the Mediterranean area, where England is employing superior forces against our allies, requires that Germany should assist for reasons of strategy, politics, and psychology. Tripolitania must be held … [2]

Hitler subsequently met with Mussolini on 18 and 19 January to formalise his Libyan intervention – codenamed Operation *Sonnenblume* ('Sunflower'). The Führer was apprehensive at this moment over the wider ramifications of the Italian military calamity in Africa. Would losing Libya compel Italy to leave the war? And would such a defeat cause the Axis partnership to collapse? Consequently, while Hitler remained fixated on invading Russia – *Unternehmen Barbarossa* – a small-scale intervention in North Africa would shore up Mussolini's shaky position and keep the British busy in the Mediterranean. It would also swing the focus of the land war to the Middle East.

Enter Erwin Rommel

Hitler appointed Lieutenant General Erwin Rommel, one of his heroes from the French Campaign, to lead his new African army. Briefed on his new responsibilities on 6 February 1941, Rommel touched down at Tripoli's Castel Benito airfield six days later to assume command of the newly formed *Deutsches Afrikakorps* (DAK). Like Wavell, Rommel would lead a coalition army. From the very beginning, however, it was an uneasy alliance. We can only imagine Rommel's thoughts as he toured Tripoli, observing the remnants of a weary and dispirited Italian army. The majority of the officers were disheartened and waiting with bags packed, ready to be evacuated. In the words of an Italian army doctor, 'We had been awaiting the British fatalistically – almost gladly. At least the whole business would be over. But the Germans came instead.'[3] As Rommel's newly arrived *aide-de-camp* (ADC), Lieutenant Heinz Werner Schmidt, detected, not unexpectedly, that 'we were tolerated rather popular'.[4]

From the outset, 49-year-old Rommel was at odds with Graziani's successor, and his nominal superior, 62-year-old General Italo Gariboldi (the former having resigned after the annihilation of his Tenth Army). Whereas Gariboldi advocated the building of a defensive cordon around Tripoli, Rommel looked hungrily to the east. Within hours of his arrival in Tripoli, Rommel was airborne again, in a German Heinkel He III bomber, scouting the unfamiliar desert terrain that lay ahead. Since Libya fell within the Italian sphere of interest, Berlin had accumulated only scant information prior to Rommel's arrival. Former-DAK intelligence officer Hans-Otto Behrendt recalled that 'rarely has one general known as little as about an enemy and his territory as Rommel [now] did.'[5] His knowledge of Wavell's forces amounted to a single captured map, which alerted the Axis camp of the departure of the 7th Armoured Division and its replacement by the less-capable 2nd Armoured Division. Not content merely to build up a defensive ring around Tripoli – as ordered by both the Italian and German High Commands – Rommel set himself to action.

No sooner had the initial elements of the 5th Light Division, the battle-hardened 3rd Reconnaissance Battalion, and the 39th Anti-Tank Battalion disembarked from their transports, than they were paraded around Tripoli multiple times – to bluff enemy agents – and ordered forward to Sirte. It was a coastal village halfway between Tripoli and El Agheila, and the site where O'Connor's push had finally halted. At the same time, in Cairo, a faulty British intelligence evaluation on 23 February found no indications of 'an enemy advance from Tripolitania'.[6] Greece had formally accepted the offer of a British expeditionary force on the same day, and with Wavell's command stretched by this new intervention and the need to drain troops from his army in North Africa, the timing was perfect for Rommel to strike.

Misreading Rommel

The opening round of the Desert War quickly unfolded. German troops first made contact with a British patrol, caught off guard in a skirmish near El Agheila on 24 February. The Libyan capital was, for the moment, safe. This was, perhaps, an opportune moment for Hitler to have consolidated his Mediterranean venture by neutralising Malta. Situated midway between the key RN naval bases at Gibraltar and Alexandria, Malta provided security for Britain's 13,000-mile maritime supply route to Egypt. The tiny British bastion would also be a curse to Italian convoys labouring to supply Rommel's needs.

Cairo wondered whether Rommel's initial push was the beginning of a German-led drive east, toward the Egyptian frontier? Given the magnitude of events unfolding in the Balkans, Wavell believed otherwise. He advised Churchill that Rommel would not attempt to recover Benghazi before summer. Cyrenaica, he believed, was secure for the moment. Wavell's assessment, however, ran counter to an astute appreciation from his intelligence director, Brigadier John Shearer, who suggested that the new German armoured formation was, in fact, quite capable of retaking the whole of Cyrenaica. Yet Wavell rejected Shearer's warning, believing the evidence to be 'far from conclusive'.[7] On 6 March he issued a document, entitled the 'Defence of Cyrenaica', which concluded that 'it should not be difficult to produce a perfectly adequate answer to the German threat', an analysis based on the enemy 'holding force' having to finish its desert training before engaging in any major operation.[8]

Rommel had, in fact, already begun planning an offensive, to start before the arrival of the hot summer weather. In Wavell's defence, however, was one factor that could not have been anticipated – the audacious and unpredictable nature of his new opponent. Here was an opportunist with the energy and enthusiasm of a man half his age, a superb tactician who judged the situation in Libya independently, and often in complete disregard of orders from both Berlin and Rome. While the British were intercepting some of his communications (at this time only the signals from the Luftwaffe's X *Fliegerkorps* could be read, the army codes still undecipherable) and reading his troops' movements, they could not second-guess the threat posed by this unknown adversary.

Despite feeling secure, Wavell's desert command was weakened by the loss of O'Connor, who was in Palestine recovering from a stomach complaint, and General Maitland Wilson (the short-lived military governor and commander of the newly established Cyrenaica Command), who was appointed to lead the expeditionary force to Greece. Wilson's replacement was Lieutenant General Philip Neame, a relative newcomer to both the desert and armoured warfare. Wavell knew little of Neame, other than that he was a Victoria Cross recipient, a staff college instructor and the author of a book on military strategy. Neame's Cyrenaica Command faced a host of problems in the face of Rommel's advance. With XIII Corps disbanded, its units and personnel dispersed, Neame lacked the trained staff and communications needed to co-ordinate mobile operations over the vast reaches of the Western Desert. On such a failing, O'Connor later remarked that, 'a battalion is not put into battle without being trained in its duties, yet the authorities never seem to hesitate to land a campaign with an entirely new staff, who may never have met before and know nothing of each other's responsibilities.'[9]

Wavell flew from Greece on 16 March to meet with Neame and assess the situation unfolding the desert first-hand. He found Neame 'pessimistic and asking for all kinds of [unavailable] reinforcements'.[10] Neame's defending troops were also new to the desert, untried in battle, and beset by numerous organisational troubles. They had been stripped of Mackay's experienced Australian 6th Division, which was sent to Greece, and the British 7th Armoured Division, which was refitting in the Nile Valley. The British 2nd Armoured Division, half of which had been transferred to Greece, was now reliant upon captured Italian medium tanks, British light tanks and cruiser tanks beset with mechanical troubles.

Neame's main infantry formation, the Australian 9th Division, was in a state of uneasy change. Composed wholly of volunteers, many of whom had enlisted after the fall of France in 1940, the division's partially trained 18th and 25th Brigades were exchanged with the 20th and 26th Brigades from the Australian 7th Division, and sent to Greece. The 9th Division's newly appointed commanding officer, General Leslie Morshead, now faced the daunting task of quickly turning this composite formation into a cohesive fighting unit. Originally part of a British 'holding force' scheduled to finish its training in Cyrenaica before engaging in any major operation, the 9th Division would actually fire its first shots against some of the Germany Army's most experienced units.[11] Reserves were scarce. At the end of March, Wavell sent Neame his only available formation – the 3rd Indian Motor Brigade. He also hoped to send at least one more division from East Africa once the fighting had ceased. But this left Neame relatively exposed in a new arena with inexperienced troops and insufficient armour.

Neame's questionable leadership now came into play, underscored by his 'crazy' tactical positioning of the Australian 20th Brigade on the desert plain between El Agheila and Benghazi, devoid of transport. With both flanks exposed, the immobile infantry would have been easy prey for an enemy armoured column breaking through at El Agheila. Wavell, at Morshead's insistence, immediately transferred the brigade to a more defensible position east of Benghazi – a move that ultimately saved it.

Further disappointment for Wavell lay in the pitiful state of the 2nd Armoured Division's cruiser tanks. Of the fifty-two available armoured vehicles, half were in the workshops, and the remainder subject to frequent breakdowns. Britain's weakness on the ground was matched in the air, again because of the mission to Greece. Against the thirty RAF aircraft in Cyrenaica, the Germans could muster ninety Messerschmitt fighters and more than eighty bombers.

'Anxious and depressed',[12] Wavell returned to Greece to oversee the deployment of the British expeditionary force – his primary task at this time. Rommel, meanwhile, flew home on 19 March to receive further orders and the award of 'Oak Leaves' to his *Ritterkreuz* for meritorious action during the latter part of the French Campaign. Eager to strike in Libya with 'utmost energy', Rommel was warned at Hitler's headquarters not to strike a 'decisive blow' and reminded that no extra reinforcements would be available until after Barbarossa. Libya was, after all, a small defensive brushstroke on Hitler's much broader strategic canvas.

The Führer's instructions, however, fell on deaf ears, and, disregarding orders to remain on the defensive, Rommel ordered the 5th Light Division to occupy El Agheila on 23 March, as a forward base for his next push. The attack began at dawn the next day; the garrison was easily overcome, and the weak British force retired 30 miles east, back to Mersa Brega. Monitoring events in London, Churchill pressed his commander-in-chief to give the enemy 'an early taste of our quality', even though Wavell still felt that no serious danger to Egypt existed.[13] In fact, Rommel's desert foray was thought to be little more than a major, well-timed diversion preceding a new German offensive in the Balkans.

Unrest in the Balkans

Before entering the Balkans, Hitler needed to secure the passage of his troops through Bulgaria. Despite King Boris III's desire to remain neutral, the Bulgarian government threw its support behind Germany and joined the Tripartite Pact on 1 March 1941. The first contingent of German troops crossed the Danube en route to Greece the next day. Moscow's apprehension was soothed with advance notice that the transfer was directed solely toward the Greek theatre.

With Bulgaria now firmly entrenched in the Axis camp, Yugoslavia found itself alone and surrounded by covetous states disputing their territorial boundaries. As noted earlier, Germany was heavily reliant upon Yugoslavia for its raw materials, with Prince Paul (ruling on behalf of the young King Peter II) obediently accommodating Hitler's escalating needs. Toward the end of 1940, Hitler increased the pressure on Prince Paul to also sign the Tripartite Pact and, faced with little alternative, Yugoslavia succumbed and became a signatory on 25 March 1941. Opposition to the Axis union was immediate, and within 48 hours, Serbian nationalists seized power. The regency was abolished and teenage Peter proclaimed king. A new government under General Dušan Simović was also installed.

Churchill, who earlier had hoped that Yugoslavia might join the Allies, now spied an opportunity to align Greece *and* Yugoslavia with Britain – a union that might dissuade Hitler from invading Greece. The Belgrade *coup d'état*, however, enraged the Führer. Within hours of receiving the news, he issued Directive No. 25, ordering the *Wehrmacht* to crush the revolt in Yugoslavia 'as quickly as possible'.[14] Operation *Marita*, accordingly, was expanded to cover the invasion of both countries. Interestingly, the coup had opened up a new dialogue between Belgrade and Moscow, with a pact of friendship signed just prior to the invasion. In many ways a strange and defiant move by Stalin, his overture played into the hands of the Nazi Foreign Minister Joachim von Ribbentrop, who later cited it as an example of Soviet 'hostile policy' in the lead-up to Barbarossa.

'Things Are Happening in Africa'

As late as 27 March 1941, Wavell remained adamant that his new rival would not strike before the end of April. A British intelligence report three days later provided further reassurance that Rommel was incapable of launching an offensive 'in the near future', regardless of Ultra intelligence decrypts pointing to the contrary.[15] In reality, Rommel was planning to reverse the British tide in North Africa, despite a repeated warning from Berlin in early April prohibiting offensive operations, even after the 15th Panzer Division and its 120 tanks reached him in May.[16]

'There'll be some worried faces among our Italian friends,' Rommel mused in a letter to his wife.[17] Ignoring the objections of his nominal Italian superiors, he planned to open a full-scale offensive. Contradicting British expectations and his own Axis directives, on 30 March, Rommel ordered General Johannes Streich, commander of the 5th Light Division, to march on Marsa Brega. After a fierce battle the next day and Luftwaffe reports of a British withdrawal, Rommel harried his Panzers forward. Upon his return from the front lines, Rommel was 'berated violently' by General Gariboldi for disobeying orders from Rome, and for failing to take into account the vulnerable supply situation. Though as Rommel later wrote, he had no intention of 'allowing good opportunities to slip by unused'.[18] The two men were in the midst of a heated argument when a message (in German) arrived from OKW in Berlin. Seizing the moment, Rommel duplicitously declared it to be a signal sanctioning his 'complete freedom of action'. It was, in reality, a stern rebuke emphasising other major Axis commitments, warning of the delayed arrival of the 15th Panzer Division, and demanding that Rommel halt the march of the *Afrikakorps*. Further movement was prohibited, unless it was established 'beyond any doubt that the enemy is withdrawing most of his mobile units from Cyrenaica'.

Rommel, instead, directed his 'Afrikaner' forward. Wavell only added to the escalating confusion in the British camp – confronted by this unexpected advance – by dispatching orders and counter-orders that, often, were received too late. With Churchill's prodding, he recalled and haplessly appointed

O'Connor – Britain's most experienced desert general – as a replacement for Neame. Still unwell, O'Connor was reluctant to supersede Neame, a personal friend, and although he advised the Australian 9th Division that he would remain liaison officer to Neame, both officers continued to issue orders from the field, encumbering control of an increasingly chaotic situation.[19]

Sensing an opportunity, Rommel threw conventional wisdom to the wind and split his combined Italo-German force into four columns, to race across the protruding area of the Cyrenaican coast that Allied soldiers called 'The Bulge'. Control of the 'Bulge' airfields was crucial for both sides: The RAF could safeguard the passage of convoys sailing from Alexandria to Malta; alternatively, the Luftwaffe could dominate the skies over Malta, the prelude to an aerial invasion, and protect Italian convoys plying the central Mediterranean. That, then, was Rommel's destination. Urging his men onward, he hoped to deceive his enemy as to his true strength until he intercepted the retreating British formations. 'Things are happening in Africa,' he wrote home to Lucie. 'Let's hope the great stroke we've now launched is successful'.[20]

The remaining armour of Major General Michael Gambier-Parry's 2nd Armoured Division fell back toward Mechili (though all its tanks were lost in the withdrawal, through breakdowns and lack of fuel), where they were joined by the 3rd Indian Motor Brigade, the 2/3rd Australian Anti-Tank Regiment (less two batteries), and the 3rd RHA Anti-Tank Regiment. Watching the movement closely, Rommel prioritised the capture of Mechili.

Fighting continued along the coast, with Benghazi falling on 4 April. Australian infantry (from the 2/13th Infantry Battalion) encountered the Germans for the first time on the escarpment east of Benghazi, and had to fight a strong rearguard action. The unblooded men of the 9th Division were keen to prove themselves in battle, especially after the recent exploits of their sister division against the Italians.

Rommel's Corps d'Élite

Rumours began circulating among the British that Rommel was leading a *corps d'élite* of specially trained desert warriors. In reality, the DAK was hastily formed 'without experience' or any formal training in desert warfare. It was, in essence, a standard *Wehrmacht* unit, albeit one totally reliant upon mechanised transport. Its preparation prior to leaving Europe consisted of little more than lectures on tropical medicine and briefings by officers who had visited Africa.[21] The DAK's first lessons in desert warfare, consequently, were learned through trial and error. As an example, Rommel flew over the former Ottoman fort at Mechili on the morning of 7 April, in search of a missing armoured column. He eventually located it, some 15 to 20 miles further south than expected. Landing among the vehicles to criticise their tardy progress, he heard that they had earlier attempted to cross a salt marsh, and made a detour around a large expanse of water to their east – a mirage. Later the same day, an exasperated Rommel again found the vehicles held up, this time while crossing across the open desert and unaware of a nearby road. Drivers would also become disoriented and lost in dust storms while fuel shortages froze German columns for long periods.

Thrown headlong into a harsh and unfamiliar environment, the DAK was forced to adapt and operate under a myriad of difficulties. The first German vehicles unloaded on to the wharves at Tripoli still retained their dark grey European colour scheme, while the low-grade fuel supplied by the Italians was unsuitable for their engines. Operating without appropriate air filters halved the average life of a tank engine – a problem compounded by the need to operate in low gear for extended periods. Without special lubricants, Rommel's Panzers needed an overhaul after 600 to 900 miles – the distance from Tripoli to Tobruk – and an engine replacement after only 2,100 miles, compared to 5,000 under European conditions.[22] Designed for combat across Europe, the German wheeled and tracked armoured vehicles experienced considerable trouble negotiating the difficult Libyan landscape. Marshalling his men to seize at Mechili, Rommel found his plan (originally set for 6 April) delayed by two days while his tanks negotiated the stony terrain. Eventually, eight tanks from the 1st Battalion, 5th Panzer Regiment arrived – seven of which were small Mark IIs, with only a single, more formidable Mark IV vehicle.

Before we continue, it would be wise to examine Germany's supposed superiority in armoured vehicles. 'The idea of the tank was a British conception.' Churchill said in a July 1942 speech, delivered in the debate over his handling of the war. 'The use of armoured forces as they are now being used was largely French, as General de Gaulle's book shows. It was left to the Germans to convert those ideas to their own use.'[23] Were Hitler's tanks, therefore, in any way superior to the British vehicles of this time, or was the early German success in mobile warfare due to the way in which their armour was handled?

Such an assessment begins in the interwar period, when cutbacks in military spending curbed Britain's development of new tanks. Germany, on the contrary, devoted considerable resources to the design and development of a range of tanks specifically designed to accommodate heavier guns and thicker armour over time. When the Germans finally surrendered to the Allies in Tunisia in May 1943, for example, up-gunned versions of the Mark III and IV Panzers were still in front line service, unlike the British, who were now using entirely different vehicles, including the ubiquitous American-made M4 Sherman. Unlike the various models fielded by the Allies in 1941, German tanks were designed to use parts standardised across several models and produced by a large number of firms. They were also powered by reliable, purpose-built engines, in contrast to the early British and American designs forced, by necessity, to draw upon existing truck and aircraft engines.

We have already looked at the three classes of British tank in North Africa in 1941. Germany, in comparison, initially shipped four different tank models to North Africa. Divided into three classes on the basis of their armament were two light tanks: the 5.4-ton Panzer I, armed with two 7.92mm machine guns, and the heavier 8.9-ton Mark II, which was armed with a 2cm cannon. The 20-ton Panzer III was a reliable and versatile 'medium' tank, armed with a 50mm gun. The larger, 25-ton Panzer IV, with a five-man crew, was classed as a 'heavy' tank because of its large-calibre 75mm gun. Yet, as it stood, almost 50 per cent of Rommel's tanks were either obsolete or useless when compared to their British equivalents. A contemporary German summary on the Panzer I, which made up a quarter of Rommel's armoured strength, dismissed it as too weak, too slow and totally unsuitable for the Western Desert. Although the heavier German tanks, the Panzer III and IV, enjoyed a similar thickness of protection to their British rivals, they had a distinct advantage of face-hardened armour – a metallurgical advance that helped to deflect the kinetic energy of solid shot projectiles. A number of DAK tanks also had additional face-hardened armour plates bolted on to the hull front and superstructure of the tank, affording even greater protection. The British and Italian tanks, by comparison, were protected by less effective homogeneous armour.[24]

The Germans also held a distinct advantage in terms of intelligence. A comprehensive understanding of the strengths and weaknesses of every British tank in service up until June 1941 (when the Cruiser Tank Mark VI was introduced) was gleaned from combat during the French campaign. German anti-tank crews therefore appreciated the critical ranges at which to engage these vehicles, unlike British tankers in the opening rounds of the desert war, who had trouble identifying German individual tank models and the optimal range at which to engage them. It was only after several tanks were captured at Tobruk on 14 April that British intelligence was able to measure the type and thickness of the German armour. And not until the following month were tables issued showing the maximum range for the standard 2-pounder gun against the heavier German tanks.

The '2-pounder', so named because of the weight of the projectile, was the standard British anti-tank gun until November 1941, when its replacement, the 6-pounder, was introduced in limited quantities (only 100 of these new guns had reached the Middle East by the end of May 1942). Outdated, the British 2-pounder guns – 'which nearly lost the British the Middle East' according to one British general[25]– could only fire heavy, solid-shot projectiles, which, although adequate against thin armour at close range, were unable to penetrate the armour of the heavier German tanks beyond 500yd. These projectiles also had the distinct disadvantage of being non-explosive when used against soft-skinned vehicles, anti-tank guns, field guns and infantry positions. Because of the heavy equipment losses sustained during the battle of France, Britain had no choice but to continue manufacturing this outmoded weapon. Work on a much larger anti-tank gun, the 17-pounder, began in April 1941, though this formidable weapon did not see action in North Africa until 1943. Stopgap weapons, such as the spigot mortar, saw limited use in the desert in 1942. Solid-shot ammunition was also issued for the British 18-pounder and 25-pounder field artillery, which obviously were not as mobile as tanks, and it was not until US-manufactured tanks arrived in North Africa that British tankers could reply with high-explosive ammunition.

The heavier German tanks, by comparison, could fire a range of ammunition. The Panzer III, for instance, was supplied with both armour piercing and high explosive ammunition; the Mark IV could also fire smoke and high explosive shells more than 3,000yd. All German armour piercing ammunition above 37mm in calibre was available with both high explosive and delay-fuse options. Upon striking a British tank, these projectiles were frequently associated with irreparable mechanical damage and horrendous injuries to the crew, unlike solid-shot, which often wounded the occupants but rarely destroyed the tank through fire or severe damage. German tanks could therefore act as both mobile artillery and tank killers. Junkers Ju 87 (Stuka) aircraft also helped to reinforce Rommel's superior battlefield firepower.

Flawed British armoured doctrine also had a profound influence on the battlefield. It was standard practice for British tanks, in the absence of hull-down, or partially hidden firing positions, to fire on the move. Some idea of the poor accuracy obtained in this manner is found in a 1938 British report claiming a 21 per cent chance that a 2-pounder gun could hit a large target at 650yd while moving at 10mph. German and Italian tank crews, alternatively, were instructed to fire only when stationary, regardless of available cover. While it was true that the German tanks were wary of attacking their British equals, which they respected, it was the fundamental responsibility of German anti-tank gunners to engage British tanks, *not* the Panzers. It was only in time that this tactic was appreciated by the British, who had had lost most of their precious armour to cleverly sited anti-tank guns, in particular the deadly 88mm anti-aircraft gun, in its ground attack role, and the 50mm (*Panzerabwehrkanone* or *Pak*) Pak 38 anti-tank gun, rather than to German armour.

Developed as an anti-aircraft (*Flugzeugabwehrkanone* or *Flak*) gun during the First World War, the long range and precision optics of the 88mm gun also made it a deadly anti-tank weapon. First tested in a ground attack role against armour and bunkers by Germany's *Condor Legion* during the Spanish Civil War, it is said that Hitler suggested using the gun in this novel manner. It was at this time that armour piercing ammunition was developed for the gun, and since no British or French armour fought in Spain, its lethal potential seems to have been overlooked by the Allies. Although hampered by a high silhouette, the 88mm gun could be brought quickly into action, and was fearsome in the hands of an experienced crew. In the desert, it could knock out the formidably armoured British Matilda at ranges up to 2,000yd, with a practiced crew firing up to twenty-five rounds a minute.

There was a British weapon in Libya in 1941 that had, perhaps, the potential to tip the balance against Rommel's Panzers: the QF 3.7in (94mm) anti-aircraft gun. Primarily retained in its archetypal role at this time because of conservatism in the British Army, there were also inherent problems of heavier weight, optics not designed for a ground attack role, and the strain on the mounting and recuperating gear when fired at low angles. Nevertheless, when finally utilised in anti-tank capacity in the defence of Tobruk in 1942, the weapon proved highly formidable against Axis armour.[26]

Regardless of the reliability under European conditions, we must remember that the majority of tanks operating in the Western Desert were lost to mechanical breakdowns and damage, rather than the effects of enemy fire.[27] In this harsh environment, the Germans excelled at battlefield recovery and repair. The British, on the other hand, initially lacked appropriate recovery equipment, and were more often forced to abandon damaged, yet repairable, tanks. The DAK therefore held the edge in armoured combat during the opening rounds of the desert war – a battlefield that more often resembled a naval engagement than a traditional land battle.

Mechili Falls

After a short, sharp battle on the morning of 8 April, the encircled British forces inside the old stone and mud fort at Mechili surrendered. The victory brought Rommel's first desert windfall. Although a significant number of defenders, including a battery of the RHA, managed to slip through the enemy cordon, some 3,000 prisoners were captured, including Major General Gambier-Parry and his headquarters staff. Valuable supplies, vehicles and equipment were also appropriated, much to the Germans' delight. Surveying the scene, Rommel spotted a pair of British sand and sun goggles. 'Booty – permissible, I take it, even for a General,' he remarked, placing the goggles over the rim of his peaked cap – the iconic motif of the future 'Desert Fox'.[28]

Mechili, however, proved to be rather expensive. Rommel's forward troops, at one point, were only 48 miles south of Derna, while the majority of the Australian 20th and 26th Brigades were perilously still more than 100 miles to the west of Tobruk. A thrust to the coast at this time could potentially have sealed the fate of the Australian 9th Division. Had Rommel moved to block the coast road, a stand by the Australians in the open without armour, artillery and anti-tank guns would have been disastrous. As it happened, though, he decided to consolidate his forces and overwhelm the resistance at Mechili, and in doing so provided a window of opportunity for the retreating British forces to withdraw into the former Italian fortress at Tobruk. It was a mistake.

But it made Tobruk Rommel's next objective.

Hitler's Balkan Onslaught

Exacerbating Britain's unforeseen North African crisis was the decision to rush an expeditionary force to Greece. Intervention in the Balkans had been agreed upon after secret talks on 22 and 23 February between a British delegation, including Wavell, Eden and General John Dill, Chief of the Imperial General Staff (CIGS), Alexandros Koryzis (Metaxas' successor), King George II, and the Greek commander-in-chief, General Alexandros Papagos. Mussolini launched a new offensive a week later and hurled twenty-eight divisions on to the

Albanian front. Although the advance was quickly checked, the Greeks were weary and disheartened by the looming German attack and Yugoslavia's decision not to side with them.

Hitler simultaneously invaded Greece and Yugoslavia on the morning of 6 April 1941. Attacking from Bulgaria, Field Marshal Siegmund List's Twelfth Army poured into southern Yugoslavia and Greece. Shortly afterwards, a military consortium of German, Italian and Hungarian soldiers marched into northern and central Yugoslavia. Bulgaria, for its part, was not obliged to participate for its share of the spoils. In total, fifty-two Axis divisions flooded into Yugoslavia, twenty-four being German. The beleaguered Royal Yugoslav Army, though numbered at 700,000 men and the largest army in the Balkans, was hindered by obsolete equipment, dissension and mutiny. It didn't stand a chance. Heavily bombed, the open city of Belgrade fell on 13 April. Finding suitable dignitaries to sign an instrument of surrender proved difficult, however, with King Peter and the majority of his ministers in Greece, and en route to exile in London. An unconditional surrender was finally signed on 17 April and the country apportioned, with the exception of the puppet state of Croatia, between the four invading Axis nations.

Yugoslavia's collapse, for the cost of 151 German lives, enabled List's German 40th Corps to enter Greece, where it outflanked and encircled the Greek divisions that Papagos had earlier failed to withdraw from the Albanian front, and which the Italians had pinned down. Simultaneously in the north, the German 18th Corps penetrated the so-called Metaxas Line and captured Salonika. This left three Greek divisions and the recently arrived British expeditionary force (comprising the 6th Australian Division, 2nd New Zealand Division and the British 1st Armoured Brigade) under 'Jumbo' Wilson to hurriedly secure a defensive line south of Salonika.

Faced with the threat of the advancing 40th Corps, and assisted by Ultra intercepts, Wilson successfully withdrew his forces south to Thermopylae. With the main body of the Greek army – already bled white from fighting the Italians – therefore split from Wilson's forces, Wavell decided on 21 April to withdraw his expeditionary force from an increasingly doomed position.

The previous day General Georgios Tsolakoglou, commander of the Greek army in Epirus, approached SS General Josef 'Sepp' Dietrich with an offer of surrender rather than face the humiliation of capitulating to the Italians. A second accord was signed the next day after it was realised that the unfortunate Tsolakoglou had authority only over his own troops. Mussolini exploded upon hearing the news and demanded that the Greeks capitulate to him, too. Greek honour duly took second place to preserving Italo-German unity as a third armistice was signed on 23 April in the presence of joint Axis representatives.

The Duce's Greek campaign – at some 150,000 casualties – was even more disastrous than his Egyptian enterprise. German losses, by comparison, amounted to 1,160 killed, 3,755 wounded and 345 missing. Save for honour, Churchill's Balkan intervention was another expensive fiasco, with 903 men killed, 1,250 wounded and 13,958 men taken prisoner. Like Dunkirk, a sizeable volume of fighting equipment had been abandoned, though 50,732 troops from several armies, including Greeks and Yugoslavs, were rescued from the beaches by Admiral Cunningham's overtaxed fleet. The majority of those saved were ferried to Crete, 160 miles distant. Providentially, the Italian fleet, presumably after its stunning defeat by the RN in the Battle of Cape Mattapan on 28 March, was absent during the evacuation.

In the end, *Marita* may have secured Germany's southern flank, but at what price? Although it has been argued that the Balkans campaign delayed the launch of *Barbarossa* from May to June, it is widely believed today that the operation had minimal impact. In actuality, the postponement resulted from either the need to establish the Luftwaffe's forward air-fields, bring forward fuel reserves, or to assemble the necessary motor transport pool. A late thaw may also have been a prime factor. For nearly all the armies involved, the Greek campaign was messy and expensive, with a comparatively minor effect on the war itself.

Britain's Fiscal Crisis

For Churchill, the events of April 1941 were almost as calamitous as those of the previous year, when his expeditionary forces were evacuated from France and Norway. Rommel was now threatening his position in North Africa; shipping losses in the Atlantic to U-boats continued to rocket – Churchill later said that the U-boat threat was the only thing that ever really frightened him – and the Luftwaffe was pounding Britain's cities and ports. Roosevelt was also unconvinced at this time of the premier's leadership qualities, as were many British politicians, senior military leaders and businessmen. Unbeknown to the majority of Churchill's doubters, however, there was another battle being waged behind closed doors – the funding of Britain's military effort.

On 8 December 1940 – the day prior to the launch of Compass – Churchill dispatched a frank 4,000-word letter to Roosevelt, outlining the precarious nature of Britain's financial situation at the heart of a war that was far from won. He spelt out the crippling shipping losses being sustained in the North Atlantic, and the fatal consequences for Britain should Hitler's U-boats continue to decimate convoys. He also warned of the danger from the powerful new German battleships, *Bismarck* and *Tirpitz*, once they became operational.

For America, news that the mighty British Empire was fast running out of cash was, at first, difficult to fathom. With the majority of Americans wishing to stay out of this new conflict, a British victory, and at the very least Britain's survival, was imperative to keep the US out of the war. Returning from the Caribbean, where he had visited newly leased British naval bases, Roosevelt announced on 17 December 1940 that a new lifeline would be thrown out to Britain. America's assistance, though, would not be in the form of 'silly, foolish' dollar signs, but as an act of goodwill. He used an allegory of one neighbour helping another to fight a fire. Rather than selling Britain a garden hose, he would lend her one. Once the fire was extinguished, it would be returned. No invoice would be sent. This overture was the origin of 'Lend-Lease': an enormous programme to assist Britain – and later other Allied countries – whose protection was 'vital to the defence of the United States'. In Roosevelt's words, America would become 'the great arsenal of democracy', leveraging her immense economic resources to fight Hitler, but without sending her men off to war.

The day after the Lend-Lease bill (patriotically numbered H.R. 1776) was passed on 11 March 1941, despite isolationist Republican opposition, Roosevelt secured US $7 billion for the manufacture of aircraft, armour and plant, the production of food, and the procurement of raw materials. Churchill was now guaranteed American arms and oil in his fight against the Axis, but at an enormous cost. Tottering on a financial precipice, Britain had exhausted centuries of wealth to fund the war effort. Churchill was now fiscally dependent upon the United States, which since 1918 had become the world's fastest growing and most powerful economy. Up until this time, the purchase of American-made arms was on a 'cash and carry' basis through the American Neutrality Acts. A total of US $4.5 billion had been paid to Washington, and with a reserve of somewhere more than US $2 billion in assets not readily marketable – the Suez Canal, for example. Huge orders for additional materiel – all of which primed America's wartime economy, having already rescued Washington from the Great

Depression – now outstripped the value of all available British investments and cash reserves, should they be realised. As Churchill's ambassador to Washington, Lord Lothian, declared: 'Britain's broke.'[29]

Behind closed doors in London, the British were aghast. An audit of all assets was demanded, with no subsidy to be paid until Britain's foreign exchange and gold reserves were drained. As Churchill complained in letter drafted to Roosevelt, but never sent, the US was behaving like 'a sheriff collecting the last assets of a helpless debtor'.[30] In all, London had underestimated negative American sentiment toward Imperial Britain and its despised knack at getting other nations to fight its wars. By 1945, Britain would stand as one of the world's biggest debtors, however, for the moment Churchill could rest easily over the supply of additional arms and vehicles needed to fight the war.

Tobruk: 'To Be Held to the Death without Thought of Retirement'

By early April 1941, Rommel had taken most of Cyrenaica, with the exception of Tobruk – a feat as astonishing, and even more rapid, than O'Connor's drive. As had happened in France, the British were overwhelmed in the desert by the combination of superior German firepower and tactics. Apart from the British units forces in and around the now-isolated fortress, the only other formations standing between Rommel and Cairo were 'Strafer' Gott's 7th Armoured Division's Support Group (containing two motorised infantry battalions, a field regiment, anti-tank and anti-aircraft artillery), south of Tobruk at El Adem, the motorised infantry of the British 22nd Guards Brigade at Mersa Matruh and a Polish infantry brigade at Alexandria.

In one of the greatest misfortunes of the whole campaign, a small German reconnaissance party pulled over a British staff car on the night of 6 April. They'd been caught hurrying east in darkness toward Derna. Inside were Neame and O'Connor, who were now made prisoners of the German Army. Greatly affected by the loss of one of Britain's finest generals, Wavell placed Major General John Lavarack, his only available senior officer, in charge of Cyrenaica Command.

An experienced artillery officer, Lavarack had fought in France and Greece during the First World War before heading up the Australian Army from 1935 to 1939. One of his first decisions now, in the face of the Axis advance, was to defend Tobruk. Its reputation – even at this early point in the campaign – weighed heavily on his mind; on the grounds of prestige alone, he demanded that if 'Tobruk could be regarded as even only possibly defensible, it should be held'.[31]

In Cairo, Wavell met with Eden and his fellow commanders-in-chief on 6 April, to discuss the same. The atmosphere was tense. On top of the German onslaught in the Balkans and the outflanking of Mechili, a race against time was under way along the coast. Would the retreating Australian columns even reach Tobruk? Moreover, was defending the Italian fortress the best course of action? Admiral Andrew Cunningham and Air Chief Marshal Longmore both supported Wavell's assessment that Tobruk should be held. Such a stand would not only keep Rommel at bay, but also – hopefully – prevent the Luftwaffe from acquiring forward landing grounds, from where its bombers could target the British fleet at Alexandria. Locking up a garrison within the remote fortress would be an expensive exercise, Eden believed, though Cunningham was convinced that his ships could sustain its needs.[32] With the decision made, it was agreed that Tobruk would be held for up to two months, allowing sufficient time for an armoured counter-attack to be mounted from Egypt.

A communiqué to London outlined Wavell's ruling, with a request for additional cruiser tanks, anti-aircraft and anti-tank guns, and trucks. Meanwhile, in desperate need of a victory,

Churchill cabled Wavell separately, presenting *his* rationale for holding Tobruk: it was 'a place to be held to the death without thought of retirement'.[33] The British historian Sir Basil Liddell Hart surmises that Churchill was far enough removed from the confusion of the British retreat, the associated shaken confidence and exaggerated view of the enemy's strength, to be in a superior position to analyse his enemy's strategic and numerical handicaps.[34] Such a view, however, neglects Churchill's proclivity toward strategically unsound operations or 'diversions'. Churchill possessed a poor understanding of the logistical difficulties faced by modern armies, especially in an arena such as North Africa, and his ideas about the tactical conduct of warfare were outdated and largely based upon his experience fighting in South Africa during the Boer War.

As it was, Churchill's decision was far from universally well received. Australia's prime minister, Robert Menzies (then in London to discuss the limitations of the Singapore Fortress' defences), was anxious about the Australian divisions serving under Wavell's command, the quality of Britain's military leadership and even Churchill's suitability as leader. Sensing yet another military catastrophe, Menzies challenged whether Tobruk was the 'right place to make a stand' following a War Cabinet meeting on 11 April, only to be told by Britain's top soldier, General John Dill, that it *could* be successfully defended.[35] Quite the opposite view was held by Britain's director of military operations, Major General John Kennedy, who was 'astonished' by Wavell's 'absolutely wrong' decision. A better course of action, he argued, would be to fall back, 'as we did originally with the Italians', wait for Rommel to become overextended and then 'fall upon him'. Kennedy also believed the small size of the British garrison would prevent it from breaking out, should it be invested.[36]

With the decision to hold Tobruk settled, Wavell flew there with Lavarack aboard an RAF Lockheed Lodestar on the morning of 8 April to organise its defence. Touching down amid a *khamsin*, the passenger aircraft disappeared into the swirling sands for nearly an hour before the ground party finally reached it. Wavell's first stop was a meeting at command headquarters. Arriving independently, Morshead (the senior military commander in the field) delivered the welcome news that the 9th Division was safe, having suffered few casualties, although a considerable proportion of the men were still outside Tobruk's outer perimeter. Less welcome news was the unfortunate state of the 2nd Armoured Division and the trickle of vehicles that had so far managed to reach Tobruk. Generals Neame and O'Connor were presumed captured.[37] After examining reports from Brigadier John Harding and Morshead, and briefly studying a map of Tobruk, Wavell appointed Lavarack as commander-in-chief of Cyrenaica Command, with orders to hold Tobruk for a period of up to two months and halt Rommel's advance. Morshead was appointed fortress commander.

Wavell's pencilled a series of directives to Lavarack:

1. You will take over command of all troops in Cyrenaica. Certain reinforcements have already been notified as being sent to you. You will be informed of any others, which it is decided to send.

2. Your main task will be to hold the enemys [*sic*] advance at Tobruk, in order to give time for the assembly of reinforcements, especially armoured troops, for the defence of Egypt.

3. To gain time for the assembly of the required reinforcements it may be necessary to hold Tobruk for about two months.

4. Should you consider after reviewing the situation and in the light of the strength deployed by the enemy that it is not possible to maintain your position at Tobruk for this length of time, you will report your views when a decision will be taken by G.H.Q.

5. You will in any case prepare a plan for withdrawal from Tobruk, by land and sea, should withdrawal become necessary.

6. Your defence will be as mobile as possible and you will take any opportunity of hindering the enemy's concentration by offensive action.[38]

Later, Lavarack and Morshead wrangled over the decision made at this critical time to hold the fortress.[39] Today, the former's vital role in undertaking and organising the defence of Tobruk, rather than endorsing a withdrawal, remains largely unrecognised. Despite his recommendations, Wavell harboured doubts about whether Tobruk could actually hold out. He notified the Australian and British high commands of his apprehension, highlighting that 'Tobruk is not a good defensive position. [Its] long line of communication behind is hardly protected at all and is unorganised.'[40] In consultation with his Chiefs of Staff, Churchill wasted no time in drafting a typically stern response, spelling out the potential menace Tobruk would pose to Rommel's flank and any Axis movement into Egypt. However, before this communiqué was dispatched, a cable arrived from Wavell, confirming his intention 'to hold Tobruk'. The premier 'cordially' endorsed it with the promise to 'do all in our power to bring you aid'.[41]

Wavell's biographers have lauded his judgement, though in retrospect he was left with little alternative. With characteristic modesty, he later avowed that, 'I have been praised for my decision to hold Tobruk but I doubt whether I really had much option.'[42] The 9th Australian Division had managed to retreat east at a gallop – in what became known as the 'Benghazi Handicap' – with far fewer vehicles than what the 6th Australian Division had available.[43] Of its nine battalions, only five had first-line transport. Many of its vehicles were captured Italian ones and practically unserviceable, leaving the division with little option but to withdraw into and defend

Tobruk.[44] Lavarack and Morshead agreed – they doubted whether a retreat could have been organised in time.[45] A different course of action would have invited disaster, given the shortage of equipment, field artillery and anti-tank guns.[46] And thus, through lack of options and some desperation on behalf of the British leadership and imperilled Australian troops, the stage was set for the next siege of Tobruk.

'There'll Be No Dunkirk Here'

'It is the general opinion that it was most severely fought battle of the whole war.'
  – Lieutenant Joachim Schorm, 5th Panzer Regiment, 1941

The period from December 1940 until March 1941 marked the pinnacle of Wavell's accomplishments in the field. Having achieved two remarkable feats of arms against the Italians in the Western Desert and East Africa, he is remembered for directing Britain's first victories on land against the Axis. Only weeks later, the tables were turned, following German triumphs in the Balkans and Libya. Further cause for alarm would surface after a pro-Axis *coup d'état* in Iraq and a lingering doubt over the Vichy French states in Africa and the Levant. It was in the middle of this strategic tumult that the defence of Tobruk came to the forefront.

Fortress Tobruk

Wavell may have been left with little alternative but to defend Tobruk, but did he really appreciate the fixed defences that he

hoped would stave off Rommel? He first inspected the fortress on 23 January 1941, in order to judge its importance as
a base for possible future operations. As we saw, he returned
on 8 April, under different circumstances, to co-ordinate its
defence. Surveying the expansive area, he shared Lavarack's
fear as to whether the lengthy 28-mile outer perimeter
could be held. Alternatively, he suggested holding the 'area
within the inner perimeter'.[1] But this inner defensive line,
as Morshead explained, existed 'only on a map'.[2] Ignoring
Wavell's advice regarding the illusory inner defensive line,
Lavarack selected the outer anti-tank ditch as the primary barrier. But what was actual the state of Tobruk's fortifications?
As early as March 1941, the Australian 24th Brigade, which
had been stranded in Tobruk through a lack of transport, had
begun strengthening the original Italian defences. The brigade's newly appointed commanding officer, Brigadier Arthur
Godfrey (who was present as a battalion commander during
the capture of Tobruk in January) was appointed base commander in February, when the port was supplying O'Connor's
push on Benghazi. Deeply aware of Tobruk's strategic value,
and upon learning of Rommel's advance, Godfrey reconnoitred the former Italian field works and proposed a protective
perimeter based on the existing Italian defences.[3] The outer
semi-circle of perimeter posts were, however, in a deplor-
able state, filled, according to one observer, with the 'filth
and squalor – mute, if unpleasant evidence, of the unhygienic
habits of the recently departed Italian soldiery'. History had
shown that disease and hunger can undermine the strongest of
fortresses, and a fear of dysentery remained high following the
earlier Australian experience at Gallipoli.[4]

   Plenty of work was needed to ready the fortress before a
concentrated Italo-German attack. Numerous gaps punctuated the outer barbed wire entanglements, which were
also rusting from age and exposure to the corrosive salt air.[5]
The anti-tank ditch along the southern and eastern parts of

the perimeter, which the Italians never completed, had caved in and silted up. It now varied from a well-constructed pit 14ft deep and 15ft wide to an ineffective shallow trench just 2ft deep.[6] The subterranean defensive posts, though armed with automatic and anti-tank weapons and offering good protection against shellfire, were nevertheless viewed by the Australians as 'death traps'.[7] Considerable effort was expended digging subsidiary and alternate positions, as well as new communications trenches.[8]

Mackay's assault had exposed Tobruk's lack of defence in depth – a fundamental weakness that Lavarack set about correcting. Under his direction, three concentric lines of defence were constructed. The first – dubbed the *Red Line* – incorporated the original Italian outer perimeter, together with new obstacles and minefields to repel enemy tanks and infantry. Approximately 4,000yd inside the outer perimeter, a second defensive barrier – the *Blue Line* – would provide defence in depth, and prevent further penetration should the enemy breach the Red Line. The third and final defensive barrier – the *Green Line* – was constructed in an arc approximately 2 miles from the harbour. This was a 'last resort' field of defence, should the garrison face evacuation by sea.[9]

As early as January 1941, when Tobruk was still under Italian tenure, Hitler had sounded the importance of protective minefields at Tobruk.[10] Under new ownership, hundreds of additional anti-personnel and anti-tank mines were sunk into the ground as an integral part of the defences. Given the obvious value of minefields in defending the outer perimeter and providing defence in depth, one of the first tasks for the Australians was to augment the original fields in front of the Red Line, since many of the original Italian mines had been lifted. Extensive tactical minefields were also laid in the area, sandwiched between the Red and Blue Lines. The western field, in particular, was to prove crucial in halting the final Axis attack in May 1941. Later during the siege, nightly patrols would venture outside the perimeter wire and steal enemy mines to bolster the perimeter defences. One particular Australian patrol was responsible for 'delousing' and recovering no less than 600 enemy mines.[11] A number of 250kg and 500kg aerial bombs were also buried in front of the outer defensive posts.[12]

Some idea of the work carried out to bolster Tobruk's defences is illustrated by the efforts of the Australian 2/12th Battalion. Taking over the 7,500yd western perimeter position, known as the 'Fig Tree Sector', on the night of 12 May, until its relief on 6 June, the battalion installed nearly 3,000 coils of barbed wire, 15,000 pickets, 15,000 sandbags and 2,500 anti-tank mines.[13]

Meanwhile, the last runners in the Benghazi Handicap crossed the line into Tobruk under cover of a *khamsin* on the

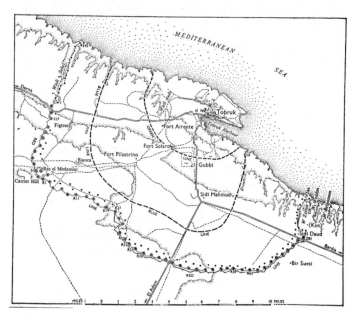

Defence in depth. The three defensive lines – outer red, inner blue and green – established at Tobruk in 1941.

night of 9 April. The clouds of dust had settled by noon the next day, affording the new occupants the opportunity to familiarise themselves with their new fighting positions and the area that lay ahead – a zone soon to become no-man's-land. Many of these raw Australian troops were novices hurriedly learning the ropes of combat. Some had never received basic weapons training; some had never seen a 'live' grenade and had to be shown its lethal radius. During the evening stand-to, men would practise their marksmanship by taking pot shots at tin cans. Directions were issued about how to disable enemy tanks using a heavy iron bar to jam the tracks while other troops climbed on top, forced the turret open with a crowbar and dropped a grenade inside. A more unusual instruction called for a battalion's musical instruments to be buried, much to the amusement of the men as far more appealing booty awaited the enemy.[14]

Monitoring happenings in Cairo, Wavell and his staff were positive that Morshead could hold out; his four brigades already inside the fortress were considered to be of sufficient size to put up 'an active defence'. Morshead readied his garrison for the forthcoming battle, instilling a sense of resolve. Each man, regardless of his role, was to stand and fight. Briefing his officers, Morshead warned that 'there'll be no Dunkirk here. If we should have to get out, we shall fight our way out. There is to be no surrender and no retreat.'[15]

Opposing Armies

Morshead's defensive arrangement was based upon four cardinal principles: the garrison would dominate the no-man's-land outside the perimeter, no ground would be yielded in the event of attack, every effort would be spent in improving the defences and the fortress' defence would be organised in depth. If attacked by tanks, the infantry were ordered not to attack or attract their attention, but to wait in their shelters until they had passed, and then open fire on the infantry following behind on foot. A single infantry brigade would man each of the three outer perimeter sectors – eastern, southern and western. A fourth brigade, held in reserve, would occupy key tactical positions such as the El Adem (King's Cross) junction, the area around Pilastrino, and the aerodromes, should the enemy use airborne troops. Given the total area of the fortress and the distance of the outer perimeter, few troops could be spared to guard against a sea-borne assault. Apart from two elderly Italian 149mm guns and a small assortment of pieces, the only realistic defence of the 20 miles of coastline rested with the RN.

Inside the fortress were 35,307 British personnel, including a number of non-combatant RN and RAF personnel. One of Morshead's primary concerns was the evacuation of rear-echelon unnecessary personnel and prisoners of war, so that by 21 April the garrison had contracted to 33,109 men: 14,817 Australians and 18,292 troops of British or Indian origin.[16] Controversially, he ignored the pleas from the medical staff and transferred the nurses out of Tobruk on the (personally held) grounds of unacceptable behaviour under enemy fire![17]

The principal formations left were the 9th Australian Division, comprising the 20th, 24th, and 26th Brigades (each of three battalions, though the 24th Brigade's 2/32nd Battalion did not arrive until 4 May), and the 18th Brigade, 7th Division, which had been rushed forward from Alexandria. Morshead's four infantry brigadiers had all served with distinction during the First World War and were well prepared for this fight. Other Australian supporting units inside Tobruk included the 2/1st Pioneer Battalion, 2/12th Field Regiment and 2/3rd Anti-Tank Regiment. Non-Australian formations included the 18th Indian Cavalry Regiment (dismounted), 1st Royal Northumberland Fusiliers Machine Gun Battalion, the 1st, 104th and 107th Regiments of the RHA, and the British 51st Field Regiment.

Morshead's small armoured force was scraped together from the remnants of the 3rd Armoured Brigade, the recently arrived 1st RTR and a miscellany of other units. On 10 April, this scratch force could muster only four Matilda tanks, six cruiser tanks and twenty light tanks.[18] Two days later, a welcomed signal from Wavell (in consultation with Lieutenant General Sir Thomas Blamey, commanding officer of the 2nd AIF), advising that eight Matildas would be delivered by sea. These tanks were especially welcomed, since German tanks had already begun probing Tobruk's southern perimeter. By the end of the month, Morshead's tank strength had grown to thirty-five Matilda and cruiser tanks in various operational states.[19] Lavarack later declared that the fortress could not have been held in 1941 without tanks, especially in the beginning before the defences had been thoroughly organised and tested.[20]

On 9 April, as Rommel's threat to Tobruk intensified, its aerial defence was boosted by the arrival of the Hurricanes from the RAF's No. 73 Squadron, joining No. 6 Squadron (Hurricanes and Lysander tactical reconnaissance aircraft) at El Gubbi, one of four landing grounds inside the fortress. The next day, an additional seven Hurricanes arrived. These aircraft provided invaluable ground support; for example, No. 73 Squadron undertook twenty-three ground strafing sorties on Good Friday (11 April), destroying eleven enemy transport vehicles and damaging many more.[21]

The fortress, however, was also poorly equipped in terms of anti-aircraft artillery. Of the seventy-five available guns, fifty-nine were small-calibre weapons. A shortage of field artillery and anti-tank guns was, to some extent, offset by a vast array of abandoned Italian artillery pieces. Beginning in March, the Australian infantry started learning to use captured anti-tank guns taken at Bardia, as well as the motley collection of Italian field pieces abandoned at Tobruk. Lacking sights and other instruments, the colourful collection of corroding guns – soon to be christened the 'bush artillery' – were nevertheless of great value in boosting the besieged garrison's morale, protecting the lengthy outer perimeter and repelling enemy raiding parties, counter-battery work and disguising the real strength of the garrison's artillery.[22]

On the other side of the wire, Rommel's combined Italo-German force comprised the German 5th Light Division, the leading elements of the 15th Panzer Division, the Italian 'Ariete' Armoured Division and the 'Trento' and 'Brescia' motorised Infantry Divisions. The number of operational German tanks had dwindled to some twenty-five light and medium Panzers, ten self-propelled anti-tank guns, plus an assortment of the less capable Italian medium and light tanks. As the veteran German armoured columns neared Tobruk, Rommel directed General Johannes Streich to attack 'with everything we have ... before Tommy has time to dig in'.[23] But as we have seen, traversing the desert had taken a heavy toll on his tanks. The 5th Light Division arrived at the fortress short of ammunition and fuel, having left a trail of broken-down vehicles and equipment stretching back across the Cyrenaican desert. Nevertheless, the idea of another quick victory at Tobruk now presented itself, and the gambler in Rommel was keen to try his hand before consolidating his forces for a march on Cairo.[24] Aerial recon-naissance, after all, had disclosed a large enemy force inside Tobruk and numerous ships in the harbour; was it another British evacuation? Rommel thought so, though the assem-bled shipping was, in reality, disembarking reinforcements – the infantry of the Australian 18th Brigade.[25]

Perhaps Rommel sensed an opportunity to emulate his ear-lier victory on 12 June 1940, during the French Campaign, when he had seized the small port of St Valéry, netting 12,000 prisoners, including four generals, fifty-eight tanks and 1,133 trucks – his greatest triumph to date. On 10 April, he was convinced that the British were actually avoiding contact and issued an order to 'pursue him with everything we have'. His objective was made known to every man – the Suez Canal.

Rallying his troops, he called for the offensive against Tobruk 'to be pushed ahead by every means possible'.[26]

10 April: The First Shots 'Cock 'em up a bit, Boys'

Tobruk was enveloped in dust for most of 10 April, as individual units moved out to their assigned positions. An Australian serviceman turned to his diary on this, the 'filthiest' of days:

> The day had turned hot and muggy, and by lunchtime we were in the middle of a hell of a sandstorm. It was bloody awful, we could not see a thing six feet away, the cookhouse was about fifty yards away but I would not risk looking for it, and wandering round out in the desert, perhaps to die of thirst, so I opened a tin of bully and picked it out with my fingers and ate it. It was lousy. Each piece was covered with sand before I could get it into my mouth.[27]

For the artillery officers, it proved impossible to survey the approaches to the perimeter, while infantry officers tried in vain to familiarise themselves with the territory they would soon attempt to defend. Infantrymen shovelling sand from their trenches quickly realised it was a futile task. Heightening the anxiety of the men staring ahead into the unknown was news of the enemy advance. When and where would Rommel strike?

That afternoon, men of the Australian 2/28th Battalion spotted an enemy column advancing along the road from Derna. Quick to react, sappers blew up a road bridge outside the perimeter, while captured Italian 75mm and 105mm guns of the bush artillery, manned by a battalion carrier platoon, opened up. Lacking sights, but compensating for imprecise aiming with boyish enthusiasm, the novice gunners peered through the gun barrels to gauge the range and direction of their first target. Overseeing the shelling was a British colonel from the RHA who had recently given the Australians a crash course on the science of gunnery. Having loaded their guns, which were prone to dangerous premature detonation, the crews retreated to a safe distance before firing them, using a lengthy rope lanyard. Through trial and error – 'cock 'em up a bit, boys', the amused colonel instructed – the shells soon found their mark close to the leading German vehicles, which quickly retired.

Later, another bush battery joined with the 25-pounder guns of the 51st Field Regiment in a longer engagement. Though the Axis claimed two artillery pieces and two Bren Gun Carriers in this skirmish, the defenders destroyed two German armoured cars and seven other vehicles. Among those killed in the clash was the commanding officer of the 15th Panzer Division, Major General Heinrich von Prittwitz und Gaffron, who had recently arrived at the front ahead of his division, and been given command of an improvised pursuit force containing the German 3rd Reconnaissance Battalion, 8th Machine Gun Battalion and 605th Anti-Tank Battalion.

The 2/13th Battalion, in position along the southern perimeter, forced advancing enemy infantry to withdraw using small arms fire. At the same time, reports were received of Axis tanks approaching from the south-east, while RAF aircraft attacked the large column of approaching vehicles. Desultory fire continued along the western perimeter sector throughout the afternoon and into the night. Enemy troops were heard outside the wire, moving into position, though no strike was launched. Craning their heads skyward, the defending infantry watched a 'giant fireworks display' burst over the town and harbour as anti-aircraft guns and probing searchlight chased enemy bombers. Inside command headquarters, Lavarack requested that Cairo dispatch the remainder of the 7th Division in order to build the garrison's strength up to two infantry divisions.

11 April: The First Easter Battle

Good Friday, 11 April 1941, was another hot and sultry day. By noon, Italo-German forces had blocked the Bardia road, leading out of Tobruk to the east. The Italian 'Brescia' division took up position around the western perimeter sector; the 5th Light Division formed up in the south.

Opening his attack, Rommel directed the 700-odd men of the 8th Machine Gun Battalion and all available tanks to assault a south-easterly section of the perimeter. Overly optimistic reports circulating within the German ranks suggested that the defending infantry would retire as soon as the Panzers appeared. In reality, the German tanks were moving blindly into battle, totally unaware of the formidable defences and staunch resistance that lay ahead.[28] Colonel Dr Herbert Olbrich, the commanding officer of the German 5th Panzer Regiment, later reported that 'nothing was known' about the 'old Italian anti-tank ditch, nor of the British artillery and anti-tank guns'.[29] Regardless, the German troops advanced assuredly, in the words of one, with 'firm confidence and iron determination'.[30]

Tobruk's unforeseen opposition quickly sprung up, as ten German tanks approached perimeter Post R59 (defended by the Australian 24th Brigade). The guns of the 24th Anti-Tank Company knocked out five, the remainder quickly forced to withdraw. A column of between twenty to thirty trucks then rolled up before the nearby Post R63. They too were driven off by concentrated artillery fire from 104th RHA, as were a platoon of German soldiers advancing on foot. Confronted by this unexpectedly stubborn resistance, groups of enemy soldiers began digging in. Seven more tanks approached Post R31 (to the west of the El Adem road) before the RHA once again sent the enemy armour scuttling for safety.

The harbour, already cluttered with numerous semi-submerged wrecks from earlier fighting, was targeted in seven air raids, included dive-bombing attacks against shipping in the harbour. One vessel, the cargo steamer SS *Draco*, sunk after a direct hit.

Recoiling, the Germans launched their heaviest armoured attack so far was late in the afternoon. Approximately twenty tanks advanced through an artillery barrage toward Post R33 – a potentially vulnerable zone on the outer perimeter. The anti-tank ditch here was shallow, the minefield laid hastily and only a few anti-tank guns were on hand. But with every available weapon brought to bear, the enemy tanks were forced to sheer off and wheel east. Several were hit, including an Italian M13/40, put out of action, using a captured 47mm anti-tank gun. Cruiser tanks of the 1st RTR engaged the remaining tanks, now running. Axis tanks losses numbered seven, the British two.

A new German infantry assault followed the abortive tank battle. Recalling the episode, Major John Balfe, responsible for the 2/17th Battalion's defence of Posts R30 to R35, described how 'the RHA let them have it again, but, even though some of the shells fell right among them, they still came on. In later months our patrols in no-man's-land found scores of German graves, marked by crosses dated April 11th.'[31]

With dusk approaching, another group of German infantry moved up toward the wire. 'Going to ground' as the perimeter posts opened up against them, they inched forward to the anti-tank ditch, which provided shelter for the mortars they quickly brought into action against the adjacent posts. Bringing forward their own reserves and mortars, Australian infantry counter-attacked – once again the aggressors were compelled to withdraw. The DAK war diary afterwards denigrated its failure to breach the outer defences as a mere 'reconnaissance advance'.[32]

Tracer from sporadic machine gun fire illuminated the front lines after nightfall. Moonlit German tanks moved forward to survey the anti-tank ditch in front of the 2/13th Battalion, hoping to locate suitable shallow points. Morshead intervened to make rolling up the perimeter even more troublesome.

Orders were given for aggressive patrolling outside the perimeter to begin. The dividends were immediate; one patrol broke up an attempt by German combat engineers, armed with demolition charges, to blow a passage through the perimeter wire and establish a bridgehead. To counter the next wave of attacks, Lavarack directed the newly arrived Australian 18th Brigade to move up during the night to the El Adem sector: so far, the fortress was holding.

12 April: 'Outstanding Accuracy'

First light on the morning of Saturday 12 April revealed another tortuous day of driving wind and sand. This was a blessing for the Germans, who had no need to 'concern ourselves about aimed British artillery fire';[33] the garrison's artillery had come as a nasty shock the previous day. Partly cloaked by nature, German infantry succeeded in digging in some 400yd beyond the perimeter, in front of Major Balfe's company, whose accurate sniping disrupted the positioning of seven enemy anti-tank guns later in the morning. Assembled Axis tanks and infantry riding trucks beyond the front lines were bombed by three RAF Bristol Blenheim bombers and harassed by RHA gunfire. Newly sited anti-tank guns along the perimeter more than proved their worth by driving off twelve approaching tanks, with what the Germans described as 'outstanding accuracy'.[34]

It was only now – fighting having already begun – that the Italians furnished two 1:400,000 scale maps of their former fortifications, though without any accompanying briefing. The imprecise nature of Italian cartography proved problematic, leading on one occasion to the 'Brescia' Division incorrectly reporting its uncontested occupation of Point 187, the high ground north of the Ras el Medauuar, *inside* the fortress.[35] German troops too found the maps difficult to decipher. The chain of concrete perimeter emplacements labelled as 'bunkers' were, as we know, flush with the ground, and unlike the typical 'blockhouse' strongholds with embrasures that characterised the German *Westwall* (also known as the Siegfried Line) or French Maginot Line. Even so, the Italian fortifications both impressed and troubled many senior German officers. Rommel was suitably 'impressed' by the skilful siting of the Italian posts and the unexpected depth of the defences; Streich, alternatively, was suddenly mindful of the difficult task that lay ahead.[36] Having won Rommel's unqualified appreciation, in May 1941 he designed the fortifications at the Sollum front based on the Italian-pattern posts at Tobruk. Such was their influence on German thinking, by the time of the Allied invasion of France in June 1944, 'Tobruk' emplacements, as they were known, had become a standard weapons pit along the entire length of Hitler's Atlantic Wall.[37]

The Luftwaffe returned, flying reconnaissance sorties and bombing the harbour seven times. Three dive-bombers fell prey to the handful of Hurricane fighters from No. 73 Squadron still operating from El Gubbi aerodrome. Enemy leaflets also rained down on the garrison, urging it to surrender. Historically, many sieges have begun with attractive terms of surrender or efforts to break the spirit of the defenders. The German flyers similarly warned the garrison that it was surrounded by 'strong German forces' and the promise that 'single soldiers waving white handkerchiefs' would not be fired upon. Quite the opposite of their intended effect, the leaflets became prized souvenirs; not that the men in the front lines possessed white handkerchiefs anyway, thanks to the all-pervading dust and the absolute need to conserve water.

With the onset of darkness, Balfe called upon the RHA to shell a number of silhouetted enemy vehicles, some towing artillery. When the dust and smoke cleared from the devastatingly accurate 400-shell barrage, not a single vehicle could be seen. Intermittent machine gun and mortar fire continued throughout what otherwise was a quiet night.

13-14 April: 'Bravo Tobruk'

Balfe's men awoke on Easter Sunday, 13 April, to find the dust storm still howling, partially obscuring the enemy activity before them. They nevertheless 'had a crack' at a group of vehicles grouped some 2,000yd distant, in what appeared to be a new headquarters. Fortune favoured the anti-tank gunners, who scored hits against two motorbikes and a staff car.

Guided by the Italian charts, Rommel's artillery began hammering the perimeter posts. A slow-moving German reconnaissance aircraft circled the front lines at midday, monitoring the garrison's defences. Hours later a brief barrage laid down preparation for the next incursion by tanks and the accompanying infantry of the German 8th Machine Gun Battalion. Beaten back once more by Tobruk's artillery, the DAK war diary attributed this latest reversal to the difficulty in overcoming the 'anti-tank ditch and wire'.[38] Rommel was quick to excuse himself from any culpability, laying blame on the 5th Light Division, which had 'lost confidence' and 'was unwarrantedly pessimistic about my plan to open our main attack' the following day.[39]

Tobruk's stubborn defence was already frustrating Rommel's ambitious drive. His forward troops had seized unoccupied Bardia and were moving across the Egyptian frontier. But, as General Franz Halder, Chief of Staff of OKW noted, an Axis drive on the Suez Canal at this time would be little more than a raid. There were simply insufficient troops and supplies to occupy Libya while Tobruk held out. A communiqué from Wavell advised Morshead of the seriousness of his situation, affirming how 'the defence of Egypt now depends largely' on his garrison. Churchill upped the ante (in a cable to his commander-in-chief), proclaiming that Tobruk was 'one of the crucial fights in the history of the British Army'.[40] Monitoring events in North Africa closely, the premier pored over photographs, a large-scale plan and scale model of the fortress. Emphasising its importance in a letter to Roosevelt, he assured the president of Britain's intention to fight for the Nile Valley. Tobruk would be steadfastly held. Of interest to us is the anti-British sentiment across the Middle East at the time. Through his father-in-law, the Egyptian ambassador to Iran, Egypt's King Farouk made an approach to Berlin in antici- pation of seeing 'victorious German troops' liberating Egypt 'from the unbearably brutal English yoke'.[41]

Restrained, for the moment, from pressing onward to Cairo, the bulk of Rommel's forces assembled at Tobruk in readi- ness for his next assault. German intelligence reports painted a picture of a shattered foe whose 'artillery was weak' and whose 'morale was low'. Turning to his diary, Olbrich recorded his 'conviction and unbending determination to smash the enemy and take Tobruk'.[42] Second-guessing Rommel's intentions, every sign pointed to an attack against the sector manned by the 2/17th Battalion. Forewarned, the defending infantry were growing in experience, and confidence.

A mortar bombardment before 11.00 p.m. (on the night 13/14 April) covered the advance of a small party of German infantry, armed with two small field guns, a mortar and machine guns. Penetrating the outer wire to the east of Post 33, they dug in and began firing at the Australian posi- tion. Once a foothold was established, nearly forty tanks from Colonel Olbrich's 5th Panzer Regiment would drive north toward the harbour. Following closely behind would be the 8th Machine Gun Battalion, under Colonel Gustav Ponath.

After small arms fire failed to dislodge the raiders, Lieutenant Frederick Austin Mackell, the platoon com- mander of Post 33, wasted no time in responding. While the balance of his men pinned down the intruders with heavy fire, Mackell gathered a party of six men to tackle the entrenched German advance party. Their flanking advance, however, was detected, forcing them to ground. Responding with a volley of hand grenades, the Australians rose to their feet and charged, yelling loudly, bayonets fixed. Corporal Jack Edmondson, a grazier from country New South Wales, was sprinting forward when a burst of machine gun fire wounded him in the stomach and neck.

Though mortally wounded, Edmondson reached the enemy position where he killed several Germans. Mackell, for his part, was wrestling with a German soldier on the hard desert floor when another appeared, brandishing a pistol. Screaming 'Jack', Edmondson ran to Mackell's aid, bayoneting both assailants. He went on to bayonet 'at least one more'. No fewer than twelve Germans were killed, and one taken prisoner, during the brutal skirmish. Covered in blood and unable to stand, a weakened Edmondson was helped back to his post, where he died early the following morning. His heroic stand was duly recognised with a posthumously awarded Victoria Cross – Australia's first of the war.

Other Australian patrols manning different perimeter sections similarly drove back small groups of probing attackers. A curious Panzer examined the shallow portion of the anti-tank ditch near Post R33 after midnight, while German pioneers began lifting and neatly stacking mines. Behind the lines, Rommel took a moment to pen a sanguine letter to wife. With the din of combat in the background, he reflected how today 'may well see the end of the Battle for Tobruk. The British were very stubborn and had a great deal of artillery. However, we'll bring it off.'[43]

Some 200 enemy infantry were sighted at 2.30 a.m. near the vicinity of Post R33. Balfe called for the RHA to heavily shell the Germans, who were attempting to re-establish a foothold at Post R33. Tanks from the German 5th Panzer Regiment began moving forward, though bad fortune dogged their advance. Wrongly directed to a position beyond where a gap in the wire had been cleared, Olbrich later explained that his tanks were 'unexpectedly held up by an impassable anti-tank trench'. Ordered to 'right turn', his tanks advanced for a further 2.5 miles 'along the trench under heavy anti-tank fire and extremely well directed artillery fire', in search of a suitable crossing point.[44] Lumbering west, parallel to the perimeter, Olbrich's tanks had, by this time, squandered surprise and the preliminary bombardment delivered to support their thrust. Not until 5.20 a.m. did the first wave of thirty-eight tanks and three self-propelled guns successfully infiltrate the perimeter, close to Mackell's post, before driving directly toward Balfe's headquarters.

As practised in battles across Poland and France, the German tanks would now push ahead, while the infantry would follow, stopping to neutralise any opposition. Dust thrown up in the first rays of dawn by a second wave of tanks (2nd Battalion, 5th Panzer Regiment) presented an inviting target for the RHA's versatile 25-pounder guns, positioned in the Blue Line. Massing through the bottleneck perimeter breach, the advancing German armour came under intense artillery fire; the majority of the machine gunners riding into battle on the tanks were either killed or wounded.

Meanwhile, the first wave of German tanks had advanced 2 miles beyond the wire. In stark contrast to the previous defence of Tobruk, the assaulting force now faced staunch defence in depth, and promptly deployed armour. As one, the 2-pounder guns of the Australian 2/3rd Anti-Tank Regiment, the 25-pounders of the RHA, mobile 2-pounder guns mounted on the back of trucks (known as portee), and the promptly deployed, counter-attacking cruiser tanks of the 1st RTR opened fire.

The German response was methodical and practised. The Panzers, having been earlier dispersed, closed in tight formation, and began 'leapfrogging' toward the guns of the 1st RHA – one group pausing to fire while a second proceeded past the stationary tanks until they too paused to fire. The light tanks supplied continuous cannon and machine gun support. Firing over open sights – that is, point-blank range in which no elevation of the gun barrel is required – the British gunners quickly disposed of five oncoming tanks. Two more were stopped by the 2/3rd Anti-Tank Regiment after they veered off to the right. Having steadfastly remained in their underground posts, the Australian infantry now emerged to battle the oncoming enemy infantry and prevent them from bringing forward field artillery and anti-tank weapons. Accurate sniping prevented the German supporting artillery from firing a single shot. German troops forming up outside of the perimeter were shelled; those who had managed to slip inside the perimeter were swiftly 'dealt with'.

Wheeling east, the Panzers became the target of every available gun within range, including four Matildas – a particularly nasty surprise for the German crews, who held this British tank in high regard. The first wave of tanks now turned to retreat, and in doing so ran into the path of the approaching second wave.

Lieutenant Joachim Schorm (5th Panzer Regiment) described the scene: 'Our heavy tanks fire for all they are worth, just as we do, but the enemy, with his superior force and all the tactical advantages of his own territory, makes heavy gaps in our ranks.'[45] Overhead, outnumbered RAF Hurricane fighters fought bravely overhead, and two Italian aircraft were sent careering down on to the violent battlefield below. Ordered to withdraw, the embattled tank hastened back across open terrain, toward the gap in the wire, all the time under unremitting fire. As they neared the perimeter breach, several stopped in an attempt to force the Australian infantry, who were 'mopping up' the German infantry, to surrender. Raked by machine-gun fire, however, the Panzers quickly 'closed up', forcing the German troops who had hitched a ride to jump for cover. Frustrated tank crews and accompanying infantry scurried to escape from what one soldier described as a 'Witches' Cauldron'. 'The driver cannot see a thing for the dust ... we drive by instinct,' Lieutenant Joachim Schorm later wrote.

Major Balfe detailed the 'terrible confusion':

> Into this cloud of dust and smoke we fired anti-tank weapons,
> Brens, rifles and mortars, and the gunners sent hundreds of shells.
> We shot up a lot of infantry as they tried to get past, and many,
> who took refuge in the anti-tank ditch, were later captured.[46]

Mopping up continued throughout the night. Stranded on the battlefield, the German machine gunners put up a valiant fight until their ammunition was exhausted. Then an armada of forty Ju 87 dive-bombers and Messerschmitt fighters arrived over the harbour early the following morning in what should have been a knockout blow for the garrison. Instead, Tobruk's remaining Hurricane fighters took to the air, shooting down six intruders; the ack-ack (a British term for anti-aircraft artillery) destroyed another four.

All fighting had ceased by 8.30 a.m., and Rommel's largest attack to date had ended in abject failure. More than 100 dead Germans lay on the battlefield, including Ponath (recent *Ritterkreuz* recipient). A further 254 Germans were taken prisoner. Shattered, Sergeant Rudolph Liessmann (8th Machine Gun Battalion) wrote: 'I was not the only one with tears in my eyes, and we did not need to be ashamed of it ... Our march to Tobruk continued, but as prisoners of war.'[47]

Olbrich tallied up his loses inside the 'Hell of Tobruk':

38 tanks went into battle
17 tanks destroyed by the enemy
2 officers are missing and 7 wounded
21 N.C.Os and men are missing
10 N.C.Os and men are wounded; this means a total loss of 50 per cent.[48]

The defenders suffered surprisingly few casualties, with only twenty-six men killed and sixty-four wounded. Two cruiser tanks, one 25-pounder gun and two precious Hurricanes were also lost. Morshead circulated a congratulatory signal from Churchill to Wavell – *Bravo Tobruk!* [49]

Lavarack congratulated the garrison in a special order of the day: 'Everyone can feel justly proud … well done Tobruk.' He also highlighted the reasons for the Axis rout: the refusal by the perimeter posts to give up their ground, the rapid counter-attack by reserves of the 26th Brigade, competent shooting by the artillery and anti-tank guns, in combination with the armoured counter-stroke that halted the advancing Panzers and then drove them back in disorder. He praised the gallant efforts of the RAF and the anti-aircraft defences, acknowledging how 'prompt action and close co-operation by all arms ensured the enemy's defeat'. [50] It was, however, a bittersweet day for Lavarack. Cyrenaica Command was to be absorbed into Western Desert Force command, under Lieutenant General Beresford-Peirse (who had led the 4th Indian Division against the Italians at Sidi Barrani). Lavarack would therefore return to his position as commander of the Australian 7th Division (minus the 18th Brigade, which was inside Tobruk). He was to take a step down, even after this gallantly fought battle.

Across no-man's-land, a furious Rommel blamed his tanks for leaving the infantry 'in the lurch'. [51] Yet he was responsible for thrusting the diminutive attacking force against the larger garrison, with its superior firepower. Inviting further failure, he now ordered the Italian 'Ariete' Division to seize a raised perimeter sector south of Ras el Medauuar (also known as Hill 209 and Fort Lloyd), which sat some 600ft above sea level. [52] Escorting the Italians in person, he was shocked to witness several incoming artillery rounds throwing the division into 'complete disorder' and 'indescribable' confusion. [53] In frustration, Rommel called for a second, German, attack that evening, until he backed down following protests from Streich and Olbrich. Rommel's riposte was that his senior officers 'lacked resolution'. [54] A victim of Rommel's wrath, Streich was relieved of his command in July, on the justification that he had failed to come to the aid of the isolated 8th Machine Gun Battalion as ordered.

The frustrated Italo–German force at Tobruk was now in a precarious position. General Streich explained to Rommel's operations officer that had the British possessed the least daring, they could have pursued the retreating Germans through the perimeter breach, overrun the remainder of his division and potentially captured the entire *Afrikakorps* headquarters. Meanwhile, in London, Churchill's leadership was still under question by the Australian prime minister, Robert Menzies, who believed the British Empire was headed for defeat. His concern over the safety of Australian troops and ineptitude within Whitehall was vented in a caustic diary entry (dated 14 April) following a War Cabinet meeting:

> The Master Strategist – 'Tobruk *must* be held … With what?' says I, and so the discussion goes on. Wavell and the Admiralty have failed us. The Cabinet is deplorable – dumb men most of whom disagree with Winston but none of whom dare to say so. This state of affairs is most dangerous … Winston is a dictator; he cannot be over ruled, and his colleagues fear him. The people have set him up as something little less than God, and his power is therefore terrific.[55]

15 April: The Italians Strike in the West

Ruminating over the defeat, Schorm noted in his diary (on the morning of 15 April) that Tobruk's artillery had opened up early and split the assault. 'We simply cannot understand how we ever managed to get out,' he wrote. A veteran of the earlier European *Blitzkrieg*, Schorm concluded that 'it was the most severely fought battle of the whole war.'[56]

Regardless of the fact that his own troops were incapable of storming Tobruk, and loathe to admit that his combined forces were unequal to the task, Rommel now rallied the Italians for a new assault, this time along the western perimeter. Shortly after dawn, an Italian patrol came into view in front of the 2/48th Battalion's position in front of Ras el Medauuar. Though the first party was driven away with Bren Gun fire, other parties continued to reappear throughout the morning, only to be rebuffed by artillery. Later, during the heat of the afternoon, roughly 1,000 troops managed to breach the wire in front of the 2/24th Battalion, to over-run one of the former perimeter posts. A counter-attack by a company from 2/23rd Battalion and the steady machine gun fire of the 2/24th held the enemy back. By 6.15 p.m. the only Italians still inside the wire were the fallen and the 113 taken prisoner.

Rommel's misfortune continued at sea. Four RN destroyers, sailing from Malta, intercepted Italian Convoy 20 and sank five merchantmen, sending the core elements of the German 15th Panzer Division to the seabed – losses that the DAK could ill afford. A further blow came on the morning of 19 April, when battleships HM *Warspite*, HM *Barham*, HM *Valiant* and HM *Gloucester* trained their large-calibre guns on Tripoli's harbour, sinking at least five supply ships without loss. Stalled at Tobruk, Rommel's advanced units near the Egyptian frontier at Capuzzo, Halfaya, Sollum and Bardia were also engaged by Brigadier Gott's mobile force, reinforced with tanks and the infantry of the 22nd Guards Brigade. His troops would not be celebrating by the Nile any time soon.

16 April: 'Well Done Indeed'

Rommel, in the midst of these setbacks, remained misguidedly hopeful. In a letter to his wife (on 16 April), he mistakenly boasted that the 'enemy is embarking' and that he expected the 'fortress to be ours very shortly'.[57] To this end, he planned to launch the Italian 'Ariete' and 'Trento' Divisions, plus several German companies, at the high ground of Ras el Medauuar.

All signs of Axis activity on this hot and dusty day pointed to a repeat attack from the west. For the first time, a large-calibre German gun (nicknamed 'Bardia Bill' by the Australians) began lobbing shells deep within the fortress. Along the perimeter positions, the infantry and gunners watched and waited. At 5.00 p.m., eighteen Italian tanks (six medium and twelve light vehicles) from 'Ariete' Division appeared in a formation, moving toward Hill 187. Reaching the highest point, the Italian tanks halted – a tempting target for the British artillery, whose quickly shells soon fell among them. Retiring at speed to the shelter of a nearby wadi, Rommel was unsuccessful in goading the Italian tank commander to resume his advance. An infantry battalion from the 'Trento' Division later mounted a 'half-hearted' assault before scattering under a bombardment from the guns of the 51st Field Regiment.

As the Italians retreated, a number of 'spiteful' rounds landed in their midst from disapproving German gunners. The contemptible act so infuriated an Italian colonel, captured shortly afterwards, that he helped draft a surrender leaflet to his compatriots. Dropped the next day, it urged 'Soldiers of Italy' to 'end it all' and follow his example.[58]

Once the shelling had ceased, Bren Gun Carriers of the 2/48th Battalion 'rounded up' a large number of the enemy outside the wire. The troops manning the perimeter posts, to quote the 2/48th Battalion's diarist, were greeted by 'the ludicrous sight of a battalion of infantry being herded like so many sheep through a gap in the wire into our hands'.[59] Again, Morshead had suffered minimal casualties while the Italians lost twenty-six officers and 777 other ranks.[60] When later questioned, many of the thirsty and underfed Italians were found to be unaware of any actual objective. Believing that armour from the 5th Panzer Regiment was to have supported them, they did little to conceal their scorn.

Hearing of the day's success, Wavell congratulated Morshead – 'well done indeed,' he signalled.[61] Support was promised for Morshead's 'boldest action', though the fortress commander was reluctant to undertake any large-scale operations beyond the perimeter.

A gloating Churchill also cabled Roosevelt to relay news of Tobruk's latest triumph, a 'small fierce fight in which the enemy lost prisoners, killed, and tanks, together with aircraft, out of all proportion to our losses'. For the 'first time they have tasted defeat', the premier crowed.[62]

Such an abrupt reversal was cause for some alarm within senior Axis circles, however. Since Rommel's impetuous advance on the Egyptian frontier was beyond all expectations, and orders, an increasingly intolerant German High Command, whose attention was fixated on the forthcoming invasion of Russia, vetoed his appeal for reinforcements. The Italians similarly disregarded his appeal for two extra divisions to be brought forward; even if they'd been willing to supply more men, their transport capacity was simply not up to the task.

Inside Hitler's headquarters, Halder was especially critical of the situation unfolding at Tobruk: 'Now at last he [Rommel] is constrained to state that his forces are not sufficiently strong,' an 'impression we have had for quite some time over here.'[63] Dr Joseph Goebbels, Hitler's minister of propaganda, recorded the quandary in his diary: 'We have our hands full trying to hold him back.'[64] Yet Rommel's hands remained untied.

17 April: All Attempts 'Had Failed'

Unrelenting Axis shelling through the night of 16 April, into the morning of 17 April, suggested a renewed attack would be made along the western perimeter. Numerous vehicles were spotted outside the perimeter in the morning, with Italian infantry seen disembarking from trucks shortly after midday.

Tanks from the 'Ariete' Division tailed the infantry across a minefield, possibly cleared the previous night, before breaking through the wire near Post R2. But only ten Italian tanks were on hand, the other ninety-odd having succumbed to mechanical failure. Rommel later wrote that, 'It made one's hair stand on end to see the sort of equipment with which the Duce had sent his troops into battle.'[65]

On that day, it was the 2/48th Battalion's rotation to hold the perimeter. An Australian officer narrated how:

> The tanks came on through the shelling and forced their way over a broken down part of the wire. One Italian 'light' blew up on the minefield, and two more were knocked out by our anti-tank rifles before they got very far.[66]

With an artillery barrage obstructing the progress of the Italian infantry, their tanks, contrary to orders for them to remain at the rear and accompany the soldiers forward, set off alone. Now, lacking radio sets, they had no way of communicating with their compatriots on foot.

A miscellany of weapons, including the 2-pounder guns of seven cruiser tanks from the 1st RTR, now opened up against the Italian armour. Five enemy tanks were swiftly disposed of; one escaped through the wire and four more were abandoned outside the perimeter. Captured crew members from one tank later confirmed that their objective was to capture and hold Hill 209, their confidence apparently unshaken by the abortive Easter fighting.

Meanwhile, the isolated Italian infantry, unable to pursue the armour, remained on the open ground outside the wire, despite the best efforts of Tobruk's artillery to repel them before dark. A further three enemy tanks were destroyed by British cruisers in a running battle along the southern portion of the perimeter, and although discussed, no counter-attack was launched.

18 April: A Desultory Push

First light on 18 April revealed the movement of enemy vehicles and tanks again, directly in front of the 2/48th Battalion, apparently covering the withdrawal of the Italian infantry (from the previous day's assault), still astride the perimeter. Later in the day, Italian troops made yet another desultory push before the guns of the 51st Field Regiment checked their progress, throwing the infantry into disorder. Subsequent movements outside the wire indicated yet another assault, and Morshead gave orders for a counter-attack to be prepared, though as it happened, no fighting eventuated.

A relative calm descended now upon the fortress, releasing manpower for work on the Blue Line and in re-laying mines lifted by the enemy where he had broken through. An Australian soldier confided in his diary:

> Today is a miserable day. It is raining and cold as blazes. I have a bit of covering over my dugout, but every now and then the rain drips though. However the enemy have been very quiet all day, which is a relief, but it makes one a bit suspicious when he is quiet.[67]

Visiting the garrison repair shops, a British war correspondent found a German Mark IV Panzer, retrieved from the battlefield, and went in for closer examination. He found an inscription painted on the front of the dark grey hull, paying respect to a decorated crew member killed on the third day of the war nineteen months earlier.[68] Victorious in the Polish and French campaigns, the tank's crew could not have imagined combat against British forces in North Africa, let alone suffering defeat. The Tobruk garrison had won the first round.

The 'May Show'

'We had failed, despite all efforts, to take Tobruk.'
— Lieutenant General Fritz Bayerlein

The lull in the fighting after the Easter battles gave Morshead the opportunity to reorganise and prepare for the next onslaught. In a matter of weeks, 'Ming the Merciless', as his men had nicknamed him, had successfully risen from a brigade commander, leading 2,500 troops, to a major general. Only weeks earlier, he had observed the capture of Tobruk by the Italians and now has was practically a corps commander in charge of a mixed fortress garrison, comprising 33,000 soldiers, sailors and airmen. Morale within the garrison was high; the men had withstood their first test.

It was a different picture across no-man's-land, where captured diaries and interrogated prisoners evoked flagging spirits and friction within the besieging army. Rommel conceded that:

All further attempts to penetrate into the British positions had failed. It was now finally clear that there was no hope of doing anything against the enemy defences with the forces we had, largely because of the poor state of training and useless equipment of the Italian troops. I decided to break off the attack until the arrival of more troops.[1]

Morshead's Offensive Defence

Taking advantage of his enemy's malady, Morshead issued orders for three simultaneous daylight raids to be undertaken against the Italians – who now outnumbered the Germans outside Tobruk – on 22 April; the objective being to unnerve the enemy force, and with any luck, 'bag' as many prisoners as possible.

C Company, 2/48th Battalion, undertook the largest of the three raids. The objective lay more than 1,000yd beyond the wire behind a small rise, known as Carrier Hill (so-named because of an abandoned Bren Gun Carrier there), where the Italians had dug in. Recent reconnaissance revealed that the hill was shielding a significant body of men, some forty vehicles, an artillery battery and four tanks – an attractive target. The Australian infantry set off at 6.40 a.m. supported by five Bren Gun Carriers, three Matilda tanks, four mobile anti-tank guns, the guns of the unfailing 51st Field Regiment and RAF fighter cover. Advancing behind a heavy artillery barrage, the Australian troops surprised the Italian defenders, who were focused on engaging the tanks, by appearing from the south. The Italians stood their ground, though, swinging their weapons on to the Australians, who began charging with fixed bayonets. Its nerve shattered, the 'Fabris' Battalion promptly surrendered. In all, 368 men, including eighteen officers, were brought back into Tobruk, together with their trucks, motorcycles, maps, weapons and prized artillery sights for the bush artillery. The particularly successful raid cost Morshead nine Australian casualties, including three dead.

A curious Rommel and his ADC later explored the silent battlefield. Schmidt recalled:

> As we approached the sector we thought it completely calm and were ready to conclude that the reports of enemy activity overnight had been, as so often before, exaggerated by our Allies. Even the enemy artillery in Tobruk seemed quiet. But the puzzle was soon solved: we found not a single Italian in the whole sector, barring a few isolated artillery batteries in the rear, entirely unprotected by infantry. We peered cautiously over a rise and were met by the sight of hundreds of discarded sun-helmets gaily decorated with multi-coloured cocks' feathers – *Bersaglieri* helmets. The Australians must have 'collected' the entire battalion of our Allies.[2]

The second Australian raid also met with considerable success. This time a patrol from the 2/23rd Battalion, also at company strength, advanced along a wadi that extended west from the perimeter line. Again, the combined effect of fixed bayonets, grenade blasts and swiftly moving carriers proved too much for the forty or so Italians, who were caught unaware and promptly taken prisoner.

A third raid, also undertaken by men of the 2/23rd Battalion, targeted an Italian anti-tank/anti-aircraft battery and nearby field artillery. Enemy opposition was far more determined this time and a bitter 4-hour fight ensued. The Australians sustained 80 per cent casualties, and were unable to overrun the enemy position, though eighty-seven prisoners were taken and the same number wounded or killed. Although the raid had failed to neutralise the enemy, Morshead described it as 'an epic worthy of the finest traditions of the AIF'.[3] The raids imbued the troops with confidence and experience, though Morshead cautioned them 'to remember that continued vigilance is necessary and that most of our patrol successes have been against the Italians'.[4]

'This Soldier Gone Stark Mad'

Meanwhile, in Berlin, an increasingly unsympathetic Halder recorded his misgivings about the conflict in Libya; the hand that guided the *Afrikakorps* was now under increasing scrutiny. Since arriving in North Africa, Rommel had become a some-thing of loose cannon in Halder's eyes, a general who needed reining in. Halder's growing frustration reads in a diary entry of 23 April:

> Rommel has not sent in a single clear report, and I have a feel-ing that things are in a mess ... All day long he rushes about between his widely scattered units and stages reconnaissance raids in which he fritters away his strength ... the piecemeal thrusts of weak armoured forces have been costly ... His motor vehicles are in poor condition and many of the tank engines need replacing ... It is essential to have the situation cleared up without delay.[5]

To investigate this 'mess', a senior representative from Germany was sent to examine and report on the situation. He would also be in charge of briefing Rommel regarding the finite resources available to him. The officer selected, Lieutenant General Friedrich Paulus, was on good terms with Rommel and, as Halder thought, 'perhaps the only man with enough personal influence to head off this soldier gone stark mad ...'[6]

At the same time, Rommel was updating Berlin about the hazardous situation confronting his men at Tobruk and Bardia (even though the British threat along the Egyptian frontier had eased considerably). His report warned that if Sollum or Bardia fell, or were to become isolated, then the siege of Tobruk would have to be raised to meet a new British threat – a circumstance Halder wished to avoid, primarily for fear of a propaganda backlash. The solution, Rommel proposed, was for air-lifted reinforcements, additional aircraft, particularly fighters, and U-boats to patrol the Mediterranean. It was, he believed, the perfect moment to match the British in Libya and prevent their strengthening, especially after their misfortunes in Greece.

Churchill, too, wanted to see action in the desert, though Wavell – also under intense scrutiny – was hard-pressed to undertake any large offensive at this chaotic juncture. A new headache had also developed in the Middle East. Earlier on 3 April, the former Iraqi prime minister, Rashid Ali Al-Gaylani, had seized power in Baghdad – the recent British setbacks in Libya a key factor in his timing – with the support of army officers, and formed a new pro-Axis cabinet. German aid was openly invited. As well as reaffirming sympathy for the Arab cause, Berlin promised, at the very least, diplomatic and propaganda support. When asked if he could spare troops to intervene in Iraq, Wavell, who had foreseen its importance, replied that he could only spare a single battalion from Palestine. His strained resources were already stretched across Libya, Greece and East Africa. Wavell believed that the situation could, alternatively, be defused through diplomacy and the use of the RAF. Wavell had already, in fact, discussed using Indian troops with General Claude Auchinleck (commander-in-chief of India since February 1941), in the event of Axis infiltration into Iran and Iraq, and no doubt felt a sense of relief on 18 April when London advised him not to 'worry about Iraq for the present'.[7]

The shaky state of affairs in Iraq, however, only served to further heighten Churchill's mistrust of his senior Middle East commander. Wavell's apparent reluctance to extend his forces into this new theatre irritated Churchill immensely; it smacked of indecision and an aversion to risk-taking.

Churchill's suggestion to transfer Auchinleck (who had gained the premier's respect through his readiness to act and take the initiative) to the Middle East as Wavell's second-in-command was rejected by General Dill (CIGS), because it intimated succession. It would also undermine Wavell's confidence and performance at this critical moment. 'I realise too that he has many balls on which to keep his one eye,' Dill contested, but compared with Auchinleck, he 'is more versed in the conduct of military operations under modern conditions'. But, as he added, 'the minute you lose confidence in Wavell, or should anything happen to him, Auchinleck should at once succeed him.'[8]

The same day (18 April), Wavell alerted Dill to the substantial number of German tanks, at least 150, believed to have recently arrived in Cyrenaica. British Intelligence warned that the parent formation, 15th Panzer Division, would reach Tobruk around the beginning of May. This was a complete armoured division, with its full complement of tanks, and not, as previously thought, a second light division. The main formation, the 8th Panzer Regiment, a veteran unit of the French campaign, had successfully slipped across the Mediterranean in three convoys, bringing forty-five Panzer IIs, seventy-one Panzer IIIs and twenty Panzer IVs. Many of these tanks were also the latest models, fitted with additional reinforced frontal armour or extra armour plates bolted on to the turret and hull front for increased protection. Wavell was equally unsettled by the small number of operational British tanks in North Africa – the small mixed force inside Tobruk and a squadron of cruisers based at Mersa Matruh. Jolted into action by Wavell's reports and revelations gleaned from Ultra, Churchill magnanimously called for the dispatch of 'tanks with all speed and at all cost'.[9]

A fast convoy left Britain five days later. Disregarding 'admiralty reluctance', the ships would sail directly through the Mediterranean to Alexandria, shaving forty days off the usual sailing time around the Cape. The journey would be, however, fraught with the danger of Axis sea and air attack. Dubbed Operation Tiger, the precious cargo of 295 tanks – what Churchill called his 'tiger cubs' – plus fifty-three Hurricane fighters, was due to arrive in Alexandria in mid-May. 'Speed is vital,' the premier stressed.[10]

Readying for Rommel's Next Onslaught

Inside Tobruk, Morshead instructed his men to continue strengthening the defences and to prepare for Rommel's next assault. The fortress's firepower was increased through the issue of additional captured weapons, though the small number of tanks and a chronic shortage of anti-tank guns increased his reliance upon minefields. The Easter battles had demonstrated how easily the outer anti-tank ditch could be breached, and how readily the mines laid outside the wire could be lifted. Accordingly, the mines outside the perimeter entanglements were retrieved and re-laid in front of the perimeter posts, and in the area extending between the Red and Blue lines. Mines were also re-laid in the gap along the western sector, where the Italian tanks had earlier penetrated. Priority was given to the zone around Ras el Medauuar, where it was assumed Rommel would strike next. Work on the Blue Line minefields and another immediately behind Hill 209 was also intensified, while the sensitivity of existing fields was improved by modifying them for hair-trigger detonation.

Telephone poles lining the main roads into the town were cut down to prevent them acting as 'signposts' toward the harbour. Communications, in general, remained problematic since the majority of the infantry battalions had never received their full allocation of equipment. One battalion, in fact, had arrived at Tobruk with little more than signal flags. Other formations had lost their makeshift, mainly captured, equipment during the retreat across western Cyrenaica. In the absence of wireless sets, telephone communication with the perimeter posts was upgraded by installing signal lines and using reconditioned Italian sets.

The commander of the fortress anti-aircraft artillery, Brigadier John Slater, introduced an 'umbrella barrage' to counter the growing intensity of Axis air raids. The new tactic, which shrouded the harbour with a screen of projectiles set to explode at a particular altitude, brought immediate success, with six of the thirteen aircraft that attacked the harbour on 23 April shot down. To give some idea of Axis air activity over the fortress: During the last three weeks of April, Tobruk's harbour and surrounding areas were attacked by 677 aircraft in fifty-two separate raids. By the end of the April 1941, the fortress ack-ack gunners had brought down thirty-seven aircraft, probably destroyed sixteen more and damaged another forty-three. The steadfast gunners, though, had also suffered. Drawing increasing enemy attention, they had suffered nearly fifty casualties during attacks on 27 April alone.

Then, on 25 April, much to Morshead's annoyance, RAF command transferred the few remaining fighters out of Tobruk to assist in the British rearguard action in Greece. (In the timeline of the larger war, the Greek government had capitulated the previous day, and only added to Britain's escalating turmoil). Only five out of the original thirty-two Hurricanes were still airworthy, though one flight was retained inside the fortress until 8 May for reconnaissance duties. The relative quiet along the perimeter was shattered the same day by a fresh Italian infantry attack. Following hot on the heels of the heaviest enemy artillery bombardment to date, a tightly grouped enemy pushed across the wire to where the 2/23rd Battalion was positioned, close to the Derna Road. As in earlier encounters, the attackers were soon blocked by concentrated artillery fire and the deadly response from the perimeter posts. A second attack against Ras el Medauuar also drew intense fire before the waving of numerous white flags signalled the Italians' wish to lay down their arms, forty of their own already dead. Australian parties later returned with 107 prisoners. In their first appearance on the western sector, around forty Germans launched a separate attack at noon. They were also forced to ground before withdrawing in the face of strong fire, and seven were captured.

Meanwhile, alarming verification that the 15th Panzer Division had arrived was exacerbated by British Intelligence reports confirming that a battalion from the motorised Italian infantry 'Trento' Division and two infantry regiments from the 'Brescia' Division had also moved into position around the western perimeter.

A *khamsin* on 26 April, though, brought natural hardship for all. Visibility, in the words of one Australian soldier, was 'about the length of a cricket wicket'.[11] Due for rest, the 2/48th Battalion, which had tenaciously held its 5-mile western perimeter front (pre-war teaching in the Australian Army had taught that one battalion in open country with good 'machine gun slopes' could hope to successfully defend 2,000yd) was transferred at night to its new position on the interior Blue Line. Its replacement battalion, the 2/24th Battalion under Lieutenant Colonel Allan Spowers, would occupy Posts S11 to R10 (the prefix of posts north of Hill 209 was 'S' and to the south 'R'). To Spowers' right was the 2/23rd Battalion; to his left the 2/15th Battalion.

Spowers' men set to work enthusiastically, deepening trenches and reinforcing sandbagged positions. But although Tobruk's defences were now stronger than ever, Morshead's 24th Brigade was still missing one of its three battalions, the 2/25th. To bring the 9th Division up to full strength, Cairo ordered the 2/32nd Battalion to Tobruk by sea. Owing to bad weather at Mersa Matruh, however, only a single company aboard HMS *Chakla* arrived on 28 April (the vessel was later sunk during an air raid the same day).

Three RN 'A' lighters also slipped into the harbour, carrying six new Matilda tanks, before returning to Alexandria with captured Panzers to be shipped to England for evaluation. Tobruk was the first combat zone where the invaluable, shallow draft tank landing craft (later known as LCTs) saw action. Built at Churchill's insistence, LCTs could deliver armour directly on to a beach, and would later spearhead the Allied invasions at Sicily, southern Italy and Normandy. Originally sent to the Middle East for the aborted invasions of Rhodes and the Dodecanese islands (and dubbed 'A' lighters for security), they now became part of a newly formed 'Western Desert Lighter Flotilla'. An extraordinary collection of small ships, minesweepers, gunboats, sloops, whalers and trawlers from the Naval Inshore Squadron also plied the treacherous waters between Alexandria and Tobruk. The motley armada kept the fortress well provisioned for the agreed period of two months, though the likelihood of a protracted siege now lay ahead.

'We Intend to Take Tobruk'

Back at the Egyptian frontier, the Germans were recapturing lost ground at Sollum and Halfaya Pass – strategically important territory on Rommel's eastern flank, from which to challenge any British attempt to relieve Tobruk. With this forward position secured, Rommel could now return to crushing Morshead's stubborn fortress: A blight tying down valuable resources and obstructing all progress into the Nile Delta. During the final days of April 1941, he busily assembled a reinforced army in readiness for his next push, though he was constrained by the Luftwaffe's forthcoming aerial invasion of Crete, the disturbing loss of Italian transports ('There must be a whole lot of post lying at the bottom of the Mediterranean,'[12] he informed his wife), and a shortage of road transport to shuttle supplies, especially ammunition, forward from Tripoli. The alternative option of ferrying provisions by air to airfields near Tobruk was deemed too dangerous by the Luftwaffe's African commander.

Meanwhile, in a rousing ovation to the House of Commons on 27 April, Churchill delivered a measure of hope. 'Tobruk – the fortress of Tobruk – which flanks any German advance, we hold strongly,' he exclaimed proudly. 'There we have repulsed many attacks, causing the enemy heavy losses, and taking many prisoners.'[13] But could Tobruk withstand its hardest test to date?

Paulus arrived at Rommel's headquarters the same day. Studying the situation first-hand, and, with Gariboldi's backing and a disingenuous assurance from Rommel that supplies (including ammunition) were adequate, he sanctioned a new thrust. Rommel's ensuing order read: 'The *Afrikakorps* will force a decision in the battle round Tobruk during the night 30 April–1 May by an attack from the west.'[14] The plan was simple: Shock troops and tanks would infiltrate the western perimeter at Ras el Medauuar after dive-bombers and artillery had pounded the outer fortifications.

A battle group formed from the bulk of Streich's 5th Light Division was placed under the command of Major General Heinrich Kirchheim, his predecessor having been removed by Rommel after his trouncing in the Easter battles. The 5th Panzer Regiment now contained 81 operational tanks, half of which were medium and heavy tanks – thirty-six Panzer IIIs and eight Panzer IVs – and twice the number available on 14 April. Extra support would come from the 'Ariete' (armoured) and 'Brescia' Divisions. Although the newly landed tanks of the 8th Panzer Regiment would not reach Tobruk in time, several battalions from the 15th Panzer Division would participate: one tank destroyer, two rifle, one motorcycle and one engineering battalion.

Lieutenant Schorm became the proud recipient of a new tank – No. 634 – just prior to the battle. Together with his tank commander, he drank a last bottle of Chianti. More would await the victor. Self-assuredly, he recorded in his diary: 'We intend to take Tobruk.'[15]

April 30 dawned cloaked in a cloud of swirling dust. Through the mustard-coloured desert haze, Australian troops manning the western perimeter posts could discern Axis activity several miles distant – massed tanks and artillery, infantry alighting from trucks. That evening, as the mirage disappeared and a wind kicking up dust waned, gunfire could be heard. It was more intense than usual. The screaming sirens from the first wave of Stukas heralded the beginning of an assault. It was around 7.15 p.m.; the setting sun had just dipped below the horizon. One of the ungainly German dive bombers never recovered from its vertical drop and ploughed into the desert floor, exploding on impact. The physical stress on the pilot's body was immense. Perhaps he had switched off the automatic pull-out, as German pilots occasionally did to prevent Allied ground defences from predicting their recovery path.

After some 50 minutes of unopposed dive-bombing and machine gunning (not until later did RAF fighter aircraft from Nos 73 and 274 Squadrons in Egypt fly patrols over the battlefield) – in what the men of the 2/24th Battalion referred to as the 'May Show' – Axis artillery began targeting positions on either side of Ras el Medauuar (Hill 209). In a replay of events earlier in the month, ill-prepared German troops were now thrust directly into battle, without adequate rest or rations. To maintain surprise, Rommel prohibited *any* reconnaissance, leaving the newly arrived troops to advance across unfamiliar terrain against unknown defensive positions. (Kirchheim's group, who ignored this order, made the best progress until it encountered a minefield.)

German shock troops cleared a path through the deadly field under the cover of approaching darkness and the dust thrown up by bombing and shelling – 'for over an hour we received a generous ration of Axis ironmongery', Lieutenant Frederick Geale (2/24th Battalion) narrated. Several gaps were blown in the outer wire and moving into position behind

Posts S5 and R1. Here the infantry of the 2nd Machine Gun Battalion set up their weapons and, overcoming resistance, established a bridgehead stretching from Posts S3 to S7.

From his 'ground stand seat' position, Geale watched S7, now completely surrounded, and 'mortared all through the morning':

> Jerry's medium machine guns must have made their lives hell. In the lulls of the fighting we could hear their Bren gun rat-tattling, and that the enemy were not getting any closer to the position. Now and again parties of the enemy infantry attempted to storm their objective, but from inside the post always came that rat-tat-tat of fire, and then we could discern figures sprawled out across the open ground used by the attackers. We estimated the dead in that area from 75 to 100, so the fire from S7 must have taken a terrible toll. [Once their ammunition was exhausted] there was a concerted rush from all sides, and the defenders were overwhelmed by sheer weight of numbers.

Perimeter posts had clearly fallen, but which ones? The telephone at Spowers' headquarters, 3 miles inside the perimeter had gone dead and not until 11.20 p.m. did indeterminate news of the fighting eventually reach divisional headquarters; recorded in the log as: 'Penetration 2/24th Battalion area possible but situation not certain.'[16] While the garrison's resistance was 'stubborn as ever',[17] fortress command had no clear understanding of the enemy's headway. Patrols sent out into the darkness to clarify the situation were hampered by the veil of thick mist that had descended upon the battlefield.

Morshead retired for the evening. In his absence, Colonel Charles Lloyd ordered the 24th Anti-Tank Company forward to buttress the 2/24th Battalion, which was equipped with only ten guns to protect a 5-mile perimeter stretch. Lloyd also ordered the 3rd Armoured Brigade to move forward into position behind Spowers' headquarters.

The blanket of fog began to lift after first light on 1 May. Through his binoculars, and much to his surprise, Spowers counted some forty Panzers on the eastern slope of Ras el Medauuar (Hill 209); Rommel had already established a bridgehead approximately 1.5 miles wide, and captured seven perimeter posts. Similar to Mackay's January assault against the Italians, heavy shelling had kept the posts quiet while Rommel's infantry reduced them individually.

Still lacking satisfactory facts about the Axis break-in, Morshead chose not to counter-attack. The incursion, he believed, may have been a feint to draw his forces off from a main assault to be launched elsewhere. Fortunately, the invading force now made a fundamental error. Rather than pressing onward toward the town, the infantry turned to consolidate their bridge-head and roll up adjacent perimeter posts before advancing on the Blue Line. Confused, bloody fighting broke out along the perimeter as the Germans began neutralising individual strong-holds. A young soldier from country Victoria recalled the clash:

> Thirteen tanks approached our post. Two were perched about thirty yards away from which constant fire forced us to keep our heads down. My mate started to throw 'Molotov cocktails' but he couldn't make the distance as the tanks drew off. He crept out to get nearer to them but was shot while hurling another 'cocktail'. More tanks came up and their fire was so severe we had to keep down.

Posts S1, S2, S5, S3, R0, R1, R2, S6, S4, R3 and R4 had all succumbed by noon. As we saw, Post S7, to the north, proved especially troublesome for the Germans, with heavy casualties sustained before the Australians surrendered due to a lack of ammunition. Rommel later bemoaned how, 'this should really have been a job for a few storming parties'. Moreover, it was a, 'great mistake to allow oneself to be diverted from the main line of one's plan by relative trivialities'.[18]

Rommel, who may have missed the opportunity to reach deeper into the defenders' lines, watched with interest as a group of Australian prisoners were marched past him – 'immensely big and powerful men, who without question represented an élite formation [*sic*].'[19] Major Len Fell, 2/24th Battalion, was one of the Australian officers captured and taken to the German headquarters. He observed how confident Rommel's staff were, 'convinced' that the fortress would fall within a matter of hours. After the war, he recalled the 'correct' behaviour of his German captors, how the wounded were cared for and how the looting of prisoners was forbidden. Whereas the Germans had expected the occupants of the perimeter posts to have surrendered immediately after the Stuka onslaught, as Fell wrote, 'We had no place to go, whatever the inclination.'[20] An Australian officer and his men, 'winkled out' of their post, were now prisoners. Escorted away, they were 'dumbfounded, incredulous and shocked' by the large number of dead 'Jerries' littering the battlefield.[21]

German tanks appeared from behind Ras el Medauuar at 8.00 a.m. before turning east and proceeding along a narrow frontage. Schorm: 'We file through the gap where many of our comrades have fallen. The British artillery fires on us. We attack …'[22] Again, every available British weapon began hammering the intruders. Corporal Felix Aston of the 24th Anti-Tank Company promptly knocked out three Panzers, including a Mark III, before his gun's dial sight was damaged by a machine gun bullet and his gun received a direct hit from an enemy projectile. Two adjacent guns were also destroyed. Pressing forward through the shellfire, the enemy tanks stumbled into a minefield. In a matter of minutes, around seventeen Panzers were disabled, mainly through broken track links. Since the mines were not powerful enough to pierce the hull or kill the occupants, a number of tanks were recovered. (Schorm noted in his diary with satisfaction that two Panzer IIs from his company were salvaged from the battlefield the next day, a feat saving the

Fatherland about 800,000 Reichsmark![23]) Five more stationary tanks remained on the battlefield as makeshift pillboxes.

Mercilessly shelled by the 51st Field Regiment, a battalion of German infantry were unable to follow the Panzers forward. The remaining tanks in the leading spearhead now re-formed and joined in the task of silencing those posts still holding out. High-explosive shells were fired at point blank range, while *Flammpanzers* (a field variant of the Panzer I mounting a portable flame thrower) helped flush out the infantry.

A second column of roughly thirty Panzers that broke through the perimeter south of Post R3 became the targets of the 3rd RHA's guns and three British cruiser tanks. Several Panzers were hit before smoke was laid, allowing them to withdraw. Ten cruiser tanks later registered hits against a number of Panzers parked inside the perimeter; the ever-accurate artillery fire by the 1st and 107th RHA forcing them to shelter behind Ras el Medauuar. A sandstorm in the early afternoon was surely welcomed by the retired tank crews, who took the opportunity to replenish their fuel and ammunition. Morshead now counter-attacked with a piecemeal armoured force comprised of three cruiser and five Matilda tanks. His straightforward plan called for the armour to advance from the west. When they neared Post R12, the tanks would turn and continue between the double rows of perimeter posts toward the enemy. Three infantry companies would advance toward Ras el Medauuar near Post R2, and from the north, between Posts S4 and S6. Post R8 was found to still be in Australian hands, though many of its occupants were severely wounded. Two Matildas were stationed to guard this post, while the remainder trundled forward toward R6, also found to be under Australian occupation. A lopsided tank battle then forced the outnumbered British vehicles to break off the engagement, with only three 'runners' returning to Post R14.

The German advance had now been checked on the northern side of Ras el Medauuar. Fifteen posts had been captured, though at considerable cost against a determined enemy. Schorm described the unexpected situation he and his fellow soldiers now faced:

> It is beginning to grow dark, which is friend, which is foe? Shots are being fired all over the place, often on our own troops and on tanks in front, which are on their way back. Suddenly a wireless message – 'The British are attacking the gap with infantry'.[24]

Morshead ordered the 2/48th Battalion to move out at 7.15 p.m. and counter-attack the enemy bridgehead. The troops, however, were delayed in reaching the starting line through a lack of transport, a *khamsin*, and low-level strafing by enemy fighters. Dismounting late, in the middle of the sandstorm, and with no time for reconnaissance, the Australians finally began their westward march on Ras el Medauuar. Close artillery support was wasted owing to the belated arrival of the infantry, their tough assignment a challenge for even a full brigade. Marching into the glare of the setting sun, which helped conceal the German tanks and machine guns awaiting them, they were devoid of cover, armoured support and sufficient firepower. Fifty-two troops fell. Only modest headway was made before Brigadier Raymond Tovell (commanding officer of the 26th Infantry Brigade) called for the attack to halt and resume the next morning.

Morshead's counter-attack was, on the whole, a failure. The Australian 2/48th battalion was withdrawn to the Blue Line to recuperate.

The Salient

Tobruk was again blanketed by a heavy sandstorm on 2 May. Paulus' initial optimism was waning and, in consultation with Rommel, he stopped the attack. Instead, the Axis troops would concentrate on widening the bridgehead from Posts S7 to R14. Inconclusive fighting continued in the afternoon, with the assistance of Italian armour and infantry. Although Rommel's latest assault had foundered, he now occupied a bulging dent along the fortress' western perimeter, including the all-important high ground of Ras el Medauuar – a protrusion that became known as 'The Salient' – for the loss of more than 1,200 men killed, wounded and missing. Out of the eighty-one German tanks that had started out, twelve were damaged beyond repair and only thirty-five were still running. Shocked by this latest reverse, an entry in a German officer's diary read: 'What we experienced in Poland and the Western Front was only a promenade compared to this.'[25] Ruminating on yet another failure to storm Tobruk, Rommel admitted that:

> We were not strong enough to mount the large-scale attack necessary to take the fortress, and I had no choice but to content myself with what we had achieved, namely, the elimination of the threat to our supply route from enemy positions on the Ras El Medauar [*sic*]. It was now impossible to contemplate anything more for the present than isolated operations against individual strong points.[26]

On the other side, Morshead's tank losses were relatively light. Out of the twelve Matildas sent out, two were destroyed and a further two damaged; out of the nineteen cruisers, three were destroyed and one damaged. The 2/24th Battalion, however, had suffered heavily with 318 men missing, mostly taken prisoner, and at least twenty-two killed and thirty-five seriously wounded.

Axis 'artillery fire very severe', Schorm noted on the night of 2–3 May: 'ten batteries are firing ceaselessly. Something is in the wind. Naturally the enemy answer equally briskly.' Morshead, as the German lieutenant suspected, launched a new counter-attack on the night of 2 May, using two battalions from the 18th Brigade to assault the flanks of the Salient, recapture fallen posts and blunt the German spearhead. Word reached Schorm at 1.15 a.m.: 'Australians have penetrated the defences R1–R7. Immediately counter-attack and cover.' Chaos followed:

> Oh hell! Where to? No Idea. Italians argue and gesticulate wildly. I start by going as far as the gap, and then turn right. No officer knows the position. Near R7 an Italian tank is burning.

Little headway was made under intense enemy fire, 134 casualties were suffered and, shortly after 3.00 a.m., the operation was rescinded so that the infantry could retreat rather than be caught in the open at dawn.

Unable to retake the Salient, Morshead had nevertheless foiled Rommel. The Axis troops, however unwilling, were to strengthen their positions and remain on the defensive for the remainder of the siege.

Stalemate at Tobruk

Frustrated at Tobruk, Rommel's single-minded plan to reach the Suez Canal was now dashed. News of the Axis setback was widely circulated, though with varying degrees of accuracy. London's *Times* depicted the fortress as 'a perpetual menace and an irritant on the flank of the Italo-German forces operating on the border of Libya and Egypt'. Like a lance 'stuck into the bull in the early stages of a bullfight, [it] eventually can lay the animal low with exhaustion'.[27] Across the Atlantic, the *New York Herald Tribune* reported on the 'first time anything like that had ever happened to German tanks in the eighteen months of victorious advances. It was their first defeat.'[28] It should be remembered, however, that the German XVI Corps (containing the 3rd and 4th Panzer Divisions) was stopped in its tracks a year earlier in Belgium, during the (little-known) Battle of Gembloux (14 to 15 May 1940) by General de Fornel de La Laurencie's French III Corps and General Henri Aymes's IV Corps (French First Army). By the final day of fighting both sides were withdrawing from the battlefield. The German commanders subsequently viewed the French withdrawal as indicative of victory, when in fact the French First Army only retreated after being outflanked in the south.[29] One of the hardest fought battles of the French Campaign, Gembloux had shown how the German *Blitzkrieg* could falter against a combination of fixed defences, defence in depth, stubborn and determined infantry, mobile reserves and effectual artillery and antitank fire.

After the war, Major General Horace Birks, commander of the British armoured brigade at Tobruk, questioned why a general of Rommel's ability was unable to overrun the fortress in April 1941, when its defences were incomplete and the garrison incapable of defending the extensive perimeter.[30] What was more, why had Rommel failed when General Iven Mackay's troops had taken the fortress with relative ease only three months earlier?

A 1941 Australian Army report tabled a series of tactical reasons for Morshead's success. It found that victory stemmed from a combination of elements: The forward infantry manning the Italian perimeter posts held their ground and went to cover as tanks passed over, emerging afterwards to engage the oncoming infantry with every available weapon; the forward anti-tank weapons were able engage the Panzers from both the front and the rear; and weapons were sited in depth with reserves in readiness to counter-attack. Because of the infantry's grit in holding their posts, enemy successes were localised and dealt with by the British tank reserve. A combination of minefields and, where possible, a small mobile reserve obstructed enemy tanks withdrawing. And finally, all enemy movements were immediately reported, enabling a response against deep enemy penetration.[31] Morshead also acknowledged the significance of preventing enemy infantry from keeping up with their tanks – an operational separation that forced the Panzers to retire. In short, the disciplined Tobruk garrison was better prepared than its overly confident German counterpart, who was thrust blindly into battle in the expectation of whitewashing its foe.[32]

Morale

We have studied the dichotomy of fighting spirit that divided the British and Italian forces at Tobruk. Reflecting upon the fundamental importance of morale in war, Wavell believed:

> The final deciding factor of all engagements, battles and wars is the morale of the opposing forces. Better weapons, better food, superiority in numbers will influence morale, but it is sheer determination to win, by whomever or whatever inspired, that counts in the end.[33]

Brigadier Raymond Tovell also observed first-hand that 'handfuls of determined men can turn the tide, when the odds seem all against any success …'[34]

The cohesiveness of Tobruk's mixed garrison stood in contrast to the Axis camp. Morshead noted how the 'garrison was quickly welded into a team and the team spirit prevailed to a marked degree manifested equally by British, Australians, Indians and, later, the Poles. Each had confidence in the other and a high regard and everybody played their part.'[35] There was also a high degree of respect among the various units. Without the mutual admiration between the infantry and other arms such as the artillery, ack–ack and the tank corps, it is perhaps doubtful whether the bastion would have survived in 1941.[36]

Positional Warfare

Unaccustomed to protracted engagements and defeat, Rommel instigated 'feverish training' among his troops following their defeat in the Easter battles. Culpability, in his eyes, lay with his men, as it had 'become only too evident' that their training in positional warfare was inferior to that of his enemy.[37] This became a common theme. Rommel later justified the 1,200 casualties suffered in May fighting as a consequence of the switch from mobile to localised fighting.[38] A German battalion commander protested in June that:

> Our people know nothing about the construction of defences. We have scarcely any exercise in this phase of warfare in our peacetime training. The junior commander does not realise that positional warfare is 60 per cent with the spade, 30 per cent with the field glasses, and only 10 per cent with the gun.[39]

A captured report, written by Major Ernst-Otto Ballerstedt (115th Motorised Infantry Regiment), likewise believed that the Axis setback was due to the actual type of fighting as opposed to the more fluid battles that had characterised Germany's earlier success across Europe:

> The Australians, who are the men our troops have had opposite them so far, are extraordinarily tough fighters. The German is more active in the attack but the enemy stakes his life in the defence and fights to the last with extreme cunning. Our men, usually easy-going and unsuspecting, fall easily into his traps, especially as a result of the European campaign.[40]

But while the transition from open to static warfare may have been new to the *Wehrmacht*, the British forces within Tobruk, especially the infantry of the 9th Australian Division, were not only new to defensive warfare but to battle itself.

Artillery and Dive-Bombing

Tobruk's gunners merit special praise. As we have seen, British artillery support, especially counter-battery fire, played a cardinal role in the capture of Tobruk from the Italians in January 1941.[41] Again in April, the British artillery (under Brigadier L.F. Thompson) had fundamentally decided the course of the fighting. A contemporary Australian Army report cited the 'effective fire of [the] Royal Artillery' as an 'outstanding feature' of the Easter battles.[42] Even Roosevelt was notified of the German prisoners' low morale, how they were short on food and water, and 'badly shaken' by the garrison's artillery firepower.[43] A captured German prisoner concurred: 'If only we had artillery to reply to yours, but now it is just a question of holding on after every salvo from the Tommies.'[44]

Confronted by the unfamiliar task of disseminating the news of a military reversal, the Nazi press blamed the Axis setback at Tobruk on the disproportionate toll taken by the British heavy artillery. The impact of the incessant shelling was likened to the colossal bombardment at the beginning of the Battle of the Somme during the First World War.[45]

From the outset, the irregular Australian 'bush artillery' was a foremost feature of Tobruk's defence. With almost unlimited quantities of ammunition on hand, there was no shortage of eager volunteers to collect it and operate the guns. Hundreds of rounds were fired at suspected or known positions each day. At the first, the enthusiastic efforts of the greenhorn gunners were to the mild amusement of the RHA specialists who oversaw their spirited actions. But the Italian 149mm guns could outrange the British 25-pounders, and as the bush gunners became more adept, their value was quickly realised, with fire support formally requested for targets beyond the reach of the RHA's guns.

This was also appreciated in the Axis camp. A *Gruppe* of Ju 87 dive bombers was transferred to Libya from Sicily in

April 1941, to compensate for Rommel's deficiency in artillery. Yet the impact made by these ungainly aircraft was rather minor. Morshead felt that the 'dive bombing attacks were remarkable for the relatively small number of casualties caused, the small amount of material damage and their inaccuracy against a point target. But they can have a considerable moral effect on troops in the target area.'[46] A British report written at the end of 1941 similarly concluded that 'dive bombing on average does practically no damage'.[47]

The considerable psychological effect of being dive-bombed, to which we return to later, was contained in a letter home from one soldier:

> 2 bombs landed in the middle of my section line but by the grace of God only the first (and smaller) exploded. The second weighed a ton but happily was a dud. Two dugouts were ten feet away from the first but fortunately the inmates were elsewhere – every scrap of their clothing was torn to shreds – blasted away but no one was hurt. I was cowering in a hole about 50 yards away listening to the fiendish whistle of the bombs falling – that is the worst of the lot and fear does not diminish in each succeeding raid ...[48]

Rommel as Military Commander

Rommel's knack for calculated flexibility and tactical prowess on the battlefield, often earning him victory from seeming defeat, shaped the reputation that continues today. Yet his performance during the Easter battles at Tobruk is certainly questionable. What shadow, therefore, does Tobruk cast upon the legendary status of the general later celebrated as the Desert Fox?

To understand the 1941 'miracle of Tobruk' is to appreciate Rommel's character, his often reckless behaviour, and the

'Outside Tobruk', reads the headline on the cover of *Die Wehrmacht*, 21 May 1941.

perilous position into which he frequently thrust his men. Here was a commander choosing to ignore 'unpalatable' information, underestimating the enemy and overestimating the capabilities of his own army. While censuring those around him, he failed to ensure proper reconnaissance, with disastrous results. His troops had marched into an unanticipated hail of fire at night, from an unknown enemy, ensconced in unknown positions. Yet in the aftermath of defeat, he cast aside personal responsibility for the reverses and heavy casualty rate. It was, he explained, down to the difficult conditions faced by his men in having to dig in around Tobruk 'and their lack of training'.[49]

Writing in the *London Gazette* in 1948, General Harold Alexander (Claude Auchinleck's replacement as the Commander-in-Chief of Middle East Command in August 1942) praised Rommel as a 'tactician of the greatest ability' before challenging his 'strategic ability'.[50] Alexander doubted 'whether he fully understood the importance of a sound administrative plan'. In his opinion, Rommel was happiest while directing a mobile force, though he was 'liable to overexploit immediate success without sufficient thought for the future'.[51]

Although sufficiency was obviously a prime requisite in the vast and fluid arena of desert warfare – 'a real knowledge of supply and movement factors must be the basis of every leader's plan',[52] Wavell taught – Rommel took the operating efficiency of his overly taxed supply system for granted.[53] After the war, Johannes Streich apportioned blame on Rommel for the recurrent fuel shortages: 'There just wasn't any gasoline for Rommel's pipedreams. And that wasn't the fault of "some of" his commanders, but of Rommel himself.'[54] When questioned by Halder about maintaining his ever-extending supply lines, he snapped, 'That's quite immaterial to me. That's your pigeon.'[55] But as Paulus informed OKH, 'The crux of the problem in North Africa is not Tobruk or Sollum, but the organisation of supplies.' After a briefing from Paulus, Halder documented Rommel's culpability: 'Situation in North Africa unpleasant.

By overstepping his orders Rommel has brought about a situation for which our present supply capabilities are insufficient. Rommel cannot cope with the situation.'[56]

Rommel, in turn, blamed the Italians for the shortfall in supplies, when in fact their convoys were being decimated by British aerial, surface vessel and submarine attacks as a consequence of intercepted German transmissions. Criticism levelled at Italian quartermasters for unloading supplies at Tripoli instead of using the closer port facilities of Benghazi ignored the fact that there simply weren't enough trucks on hand to haul Rommel's supplies forward. Only in time did he come to realise the fundamental importance of logistics in this most desolate and unforgiving theatre of war. Certainly, the rationale and scale of the initial German intervention in Libya was never designed, nor prepared, to support a protracted siege at Tobruk.[57]

We have seen how Rommel was just as quick to censure the Italian soldier, denouncing what he saw as a 'very serious inferiority complex'.[58] This prejudice dated back to his experiences during the First World War. In a letter to his wife on 23 April, he groaned, 'There's little reliance to be placed on the Italian troops. They're extremely sensitive to enemy tanks and – as in 1917 – quick to throw up the sponge.'[59] Yet he flung them against Tobruk's outer defences after his own men had failed – but they too made no impression. In situations where the Germans had failed, the Italians became convenient scapegoats. He even issued an order 'much discussed and disputed in high Italian circles' that in the future, he would 'expect the immediate execution of officers who showed cowardice in the face of the enemy'.[60]

But is such criticism warranted? To be fair, the Italian army in North Africa struggled under inferior leadership, mediocre training and, as we saw earlier, generally obsolete weaponry. 'As regards our Italian allies,' former staff officer Friedrich von Mellenthin wrote after the war, 'I have no sympathy with those who talk contemptuously about the Italian soldier, without pausing to consider the disadvantages under which he laboured.'[61] In Schmidt's opinion, the Italian soldier was helpful and eager to co-operate and 'would fight bravely if well-equipped and efficiently led. But the equipment and leadership were seldom there.'[62]

Frustration over Rommel's leadership style, however, surfaced long before the legend did. Unlike the charismatic image so often projected, Rommel was a demanding, often maddening commander to work under. Quick to apportion blame on subordinate officers who failed to meet his demanding, sometimes unrealistic, expectations, Rommel sent many home packing. In a report to Berlin in July 1941, he charged that:

> During the offensive in Cyrenaica and particularly during the early part of the siege of Tobruk, there were numerous instances when my clear and specific orders were not obeyed by my commanders, or not promptly; there were instances bordering on disobedience, and some commanders broke down in face of the enemy.[63]

Never a fan, Halder noted in July 1941 that his 'character defects make him extremely hard to get along with, but no one cares to come out in open opposition because of his brutality and the backing he has on top level'.[64] Stressing the value of front line leadership – 'the commander must go up to see for himself; reports received second-hand rarely give the information he needs for his decisions' – Rommel was often absent from his headquarters for extended periods, much to the frustration of his Chiefs of Staff, who were often unaware of his exact position. Moreover, his habit of giving of orders to the person on the spot, or changing plans impulsively to meet new circumstances, was a 'real thorn in the flesh' for his subordinate commanders, who 'resented it bitterly'.[65]

The cost of Rommel's command came high. The German commander at the Egyptian frontier, Colonel Maximilian von Herff (later to serve in the *SS* as chief of Heinrich Himmler's personal staff), protested over the needless slaughter:

> Nobody here understood these first attacks on Tobruk: although the strength of the garrison and fortress were known, each newly arrived battalion was sent into attack and naturally enough didn't get through. The result is that there isn't a unit at Tobruk that hasn't taken a mauling.[66]

The heavy losses at Tobruk also stirred up painful memories for Kirchheim: 'I do not like to be reminded of that time, because so much blood was needlessly shed.'[67] It should also be borne in mind that Rommel's 7th Panzer Division suffered the highest casualty rate of any German formation in the French campaign during its dash to the English Channel.[68] Perhaps the Axis setback at Tobruk was best summarised in a letter home from Rommel's adjutant, Hans Joachim Schraepler: 'This outcome was caused by Rommel's error ... One should have realised that such an attack could only have been done after careful preparation and planning.'[69]

9

Threatened in All Directions

'Tobruk: the indispensable preliminary to serious invasion of Egypt.'
– Winston Churchill

Tobruk was a rebuff to the Axis of which Britain could be justly proud. Churchill could boast to his critics in the House of Commons in May 1941 that its strategic significance was 'obvious from the first and anyone can see now how irresistibly it has imposed itself as a magnet upon the enemy'.[1] And to his private secretary, John Colville, the premier enthused how it 'was playing the same part as Acre [besieged former Ottoman city, now Akko in northern Israel] did against Napoleon. It was a speck of sand in the desert, which might ruin all Hitler's calculations.'[2] But while Churchill gained solace from Tobruk's stubborn defence, Wavell's Middle East command was a house of cards, threatened from all directions and on the verge of collapse.

Brevity

Rommel at this time faced an impasse in the Western Desert. Standing on the threshold of Egypt, but having failed to take

Tobruk, he was restrained from moving ahead until reinforcements – and authorisation – reached him. Paulus' detailed
situational report on North Africa, which Churchill received
courtesy of Bletchley Park, described the most recent attack
against Tobruk as an 'important success'.[3] It also contained
a damning indictment of Rommel's heavily overextended
supply lines, the chronic fuel shortage and lack of ammunition. 'The crux of the problem in North Africa is not Tobruk
or Sollum [on the Egyptian frontier] but the organization
of supplies.'[4] In Paulus' judgement, *no new attempt* to capture
Tobruk was to be undertaken unless the British garrison was
evacuated. Hence, Rommel's principle task was restricted
to holding Cyrenaica, regardless of which army held Bardia,
Sollum or Tobruk. Forced on to the defensive, Rommel was
left with little option but to await the arrival of Major General
Walter Neumann-Silkow's 15th Panzer Division – and permission from Berlin – before he could commence any new
offensive action.

Churchill, on the other hand, was spurred into action.
On 7 May he cabled Wavell, calling for a fresh offensive in
Cyrenaica, for 'Those Hun people are far less dangerous once
they lose the initiative.'[5] An immediate counter-attack, it was
reckoned, could tip the balance in the desert, possibly relieve
Tobruk, and in so doing ease the RN's dangerous supply
burden. Raising morale after the Balkans fiasco would shore
up Churchill's standing, and support Britain's uncertain situation amid growing instability in Iraq, Syria and Palestine.

Operation Brevity, as it was fittingly dubbed, was a rushed
and ill-prepared attempt to pit all available armour – two
Matilda squadrons, two cruiser squadrons, plus a number of
light tanks – against Axis formations spread along the frontier,
Bardia and Tobruk before the 15th Panzer Division reached
its full strength. Churchill's 'cubs' were still in transit and not
expected to arrive in Alexandria before 12 May. Even then,
the tanks would need several weeks in the workshops before

they would be considered 'desert worthy'. On 1 May, already hard-pressed to organise the defence of Crete and eliminate Gaylani's threat in Iraq, Wavell notified General Sir Noel Beresford-Peirse (newly appointed commander of the Western Desert Force) of his intention to attack Rommel as 'soon as our resources permit'.[6]

Entrusted to Brigadier Gott, Operation Brevity involved three parallel assaults designed to recapture the Halfaya Pass, drive the enemy from the Sollum and Capuzzo areas and deplete Rommel's forces. A lesser objective was to advance toward Tobruk, though only as far as supplies would allow without jeopardising the operation.

Rommel's own radio intelligence company, *Nachrichten Fernsehsendung Aufklarung Kompanie 621* (Signals Intercept Company 621), had given ample warning of the assault, the British being notoriously lax in their own radio procedure. Forewarned, Colonel Maximilian von Herff directed a small ad hoc *Kampfgruppe* (battlegroup) to expect an attack, though the British strike on the morning of 15 May still took his men by surprise. The British nevertheless suffered heavy losses, and Gott nervously withdrew his infantry to Halfaya Pass while Herff, uncertain as to the size of the British force, withdrew west. Herff counter-attacked the following day, leaving the British with the strategically important Halfaya Pass as their only gain (until it fell to another German counter-attack two weeks later). Gott's force suffered 160 casualties. Five Matilda tanks were destroyed and another thirteen damaged. The modest losses on the Axis side amounted to: three tanks, twelve killed, sixty-one wounded and 185 men listed missing.

An utter failure, Brevity had lasted 36 hours. Crucially, the British had thrust their tanks into battle, squadron by squadron, without co-ordinating the movement of individual units. Future British operations would require a dramatic revision of preparation and tactics. Rommel, meanwhile, consolidated the Sollum front on 16 May by transferring the bulk of his

mobile forces there, laying minefields and emplacing deadly
88mm guns in an anti-tank role. Concentrating his skills on
this single front, the British, conversely, were being drawn into
new theatres of war across the Middle East.

Iraq's Pro-Axis Revolt

Returning to Berlin from their Balkan campaign field headquarters, Germany's Operations Staff were presented with the
news of events in Iraq. Hitler had earlier stated that Baghdad
could receive direct military support – 'weapons of all kinds'
– though no time frame was specified.[7] Neighbouring Kabul
also voiced its willingness to help with transporting Axis arms,
an idea that was floated with the Japanese, though Tokyo
rejected the idea outright.

While the Axis dallied Whitehall made the first move. On
17 April 1941, Britain's 1st King's Own Royal Regiment was
flown (in the first ever airlift of British forces) to the RAF's
base at Shaibah in southern Iraq. The 20th Indian Infantry
Brigade (10th Indian Division) and divisional headquarters
disembarked at the port of Basra. A stand-off was developing.
Gaylani (Iraq's nationalist prime minister following the 3 April
coup d'état) appealed to Germany for weapons and support.
Berlin, for the moment, bided its time. Were the Iraqis really
prepared to fight?

Hostilities were liable to break out at any moment, and with
German intervention in Syria possible, Wavell had yet another
theatre in which to commit his finite resources.

Fighting began at 5.00 a.m. on the morning of 2 May.
The miscellany of British training aircraft at Habbaniya, hastily converted into makeshift bombers, took to the air and
attacked the besieging Iraqi troops, who responded with artillery and anti-aircraft fire, shooting down twenty-two aircraft.
Upon hearing about the bombing, Haj Amin al-Husseini,

the Grand Mufti, who had fled Jerusalem for Iraq in October 1939, declared a *jihad* against Britain while Baghdad cut the flow of oil to the British refinery at Haifa.

A fresh appeal for German assistance was sent. This time Berlin agreed to dispatch aircraft, though primarily for propaganda purposes. On 6 May, General Henri-Fernand Dentz, commander-in-chief of the *Armée du Levant* (Army of the Levant) and Syria's Vichy high commissioner, received an order from Admiral (Jean) François Darlan to provide 'every facility'[8] to Luftwaffe aircraft, freshly adorned with Iraqi insignia emblems painted over with the German *Balkenkreuz* (bar cross) emblem. They would be flying to Mosul via Syria, in what was the pinnacle mark of Vichy–German collaboration. An agreement was also made for the transfer of French arms to Iraq.

The Arab world watched closely, particularly in light of Germany's recent victories over the British in Greece and across Cyrenaica. On a local level, the uprising in Iraq incited one of the worst wartime Arab atrocities against Jews in North Africa with eight Jews killed and twenty injured in the Tunisian town of Gabès.[9] Gaylani's revolt also encouraged Egyptian Lieutenant Anwar Sadat (a member of the Free Officers Movement) to press nationalist leader and former Chief of Staff of the Egyptian army, General Aziz El Masri, to make Egypt a 'second Iraq'. Sadat had already contacted Sheikh Hassan El Banna, the founder of the paramilitary Muslim Brotherhood, and the German headquarters in Libya, which was monitoring the Iraqi rebellion with interest as the first signs of a greater Arab movement. Masri, a pro-German veteran of the Balkan Wars, who had fought with the Turks in Libya during the First World War, firmly believed that the Egyptian army was the means to his country's 'liberation'. But the veteran general, upon whom Sadat had pinned his hopes of securing German support, was not enthused; as Sadat later wrote, the 'Egyptian people remained latent and suppressed'.[10] The key to Egypt's liberation lay instead with Rommel.

Fearful that the growing Iraqi emergency might imperil Egypt and Palestine, Wavell renewed his call for negotiations with Gaylani in an attempt defuse the crisis; a suggestion that 'deeply disturbed' Churchill. 'What matters is action,' the premier underscored, noting that his commander-in-chief leaves the 'impression of being tired out'.[11]

The possibility of Italy also intervening in Iraq and Syria was raised by Ribbentrop (Hitler's Foreign Minister), in Rome on 13 May. Mussolini, it was reported, was outwardly enthusiastic about dispatching aid and opening one more front against Britain. In the meantime, Germany's diplomatic representative, Fritz Grobba, one-time German ambassador to the Kingdom of Iraq, had flown into the Iraqi city of Mosul with two Heinkel He III bombers, followed shortly after by a further twenty-two aircraft. Grobba met with Gaylani and other members of the 'Golden Square' in Baghdad, where it was decided that British reinforcements must be prevented from reaching Habbaniya.

As a British relief force approached the Iraqi capital, Hitler issued a belated interventional order: Directive No. 30 – Middle East, which qualified the Arab Freedom Movement as a 'natural ally against England'.[12] The Iraqis were about to start fighting back, with Germany's help. The coup leaders also called upon Ibn Saud, the Saudi Arabian monarch, for assistance, which he refused on the grounds that it would be a treacherous act against the British. Conversely, Afghanistan's economics minister, while indulging himself at a German spa, pledged (unofficial) close co-operation with the Third Reich. His enthusiasm, however, soon disappeared, as did his offer to support a guerrilla conflict along the frontier with India, once the Iraqi insurrection began to flounder.

By 18 May, the Luftwaffe's Iraqi force had dwindled to just eight operational Messerschmitt Bf 110 fighters, four Heinkel He III bombers and two Junkers Ju 52 transports. On Berlin's invitation, twelve Italian Fiat CR.42 fighters arrived at Mosul on 27 May, but little would be achieved. The heavily outnumbered British force had already seized Fallujah and was nearing Baghdad. Nervous, Grobba called upon the Luftwaffe to stem the advance, however only a single German bomber was available at Mosul. In a game of bluff, fantastic rumours began spreading through the city streets regarding the strength of the approaching British columns. No fewer than 100 enemy tanks were advancing! Unnerved, the new government abruptly crumpled. Gaylani fled to Iran on 30 May before making his way to Germany;[13] an armistice was signed the next day. The Axis, in the end had done little for their protégés in the Iraqi rebellion, despite Hitler's grand statements.

Churchill later reckoned that Hitler had forgone the chance of taking a 'great prize for little cost', though as we know, German military intervention in the Middle East was always secondary to Barbarossa, centrepiece of Hitler's strategy. Field Marshal Keitel later (accurately) explained to General Ugo Cavallero, chief of the Italian Supreme Command, how unfortunate timing affected the Iraqi revolt:

> The Iraqi government attacked too soon. Support was not made ready in advance. Germany and Italy were determined to make effective help available, [but] this failed on account of too rapid a collapse of the Iraqi will to resist and difficulties in transporting troops, weapons and supplies.[14]

Still, as Halder conceded, whatever the outcome, Iraq had forced Wavell to spread his resources even more thinly at a time when Rommel's situation in Cyrenaica was 'rather precarious'[15] and the battle for Crete hung in the balance.

Crete

Hitler's gaze had turned to Crete following Greece's collapse. Strategically important for both sides, this small rugged, mountainous island – 160 miles long, 35 miles wide, and only 60 miles from the Greek mainland – would complete Germany's Balkan crown. Conversely, for Churchill, Crete held the promise of becoming another Alexandria, Malta or Tobruk.

Unlike their earlier campaigns, the Germans would assault Crete chiefly from the air, using General Kurt Student's elite XI Air Corps. Plans for what would be the largest airborne operation to date were presented to Hitler by Göring on 21 April, the latter surely hoping to redeem the reputation of his Luftwaffe after its disappointing performance in the Battle of Britain. Hitler's Directive No. 28, issued four days later, stipulated the capture of Crete – Operation *Mekur* ('Mercury') – as a 'base for air warfare against Great Britain in the Eastern Mediterranean'.[16] The daring undertaking, however, rankled many of Hitler's senior advisers, who believed that Malta was a superior option and would secure Axis sea-lanes between Tripoli and Italy.

OKW had studied invading Malta in February 1941, but the operation was deferred by Hitler until after the Soviet Union had collapsed. In his eyes, Crete represented a greater danger because British possession of the island would place the Ploesti oilfields – so important to his war machine – within range of RAF bombers. In the end, it was Student's insistence that Malta was too strongly defended that sealed Crete's fate.

Wavell flew to Crete on 30 April to organise its defence. Under General Bernard Freyberg (a veteran of the Gallipoli landings and Western Front), the mixed British–Greek defending force of 35,000 men lacked arms, transport and signals equipment. The 5th Cretan Division had been captured on the mainland, leaving only local reservists and civilians on the island. These men began arming themselves with makeshift weapons. Freyberg's armour stood at nine Matildas and sixteen light tanks. A regiment's complement of artillery was on hand, though it was made up mostly of captured Italian pieces taken during Compass, many without sights. Air cover was unavailable.

The Luftwaffe expected the Cretan invasion to be brief, a stepping-stone to Cyprus and, ultimately, the Suez Canal. The Germans were badly misinformed as to the true strength of the British garrison on Crete, however, and Freyberg held the intelligence advantage. Tipped off by Bletchley Park, which had deciphered the Luftwaffe's 'Red' key, the British were given an extraordinary insight into preparations for the joint airborne-amphibious landing. Examining the enemy intercepts, Churchill smugly signalled: This 'ought to be a fine opportunity for killing the parachute troops'.

The assault began on the morning of 20 May. Gazing skyward, Freyberg calmly pronounced: 'they're dead on time'. A hail of bullets met the parachutists, many of whom were killed before they hit the ground, their limp bodies later dangling among the olive groves. Student's men suffered heavily in the bloody first day of fighting, and gained only two small footholds, including the crucial Maleme Airfield. The airlift of the German 5th Mountain Division the following day finally tipped the scales against Freyberg, whose position became increasingly hopeless. Then on 24 May, at the height of the battle, Wavell was directed, regardless of his personal judgement, to intervene in Syria. Should he refuse, Churchill challenged, arrangements would be made for his relief. Another Churchill communiqué two days later implored: 'Victory in Crete essential at this turning point of the war. Keep hurling in all you can.'[17] Threatened from all directions, we can only imagine Wavell's reaction as he simultaneously juggled his forces before an increasingly angry and impatient overlord.

But the situation on Crete was becoming hopeless, and the decision was made to evacuate the embattled British force. The overstrained RN once again rallied to save the army, though at the tremendous cost of three cruisers, six destroyers and the lives of some 2,000 sailors. The aircraft carrier *Formidable*, three battleships, six cruisers and a further seven destroyers were also heavily damaged. Had the fuel-starved Italian fleet managed to join the Luftwaffe, the toll may have been far higher, possibly ending Britain's hold over the eastern Mediterranean entirely. Roughly 15,000 men were shipped to Egypt *sans* equipment. British land and air forces had lost 23,830 men killed, wounded or captured.

Ultra had cost the Germans dearly on Crete, but similar to Wavell's knowledge of Rommel's arrival into Tripoli, even the best intelligence cannot stave off defeat. German losses in what Student dubbed a 'disastrous victory' amounted to 3,985 killed or missing and 2,131 wounded. Shocked by the magnitude of these losses, Hitler would never again attempt an invasion or large-scale attack using airborne troops. Ironically, it was the Allies who grasped the potential of future airborne campaigns. The next time an airdrop of such magnitude would be undertaken was in June 1944, when the Allies invaded German-occupied France. For the moment, though, Tobruk, Malta and Cairo were safe from the possibility of a German airborne assault.

On top of the Cretan tragedy, however, Wavell had also lost the vital Halfaya Pass to a German counteroffensive – *Skorpion* ('Scorpion') – on the morning of 27 May. Three tank battalions from the newly arrived 8th Panzer Regiment devastated the solitary Matilda squadron, destroying seven tanks and capturing three, which subsequently became turncoats. Hamstrung by his perennial supply dilemma, Rommel was unable to press forward afterward, and instead began firming up his position at Halfaya. Across the frontier, Wavell was busy preparing a new offensive to relieve Tobruk, now with the added encumbrance of Syria.

The Syrian Campaign

Syria was another budding nightmare for the British. The passage of German aircraft through the Levant to Iraq in

May 1941 had heightened Allied concerns regarding Hitler's intentions in the region. What if Syria became an Axis platform for strikes against the Abadan oil refineries, Cairo, the Suez Canal (already under attack from Luftwaffe units in the Dodecanese) and the army's lines of communication extending across Palestine and Iraq? What would happen, as Anthony Eden (Britain's foreign secretary) surmised, if the *Wehrmacht* built up a formidable army in Syria and then advanced on Egypt? And what would be the political fallout across the Middle East, particularly since a German presence in Syria and Iraq would isolate Turkey and potentially goad Ankara into joining the Axis?

Eager as ever for battle, Churchill called for a 'supreme effort' to frustrate any German foothold in the Levant.[18] Wavell's aversion toward intervening in Syria, however, mirrored his reluctance to act in Iraq. This foot-dragging was also to be his undoing. Churchill notified General John Dill (CGIS) on 19 May that he had finally decided that he would remove Wavell from his command (though not until mid-June). His replacement would be General Claude Auchinleck. And rather than have Wavell loitering around in London, Churchill would send him to India, where he could 'enjoy sitting under the pagoda tree'![19]

The following day, as German paratroopers descended on to Crete, Wavell – still unaware of Churchill's verdict – received a notification from the Defence Committee in London that Syria was an opportunity 'too good to miss'. His orders were to provide General Georges Catroux, General Charles de Gaulle's Free French deputy in the Levant, with trucks, drivers and 'as much military and air support as possible'.[20] Wavell's curt response (sent on 21 May) underscored his belief that any action undertaken by the Free French alone was likely to fail. British ground forces would be needed. Moreover, he called for his personal judgement to be trusted and threatened to step down from his command.

A subsequent cable to Wavell – at the height of the fighting in Crete – dictated that 'Nothing in Syria must detract at this moment from winning the battle of Crete, or in the Western Desert ...' But it also reiterated the War Cabinet's support of intervention in Syria and, in a direct challenge, offered to make arrangements should he wish to be relieved.[21] Wavell chose to remain. Concurrently with Britain's waning position in Crete, he circulated plans for an invasion of Syria and Lebanon – codenamed Exporter – with the primary objectives of seizing Damascus, Rayak and Beirut (Lebanon's capital).

Without compromising his forthcoming Western Desert offensive or the security of his Cyrenaican front lines, Wavell assembled a combined British–Free French force under Lieutenant General 'Jumbo' Wilson, who had been appointed commander of Palestine and Transjordan after the fall of Greece. Wilson's force comprised the two brigades of General Lavarack's Australian 7th Division, two regiments of the 1st British Cavalry Division, the 5th Indian Brigade (fresh from East Africa), a commando unit, and the six battalions of the 1st Free French Division under Major General Paul Legentilhomme. No strong reserve was available.

But the Vichy army had plenty of time to prepare its defences, and intimate knowledge of the Syrian terrain, which heavily favoured defence. General Henri-Fernand Dentz's Vichy army numbered some 45,000 troops, both local and French colonial, including four French Foreign Legion battalions, ninety tanks and 120 artillery pieces. In the air, he had sixty fighters and thirty bombers; at sea, two destroyers and three submarines were based at Beirut. The nearest Luftwaffe aircraft were based in Greece or the Dodecanese, though, and stretched to the limits of their operational radius. Although Syria's sequestered Vichy forces outnumbered Wilson's in armour, men and aircraft, prolonged resistance would be compromised by the inability to receive extra arms and stores. And while Vichy France was permitted to send additional arms via

Greece, the British blockade of Syrian–Lebanese waters effectively halted any seaborne supply. The Turkish government's neutrality policy also prevented the transport of supplies along the only available land route.

Exporter did at one point come close to being cancelled. Doubts were voiced over timing the operation so closely to Battleaxe, Wavell's new offensive against Rommel, while a political wrangle had erupted between London and the Free French over the future independence of the native Syrian and Lebanese populations. Meanwhile, Admiral François Darlan (Pétain's most trusted associate) requested that German personnel returning from Iraq leave Syria without delay, to avoid forcing Britain's hand. Churchill, busy fending off criticism over Crete, demanded that Wavell keep his eye on Syria and, above all, Battleaxe. He advised Roosevelt that the Syrian operation was a means of preventing 'further German penetration'.[22] It was unavoidable, but the timing was appalling.

Exporter began at 3.00 a.m. on the morning of 8 June 1941. Just how Vichy troops would react was unknown. Where would their loyalty lie? Would token defiance precede their defection en masse to de Gaulle's Free French movement? As it happened, unexpectedly stiff resistance was met, the memory of the shelling of the French fleet at Mers el-Kebir still strong. Optimistic Free French officers, advancing under a flag of truce, rapidly learned that their Vichy opposites were in no frame of mind to parley. The fratricidal fighting was especially bitter, and dogged opposition and inadequate numbers of infantry slowed Wilson's advance. Two brigades of the British 6th Division arrived as reinforcement, with arrangements made for General William Slim's 10th Indian Division to cross the desert from Iraq into northern Syria as well.

Ten days into the offensive, progress was still far from satisfactory. The second phase of the fighting (14 to 22 June) coincided with Operation Battleaxe: Wavell's last Western Desert offensive.

Battleaxe: A 'Most Bitter Blow'

Writing after the war, Churchill narrated how the evacuation of Greece, the fighting in Iraq and Syria, and the struggle for Crete all paled before the 'gleam of hope' offered by victory in Libya.[23] The key to this victory, the premier held, lay in the Tiger convoy. Although one ship carrying fifty-seven tanks and ten Hurricane fighters was lost when it struck a mine, 135 Matilda, eighty-two cruiser and twenty-one light tanks were still successfully disembarked at Alexandria. These were the machines Churchill needed to relieve Tobruk and inflict a crushing defeat. Yet Wavell begged to differ. On 28 May, he expressed his reservations to Dill:

> I think it right to inform you that the measure of success which will attend this operation is in my opinion doubtful. I hope that it will succeed in driving the enemy west of Tobruk and re-establishing land communications with Tobruk. If possible we will exploit success further. But … our Infantry tanks are really too slow for a battle in the desert, and have been suffering considerable casualties from the fire of powerful enemy anti-tank guns. Our cruisers have little advantage in power or speed over German medium tanks. Technical breakdowns are still too numerous. We shall not be able to accept battle with perfect confidence in spite of numerical inferiority, as we could with the Italians.[24]

Wavell's concerns over the operation were wholly justified. The 7th Armoured Division had lost most of its original tanks through wear and tear. The tank crews were unfamiliar with these latest vehicles, a significant number of which required an overhaul, and all of which required modifications for desert use. Regardless of any 'teething troubles' Wavell faced in readying Churchill's 'cubs' for action, the premier's impatience was only eased after receiving notification that D-Day was set for 15 June.

Operational plans were drawn up at General Noel Beresford-Peirse's headquarters at Sidi Barrani for a three-part operation: One and a half squadrons of Matilda tanks (from the 4th Armoured Brigade, attached to the 11th Indian Brigade) were to capture Halfaya, while the remainder of the 4th Armoured Brigade and the 22nd Guards Brigade overran the inland area, including Fort Capuzzo and Sidi Aziez. The 7th Armoured Division would sweep past on the left flank, link up with and relieve the Tobruk garrison, and press onward to Derna and Mechili.

Battleaxe began on 15 June. The British quickly established air supremacy. It was a different story on the ground, however, where Rommel's intelligence had given forewarning of the attack. The 5th Light Division, under its new commander, Lieutenant General Hans Ravenstein, was brought forward, to a position between Tobruk and Bardia. The expertly sited 88mm guns of the 33rd Flak regiment, under the command of an extraordinary German cleric, Major the Reverend Wilhelm Bach, wrought havoc, promptly knocking out eleven of the twelve Matildas attached to the Indian Brigade. Four more were immobilised by mines. The thrust by the 7th Armoured Division ground to a standstill after three abortive attacks and the riposte from four German 88mm guns and several smaller-calibre anti-tank weapons. Of the nearly 100 Matildas that had set off that morning, only thirty-seven were still runners at the end of the day, though a further eleven were repaired overnight. Immobile British steel hulks now littered the desert, testament that the reign of the 'Queen of the Desert' had ended. Only in the centre of the fighting had headway been achieved, where the Guards Brigade had seized both its objectives.

The second day of fighting was inconclusive. A renewed British attack meant to dislodge the Reverend and his guns fell short, while an attack by the 15th Panzer Division was beaten off by the Indian infantry and 4th Armoured

Brigade. A day-long clash between the 5th Light Division and 7th Armoured Division thwarted a German break-through, though at considerable loss. By the evening, only twenty British tanks remained operational. Beresford-Peirse regrouped his remaining armour during the night for a concerted attack the following morning. Having shrewdly second-guessed his opponent's thinking, at 4.30 a.m. Rommel swung the weight of his armour toward Halfaya – the British left flank. As he afterwards wrote, 'The decisive moment had come.'[25] The situation deteriorated rapidly for the British, and by late morning, Beresford-Peirse was forced to call off the operation. Wavell's Battleaxe had shattered; nothing had been gained. The British had lost 122 men killed, 588 wounded and 259 listed as missing. The RAF had lost thirty-three fighter aircraft and three bombers. The largest armoured clash thus far in the desert, upon which Churchill had pinned so much hope, was an expensive failure; fifty-eight Matildas and twenty-nine cruisers languished as wrecks on the battlefield. The few remaining tanks were ordered back to Sidi Barrani.

German armour losses were also high, with fifty of the 15th Panzer Division's eighty tanks destroyed or damaged. Courts martial and dismissals followed, with Rommel exas-perated by the actions of several of his senior officers. News of this latest British defeat, while minor in comparison to operations elsewhere in the Mediterranean, nonetheless struck Churchill as a 'most bitter blow'.[26] Leaving London, the pre-mier travelled to his home at Chartwell, where he wandered alone, 'disconsolately for hours', pondering the fate of his cubs and where his next move would be.[27] A report received from Wavell that 'no [follow-up] offensive in the Western Desert would be possible for at least three months' further fuelled Churchill's frustration.[28] A consequent cable from Cairo on 21 June – the day Damascus fell to Wilson's Free French and Australian troops in the second phase of the Syrian campaign – apologised for the miscarriage of Battleaxe and the loss of so many tanks. Wavell also expressed his regret that he had not deferred Exporter until larger forces were available for both operations. His tenuous position was finally terminated the same day, just hours before the launch of Barbarossa.

Syria and Lebanon Surrenders

An upshot from Battleaxe's miscarriage and the end of the uprising in Iraq was the availability of British reinforcements, including the 10th Indian Division, for the later stages of the Syrian campaign. After Australian troops had advanced to within 5 miles of Beirut on 10 July, General Henri-Fernand Dentz acknowledged that his situation was hopeless and appealed for a ceasefire. An armistice was signed four days later.

Combined British and Free French casualties exceeded 4,000 men, while the Vichy French lost more than 6,000 troops, including 1,000 killed. Longer and more costly than originally planned, Exporter delivered Britain new Middle East airfields and naval bases, plus a considerable buffer zone from which to defend the Suez Canal and the Iranian–Iraqi oilfields. Churchill's early meddling was vindicated. The operation, however, may well have ended differently had Hitler intervened directly. The planned dispatch of strong Vichy forces from France had ultimately come undone after its passage through either Tunisia or Turkey was prohibited.

The Allies were now in direct physical contact with Turkey for the first time in the war. Germany's recent victories across Western Europe, however, had already elicited a subtle change in Ankara's stance toward Berlin, with whom strong economic ties already existed. Relations further warmed after Hitler personally assured President İnönü that Turkey did not feature in his plans. A Treaty of Friendship was signed on 18 June 1941, though Turkey's foreign minister tempered London's concern with the reassurance that relations with Britain would remain unaffected. Walking a neutrality tightrope with one eye to the east, the Turks could relax four days later, as the immediate threat of either German or Soviet aggression dissolved due to Hitler's gamble in the Soviet Union.

An armed Sanusi tribesman photographed at Tobruk in 1911.

Italian dictator Benito Mussolini during a state visit to Libya in March 1937, where he opened the new coastal highway stretching across the colony from Tunisia to Egypt. The 1,100-mile long road was later christened *Litoranea Balbo* or 'Via Balbia'.

A knocked-out British Infantry Tank Mk II, or Matilda. Immune to smaller calibre anti-tank weapons, the tank was held in high regard by German troops.

Hitler awarded Rommel, his 'boldest general', with Swords to the Oak Leaves of his Knights Cross on 20 January 1942. After capturing Tobruk, Hitler promoted 49-year-old Rommel to field marshal, Germany's youngest.

Rommel, newly arrived in Libya in February 1941. Pictured on his right is Colonel Rudolf Schmundt, Hitler's adjutant and a casualty of the 2 July 1944 bomb plot.

A Panzer III Ausf. G from the 1st Company, 3rd Platoon, 5th Panzer Regiment, is lowered onto the Tripoli dock. Rommel believed that 'it was only in the desert that the principles of armoured warfare were taught in theory before the war could be fully applied and thoroughly developed'.

Devoid of cover, the typical stony terrain of a Tobruk wadi.

Launched in July 1908, the Italian cruiser *San Giorgio*, a veteran of the Italo–Turkish and First World Wars, arrived in Tobruk in May 1940 as a floating battery to bolster the fortress's anti-aircraft defences. Already damaged during RAF and RN attacks, the ship's crew scuttled the elderly vessel in the shallow harbour on 22 January 1941.

Victorious Australian infantry inside Tobruk, January 1941. The RE on the fuel drums stands for *Regio Esercito* (Royal [Italian] Army).

Above: A German soldier's 1941 snapshot, captioned simply: 'outside Tobruk.'

Left: Major-General Leslie James Morshead, General Officer Commanding the Australian 9th Division and Tobruk Garrison. Morshead was knighted on 6 January 1942 (Knight Commander in the Order of the British Empire) by King George VI for his part in defending Tobruk.

Inside the wire: 'Rats of Tobruk' posing before a captured Fiat 666 NM truck.

The 'bush artillery'. Former Italian Cannone da 47/32 M35 anti-tank gun pressed into service with Australian Infantry.

Australian infantry along the perimeter front line, bayonets fixed on their .303 rifles.

AUSSIES

Surrender leaflet dropped during the 1941 siege. These propaganda pieces quickly became prized souvenirs among the 'Rats'.

AFTER CRETE DISASTER ANZAC TROOPS ARE NOW BEING RUTHLESSLY SACRIFICED BY ENG-LAND IN TOBRUCH AND SYRIA.

TURKEY HAS CONCLUDED PACT OF FRIENDSHIP WITH GERMANY. ENGLAND WILL SHORTLY BE DRIVEN OUT OF THE MEDITERRANEAN. OFFEN-SIVE FROM EGYPT TO RELIEVE YOU TOTALLY SMASHED.

YOU CANNOT ESCAPE.

OUR DIVE BOMBERS ARE WAITING TO SINK YOUR TRANSPORTS. THINK OF YOUR FUTURE AND YOUR PEOPLE AT HOME.

COME FORWARD – SHOW WHITE FLAGS AND YOU WILL BE OUT OF DANGER !

SURRENDER !

Abandoned Panzer III. Armed with a short-barrelled 50mm gun, this medium tank formed the backbone of Rommel's armour in the desert.

Australian troops pose beside a captured German 88mm dual-purpose gun, one of
the most well-known, feared and publicised weapons of the war. First used against
ground targets in the Spanish Civil War, the potent weapon proved deadly against
British armour in the desert.

Rommel stands before a QF 25-pounder, the standard RHA field gun at Tobruk.
According to a British intelligence officer 'since our standard anti-tank weapon, the
2-pounder, had neither the range nor killing power, the 25-pounder was the only
weapon on which we could entirely rely to kill a tank.'

Rommel pays his respect to the dead. Colonel Maximilian von Herff protested over the needless slaughter of men in 1941: 'Nobody here understood these first attacks on Tobruk.'

A partially cannibalised Ju-87 forced down inside the Tobruk perimeter during the 1941 siege. Stuka raids were especially disliked by ground troops.

General Johann von Ravenstein, commander of the 21st Panzer Division, photographed at Tobruk shortly after his capture by New Zealand troops on 29 November 1941. Never a fan, he spoke of the 'great losses in recent fighting, mismanagement and disorganization, and above all, dissatisfaction with Rommel's leadership'.

A casualty of the 1941 'Spud Run'. HMS *Defender* (British D–class destroyer), a veteran of the evacuations from Greece and Crete, was heavily damaged by a German bomb en route from Tobruk to Alexandria. The crippled destroyer was scuttled 7 nautical miles north of Sidi Barrani on 11 July 1941.

Aerial view of Tobruk following an air raid in June 1941.

Advancing troops of the 2nd New Zealand Division pass a Matilda from Tobruk's 32nd Army Tank Brigade during the fighting to relieve the fortress on 27 November 1941.

The long-barreled 75mm Panzer IV Ausf F2 reached North Africa in May 1942. Known by the British as the Panzer IV 'Special', it was superior to any American or British tank at the time.

Major-General Hendrik Balzazer Klopper was officially exonerated for his role in the capitulation of Tobruk. Postwar, he enjoyed a successful army career, culminating as Commandant-General of the Union Defence Forces from 1956 to 1958.

A wooden bridge is erected across the perimeter anti-tank ditch at Tobruk. In reality the silted-up ditch in front of the Indian 2nd Mahratta Light Infantry presented little obstacle to advancing enemy troops.

Rommel's Italo-German forces close on the harbour, 20 June 1942.

The concrete perimeter posts built by the Italians in their desert fortresses were flush with the ground, unlike the fortifications constructed in post-1918 Europe, such as France's Maginot Line or the German Westwall.

German troops inspect an Italian perimeter post. These subterranean posts influenced the pattern of later German fortifications in Europe called *Ringstände*, and known as 'Tobruk' pits.

Rommel in Tobruk, with smoke from a blazing fuel depot in the background.

Accompanied by Colonel Fritz Bayerlein, then Chief of Staff of the *Afrikakorps*, a triumphant Rommel entered Tobruk on the morning of 21 June 1942. 'Practically every building of the dismal place,' Rommel wrote, 'was either flat or little more than a heap of rubble, mostly the result of our siege in 1941.'

Although the exact number is unknown, official British history concluded that some 32,200 prisoners were taken at Tobruk: 19,000 British troops, 8,960 South African Europeans, 1,760 South African Natives and 2,500 Indian troops.

South African troops marching into captivity. Many of these troops manning the western perimeter had not fired a shot prior to Klopper's decision to surrender.

Rommel (left) and Colonel Fritz Bayerlein in their Horch staff car overlooking the harbour. The booty was enormous: large quantities of British and German ammunition, some 2,000 serviceable vehicles, over 2000 tons of fuel and roughly 5,000 tons of stores.

A German soldier outside Tobruk's oft-photographed Catholic church. A US war correspondent was present when the town was retaken on 12 November 1942: 'The steeple had escaped the bombs, and the bells were tolling. The soldiers paused in the streets to listen. It probably reminded them the bells were ringing in England too ...'

Italian M13/40 (*Carro armato* M13/40) tank from the 'Ariete' armoured division opposite the town and dock facilities on the northern promontory.

Hundreds of South African native prisoners were retained in Tobruk as dock labourers. Lance Corporal Job Maseko, Native Military Corps, was awarded the Military Medal for sinking 'a fully laden enemy steamer – probably an 'F' boat – while moored in Tobruk Harbour. This he did [on or about 21 July], by placing a small tin filled with gunpowder in among drums of petrol in the hold, leading a fuse therefrom to the hatch and lighting the fuse upon closing the hatch.'

Rommel (right) and Colonel Fritz Bayerlein pictured off the main road into Tobruk above the harbour. The surrender of the fortress marked the highpoint of Rommel's career and one of the worst British defeats of the war.

Tobruk harbour littered with half-sunken ships. To their disappointment, the Germans found the port's capacity to be well below what was needed to ease Rommel's logistical crisis.

10

'The Auk'

'[The defence of Tobruk] is one of the crucial fights in the history of the British Army'.

– Winston Churchill

Wavell's last decision as Middle East commander-in-chief was taken at a conference in Cairo on 18 June 1941. In the company of Air Marshal Arthur Tedder (successor to Air Chief Marshal Longmore, who had been dismissed in early May, having incurred Churchill's displeasure), Admiral Cunningham and General Blamey, Wavell discussed the possible evacuation of Tobruk – now the epicentre of Allied land-based warfare against the Axis – before an agreement was reached to hold the fortress. Four days later, however, the world held its breath as the focus of the land war jumped from the Middle East to Germany's invasion of the Soviet Union: Operation Barbarossa.

Barbarossa

Mussolini received word of Barbarossa when he was awoken at his holiday villa at Riccione early on the morning of the invasion – 22 June 1941. He immediately offered his support and declared war on Russia. As Hitler had come to his aid in Greece and North Africa, he would now reciprocate in a show of solidarity. On 26 June the Duce presided over the official farewell for the *Corpo di Spedizione Italiano in Russia* (the Italian Expeditionary Corps), or CSIR – three infantry divisions, a cavalry group of more than 10,000 mounted troops and a Blackshirt legion.[1] He savoured not only the opportunity to confront Marxism but also to reap Russia's immense mineral wealth. Stalin's demise, he believed, would rob Churchill of his only hope for a second front. Besides, the Axis situation in the Mediterranean had recently been enhanced by the capture of Crete. Still, it may be argued that part of the CSIR would have been better used fighting in the Western Desert.

Eleven days prior to Barbarossa, Hitler had confidently drafted Directive No. 32, in which he outlined the operations to take place following the Soviet collapse. Once Stalin's armed forces were crushed, the *Wehrmacht* would turn its attention to Tobruk and beyond:

> It is important that Tobruk should be eliminated and conditions thereby established for the continuation of the German–Italian attack on the Suez Canal. This attack should be planned for about November [1941] on the understanding that the *Deutsches Afrikakorps* will be by then brought to the highest possible efficiency.[2]

Hitler's post-Barbarossa strategy stemmed, in part, from an ambitious February 1941 study for an assault against British India through Afghanistan. After tying Churchill's forces down in the Mediterranean and Western Asia, a second thrust would be launched from Bulgaria, through Turkey and, if necessary, via southern Russia through Iran. Field Marshal von Brauchitsch, the overall commander of Barbarossa, reviewed a similar proposal a month after launching the juggernaut. It too outlined operations against Britain in autumn 1941, including the capture of Tobruk, Malta and Gibraltar.

'No British Commander Has Been Asked to Assume Greater Responsibilities'

Churchill – already privy to intercepted German plans – was delighted by news of Hitler's foray to the east. He now had a new ally. Stalin, in turn, appealed to Whitehall in July for the opening of a second front in either northern France or Norway. But an Allied invasion of Europe was still some time off. The more immediate problem was the security of the Middle East, now under threat from a possible German thrust through the Caucasus and Iran, or through Anatolia into Syria. In Axis hands, the vital Anglo-Iranian oilfields would substantially alleviate Hitler's fuel problems. British operations in the Middle East, on the other hand, would be paralysed.

Churchill had dispatched two telegrams in the hours preceding Barbarossa. The first notified Wavell of his dismissal: 'The public interest will best be served by appointment of General Auchinleck to relieve you in command of armies of Middle East.'[3] The second communiqué advised the viceroy of India, Lord Linlithgow, by protocol, that Lieutenant General Claude Auchinleck would take up a new responsibility in the Middle East as Wavell's replacement. As we have seen, Churchill was deeply critical of Wavell's hesitancy to intervene in Iraq and Syria and his responsibility, in part, for the recent British setbacks in Crete and the Western Desert. He justified Wavell's removal to General Sir Hastings Ismay, Chief of Staff to the Minister of Defence, on the grounds that remaining on the defensive in Cyrenaica would, in due course, lead to the evacuation of Tobruk and possible disaster. To Roosevelt, Churchill confided that 'a fresh eye and a unrestrained hand' were needed in the 'most seriously menaced' Middle East theatre.[4] One of the fiercest critics of the exchange was General John Dill, who believed that Auchinleck was best suited to a command in India while Wavell returned to Britain for a period of rest. Unable to persuade Churchill otherwise, Dill welcomed Auchinleck in a cable, though with the coda that, 'No British commander has been asked to assume greater responsibilities.'[5]

Wavell also wished his successor well, using a cricket analogy, 'I am sure that in the circumstances a change of bowling will be a good thing and that "Auk" is the man to take the remaining wickets. My bowling has been a bit expensive lately!'[6] Auchinleck wrote:

> In no sense do I wish to infer that I found an unsatisfactory situation on my arrival – far from it. Not only was I greatly impressed by the solid foundations laid by my predecessor, but I was also able the better to appreciate the vastness of the problems with which he had been confronted and the greatness of his achievements, in a command in which some 40 different languages are spoken by the British and Allied Forces.[7]

Wavell – as Churchill's scapegoat, it may be argued – was on a plane to Delhi five days after leaving his Middle East command. The repercussions of his removal were immediate, the aftershocks felt well into the following year. Although Churchill would naturally have gravitated toward the more articulate Auchinleck over the taciturn Wavell, he had 'not altogether liked' Auchinleck's attitude in Norway in 1940, having condemned his penchant for being 'too much inclined to play for safety and certainty'.[8] A questionable replacement for Wavell, Auchinleck, as Dill reasoned, was the ideal man to oversee the expansion of the Indian Army when a new war against Japan was imminent. New to the Middle East, he was also largely unfamiliar with the British Army, from whose ranks he would draw his subordinate officers. Churchill, though, wasted no time in ruthlessly pressing 'the Auk' to resume the offensive, especially after Ultra intercepts revealed Axis plans for a new offensive in Cyrenaica and the transfer of large-calibre siege artillery from Vichy Tunisia.

Agreeing in principle to a new Libyan offensive, Auchinleck was, however, adamant that it would not be feasible until later in the year. On top of his concerns over unfinished business in Syria and Iraq, he was leery about the defence of Cyprus. His curt response to Churchill's call to arms – 'No further offensive Western Desert should be contemplated until base is secure' – was a 'sharp disappointment' in the premier's unsympathetic eyes. It would, Auchinleck advised, require 'at least two and possibly three armoured divisions with a motor[ised] division' to guarantee success. He expounded on how infantry divisions were ineffective in the desert against armour, except in holding captured or even taking ground once the enemy tanks had been dealt with. Auchinleck also raised the need for close aerial support on the battlefield, which at present was 'non-existent'.[9]

Was this the new 'eye' in the Middle East that Churchill so badly needed? His riposte of 6 July spelt out the clear need for a desert victory in the short term – as soon as possible, should the Red Army collapse – and certainly not later than mid-September. Churchill was equally keen to exploit Tobruk's 'offensive value' – a favourite theme, though Morshead was unable to make any significant impression on the Axis lines after May; only 1,000yd of the Salient had been retaken by the end of June. Stretched to capacity to man the 30 miles of outer perimeter, the Tobruk garrison was simply not strong enough to break out on its own.

Auchinleck was asked on 19 July whether an offensive could be undertaken if 150 cruiser tanks and 40,000 reinforcements were immediately sent from Britain. A limited operation to relieve Tobruk could be staged, he felt, in mid-November, perhaps a fortnight earlier, if trained crews accompanied the armour. A major offensive, aiming to drive the Axis out of

North Africa, could be mounted if he received an additional 150 US-built tanks and heavy transport. But as things stood, Auchinleck would not have even a single armoured division ready for action by the end of September. Such a measured build-up, the Defence Committee reasoned, was troublingly slow. Strike now, while Hitler could least afford to syphon off resources from Russia, they argued.

To resolve the strategic standstill, Auchinleck and Air Marshal Tedder were summoned to Britain on 29 July to voice their collective grievances. A host of arguments were tabled as to why an offensive should proceed: the political and military necessity to assist the Soviets, the chance of a German drive through Turkey or the Caucasus before mid-September and Rommel's current supply predicament. Auchinleck answered that the new desert offensive – now named Crusader – could not proceed before November. Numerical strength in armour was one thing, but, as he argued, training at all levels was indispensable. He also needed to consolidate his position in Syria, Iraq and Cyprus before any new undertaking could take place in North Africa. The forum concluded with Churchill unconvinced, but with an agreement from the Defence Committee that the 22nd Armoured Brigade, 1st Armoured Division would be shipped to Egypt as soon as practicable.

Crusader was tentatively set for 1 November 1941. The scope of the operation, however, varied according to the individual. Churchill, as usual, envisaged a 'continuing path' all the way to Tripolitania, possibly Tunisia, and even onward to Sicily.[10] Auchinleck, who was more circumspect, believed the offensive would safeguard the RAF's forward airfields, ease the strain on the RN supply lines to Malta and Tobruk, lessen the threat of air attack against RN bases at Alexandria and Haifa (Palestine), and protect the Suez Canal. But regardless of what *could* be achieved, Auchinleck would *first* have to oversee yet another British intervention. This time, in Iran.

The Anglo-Soviet Invasion of Iran

Fear of a Gaylani-style coup in Iran, Rommel's reconquest of Cyrenaica and German strides in the Soviet Union prompted Allied action against Iran. Although technically neutral, the country's pro-Axis government under Mohammad Reza Shāh Pahlavi represented a strategic threat to Stalin's Caucasus oilfields, the Red Army's rear flank and the rich Middle East oil reserves. Conversely, if occupied, Iran would provide a convenient conduit for US Lead-Lease arm supplies to Russia via the Persian Gulf – the so-called Persian Corridor – in place of the treacherous Arctic Convoy route to the ports of Archangel and Murmansk. Occupying Iran would also demonstrate Britain's support for Stalin, who might otherwise act unilaterally.

Leading up to the invasion, London and Moscow jointly pressured Tehran to expel the large number of Germans, mostly workers and diplomats, from the country. The British embassy had reported in 1940 that nearly 1,000 German nationals were resident in Iran – the nucleus of a potential 'fifth column'. Reza Shāh's blunt refusal to meet his historic enemies' demands became the justification needed for a show of force. A combined British–Soviet invasion comprising some 200,000 troops, supported by modern aircraft, tanks and artillery, was launched on 25 August 1941. The Iranian Army's nine infantry divisions were hopelessly ill-equipped to meet the massive multi-front assault. History was made when the fragmentary resistance collapsed and two Allied armies linked up to join hands for the first time in the war. The four days of combat cost Britain twenty-two men killed and forty-two wounded; the Soviets suffered a similar figure. Arrested and placed in British custody, Reza Shāh was exiled in South Africa, where he died in July 1944.

Iran remained divided between Britain and the Soviet Union for the remainder of the war. A Treaty of Alliance signed in January 1942 guaranteed Tehran's non-military assistance to the Allied war effort. In the end, more than 5 million tons of US Lend-Lease materiel passed through what Churchill termed 'The Bridge of Victory'; primarily to Stalin, but also to British forces in the Middle East. In the meantime British forces in North Africa had retired behind the Egyptian frontier following the failure of Brevity and Battleaxe. Tobruk remained isolated and under siege.

The Life of the 'Rats' — 'Not without Interest'

'[The] Tobruk garrison has earned the admiration of the world
for one of the most memorable sieges in military history.'
— General Sir Thomas Blamey, 1941

Rommel's grand plan had faltered at Tobruk. Over the summer months of 1941, besieged and besieger alike consolidated their forces respectively to either relieve or seize the fortress. Inside Tobruk, Morshead's men were denigrated as 'Rats' by German propaganda. Sustained by a tenuous maritime lifeline, they eked out a simple yet dangerous existence punctuated by moments of reflection, grief and humour as they awaited relief or an end to the siege.

'The Front Liners'

Often referred to as the 'Verdun of the desert', Tobruk's front line resembled the mesh of trenches epitomising the First World War, though minus the mud and the comfortable rest billets behind the lines, save for the occasional opportunity to bathe at the beach.[1] Death and dying were never far removed, with the brunt of the danger borne by the troops manning the perimeter, especially in the Axis-held indentation known as the Salient. One soldier expressed his resentment over this disparity:

> Almost all the risk and hardship is assumed by a small fraction of the men, the front liners. If those further back did not hear the air raids from the depths of their shelters, life would be altogether too monotonous.[2]

The ever-present danger of shelling and sniping enforced a type of troglodyte-like existence. Some idea of the volume of shells fired, while not on the colossal scale of the First World War barrages, is found in the figures for the comparatively quiet period of 26 June to 6 August, when some 650 projectiles plunged toward the forward lines each day. By September, the daily average had jumped to 1,000. One of the Australian 'front liners' wrote of the ever-present danger from shelling:

> Since yesterday morning I've had the worst time I've ever had. Yesterday morning about nine o'clock the Huns shelled us with big stuff … Brian had his leg nearly blown off and I had to carry him about half a mile on my back … While I was at Company the section post was shelled again and many parts of it were completely smashed in. Bluey and Dead Eye were buried and had to dig themselves out and Ted was thrown against the wall with the force of the explosion. Most of the boys are a bundle of nerves … Anyone who reckons he's not scared is a blasted liar.[3]

This universal risk of death, another soldier wrote, produced an early philosophical attitude toward life:

> … a bloke is only alive hour by hour. A mate of mine was telling me about his plans when he got home, 30 minutes later they dropped a shell on him that's how it is here. We don't

seem to look at it on the bad side we've seen so much and been so close to death that a lot of us are 100% fatalists.[4]

The garrison's dugouts running through the area before the Salient generally held only two to three men. Up to 4ft deep at the most, due to the hard Libyan bedrock, and camouflaged with camel bush, they were joined by short crawl trenches. Since the slightest movement, even the smoke rising from brewing tea, would draw accurate mortar, sniper and machine gun fire, daylight hours were spent hidden below makeshift parapets. Here the enemy became monotony and vermin, as one defender wrote:

> You never see anyone and cannot move until dark, and every-one is starting to get on everyone else's nerves … we are up all night, every night, and you cannot sleep during the day owing to the heat and the flies. The only consolation is that the Huns must be feeling it more than we are, as they are not used to it.[5]

Rest, as we can only try to imagine, proved difficult, because of the extremes in temperature, innumerable insects, shelling and frequent sandstorms. Boredom was an inescapable adversary; 'this is a nerve racking game we're on and the worst part is the days of inactivity and waiting – waiting for one knows not what.'[6] Idle time was spent writing letters and thumbing through tattered books and magazines, and smoking. The onset of darkness brought welcome relief. Hot meals were brought forward, cramped joints were exercised and the never-ending task of improving defensive positions continued. Men who were ill or wounded could be evacuated and treated. In the absence of latrines, it was also a time to relieve oneself, as a sergeant in the South Nottinghamshire Hussars explained:

> [You] took a shovel and walked away until you found an empty area. You did whatever you had to do and covered it over again.

The men knew that they had to cover their excretia because of the flies. You lived with the flies all around your mouth and up your nose.[7]

Morshead's policy of patrolling, as we have seen, began early in the siege. After the Axis troops became established, the majority of the patrols surreptitiously set off into the enemy's lair after dark; 'when night comes the Tobruk rats show their fangs', one correspondent recorded. So successful were the patrols that from May onwards, the garrison was more on the offensive than the besieging Axis army. A special uniform was adopted. Boots padded with thick rubber soles aided stealth; one-piece overalls reinforced in the knees and elbows provided extra comfort. The soldiers, weighed down with guns and grenades, might sometimes draw on an artillery barrage to cover their furtive disappearance forward into the blackness. Carefully feeling their way, patrols were on constant guard for enemy minefields and any manner of booby traps. Bloody havoc befell one reconnaissance party that accidentally triggered an enemy trip wire:

> There was a sharp metallic click underfoot. I jumped clear, calling Alan to ground. There was a blinding red flash and he was on his knees moaning … We got Alan to his feet and half carried, half propelled him towards our own lines. Alan was groaning as we took him in and then he was silent. A sliver of shrapnel had entered his left eye and no doubt pierced his brain, because he was dead when he reached our lines.[8]

Sometimes the parties would have to cover thousands of gruelling yards before they reached enemy lines. Wary of these British intruders who might appear at any moment, Axis troops would fire flares into the sky and sweep searchlights across no-man's-land, freezing all activity until the cover of darkness returned.

On the other side, solitary tracer bullets were sometimes fired to help guide a patrol home through the darkness. One company of the 2/15th Battalion learned to manoeuvre toward the sound of a serenading saxophone emanating from the front lines.

Understandably, the mental strain from these incursions was enormous. One soldier, whose patrol had been ambushed three weeks earlier, wrote:

> The corporal of our squad … has not yet straightened up but gets about with a perpetual stoop and anxious glances enemywards; it jolted his nerve badly. Another member of the squad has been in hospital and I admit I felt jittery for a couple of days …[9]

No-man's-land in daylight hours was 'policed' by several groups of two or three men entrenched beyond the boundary, sometimes as far as 3 miles out, in small dugouts known as Bondi, Plonk, Bash, Jack and Jill. Watching and waiting, the 'silent cops' would report enemy movements by telephone or occasionally direct a patrol or artillery bombardment. In time, a 40ft observation pole was erected more than a mile out in no-man's-land to spy on Axis activity.

The 'Rats of Tobruk'

Months into the siege, complaints were understandably aired regarding the 'monotony of the landscape, the food and the dust', though life according to one soldier was 'not without interest or excitement'. [10] The repetitious diet was an especial privation. Tinned bully beef and hard biscuits were supplemented with fresh bread, along with rationed margarine and jam, until the garrison's bakery was bombed. Vitamin C tablets supplanted fresh vegetables and fruit. Daily rations were occasionally enriched for a fortunate few with fresh fish, caught using hand grenades. Mostly dirty, brackish water was drawn from various wells within the perimeter, the taste sometimes disguised with effervescent fruit salts. Home-made distilleries produced decent drinking water and other more sought-after beverages to supplement the occasional beer ration. Sustained poor nutrition invariably led to the appearance of 'desert sores' – a loosely applied term for bacterial skin infections that took weeks to heal – as well as dysentery, a scourge on both sides. Not surprisingly, most of the besieged troops had lost 2st by the time they were evacuated.

'Free time', as such, was largely devoted to digging defensive positions and maintaining weapons. Items such as tobacco were 'manufactured', while some indulged in scrounging or creating items of interest from battlefield detritus to be sent home as a souvenir. Post from home was always a high point. As an Australian soldier explained, 'There's no doubt about it, when mail arrives our whole outlook changes; no beer, no fresh food; dust; heat; flies; what do all these matter so long as our letters come to hand.'[11] By August 1941, the Australian Postal Unit in Tobruk was handling 50 tons of incoming mail each week. Outgoing mail, by and large, contained a variety of front line keepsakes. Deactivated Italian hand grenades, for example, made convenient egg cups; cut-down shell casings were fashioned into ornamental ashtrays. Enemy bayonets were especially prized. Axis prisoners were sometimes stripped of their accoutrements as souvenirs. An officer in the 2/13th Battalion diarised how, 'Some of the fellows have been pinching stuff off the prisoners, wounded and dead, pistols and so on, a lot have been going a bit far.'[12]

News gleaned from censored mail and the occasional newspaper from Cairo was complemented by garrison news-sheets such as *The Tobruk Truth: The Dinkum Oil* – a daily roneoed bulletin featuring updates that scribes would copy from BBC broadcasts. Some units also produced their own circulars, such as the 2/23rd Battalion's *Mud and Blood*. False news stories,

or those exaggerating or romanticising the garrison's existence, were particularly irritating for the men in the dugouts;
misinformation circulated in 1942, as we will learn, could be
disastrous. One particular newspaper clipping, as an example,
which maddened the garrison reported on a regular supply
of beer – a fabrication best handled with humour. A 'rumour'
within the fortress contended that so much beer had been lost
in the Mediterranean en route to Tobruk that the tidal pat-
terns had changed! Humour in this way helped to alleviate the
hardships of the siege. A solitary German soldier caught 'in the
act of performing his natural functions became the butt of a
bush gunner joke on one occasion. Sniped using an 'ancient'
telescope borrowed from the Navy, 'one or two shells fell not
far from the Nazi who continued to apply himself to the task,
not believing any gun crew could be crazy enough to range
on one man'. Not until several shells straddled him did he suddenly appreciate that he was 'indeed a military objective'.[13]

Lord Haw Haw, in reality, William Joyce – founder of the
pro-Nazi British National Socialist League – also provided an
unintentional form of light relief through his daily propaganda
broadcasts. Joyce's derogatory reference to the garrison as the
'Rats of Tobruk' was viewed as a badge of honour; 'He never
failed to cheer us', an Australian medical officer recalled.[14]
Delighted with their new epithet, the 'Rats' struck an unofficial medal, using metal scavenged from a downed German
aircraft. Repeated wireless warnings for the extermination of
Morshead's 'self-supporting prisoners' were likewise received
with laughter rather than terror. Attempts to demoralise the
garrison through airdropped propaganda leaflets also failed
miserably. The enemy handbills became instant keepsakes with
a soaring monetary value, as demand outstripped supply.

Communal worship also helped lift wearied spirits.
Attendance, according to a British gunner, varied with the
'seriousness of the situation'. After attending a service on
6 May, another serviceman wrote how it was 'only simple but

bucks us up a lot'. An Allied cemetery, an 'oasis of tombstones and crosses', was established inside the perimeter near the aerodrome. Described as a 'haven among the dust', considerable effort was expended by the men to express their condolences. Large and elaborate tombstones were erected; one batman, in particular, spent nearly a month building a suitably ornate memorial to his fallen officer.[15]

'War without Hate'

Notwithstanding the ever-present danger of two sides locked in a static battlefield, an extraordinary degree of chivalry existed between the Germans and the British forces. Both sides appreciated and respected the difficulties under which they all lived and fought. Hans von Ravenstein wrote after the war that the 'fight in Africa was fierce, but fair';[16] Rommel referred to the entire North African campaign as *Krieg ohne Hass* (War Without Hate), a theme we will return to later. 'Each side thrusts and counter-thrusts,' Schorm noted, but 'If the struggle was not so brutal, so entirely without rules, one would be inclined to think of the romantic era of a knights' Tourney'.[17] The humanity often accorded to the enemy in this theatre was recorded by an Australian soldier following the Easter fighting:

> One of the Germans, an officer came to see me. He was crying and asked if he could speak with his Captain before he died, so I took him over, but had to turn my back. The Captain died a few minutes later, and he covered him with a Swastika [flag], made a smart about turn, gave the Nazi salute, and came to me with tears rolling down his cheeks, and said 'Now I await your command'. I was terribly touched, and could not feel bitter about it, and gave them water before I handed them over.[18]

Chivalrous acts were not uncommon, nor were unofficial understandings, sometimes punctuated with humour. The diary entry of a 'Rat' (6 June 1941) detailed how:

> We throw everything at each other from daylight until about 10.30, when it starts to get hot and then both the Germans and ourselves appear to have a mutual agreement, that it is getting too hot and not a shot is fired until about 6 o'clock in the evening, then we go flat out again until about 9 o'clock, when it gets dark. Then we carry on with spasmodic fire all through the night. It is really funny how everyone stops firing around 10 p.m. ...[19]

Nonetheless, this was still war, and while far removed from the carnage on the *Ostfront*, it was often ugly. An Australian solder recalled how:

> My platoon was given the doubtful honour of rounding up a German raiding party so out we went, thirty-two of us and were surprised to find the German strength was 110 fully-armed men, with every type of modern equipment. Two of them surrendered as a decoy to us, and when I went forward to search them, the remainder opened up with machine guns. I scattered my men and gradually closed in on them. We fought for five hours and then their Commander came out with a white flag ... the outcome was that we killed five, wounded twelve and took prisoners ninety-three, and we didn't lose one man either wounded or killed.[20]

Air Raids

Enemy aircraft wrought a different type of danger in the built-up harbour area, where some 787 air raids were recorded in the first three months alone. A doctor in the hospital recorded the terror:

> Now the whistle and crash of bombs become more frequent, and at each whistle the shelter occupants, who are not now prone to much conversation, instinctively crouch, while at each crash their tension relaxes and up they bob again. There is a particularly loud and piercing whistle, and someone mutters, 'This'll be a close one.' There is a mighty crash, the shelter shakes and a great wind rushes through it like a tornado, sending the dust from the floor in swirls that cover everyone and set men coughing.[21]

The regularity of air raids led to Tobruk becoming a proving ground for anti-aircraft defence that even drew specialist officers from the US. One weapon backed by Churchill was a 3in finless rocket called a Unrotated Projectile, or UP. Fired from a multi-barrelled launcher, the rockets exploded at 3,000ft and released small bombs dangling from a parachute by piano wire that would (in theory) detonate upon contact with an enemy aircraft.[22] Numerous anti-aircraft batteries around the harbour could also saturate the sky with the equivalent of a steel curtain against enemy bombers bent on severing the fortress' maritime lifeline. Courage and cool nerves were needed to operate the guns during dive-bombing or strafing attacks. An observer beside a Scottish ack-ack crew noted how:

> There was no hurried or frantic pumping out of shells to frighten off the planes: they carefully sighted their targets regardless of their own lack of protection, and scored several hits. By an absolute miracle only one man in the gun crew was hurt, though bullet marks were scattered all over the old wall about the gun and several bullets had hit the predictor.[23]

Another ack-ack crew was commended for unwaveringly manning the gun that remained above water on the sunken

HMS *Ladybird*, a river gunboat that had survived earlier Japanese shelling on the Yangtze in 1937 before being sunk at Tobruk on 12 May 1941. They steadfastly refused to be relieved, and only later was it discovered that the newly installed army gun crew were actually diving into the wreck during quiet periods to plunder the captain's whiskey supply.

Dummy ack-ack sites, complete with bogus trucks, men and ammunition dumps, were erected around the harbour as well, to fool enemy pilots. Hand grenades were sometimes triggered via wires to produce the effect of gun flashes. Alternative positions were also built, and existing ones strengthened and counter-sunk. Casualties among the gunners dropped significantly once the Axis aircraft divided their attention between attacking real and decoy positions.

Later in the siege, a small number of Hurricanes flew reconnaissance missions out of Tobruk from two splinter-proof, specially camouflaged hangars and a third sunken hangar with a platform lift.[24] Although outclassed and outnumbered by the German Messerschmitt Bf 109F fighters, the Hurricanes of Squadron Leader Peter Wykeham Barnes' No. 73 Squadron in 1941 provided invaluable aerial protection, claiming thirty-one victories in the air, plus five probables, as well destroying eight aircraft and numerous vehicles on the ground. The pilots were often in action several times in a day, sometimes bailing out of stricken craft to fight again the following day.

A War of Nerves

For some men, the relentless strain of combat and exposure to traumatic events – a war of nerves – was simply too much. The worst cases were labelled 'bomb happy' – a condition we would call post-traumatic stress disorder today. Minor self-inflicted wounds began appearing in the first weeks of the siege as the soldiers attempted to escape from the horror of the front lines or the slide into madness from repeated bombardment. 'I was well and truly scared and hugged the bottom of my partially made dugout,' wrote one Rat.[25]

In a review of the 210 men with suspected war neurosis, Captain Alexander Sinclair categorised patients with a psychological condition into four general groups: those with a pre-existing nervous condition, those found to be suffering from mental and physical exhaustion, those experiencing their first taste of combat, and or fear of capture, and those who felt 'expendable' because every British offensive to relieve Tobruk had failed. Sinclair concluded that, 'The main cause of war neurosis is still fear. The anxiety and terror inevitable in modern warfare is the exciting cause of almost every case of war neurosis.'[26]

Exposure to war could also, paradoxically, bring out the best in a soldier. As one Australian officer noted:

> It's surprising how action changes many men; my worst and most troublesome man in camp life and the only man I've ever had under arrest is now one of my best and will do anything for me at all. Others we thought were good men, crack up quickly; but fortunately very few.[27]

The Tobruk 'Standard'

Tobruk was a 'miracle' for the Allies at a time when German pincers were driving ever deeper into Russia.[28] Dwarfed by the sheer magnitude of the Eastern Front, Tobruk was nevertheless a convenient model of military fortitude. To bolster the spirits of his resolute Russian counterparts encircled at Odessa – a city that Halder labelled a 'Russian Tobruk' – Morshead saluted them in a communiqué, closing: 'This being invested is not as bad as it sounds.'[29] As German columns closed on Leningrad in September 1941, Melbourne's *Age* applauded the 'men of Tobruk' for doing 'the toughest job of the war', for their 'courage of the highest order' and 'endurance which matches that displayed in the most famous sieges in history'.[30] Reporting on East Africa, America's *Newsweek* pronounced the 10,000 Italian and native troops under General Guglielmo Nasi, who had held out for seven months at Gondar, a mountainous corner of north-western Ethiopia, as 'Italy's Tobruk'.[31] The fortress' nascent acclaim was such that one writer was moved to recommend that the word 'Tobruk' enter the English language, as 'noun, fortress defended on landward side, and provisioned by superior naval power by sea'.[32]

The 'Spud Run'

At the beginning of the siege Tobruk had sufficient food and ammunition to last three, perhaps four months. But with no prospect of relief Morshead's lifeline with the outside world was kept alive by the RN and the Royal Australian Navy (RAN) plying the so-called 'spud [potato] run' from Alexandria. Axis aircraft made the passage in daylight a perilous task, forcing destroyers and a variety of small ships to slip in during the hours of darkness. The vessels making the 'run' were allowed a maximum time of 50 minutes to unload in the wreck-littered harbour before embarking on the dangerous return journey, all the time at risk of bombing, shelling or striking an enemy mine.

Activity around the harbour quickly settled into a simple routine governed by the lunar phases, for it was only on moonless nights that vessels could safely enter and leave the port. 'A' lighters and destroyers would mainly haul fuel and ammunition, while general provisions were lugged by a flotilla of decrepit blockade-runners and captained by a colourful collection of maritime characters. Possibly the most well-known captain in this bunch was Lieutenant Alfred 'Pedlar' Palmer,

Royal Naval Reserve. Known as the Pirate of Tobruk, Palmer won fame by successfully running supplies to Tobruk aboard the captured Italian auxiliary schooner *Maria Giovanni* from May to October 1941. A typical manifest recorded 115 tons of provisions, 50 tons of ammunition, 2 tons of mail and a number of live sheep. Regularly attacked from the air, it was said that Palmar navigated more by instinct than by instruments until the Italians lured him on to a reef by rigging false navigation lights.

Rightly described as 'a running sore' to the enemy, Tobruk was 'equally painful' to the RN.[33] Admiral Andrew Cunningham (commander-in-chief of the RN in the Mediterranean) estimated that one sailor had been lost for every 50 tons of supplies, and a ship for every 1,000 tons.[34] In the period between 11 April and 9 December 1941, twenty-six naval vessels and five merchant ships were sunk while provisioning Tobruk.[35] Another four warships and four merchant ships were badly damaged. In the same period some 34,000 tons of stores, seventy-two tanks and ninety-two artillery pieces were landed; 32,667 personnel were evacuated and 34,113 fresh troops brought in; and 7,516 wounded men and 7,097 prisoners of war were shipped out. The Tobruk garrison would not have survived without this crucial seaborne service, a factor that was to influence key British decision-making in 1942. For the moment, however, Tobruk became a rallying cry for the free world, a much-needed demonstration of defence against seemingly impossible odds.

Crusader and the
Relief of Tobruk

'Rommel, Rommel, Rommel! What else matters but beat-
ing him?'

— Winston Churchill, 8 August 1942

By the end of August 1941, it was clear that Hitler's largest
military venture had failed. Barbarossa was no replay of the
Wehrmacht's earlier triumph in the West. Only in Ukraine, where
Axis forces had isolated Odessa and reached the Dnieper River,
had satisfactory progress been made. By October, German
planners were forced to postpone their grandiose Middle East
ambitions as a consequence of the stubborn Soviet resistance,
difficulties in supplying North Africa, continued uncertainty
regarding Turkey's stance, and Japan's delay in entering the war
against Russia or seizing Britain's Far East base of Singapore.
Any thought of discontinuing the siege at Tobruk, though, was
undesirable, primarily from a propaganda perspective.[1]

Casting his eye over the world stage in mid-September,
Halder noted that any military action against Turkey was out
of the question, with diplomacy the key to winning Ankara
over. Intervention in Syria and Iraq was no longer possible
and Britain's position in Egypt would continue to improve.

Bolstered offensive forces, armed with American Lend-Lease equipment, would be built up undisturbed. In unison, the position of the Italo-German forces in North Africa would become increasingly tricky, unless the supply situation across the Mediterranean improved or Tobruk was occupied before the next British offensive. Halder also felt that Spain would not enter the war until the Axis had mastered the Mediterranean. But Germany's immediate and paramount goal was still to bring about Russia's collapse: 'On achieving that goal, we must concentrate all forces that can be spared from other fronts ... the continuance of the Eastern campaign in 1942 must be accorded first priority.'[2]

Rommel's Midsummer Night's Dream

General Ugo Cavallero visited Rommel at his Bardia head-quarters at the end of July 1941 to discuss the impasse in Libya. Both men were of the same mind that any operation to reach Egypt was out of the question until after Tobruk had fallen. But the Axis supply quandary would continue to check offensive action so long as Britain held the aerial and naval advantage in the Mediterranean. Malta, in particular, had become the bane of Italian convoys sailing for Tripoli. In July, for example, 17 per cent of Rommel's supplies were sunk; in August, the figure doubled to 35 per cent. Only 18,500 tons, out of the 50,000 tons of supplies dispatched from Italy, reached Rommel's displeased quartermasters in October. The next month, an entire convoy of seven Italian merchant ships was sent to the bottom without any loss on the British side.[3]

On the ground, Rommel's troops fought several small actions in August and September to tighten their grip around Tobruk, while his tanks languished in the scorching desert heat. A raid against a supposed British supply dump south of Sollum – codenamed *Sommernachtstraum* (Midsummer

Night's Dream) – was undertaken in mid-September by the bulk of the (newly renamed) 21st Panzer Division. Although *Afrikakorps* staff suspected that the enemy dump was in fact empty, Rommel was nevertheless eager to see his tanks in action. Early on the morning of 14 September, he personally accompanied one of the two battle groups into action, in what essentially became a wild goose chase. Forewarned by the din of the advancing German columns, the British covering force withdrew. The Panzers halted in dangerous proximity during the afternoon to refuel – an inviting target for the RAF and South African Air Force bombers, which 'carpet bombed' the Germans for the first time, nearly killing Rommel.

The remaining German armour returned west the next day, having only bagged a solitary South African office truck and three prisoners. The raid was an abject failure. To add further ignominy, several Italian-piloted *Picchiatellos* (Stukas) were captured after landing behind British lines. Moreover, the slim intelligence dividends wrongly fuelled Rommel's suspicion that British operations would not interfere with his next planned assault on Tobruk, set for 21 November.

'Hurrah, We Leave Tobruk'

Even before Tobruk was besieged, Australia's War Cabinet had voiced its disapproval to London about how the AIF was unfairly bearing the brunt of Britain's land-based fighting. Whitehall was also reminded of the 'Charter' affirming that the AIF would serve abroad as a single corps under Australian command. As it stood, by August 1941, Australian divisions and brigades had fought across North Africa, Greece, Crete and Syria, yet no two divisions had seen action together. It was with this principle in mind that Blamey, Australia's top soldier and now Deputy Commander-in-Chief of the Middle East Forces, pressed for the relief of the Australian garrison inside

Tobruk by either the New Zealand Division or 1st South African Division

Along with Prime Minster Menzies' concern over the repercussions at home should Tobruk fall, Blamey was increasingly concerned over the garrison's state of health. A formal notice from the Australian government reached Auchinleck on 18 July, calling for 'action [to] be taken forthwith for the relief of the Garrison of Tobruk'.[4] Churchill, in turn, ignored a cable from Menzies for two days, for what he pronounced as a 'needless relief'.[5] It would, however, prove difficult to substitute an entire Middle East division at this time, though the decision was made to return the 18th Australian Brigade to its parent division, the 7th, and replace it with the 1st Polish Independent Carpathian Rifle Brigade. The issue of relieving the remainder of the Australian garrison was finally resolved at a meeting in Cairo on 2 August (in Auchinleck's absence, but with his approval), with the British 70th Division slated to fill the gap.

Bowing to domestic political bickering following the disastrous Greek and Crete campaigns and the looming Pacific War, Menzies resigned as Australian prime minister on 29 August 1941. His short-lived successor, Arthur Fadden, remained committed to relieving the Australian force, though Churchill made one final attempt to convince him otherwise, appealing on 11 September to carefully weigh 'the immense responsibility which you would assume before history by depriving Australia of the glory of holding Tobruk till victory was won'.[6] The Australian government's stubborn position, however, plus an ultimatum from Blamey, even moved Auchinleck to consider resigning at one point. But like Canberra, Churchill remained fixed in his thinking. After John Curtin was elected as Australia's next prime minister on 3 October, Churchill called upon him to again reconsider Australia's position. Curtin, however, remained firm; the 'Rats' were to be progressively extracted.

Beginning in August, the 18th Australian Infantry Brigade and the Indian Army's 18th King Edward's Own Cavalry were replaced by two formations eager to avenge their countries' plights under the swastika: the Polish Independent Carpathian Rifle Brigade and the Czechoslovak 11th Infantry Battalion (East). In September and October, the British 70th Infantry Division, including the 32nd Army Tank Brigade, supplanted the majority of the remaining Australian garrison. Morshead's successor was the 70th Division's commander, Major General Ronald Scobie. RN losses, however, led to the cancellation of the relief operation, stranding the unfortunate 2/13th Australian Battalion, two companies of 2/15th Australian Battalion and 9th Division headquarters staff at Tobruk until after the siege was lifted. As it eventuated, the withdrawal of the Australians had little effect on Allied strategy in the Middle East, though this may have changed radically had the Luftwaffe decimated the relieving convoys or had Crusader – the third attempt to relieve besieged Tobruk in 1941 – also flopped.

Crusader

Auchinleck now assembled an impressive striking force to relive Tobruk. General Alan Cunningham was given command of the newly created Eighth Army, comprising the XIII Corps (formerly the Western Desert Force) under Lieutenant General Alfred Reade Godwin-Austen, the 2nd New Zealand Division, the 4th Indian Division and the 1st Army Tank Brigade. The new XXX Corps (under Lieutenant General Willoughby Norrie) comprised the 7th Armoured Division, 1st South African Division and 22nd Guards Brigade. General Ronald Scobie's garrison inside Tobruk comprised the aforementioned 70th Division, 32nd Army Tank Brigade and the Polish Independent Carpathian Rifle Brigade.

British armour had grown to 738 tanks, including 300 new cruiser – 'Crusader' – tanks, some sixty new infantry Mark III 'Valentine' tanks, and 300 new US M3 Stuart light tanks (nicknamed 'Honey' by the British). British crews welcomed the speed and reliability of this new American tank, though it had the drawbacks of limited range, thin armour and a lack of firepower from its diminutive 37mm gun. The new British Crusader tanks were equally hampered by their outmoded 2-pounder gun, thin armour and mechanical unreliability. Although it was more heavily armoured and far more reliable, the Valentine was nevertheless equipped with the same 2-pounder gun. But no firepower could compensate for inexperience and an adversary adroit in the handling of armour.

Newly promoted *to General der Panzertruppe*, Rommel's reorganised and renamed *Panzergruppe Afrika* (virtually an army command) contained the DAK, Italian XXI Corps and Italian 55th 'Savona' Division. His mobile troops included 15th and 21st Panzer Divisions, the latter enlarged from the former 5th Light Division into a fully-fledged armoured division. A new division, *Division z.b.V* (*zur besondere Verfügung* – 'for special use') *Afrika* was formed from various independent regiments and battalions besieging Tobruk. Rommel's armoured strength had dropped far below that of the British. Only forty-four new Panzer IIIs and sixteen Panzer IVs crossed the Mediterranean, making up a total of merely 249 tanks, including seventy obsolete Panzer IIs, and an additional 137 M13/40 tanks from the 'Ariete' Division.

Only a trickle of supplies was reaching the Axis front lines. The situation only worsened after a large convoy of seven merchant ships was sunk en route to Tripoli on 8–9 November. In total, 399 vehicles, 13,290 tons of materiel and 17,281 tons of fuel, to have propelled Rommel's projected 21 November offensive, were lost. The harsh desert theatre was also taking its toll. German manpower in North Africa would reach 48,500 by October 1941, though 11,066 men were reported as sick at this time, due, in part, to poor nutrition and the scourges of dysentery and hepatitis.

Libyan skies were ruled by the Western Desert Air Force. Of the 650 aircraft on hand, 550 were operational. A further seventy-four were stationed in Malta. In the month preceding Crusader, British aircraft flew nearly 3,000 sorties (not including strikes on Axis shipping). On the other side of the ledger, the Luftwaffe's then *Fliegerführer Afrika* (Flying-Leader Africa), Major General Stefan Fröhlich, had provided a dismal report on November 15: Only 140 German aircraft were available, seventy-six of which were operational. The Italian 5th Air Fleet had a further 290 aircraft, plus assistance was available from the German X Air Corps stationed in Greece. Fortune, at least on paper, appeared to be favouring the British.

Crusader was preceded by a daring British special forces raid, on a private villa thought to be Rommel's headquarters, on the night of 13/14 November. Hoping to kill or capture Rommel, the raid proved disastrous. Rommel, at the time, was in Rome having celebrated his fiftieth birthday two days earlier with his wife. The leader of the raid, Lieutenant Colonel Geoffrey Keyes, was killed and posthumously awarded the Victoria Cross for bravery. (We should note that Keyes' father, Admiral Sir Roger, a Conservative MP, had been a leading critic of Neville Chamberlain and had led the May 1940 debate that swung political support away from the then prime minister. Partially responsible for the Churchill's ascent to premier, he would be a future ally in one of Churchill's most difficult moments as prime minister when Rommel's 1942 offensive nearly toppled his government.)

By the evening of Sunday, 16 November, General Alan Cunningham was already showing the strain of his new command, smoking heavily and afflicted by a smoking-related eye condition. He had, as we saw earlier, successfully defeated the Italians in Kenya, but was both a novice in the desert and in directing armour. Of the considerable differences between the two African theatres, Sir Bernard Fergusson, Wavell's ADC, wrote:

> There could have been no more complete contrast to the swiftly-moving war of the Desert, and the mental adjustment required of Cunningham would have been difficult for any-body. It was tantamount to saying: 'If you can drive a bulldozer, you can drive a racing-car.'[7]

He had seemed 'an imaginative choice', Auchinleck later wrote.[8]

Over whiskey and soda, Cunningham outlined details of his forthcoming offensive, dubbed Crusader, to a group of war correspondents gathered in his dugout headquarters. He was confident of success, despite his appearance of stress, and predicted a drive 'deep into Libya'. In what was essentially a two-part operation, the tanks of XXX Corps were to sweep north-west across the desert, to destroy Rommel's armour before linking up with the Tobruk garrison, which would break out at a suitable opportunity and join the main assault. XIII Corps, primarily an infantry formation, was given the task of outflanking the German units along the frontier before advancing west along the coast road. Zero hour was set before dawn the following morning – 18 November.

On the eve of directing Britain's largest tank force to date, the lessons of mobile desert warfare gleaned from the earlier battles would be (tragically) ignored, and the Eighth Army's armour was once again segregated from its accompanying infantry to fight separate battles. German doctrine, in contrast, favoured the use of combined arms – integrating tanks, infantry and artillery in either mixed battle groups or massed armoured assaults. Success in desert warfare, as O'Connor had grasped, depended upon the close integration of all arms.

Surprise was on Cunningham's side (Rommel was in Athens). The British had concealed the deployment of their forces in preparation so well, with strict radio silence, that up until a day before the assault, the Germans anticipated, at best, only a strike to relieve Tobruk and not a full-scale offensive. British intelligence had also beamed false reports to Italy that offensive operations were, in fact, concealing the movement of a large force northwards to assist Stalin and protect the Middle Eastern oilfields. The subterfuge was complete with Ultra confirming Rommel's receipt of Auchinleck's 'intentions'. Last-minute British movements were also helped by a combination of perfectly timed extreme weather conditions over Cyrenaica; 'Sandstorm, thunderstorm and torrential rain' wrote the diarist of *Panzergruppe Afrika*.[9] Wadis were awash, roads blocked, vehicles and guns bogged and landing fields rendered unusable for days, though RAF aircraft could still operate from Egypt.

Surging across the frontier into Libya, Crusader met little opposition. And no counterblow materialised – depriving Cunningham of the decisive armoured bout that his planning envisioned. General Ludwig Crüwell, commanding the armoured formations of the *Afrikakorps*, recognised the beginning of an offensive following a report from the 3rd Reconnaissance Battalion of a thrust by several hundred British tanks. Rommel (recently returned from Rome) remained engrossed in the planning of his next assault on Tobruk and assumed that the push was merely an enemy reconnaissance in force. Not until the evening of 20 November did he finally concede that a major British offensive had been launched. Alerted to British intentions through a BBC broadcast from Cairo, reporting on an Eighth Army offensive to destroy the German and Italian forces in Africa, and Crüwell's protest, Rommel finally cancelled his assault on Tobruk and flung his forces against the British armoured columns endangering his offensive.

A confused Cunningham divided his tank force on the second day in search of his adversary's armour. Gott, in command of the 7th Armoured Division, believed that now was the time for the Tobruk garrison to break out. Cunningham concurred and issued the codeword: 'Pop'; the attempt would be made on 21 November even though the requisite destruction of Axis armour had not been achieved. In the meantime, the opposing armoured forces clashed in a confused series of armada-like encounters across miles of featureless desert.

A South African-born tank commander in the 3rd Royal Tank Regiment recounted his daily schedule on the battlefield:

> Up at any time between midnight and 4 o'clock; movement out of the leaguer into battle positions before first light; a biscuit and a spoonful of marmalade before the flap of orders and information; the long day of movement and vigil and encounter, death and the fear of death, until darkness put a limit to vision and purpose on both sides …
>
> Within that framework the battles were fought, the tanks were knocked out, the crews killed, or maimed or fried. At the end of each day the brief relief of the last-light pause, when the desert grew quiet and cold and the moon rose on the sand and scrub making black shadows of the escarpments and moving black shadows of the funereal columns of smoke …[10]

At Tobruk, General Scobie's break out was barely contained by the encircling German and Italian forces that had been preparing to assault the fortress. Simultaneously, the 4th Indian Division, the 2nd New Zealand Division (under General Bernard Freyberg, who had escaped from the Crete catastrophe) had smashed through the Sollum front. Cunningham ordered the latter to press forward to Tobruk.

Both sides continued to suffer heavy losses in the tough slugging match that developed. Sensing an opportunity, on 24 November Rommel ordered a reckless counterstroke (without precise knowledge of enemy dispositions) by the 21st Panzer Division, toward the Egyptian frontier, to pursue elements of the 7th Armoured Division and to force a British withdrawal.[11] This premature and hastily move – known as the 'dash to the wire' – allowed the Eighth Army to again attempt to link up with Scobie's troops and relieve Tobruk. Rommel's thrust found only open desert, though the Eighth Army's primary supply dump lay undetected only 4 miles distant; his own vehicles now dangerously low on fuel and ammunition.

Ritchie – 'Beyond His Capacity'

Nine days into the battle, Auchinleck found Cunningham in poor shape, suffering from strain, contemplating a retreat after heavy tank losses and generally unfit to command. Determining that Crusader should continue, but under new management, he selected Major General Neil Ritchie – one of Britain's youngest generals at age 44 – to lead the Eighth Army. This was yet another questionable choice, given Ritchie's inexperience as a senior field commander and in desert warfare. Having served in Cairo only as Auchinleck's deputy chief of the general staff at GHQ, Ritchie was thrust into a hugely demanding role – commanding the only British army fighting on a land front and in the middle of an offensive 'at a desperate moment, knowing little or nothing of his subordinate officers or troops'. Requested to 'retrieve an apparently lost battle', he was, according to General Frank Messervy (then commanding officer of the 4th Indian Division), 'put into a position which at the time was beyond his capacity'.[12]

Fighting, meanwhile, raged around Tobruk. The 19th New Zealand Brigade managed, briefly, to link up with the garrison on 27 November, before it was isolated again in a bitter see-sawing contest. The New Zealand Official History records the savagery of the fighting around the Sidi Rezegh escarpment, roughly 25 miles south-east of Tobruk:

The enemy forces comprised a number of Germans and troops of 9 Bersaglieri Regiment (Italian). Both were plentiful and supplies with machine guns and anti-tank guns and it was clear that our troops had had to advance right to the muzzles of these guns before their crews were dispatched and the guns silenced. There was an enormous number of dead and wounded all over the battlefield. A significant feature was the sight of many men who had been hit by solid shot of anti-tank guns, fired at point blank range. These projectiles had torn large portions of flesh from the bodies of the unfortunate victims and it would be hard to imagine a more unpleasant sight or a more heavily contested battlefield. The Bersaglieri Regt fought with much greater determination than is usually found among Italian troops and the numbers of their dead and the positions in which they lay showed that they had kept their guns in action to the last.[13]

Heavy losses were sustained by both sides before Scobie ordered the break-out to cease, and his troops (inside Tobruk) to go on the defensive.

'Tobruk Is Relieved ...'

British and South African troops re-established contact with Tobruk on 1 December, though it was not until the evening of 7 December that Rommel finally ordered his forces to abandon the siege, though contact was maintained along Tobruk's western perimeter. Having now lost the battle of Tobruk, and unable to hold Cyrenaica against the stronger British forces, Rommel was again forced to retreat. The siege, after 242 days, was finally over. Godwin-Austen, the commander of XIII Corps, signalled Cairo: 'Tobruk is relieved, but not half as relieved as I am.'[14]

General Ettore Bastico, commander of Italian forces in Libya, visited Rommel on 8 December, and found him incensed over the Axis rout, even threatening to withdrawal his divisions to Tripoli and intern himself in Tunisia. In the course of their meeting, Bastico (whom Rommel nicknamed 'Bombastico') was persuaded to approve a general withdrawal west. (The following day Rommel was given command over all Axis forces in the theatre.) On 11 December – eight months to the day after the first assault on Tobruk – Italo-German troops finally abandoned their last remaining positions at Tobruk and began pulling back westward toward El Agheila – the starting position of Rommel's initial push the previous March. Auchinleck's determination had, for the moment, removed the Axis threat to Egypt. While Crusader was a (limited) victory for the British, won mainly through overwhelming armoured strength rather than superior tactics, it proved that Rommel could be beaten in mobile combat.

The fighting had been costly for both sides. The British (up to mid-January 1942) had lost 2,900 men killed, 7,300 wounded and 7,500 missing. This amounted to 17,700 men, or 15 per cent of Auchinleck's force. German losses were 1,136 killed, 3,483 wounded in action and 10,141 missing – a total of 14,860 men. The Italians had suffered particularly badly, losing 1,036 killed, 2,122 wounded and 18,554 missing. Altogether, Rommel had lost some 32 per cent of his manpower. British tanks losses through combat and mechanical breakdowns were significantly higher than the Axis losses of 340 tanks, though many vehicles were subsequently recovered and repaired during Rommel's retreat, leaving only 278 tanks destroyed.

At this point we can consider whether Rommel's planned November 1941 assault on Tobruk would have succeeded if Auchinleck's Crusader had not pre-empted it. The pause in fighting over the winter months had given the German quartermaster breathing space to amass sufficient fuel, ammunition and rations for a renewed attack, and Rommel's projected ground-air strike against the south-eastern perimeter – both sides had chosen the same sector for the break out and break in – may well have succeeded. As opposed to his earlier attempts to storm the fortress, Rommel's men now knew what lay behind the perimeter wire, with detailed intelligence issued down to company level. Both Panzer divisions were earmarked for the assault, having been specially trained and rested, and the Italian besieging formations released the maximum number of German troops for the attack.

But it wasn't to happen. Instead, Ritchie's gave chase. His advance made better progress than O'Connor's had against the Italians. Gazala was occupied on 15 December and Benghazi on Christmas Day. But in a replay to events of the previous year, when British troops were prevented from reaching Tripoli by the fighting in Greece, Auchinleck was now unable to advance on the Libyan capital, and possibly destroy the Axis army in North Africa, as a result of his overextended supply lines and Japanese aggression in the Far East.

Pearl Harbor

Coinciding with the Red Army's counter-attack around Moscow on 6 December 1941 was a communiqué from Tokyo to the Japanese ambassador in Washington. Decrypted by US Navy intelligence it was, as Roosevelt declared, 'war'. Tokyo's projected strike against Stalin's rear had been substituted by a 'strike south' strategy to seize European colonies across Southeast Asia. The Imperial Japanese Navy, in particularly, was keen to seize the Dutch East Indies' oilfields (today Indonesia), after the US-British oil embargo that was imposed on Japan for occupying French Indochina (today Vietnam).

Now, in a carefully co-ordinated opening move, five Japanese armies would strike simultaneously: the Twenty-Third Army would invade Hong Kong; the Fourteenth Army would attack the Philippines; the Fifteenth Army would occupy Thailand (which practically resigned itself to Japanese control in advance) and southern Burma (now Myanmar); and the Twenty-Fifth Army would land on the Malay Peninsula and seize Singapore. To neutralise the threat posed by the US warships, especially in the Philippines operation, Japanese Admiral Isoroku Yamamoto insisted on a pre-emptive aerial attack to destroy the US Pacific Fleet, anchored at the American Naval base at Pearl Harbor. Zero hour was set for the morning of 7 December 1941 (Washington time).

The first wave of Japanese dive and torpedo bombers achieved complete surprise. In America's 'day of infamy', twenty-one US ships, including five battleships, were sunk or damaged in less than 2 hours. US aircraft losses amounted to 150 destroyed and another 159 damaged. Most were attacked before they left the ground. Total casualties in this darkest of days in US history amounted to 3,649, with 2,403 military personnel and sixty-eight civilians killed. (Simultaneous attacks were also carried out against Wake Island and Guam). Roosevelt cabled Churchill to report his declaration of war against Japan, assuring him that, 'Today all of us are in the same boat with you and the people of the Empire, and it is a ship that will not and cannot be sunk.'[15] It was an unfortunate metaphor, given the 'infamy' at Pearl Harbor and the sinking, on 10 December, of the British battleships *Prince of Wales* and *Repulse* as they sailed from Singapore to intercept a Japanese invasion fleet – yet another disaster that shocked Churchill and the British public. Within a week Britain, Australia, New Zealand, Holland, the Free French, and several South American nations (and even Yugoslavia) joined the war against Japan. China, in turn, declared war on the Axis states, as did most of the Latin American states.

Yet America's participation in the war against Germany – in a war that had shifted from being European to global – was still uncertain at this time. Upon hearing of the secretive Pearl Harbor attack at his Eastern Front headquarters in Rastenburg (in present-day Poland), a jubilant Führer turned to his liaison officer, declaring: 'We cannot lose the war at all. We have an ally who has not been defeated in three thousand years'.[16] Japan, the Führer confided to his henchmen, had saved Germany.[17] On 8 December he issued Directive No. 39, which suspended the winter march on Moscow and opened hostilities against the US. Three days later, on 11 December, Mussolini declared war on the US from his balcony overlooking the Piazza Venezia; Hitler's declaration followed that night at the Reichstag in Berlin. Victory, he trumpeted, would be followed by Germany, Italy and Japan 'establishing a new and just order'. OKW imprudently surmised that Germany could accomplish its objectives in the East, the Atlantic and the Mediterranean before the US could fully mobilise its military; that its allies could lift their efforts in the war and that the flanking neutral powers of Spain, Turkey, Sweden and Portugal could be induced to form a continental defensive bloc; that the US would be unable to fight an offensive war across two oceans; and that the Japanese would bleed Anglo–American forces in the Pacific for a considerable period. The German Naval War staff also felt that Britain's position in the Middle East at this critical juncture was now of even greater importance, not only because oil supplies from Japanese-occupied Borneo and Sumatra were lost, but to preserve sea communications (via the Suez Canal) and air communications with India, Australia and New Zealand.

Aftershocks from Japan's belligerence were immediately felt across the Middle East, where Auchinleck's command was tapped to buttress Britain's inadequate. Far East garrisons against the seemingly inexorable march of the Imperial Japanese Army. Within a matter of weeks, an armoured brigade group, the headquarters of the 1st Australian Corp, the 6th and 7th Australian Divisions, plus supporting units, were stripped from this theatre. Ammunition and supply reserves were also seriously depleted, with staff transfers affecting nearly all levels of command. The RN's striking power also suffered. Hitler had dispatched U-boats to the Mediterranean in August 1941 to combat the sinking of Italian convoys carrying Axis supplies. Early spoils for the German U-boats included the aircraft carrier *Ark Royal* and the battleship *Barham*, sunk on 14 and 25 November, respectively. The cruiser *Neptune* struck an uncharted minefield and sank on 19 December, the day on which the battleships *Queen Elizabeth* and *Valiant* were sunk by the courageous Italian 'human torpedoes' while at anchor in the shallow waters of Alexandria harbour. As the balance of naval power tipped in the Mediterranean, two Axis convoys, shepherded by Italian battleships, slipped safely across the Middle Sea without incident on 18 December 1941 and 5 January 1942.

Replenished and reinforced, while Auchinleck was busy rebuilding his Middle East command, Rommel once again set his sights on unleashing a new 1942 offensive, one that would overrun Tobruk and threaten the Nile Delta.

Afterword

The 242-day siege of Tobruk ranks, justifiably, alongside the great sieges of the history. Yet several senior military commanders, from both sides, questioned after the war whether Tobruk had really been besieged. Hans von Ravenstein, the former commander of the German 21st Panzer Division, argued that since Tobruk remained open to both the sea and communications with Egypt, the use of the term 'siege' was 'inaccurate'.[18] General Sir Thomas Blamey echoed this sentiment. In his view, the fortress was not besieged 'in the sense that Mafeking [in the Second Boer War] was', since it was provisioned by sea.[19]

The question of whether Tobruk was actually besieged, however, is readily answered by the definitions we saw earlier, as well as comparisons with the great sieges of history. In terms of absolute containment, it is rare that a besieging army was ever large enough to surround and completely isolate its objective. If it is accepted, especially in twentieth-century warfare, with the advent of aircraft, submarines and radio communication, that a 'watertight' containment of a besieged area is virtually impossible, then Tobruk was most definitely a siege; one comparable to the epic Soviet stands at Leningrad and Stalingrad – cities that the Germans were never able to completely invest, but which also ultimately contributed to the defeat of Adolf Hitler's Third Reich.

Synonymous with dogged victory, Tobruk was lauded internationally as the longest siege of the war to date; the longest in the history of the British Empire after the eighteenth-century investment of Gibraltar by France and Spain.[20] The fortress had become symbolic of Allied resistance against the German onslaught in the West, as the battle of Stalingrad (now Volgograd) in 1942 became symbolic of German defeat in the East. Paradoxically, this acclaim, as we shall see, would contribute to the fortress' unexpected downfall in 1942.

13

1942: The High-Water Mark of Axis Military Success

'We seem to be being completely worsted and outwitted, as usual by Rommel.'

– Sir Alexander Cadogan

The year 1942 began badly for the Allies. Germany's U-boats were indiscriminately sinking merchant shipping off America's east coast and in the Caribbean – the so-called 'Happy Time'. Gravely, more Allied ships were sunk in the first four months of 1942 than in the whole of 1941. Allied fortunes fared no better in the Far East, under the relentless Japanese advance. Hong Kong fell on 25 December. Japanese troops entered Kuala Lumpur the capital of Malaya) on 11 January, invaded Burma five days later and took Rabaul (the capital of the Australian mandated territory of New Guinea) on 23 January. Imperial Japanese troops also invaded the Solomon Islands and New Guinea on 23 January. The US was struggling to hold the Philippines, while the Soviet Union was fighting a series of bitter winter offensives against the *Wehrmacht* with German troops at the gates of Moscow. On 3 January 1942, Hitler explained to the Japanese Ambassador in Berlin, General Hiroshi Oshima, that once the weather improved he intended

to resume the offensive against the Caucasus and seize the oil
fields there as well as those in Iran and Iraq. Rommel's army,
he informed his guest, would form the southern pincer.[1]

Whitehall's attention turned to the Far East, in particular
Singapore, which was considered to be Britain's strongest
Far East bastion. After landing in northern British Malaya
(today Malaysia) and southern Thailand on the morning of
8 December, the Japanese forced the British back to the
southernmost tip of the Malay Peninsula by 30 January,
having advanced 621 miles in fifty-four days. We must
make Singapore's defence, 'as memorable and successful' as
Tobruk, Wavell (now commander of the Allied Forces in
the South West Pacific) declared in a special order of the
day on 4 February.[2] Four days later an Imperial Japanese
invasion force landed on Singapore Island. Trapped on
the south coast of the island, and confronted by disinte-
grating morale, panicking refugees and a damaged water
supply, Lieutenant General Arthur Percival's mixed British
force surrendered the 'fortress' (a contentious designation)
to Japanese General Tomoyuki Yamashita on 15 February
1942. A mortal blow to the prestige of the British Empire
– what Churchill described as the 'worst disaster and largest
capitulation in British history' – 62,000 Allied troops were
marched into captivity.

A storm of protest exploded against the Churchill govern-
ment. Closer to home, the British public was stunned by the
audacious passage of the German pocket battleships *Scharnhorst*
and *Gneisenau* and cruiser *Prinz Eugen* through the English
Channel on 12 February 1942. And the setbacks continued.
Japanese forces occupied the Dutch East Indies and invested
Burma in March 1942. By April, both India and Ceylon (Sri
Lanka) were threatened.

Malta's stoic resistance, in contrast, was inspirational.
Throughout 1941, British warships and aircraft operating
from the island had mauled Italian transports sailing for Libya.

Holding the dubious distinction of being one of the most bombed places on the planet, Malta was awarded the George Cross on 15 April, in recognition of its heroic plight, an unsinkable aircraft carrier and base of attack. Berlin and Rome both appreciated that no offensive could be undertaken against Egypt so long as Malta stood defiant and Tobruk remained in British hands. Plans, as we will learn, were therefore tentatively drawn up for the conquest of Malta once Tobruk had fallen. A decision also had to be made by the Allies on the larger direction of the war.

Germany First

Roosevelt's pre-Pearl Harbor agreement of a 'Germany-first' strategy was upheld at the Anglo-US Arcadia Conference, held in Washington from 22 December 1941 until 14 January 1942. Churchill returned to Washington the following June to discuss the opening of a second front against Germany. Strongly believing in the importance of safeguarding Britain's colonial interests in the Middle East and India, Churchill nevertheless wished to avoid any major confrontation on French soil in the short term, unless Germany's military might or morale had cracked.[3] He harboured fears of another First World War bloodbath in France, and argued against a major landing on the Continent, pushing instead for the main 1942 Allied offensive to be a landing in North West Africa. Confronted by a renewed Axis threat in Libya, the British premier provided his Chiefs of Staff with a series of impractical ideas: the occupation of northern Norway, a landing at Cherbourg, the reconquest of Burma and an invasion of Germany.[4] Upon his return home, Churchill was confronted by an anxious House of Commons, challenged by one of its gravest crises to date, and seeking an explanation for recent

British routs. This included Rommel's second unexpected charge across Cyrenaica.

Rommel's 1942 Offensive

The pendulum of the desert war had swung at the end of 1941 in Auchinleck's favour. But the see-sawing North African campaign now placed a new strain on the Eighth Army as its tenuous communication and supply lines lengthened. Rommel, in contrast, was now much closer to his own supply points: 'The battle is fought and decided by the quartermasters before the shooting begins,' he would (ironically) later reflect.[5] 'The situation is developing to our advantage,' he wrote home on 17 January; '... and I'm full of plans'.[6]

Ritchie had, like Wavell a year earlier, surmised that Rommel presented no imminent danger. For that reason, he ordered his subordinates to prepare a follow-up operation to Crusader, dubbed Acrobat, which would drive west and capture Tripoli en route to Tunisia. The Axis would be wiped from North Africa. But it was Rommel who struck first on 21 January, again catching the British napping. A combination of indifferent leadership in the field, equipment flaws and tactical errors once again saw British formations driven back east, in what colloquially became known as the 'Second Benghazi Handicap', or 'Gazala Gallop' – a striking parallel to events of March 1941. After five days Auchinleck had lost 299 tanks and armoured vehicles, 147 guns and 935 men taken prisoner. Rommel stated his own losses as fourteen men and three tanks.

The success of Rommel's retitled *Panzerarmee Afrika* surprised both OKW and the British. As one war correspondent noted, 'The unhappy, bewildered inhabitants of Cyrenaica changed their masters for the fourth time in little more than a year.'[7] Halting halfway back along the

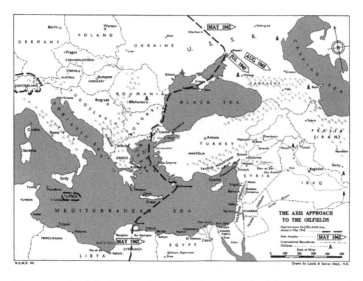

The approach of the *Wehrmacht* to the Allied oilfields of the Caucasus and Middle East.

Cyrenaica 'Bulge', British troops took up defensive positions along a new defensive line stretching from the coast at Gazala to Bir Hacheim, a remote inland oasis and site of a former Ottoman citadel. Auchinleck hoped the 73 miles of minefields and fortified positions comprising the so-called Gazala Line would shield Tobruk and provide Ritchie with a launching site for future offensives. The line's defences, however, were far from ideal. Instead of a continuous defensive belt, it contained a number of independent, heavily defended strongpoints or 'boxes'. Incapable of mutual support, each so-called 'cowpat' was surrounded by extensive minefields.[8] More than 1 million mines were laid, 'on a scale never yet seen in war', recalled Friedrich von Mellenthin,[9] Rommel's intelligence officer though many were so old as to be wholly ineffective.[10] Significantly, as we will learn, many of the land mines and defensive materials used in the construction of the Gazala Line were ripped from Tobruk.

Auchinleck's Leadership Quandary

Before we examine the fighting leading up to the next battle for Tobruk, we need to revisit the controversial issue of British Army leadership in this period, and its impact upon the events of June 1942. Churchill, disheartened by the unexpected success of Rommel's latest offensive, confided to Eden, his foreign secretary: 'I fear we have not very good generals.'[11] At one point, furious with Auchinleck's performance, he even deliberated whether he should replace him with the governor of Malta, Lord Gort.[12]

The beginning of 1942, however, was an especially difficult period for Auchinleck. Confronted by the pressing need to transfer the 18th British, 17th Indian, 6th and 7th Australian Divisions, and 7th British Armoured Brigade to fight the Japanese, he was also faced with a dilemma over the leadership of the Eighth Army. Even though Ritchie was initially cast as Alan Cunningham's temporary replacement, Auchinleck opted to retain him as commander – an equally incongruous appointment. Even so, the dismissal of a 'trusted friend and subordinate',[13] with whom Auchinleck felt 'satisfied' after Crusader, would have adversely affected morale and public opinion after such a brief period of command. According to one historian, however, Ritchie's retention after Crusader was Auchinleck's 'second great error of judgement in the Middle East', the first being his appointment of Alan Cunningham.[14]

Dissension over Ritchie's leadership now permeated the upper echelons of the Eighth Army. He was 'not sufficiently quick-witted or imaginative enough' to command an army, Brigadier Eric Dorman-Smith lambasted.[15] Brigadier G.W. 'Ricky' Richards of the 23rd Armoured Brigade, for one, was critical of 'no firm direction from the top',[16] while Dorman-Smith criticised the 'usual slap-happy optimism' within Eighth Army headquarters where the 'immobility of minds equalled

[the] immobility of formations'.[17] Announcing that he could no longer serve under Ritchie, General Godwin-Austen resigned after Benghazi fell.[18] His replacement was Lieutenant General William Gott, who, as we have seen, commanded the mobile forces outside Tobruk in 1941 and, as we will learn, would become a hapless influence on Ritchie's decision-making in coming months.

In yet another questionable appointment, Auchinleck switched his experienced Chief of Staff, Lieutenant General Arthur Smith, with Lieutenant General Tom Corbett, whom he had known in India. Unsuited to the demanding role, Corbett was unable to assert himself and manage the complex Middle East General Headquarters; his policy-making was considered indecisive and uninspired.[19] To quieten the mutterings about Ritchie's unsuitability, General Sir Alan Brooke (later Lord Alanbrooke), now CIGS, recommended his sacking to Auchinleck, who refused. Ritchie, in Auchinleck's opinion, had 'gripped the situation' and possessed sufficient drive and ability to lead the Eighth Army.[20] At the same time, Auchinleck had a poor view of his divisional and brigade commanders. He cabled the War Office in March 1942 to complain of their 'standard of leadership', a shortcoming that stemmed from an 'almost complete absence [of] systematic and continuous instruction in simple principles in peace time. Staff college training did not fill and is not filling this gap. Am convinced that we must act at once … to have [a] chance of meeting [the] enemy on equal terms.'[21]

But we must also consider Auchinleck's own competency as military commander. Possessing a 'first-class military brain and good fighting spirit', the Auk nevertheless lacked the leadership qualities needed at this desperate hour. In the eyes of South Africa's official historian, J. A. Agar-Hamilton, 'He never seemed able to get anyone to obey him … His intellect and understanding of his trade were alike excellent – his powers of command were nil.'[22] In Morshead's view, Auchinleck 'suffered from an inferiority complex and was a terribly bad picker [of commanders in the field]'.[23]

The ramifications of these leadership deficits would characterise British fortunes in the coming months; decisions that would decide Tobruk's fate.

Operation Freeborn

Churchill and his War Cabinet stood to gain tremendous political mileage by their decision to hold Tobruk in defiance of this latest Axis advance. As a 'kind of mascot' or talisman, Tobruk was a point of pride staving off the guilt from the recent losses of Singapore, Malaya and Rangoon. Beginning in early 1941, the British premier had become captivated by what he called Tobruk's 'magnetic attraction'.[24] And as the lure of Stalingrad would later dominate Hitler's thinking in the east, so Churchill's perception of Tobruk's importance would lead him to again demand its defence. Auchinleck, though, held otherwise. As early as 19 January 1942, he issued Operation Instruction No. 110, unequivocally directing that, 'It is NOT my intention to try to hold, permanently, Tobruk or any other locality west of the [Egyptian] Frontier.'[25]

Auchinleck later elaborated as to why he and his fellow Middle East commanders-in-chief were opposed to holding Tobruk:

> I did not consider I could afford to lock up one and a half divisions in a fortress. Admiral Cunningham agreed, particularly since the lengthy second siege had proved so costly in ships, as did Air Chief Marshal Tedder, who doubted whether he had sufficient aircraft to provide cover.[26]

A month later, Auchinleck softened his stance, informing Ritchie that the decision not to defend Tobruk now hinged on the 'effectiveness' of the enemy investment:

> If for any reason, we should be forced at some future date to withdraw from our present forward positions, every effort will still be made to prevent Tobruk being lost to the enemy, but it is not my intention to continue to hold it once the enemy is in a position to *invest it effectively*. Should this appear inevitable, the place will be evacuated, and the maximum amount of destruction carried out in it.[27]

Confusion within Eighth Army headquarters at this time is understandable. According to General Sir Michael Carver, then a lieutenant in the 7th Armoured Division, the consensus in Cairo was that 'if the Gazala positions could not be held, [then] the next step back would be to the Egyptian frontier'.[28] Plans were consequently drawn up for such a withdrawal – Operation Freeborn – and distributed on 10 May, after the British forces had withdrawn into the Gazala positions.[29] But when would Rommel next strike? Auchinleck initially believed that an early attack was improbable, in view of the weather, but a stream of Ultra reports hinted otherwise. A decoded Luftwaffe transmission of 25 April 1942 reported the transfer of a German parachute brigade to Libya 'for an attack on Tobruk'. A repeat request for photographs and maps of the fortress was intercepted on 5 May, with confirmation received shortly afterwards of a new Axis offensive, which included Tobruk as an objective, to be launched on 20 May.[30]

Inside Tobruk, and in accordance with Freeborn, senior regimental officers were notified of their roles in case of a withdrawal. Although disseminated in the strictest confidence, news that Tobruk might be abandoned spread like wildfire through the Western Desert.[31]

The Gazala Battles

Churchill prodded Auchinleck to resume the offensive during a subsequent pause in the fighting. But once again, Rommel pre-empted his opponent and dealt the first blow in his Operation *Venezia*. On 26 May, in the midst of a sandstorm, he steered his tanks toward the southern end of the Gazala defences while the Italians launched a frontal assault in the north. Time and again, the British allowed their isolated units to independently engage the enemy, while failing to launch a successful counterstroke. Nevertheless, they held fast. Rommel lost almost a third of his tanks, which for the first time were facing the new US (Lend-Lease supplied) Grant tank, armed with a limited-traverse hull-mounted 75mm gun (capable of firing both high-explosive and armour-piercing ammunition) and a turrent-mounted 37mm gun. Encouraged by early success, Ritchie went on the offensive on 5 June, hoping to sever the Axis supply lines. After making early headway, however, the British were beaten off with heavy losses, while Rommel withdrew into an area known as the 'Cauldron'. Ritchie chose not to continue the attack, a costly error that gave his opponent time to re-establish his supply lines and regroup his forces.

Resuming the offensive, Rommel swung his 90th Light Division (previously *Division z.b.V Afrika*) against the desert citadel at Bir Hacheim, the southern-most position of the Gazala Line, on 26 May. The encircled defenders of the 1st Free French Brigade (which had the luxury of three months in which to prepare their defences) fought bravely, refusing to surrender until ordered to withdraw on the night of 10 June. In some of the most costly fighting of the entire North African campaign, Rommel then smashed through the British lines, decimating enemy amour and overcoming the resistance of the independent fortified stronghold known as the 'Knightsbridge' box.

Two doctors later wrote of the carnage wrought. The first, a German, described an 'English troop transporter that had been blown apart by a high-explosive round. A horrible picture. Badly wounded, ripped off limbs and dead … [later] I went back with one of youngest [German] soldiers, who had been badly burnt. It was very moving how he told me about his grandmother and his home area, neither of which he would ever see again …'[32] Inside Tobruk, a British surgeon detailed the horror he faced within the hospital:

> We've worked flat out just snatching an hour's rest now and then. Once again we have all the awfulness of shattered bodies lying on the floor head to head with not an inch between them, waiting their turn to come to the surgeon. Limbs bent and unnatural in their brokenness, faces that look like smashed pulp, heads where the brain oozes out, the little room set aside for the dying, the stink, the filth, the flies, the absolute shambles, following a night's work, of blood and dressings and plaster and cut-off clothes.[33]

The Gazala Line was now unsustainable; Lieutenant General Francis Tucker (4th Indian Division) labelled the defeat: 'one of the worst battles in the history of the British Army'.[34] Auchinleck withdrew the bulk of his forces to Alam Halfa, near El Alamein in Egypt, on 14 June and ordered Ritchie, who had retreated to the Egyptian frontier, to form a new defensive line incorporating Tobruk. Three days later the 4th British Armoured Brigade was annihilated, depriving Auchinleck of any effective means of intervention as Rommel neared the fortress.

'A Nice Tidy Show'

General 'Strafer' Gott (now commander of XIII Corps) believed that the investment of Tobruk was now inevitable. He visited Tobruk on 16 June and began planning for a renewed siege, despite Auchinleck's aversion to holding Tobruk and the prospect of no naval assistance for four or five months. Misleadingly, he also notified Ritchie that Tobruk's defences were, in his opinion, 'a nice tidy show' compared to what Morshead had inherited in 1941. Gott also expressed his desire, possibly based on his own 1941 experience, to be given command of the fortress.[35] His poor opinion was accepted, his proposal rejected. Instead, Ritchie made the fateful decision of placing the relatively inexperienced and newly promoted commander of the (similarly inexperienced) 2nd South African Infantry (SAI) Division, General Hendrik Balsazer Klopper, in the role.

Born on 25 September 1902 in Somerset West, South Africa, Klopper had enjoyed a short period as a primary school teacher before joining the Union Defence Force in 1924. A popular soldier, rather than being academically gifted, Klopper rose through the army's ranks through his conscientious and hardworking attitude – admirable qualities in a peacetime army officer. Censure in one report, however, specified a need for personal development, describing Klopper as being 'a little too inclined to find excuses for things done and left undone'.[36] Attached to the College Staff of the SA Military College with the rank of captain in 1933, Klopper was duly appointed deputy director of infantry training for a period, and by January 1942 was appointed brigadier and commander of the 3rd South African Infantry Brigade. Newly promoted to major general, he assumed command of the 2nd SAI Division on 15 May 1942 – an impressive record for an officer who not yet reached his 40th birthday.

Too young to have fought in the First World War, Klopper had never commanded a brigade in battle. His fortress command at Tobruk was, unfortunately, his most challenging role to date, as well as his first combat command. Be that as it may, Ritchie rated Klopper as 'a first-class soldier', declaring that, 'I cannot want a better man for the defence of Tobruk.'[37]

'We Went through all this in April 1941'

We now turn to the week prior to Rommel's June 1942 assault on Tobruk, a period punctuated by a multitude of conflicting signals between Auchinleck, Eighth Army headquarters and London. In light of the decision to hold Tobruk only if enemy investment was 'ineffective', Ritchie informed Auchinleck on 14 June that in his view, a risk now existed of a *temporary* investment. Accordingly, he cabled the commander-in-chief for instructions: 'Do you agree to me accepting the risk of investment in Tobruk?'[38] Auchinleck's immediate response was that the, 'defences of TOBRUK and other strong places will be used as pivots of manoeuvre but on *no account* will any part of Eighth Army be allowed to be surrounded in TOBRUK and your Army is to remain a mobile field army.'[39] His signal closed by challenging Ritchie: 'If you feel you cannot accept the responsibility of holding this position you must say so.'[40]

This was an opportune moment for Auchinleck to replace Ritchie, or, as Churchill had suggested as early as 20 May, for Auchinleck to step in and assume personal control. Richard Casey, Britain's minister of state in Cairo, shared Churchill's view, although such a change, fatefully, would not occur until 25 June.[41] For a second time, Ritchie – possibly influenced by Gott's encouraging review – broached the idea of Tobruk enduring another siege. Like Auchinleck, he believed that Rommel was incapable of launching a renewed offensive, but that he could 'closely' invest the fortress. But for security's sake, Ritchie proposed incorporating Tobruk's western perimeter into a new defensive line, with a mobile force positioned to the south. Should the situation arise where Tobruk was either invested or its defenders were ordered to break out, Ritchie was confident that Klopper's garrison could fight their way out, though at a considerable cost in equipment and transport.[42] Ritchie's policy was to fight alongside Tobruk and prevent its investment. If Tobruk was *temporarily* invested, and the garrison unable to break out, he believed it could hold out for two months.

At the same time, Gott instructed the Eighth Army's chief engineer, Brigadier Frederick H. Kisch, that Tobruk was to be held with a garrison of similar size to the one of 1941,[43] though as we can imagine, and as Kisch later recalled, 'There was doubt in the minds of many of us as to whether Tobruk was going to be defended or not.'[44]

In a similar vein to 1941, Churchill pressured Auchinleck on 14 June to simply stand fast. 'As long as Tobruk is held, no serious enemy advance into Egypt is possible,' he stressed. 'We went through all this in April 1941.'[45] It was an obvious, yet, as we shall see, oversimplified and imperfect analogy. Major General John Kennedy, Britain's director of military operations, lamented in his diary, 'It is a pity that Winston's fine courage and drive cannot be harnessed in a more rational way.'[46] Swayed by Churchill's bluster, Auchinleck responded on 15 June that, 'Although I do not intend Eighth Army should be besieged in Tobruk, I have no intention whatever of giving it up.'[47] Privately, though, Auchinleck held that Tobruk would succumb to a renewed siege. With this in mind, he ordered sufficient transport to evacuate the entire garrison should a break out eventuate.[48]

Unlike Churchill, Auchinleck was wary of excessively interfering in the command of the Eighth Army and rendering Ritchie's task even more difficult.[49] Yet he continued to revise his instructions, ordering Tobruk to be 'defended without being invested' on 15 June.[50] Understanding the distinction was so critical that he requested his chief of general staff, Lieutenant General Tom Corbett, to personally deliver the order. But it was to no avail: Ritchie angrily refused to comply. At the same time, it would seem that no one deemed the danger to Tobruk serious. The British Guards Brigade arrived at the coastal 'retreat' on 15 June, seeking relaxation and bathing in the sea after the intense fighting at the

Knightsbridge Box – hardly a regrouping in readiness for Rommel's next assault.[51] Besides, as *The Times* surmised on 20 June, the primary threat lay elsewhere: 'pressure on Tobruk at present is slight, as Rommel has thrust his main forces east towards Egypt from El Adem.'

Compounding the apparent misunderstanding within the senior British ranks, and recalcitrance on Ritchie's part, were the reinterpretations of Auchinleck's original order. On 16 June, General Klopper received the updated Operation Instruction No. 28 from XIII Corp, which specified his accountability for planning a withdrawal to the Egyptian border, but with the stipulation that Tobruk must not be 'permanently invested'.[52] Ritchie flew to Tobruk on the same day in a captured Fiesler Fi 156 *Storch* liaison aircraft. His instructions were issued for the majority of the defenders to be positioned in the west and south-west. An assured Klopper – knowing little of the disorganised units from the Gazala battles spilling into Tobruk – agreed to hold the dilapidated 'fortress' for three months.

Klopper approved a provisional plan by Brigadier H.F. Johnson to co-ordinate the armour, artillery and infantry in a counter-attacking role via a combined battle headquarters. Yet at the meeting organised to discuss just this, the commanders of both Royal Tank Brigades, Brigadier A.C. Willison (a veteran of the 1941 siege) and Royal Artillery were absent. Worse still, on the same day, Auchinleck revised his original orders. He now sanctioned the possibility of Tobruk becoming *isolated*, although he remained firm in his policy of *no siege*.[53] His (contradictory) memorandum to Ritchie read: 'Although I have made it clear to you TOBRUK must not be invested I realise that its garrison may be *isolated* for short periods until our counteroffensive can be launched.'[54] Almost certainly, this was welcome news for Ritchie, who, after consultation with Gott, expressed his confidence in accepting 'investment for short periods with every opportunity of success.'[55]

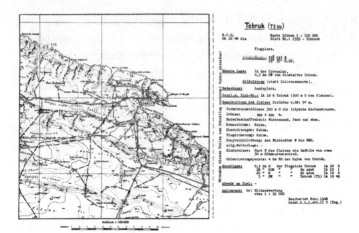

Luftwaffe map of Tobruk.

At this point, Auchinleck still believed that Rommel's troops were verging on exhaustion and that insufficient Axis forces were available to both 'invest Tobruk and mask our troops in the frontier positions'.[56] It was a view also shared by Eighth Army intelligence.[57] But on 18 June, grave news was received at Eighth Army headquarters that the neighbouring villages of Sidi Rezegh, El Adem and Belhamed had been overrun. Klopper never received the codeword 'Lamphrey' to inform him that the last troops covering his flank had withdrawn. It was only after his patrolling troops from the Umvoti Mounted Rifles discovered Axis columns nearing Tobruk that the gravity of the situation suddenly became apparent.

Further, the 21st Panzer Division reported early on the morning of 18 June that it had cut the coastal road, the *Via Balbia*. What Auchinleck had repeatedly tried to forestall since the beginning of the year had now transpired. Once again, Tobruk was invested. And once again, the free world was engrossed by events at that fortress, the only battlefield where British ground forces were in action against the Germans.

US Chief of Staff, General George C. Marshall, cabled his encouragement to Auchinleck, 'The entire United States Army is pulling for you in the gallant stand by your forces …' Now based in Australia (having fled the Philippines three months earlier), General Douglas MacArthur, Supreme Commander of Allied Forces in the South West Pacific Area, correspondingly signalled, 'We are all greatly heartened by the magnificent battle you are now waging.'[58] A confident Klopper also reported to Ritchie that 'the position was very satisfactory and that his harassing of the enemy was being effective'.[59] But while the telegraphs hummed encouragement, everything was about to get much worse.

'Tobruk, a Wonderful Battle'

– Erwin Rommel, 21 June 1942

'God bless you and may fortune favour your efforts wherever you may be …'

– General Neil Ritchie, 21 June 1942

The fortress that Rommel had branded as a 'symbol of British resistance' now lay before him.[1] 'Battle-scarred Tobruk is again besieged,' ran a newspaper headline on 18 June 1942 as the world once again looked to Libya.[2] Sir Alexander Cadogan, Under-Secretary of the British Foreign Office, and Churchill's chief advisor, noted dourly in his diary the next day that, 'Libya is evidently a complete disaster – we are out-generalled everywhere.'[3]

Rommel, meanwhile, marshalled his forces. An Operational Order for the assault was issued on 18 June. A relatively simple plan, in Rommel's words, it was:

to attack and storm the fortress according to the plan developed in 1941 but which had been forestalled by Cunningham's [Crusader] offensive. Under this plan a feint attack was first to be launched in the south-west to conceal our true design and

pin down the garrison at that point. The formations assigned
to make the main assault were to arrive in the scene unexpectedly. To this end they were to move on eastwards past Tobruk
in order to give the impression that we intended to lay siege to
the fortress as in 1941. Then they were to switch back suddenly
to the [vulnerable] south-eastern front of the fortress, deploy
for the assault during the night and, after a heavy dive bomber
and artillery bombardment, launch their assault at dawn and
overrun the surprised enemy.[4]

Reaching Tobruk on 19 June, Rommel wasted no time issuing
orders and assembling his forces prior to a final reconnaissance.
As the German artillery took up their former positions on
the El Adem escarpment, they discovered, to their amazement,
ammunition dumps containing thousands of rounds prepared
the previous November but abandoned after Crusader.[5]

Within Tobruk, it was a different story; ammunition was
about to become scarce. Klopper, who was eager to dislodge
the Axis formations from their forming-up areas, was advised
against this by Brigadier Johnson, who had only been in
the Middle East for a matter of days. Instead, Johnson suggested using artillery over infantry. The subsequent artillery
barrage proved ineffective in dispersing the Axis dispositions and may well have led to the rationing of ammunition
in the coming battle.[6] The paper war, a feature of the 1941
siege, resumed. Italian aircraft had earlier dropped propaganda
leaflets on amused South African infantry during the Gazala
fighting, urging the Springboks to 'stop shedding blood for
your English tyrants'.[7] The Germans now attempted to incite
rebellion within the Indian ranks by spreading leaflets written in Hindustani, and bearing the spinning-wheel symbol
of Mahatma Gandhi's non-violence movement against the
British in India.

On the eve of battle Auchinleck believed that Rommel
would most likely use his original detailed plan from the

previous November to assault Tobruk. Ritchie, accordingly, dispatched a copy to Klopper's headquarters. During the night of 18 June, an RAF Wellington aircraft dropped a bag of documents over the town, containing the fire plan of the artillery defences from 1941.[8] A second drop containing a copy of the German Operational Orders for the abandoned assault of the previous November is believed to have occurred the following night.[9] A subsequent signal from Cairo was received on the morning of 20 June, warning of an immediate attack, and also detailed Rommel's prior designs. Irrespective of how this intelligence was conveyed to Klopper, the important aspect is that the blueprint for Rommel's November 1941 plan was well known throughout the Eighth Army. Indeed, a junior officer gave a detailed overview to Colonel M.H. Gooler, the official United States military observer in Tobruk prior to the onslaught.[10]

A heterogeneous British 'garrison', certainly no unified body of troops, again occupied Tobruk. It was a situation made worse by a significant number of non-combat administrative personnel. Of the 33,000 men within the perimeter – at best, commensurate with Morshead's garrison of the year –10,722 were South African (including some 2,000 native non-combatants), together with 19,000 British and 2,500 Indian personnel. The principal formations were the 2nd SAI Division (comprising the 4th and 6th Infantry Brigades), the 11th Indian Brigade, the British 32nd Army Tank Brigade, the 201st Guards Brigade (the only mobile force) and four Royal Artillery regiments.

In contrast to his limited forces in 1941, however, Rommel's assault force – flushed with success – was his strongest to date: *Panzerarmee Afrika*, 15th and 21st Panzer Divisions, plus the support of three Italian Army Corps: the armoured 'Ariete' Division, the motorised 'Trieste' Division, and the 'Sabratha', 'Trento', 'Pavia' and 'Brescia' infantry Divisions.[11] Nearby, the Italian 'Littorio' armoured division was positioned near El Adem to meet an attack from the south.

Field Marshal Albert Kesselring (commander-in-chief South) reinforced the Luftwaffe in Libya with together every 'formation capable of diving' from Greece and Crete. He personally inspired his airmen on a flying visit that the 'broadcasting stations of the world' would announce their success, a sentiment echoed in an order to *Fliegerführer Afrika* Otto Hoffman von Waldau and X *Fliegerkorps* that night: 'The fate of North Africa now depends on Tobruk. Every man must know this tomorrow and act accordingly.'[12] Probing attacks, meanwhile, had begun along the western and south-western perimeter sectors in an attempt to deceive the defenders while the Axis army moved into position. Exhausted, Rommel dashed off a letter to his wife, 'Only two hours sleep last night. This is the really decisive day. Hope my luck holds ...'[13]

20 June: 'Sooner than Expected'

Lieutenant Heinz Schmidt recalled how the night of 19 June was perhaps the coldest that he had experienced in the desert. Or was it the 'suppressed excitement' of what lay ahead that made him shudder? Optimistic, he stood facing a familiar battlefield, asking himself whether this confidence was due to the current wave of success for the Axis, the certainty that Tobruk was less prepared than it had been in 1941, or the idea that DAK now had the best jumping off point for an attack?

The order to prepare for battle was passed down the line after midnight. Weapons and equipment were checked, cigarettes butted out, vehicles boarded. The German infantry alighted before the perimeter and crept silently forward, the bright North Star a navigational beacon for some. Tiny shells, relics from a time when the sea had washed over the desert, crunched underfoot. Fortunately, no landmines were detected outside the perimeter as pioneers pressed forward, cutting a corridor through the outer barbed wire entanglements.

A number of mines were lifted once inside the perimeter, however – a topic we will return to. The infantry now lay prostrate on the ground, in silence, awaiting the signal to strike.[14]

A thunderous, tightly orchestrated aerial and artillery bombardment of the outer perimeter opened at 5.20 a.m. 'Great fountains of dust plumed up out of the Indian positions, whirling entanglements and weapons high into the air,' Rommel observed.[15]

Simultaneously, Auchinleck, in Cairo, advised Eighth Army headquarters of an 'enemy movement' the previous day that would indicate an early attack from the east. A second alert an hour later advised that a 'crisis may arise in a matter of hours not days …'[16] But the warnings came too late. The 3rd Stuka *Geschwader* had already demolished the denuded perimeter barbed wire entanglements and shattered the morale of the defenders near Post 63 – a sector manned by the 11th Indian Infantry. As we saw earlier, dive-bombing was usually inaccurate, but this was more than compensated for by its morale-crushing effect.[17]

Pushing forward, the elite Italian 31st *Guastatori* (Assault Engineers) blew gaps in the wire in front of the defending Cameron Highlanders using large improvised Bangalore torpedoes detonated by German stick grenades. Pinned down by murderous fire, their advance quickly stalled. The Germans, to their right, swiftly punched through the Mahrattas.[18] The Indians, 'particularly the 2/5th Maharattas, hit back as best they could', a captain in the 115th Panzer Grenadier Regiment recounted. 'But they seemed to have been stunned by the suddenness of the attack and the shock of the Stuka bombing.'[19] Moving ahead under cover of a coloured smokescreen, the Germans recorded their surprise at the 'remarkably small scale' of resistance and the slow recovery of the defenders following the opening bombardment.[20] Their estimate, however, was not quite fair. Shortly after 7.00 a.m., the 2/5th Mahratta's reserve rifle company, assisted by the 2/7th Gurkha carrier platoon, launched a 'most gallant counter-attack'. Briefly checking the advance, however, it failed to retake any lost ground.[21]

With the partially silted anti-tank ditch bridged, the spearheading 21st Panzer Division pierced the outer wire ahead of Post 69 by 7.45 a.m., ripping open a yawning breach in the perimeter. The majority of the strong points between Posts 58 and 69 fell in quick succession. 'One position after another was attacked by my "Africans" and captured in fiercest hand-to-hand combat,' Rommel recorded[22] – a statement at odds with an account from a lieutenant in the Royal Engineers (who managed to escape):

> They did not attempt to mop up the defence posts but rushed on to the town. They halted within easy distance of the town, fanned out and swung around, covering the country behind them with fire from their guns.

To Schmidt's surprise, the garrison's artillery only began to lay down concentrated fire after 7.30 a.m., which was 'too late'.[23]

Unable to overcome the Camerons, the 'Ariete' Division followed the German formations before wheeling left. The assault, so far, had proceeded much faster than expected. Axis casualties were relatively light and the first British prisoners were being sent to the rear.[24]

'Completely in the Dark'

Klopper's senior officers were safely ensconced in their subterranean headquarters when they received news of the attack.[25] Peculiarly, up to that point, their reactions had belied the seriousness of the situation, or any forewarning of an attack. Klopper's Chief of Staff, Lieutenant Colonel P.L. Kriek, for one, dismissed the distant rumble of bombing as merely the usual morning Luftwaffe attention, while the squadron commander of the 4th RTR was allowed to sleep until 8.40 a.m.

General Hendrik Klopper's 1942 Tobruk garrison and the direction of the Axis assault.

before being rudely awakened by the news.[26] Moreover, Brigadier Andrew Anderson (11th Indian Brigade) had filed a reassuring report around 7.00 a.m., saying that the situation 'was in hand'.[27] This glib assessment surely fuelled what was described as a 'light hearted' attitude on the part of the Divisional Headquarters toward easily the most serious threat to confront Tobruk.[28]

Reverend James Chutter later described an episode he witnessed after the breakfast church services were posted on the Divisional Headquarters notice board:

> In memory stands out a rather truculent conversation with a high ranking officer: a strange and significant memory, for it

seems to suggest that neither of the participants in the alter-
cation, one planning Church Services and the other planning
not to attend them, had any realization of what the day or the
morrow was likely to bring.[29]

Remarkably, it was not until 9.30 a.m. that the British
Coldstream Guards received an order to counter-attack.[30]
Two Guards companies with six anti-tank guns arrived at the
rendezvous point – a shallow wadi 1 mile north-west of the
important King's Cross junction – approximately half an hour
later. But their supporting armour had already moved forward,
so there they waited. At around 10.30 a.m. the British tanks
were first engaged by the oncoming enemy tanks. Upon hearing of the battle, Brigadier Willison committed the remainder
of 4th RTR and ordered the 7th RTR to move to King's
Cross.[31] An eyewitness to the ensuing armoured encounter, a
major in the 2nd South African Field Battery, recalled seeing
that the tanks appeared not to fire as they moved to within
500yd of the Germans, before being knocked out one by
one.[32] The German advance was halted until heavy fire and the
support of the Luftwaffe silenced the British tanks and field
gun batteries. The 15th and 21st Panzer Divisions could now
continue their march towards Kings Cross and the harbour,
closely followed by the Infantry of the 90th Light Division.

Precious hours had been lost, from the defender's perspective. As late as at 11.00 a.m., as German columns inexorably
advanced on the town, Klopper complained that he was 'completely in the dark'.[33] He had expected the assault to begin
with a feint and – despite the intensity of the bombing and
terrific din – apparently believed this to be the case.[34] Through
a catastrophic breakdown in communication, the fortress commander had yet to receive a single report from the front line
Indian Brigade. Still unaware of the enemy dive-bombing, he
erroneously assumed that the perimeter posts were still holding out, when the German armour had in fact overrun the

11th Indian Brigade and 25th Field Regiment headquarters.[35] Little wonder then that the fortress commander maintained a 'sanguine appearance',[36] though of course this was his duty, in front of his fellow officers.

But Klopper was not the only defending officer cloaked in a veil of ignorance. A senior staff officer from the 11th Indian Brigade reporting to Fortress Command around 11.00 a.m. to present a situation report was 'received and delayed by a genial and hospitable staff officer who, despite protestations, found it difficult to understand that a cup of tea was not his immediate requirement.'[37] Arriving separately to collect orders, Lieutenant Colonel J.S. Alexander (commanding officer of the 17th Field Ambulance) was likewise struck by the cheerfulness of the headquarters staff as they returned from lunch.[38] Several hours later, at 4.00 p.m., as the advancing enemy front line was encroaching upon the fortress headquarters, tea was being brewed to celebrate the birthday of one of the Divisional staff officers! It was only now that the alarm was raised with enemy tanks 1,000yd distant.[39]

Fortress Headquarters' self-assured outlook also prevailed in the harbour area. The Senior Naval Officer, Inshore Squadron, felt so secure that he didn't request an appreciation of the battle until midday; later reports regarding the seriousness of the situation were also played down. Lieutenant Commander Walter R. Harris, South African Navy, was unperturbed after several large calibre shells landed in the harbour:

> We knew we had been surrounded for three days. But so far as the Navy in Tobruk was concerned no one expected a frontal attack so soon. This momentous day was merely regarded as another of the old siege days, and if anything, most of us felt quite elated at being in the centre of things again …[40]

At one point in the afternoon, a Springbok captain confidently assured Lambton Burn (RNVR), 'that the army had things completely under control in the front line, and the RAF had air superiority [*sic*] there.' Four Indian Mahratta soldiers who swam across the harbour from the southern shore and reported the approach of enemy tanks, found their claim likewise dismissed out of hand by the senior Naval officer in charge, Captain F.M. Smith, who initially branded them as deserters.[41] It would seem that the first Navy House knew of the breakthrough was the appearance of tanks overlooking the harbour. Only then was the order given for the miscellany of light vessel in port to hastily put to sea.

Ritchie was visiting his corps commanders outside Tobruk when, at noon, he learned of 'enemy activity' that was 'apparently against Tobruk'. Not until mid-afternoon did news of the imminent catastrophe filter into fortress headquarters – a 'scene of apocalyptic confusion and doom'[42] – via Willison's 1.00 p.m. report of the annihilation of the 4th Tank RTR. Yet an hour later, Klopper still believed that the 7th RTR remained operational when only four British tanks were 'runners'.[43] Reports received some 40 minutes later disclosed that the inner minefield had been penetrated and by 3.30 p.m. it was reported that sixty Panzers were approaching King's Cross. Willison's subsequent report, received later in the afternoon, sometime between 3.00 and 4.00 p.m., signalled the annihilation of the entire British armoured reserve force.

Orders were given for the destruction of secret documents. To his dismay, Klopper discovered that the signals centre, complete with telephone exchange and wireless sets, had also been destroyed. Symptomatic of the unfolding disaster, the 6th SA Infantry Brigade had still heard nothing from Divisional Headquarters. In his post-war history of the brigade, Brigadier F.W. Cooper described how it was only 'towards evening' that Klopper suddenly appeared in a signals van, advising that his headquarters had been overrun and ordering a mass break out for 10.00 p.m. that night.[44]

Rommel, characteristically, was in the vanguard of the advance. By 2.00 p.m. he was at King's Cross. Surveying the town and harbour, clearly his prime military objective, he later directed anti-aircraft and artillery fire on to a number of vessels attempting to flee, sinking six. As they began the descent down to the town, however, his column was slowed for a time by British artillery (9th SA Field Battery, a troop of the 5th SA Field Battery, a troop of the 231st Medium Battery RA and four 3.7in guns of the 277th Heavy Anti-Aircraft Battery RA) resisting with 'extraordinary stubbornness'.[45] Pushing through, the German 21st Panzer Division took possession of the town and harbour during the afternoon and by 5.00 p.m. Rommel's headquarters reported success, hoping to secure Tobruk 'before the day is out'. By nightfall, two-thirds of the fortress had been taken; the battle was essentially won.

Smoke now shrouded the harbour from the ad hoc destruction of provisions and vehicles, though no official order had been given. The team responsible for demolition sat through the night, awaiting an instruction from fortress headquarters to systematically destroy the food, fuel and ammunition dumps. But the order never arrived. The officer responsible refrained from taking the initiative, knowing full well that an imprisoned garrison would soon need these stores. Most of the defenders must have realised by now that hope was disappearing fast.

'Ammunition for Fifteen Minutes'

Klopper held a conference during the night at Brigadier Cooper's headquarters to review the calamitous situation. Surely disturbing was the admission from the Commander of the Royal Artillery (C.R.A.), Colonel H. McA. Richards that the artillery 'only had ammunition for fifteen minutes' fighting in the morning. An offer by Cooper to provide men and vehicles to collect and distribute ammunition from the dump was rejected.[46]

Yet the defenders still hoped they might save themselves, and perhaps even retrieve the situation. One suggestion was for the garrison to break out and, at 10.00 p.m., Klopper issued a warning order to this effect, although it was unclear exactly where the operational control of the transport lay. As an alternative, Brigadier A.A. Hayton (commander of the 4th SA Infantry Brigade) proposed that the remaining troops retire to the south-western corner of the fortress and form a new perimeter along Morshead's former Blue Line.[47] Eventually, the latter scheme of forming a new redoubt was adopted, because of an earlier order from Eighth Army recommending a delay before breaking out – 'Tomorrow night preferred' – and because it was believed that a British relieving force would soon reach Tobruk.[48] But as Cooper pointed out, eleventh-hour attempts 'to throw up fortifications were not very successful as the ground was frightfully hard. Most defences consisted of piles of rock behind which men could take shelter. The men kept at it all night, working like Trojans.'[49] Yet to be engaged in the fighting, their spirits remained high.[50]

Klopper, unable to reach Ritchie, signalled Eighth Army at 2.00 a.m. with news that it was 'not possible to hold until tomorrow. Mobile troops nearly naught. Enemy captured vehicles. Will resist to the last man and last round.' A response arrived an hour later. Ritchie, now back at Eighth Army headquarters, signalled that, 'Whole of Eighth Army has watched with admiration your gallant fight. You are an example to us all and I know South Africa will be proud of you ...'[51]

A twist developed around 3.30 a.m. between Klopper and several officers as to the best course of action. After Lieutenant Colonel E.J.R. Blake condemned the idea of the last-ditch defensive plan, Hayton, the main proponent of the redoubt plan, notified Klopper, advising that his battalion commanders now had little will to fight. This about-face, Klopper countered, placed him in a 'hell of a jam'.[52] Along with the many pieces of misinformation now circulating within the garrison, Hayton sent word that some 150 enemy tanks were massing around Ras el Medauuar in preparation for an attack along the western perimeter at first light. The South African infantry would be decimated.[53] Powerless to convince his commanders otherwise, Klopper resigned himself to the inevitable – there would be no final stand. Tobruk would fall.

June 21: 'The Decision to Capitulate Came as a Shock ...'

The seventeenth-century French engineer Sébastien Le Pestre de Vauban, skilled in the art of fortification and siege warfare, devised an etiquette that required the besieger, having broken through an enemy's outer defences, to request the fortress commander to surrender. Capitulation in such a situation was considered noble, as protracted resistance would only lead to further killing. Such a climacteric decision now confronted Klopper, some 300 years later.

By dawn on the morning of 21 June, he fatefully accepted that any continued resistance by the South African troops manning the improvised defensive line was useless: 'I am sorry boys, but we have to pack up. It is foolish to carry on. Gentlemen, I propose to surrender to save useless bloodshed.'[54] Klopper later justified his decision on the 'chaos' present and the 'concentrations of thousands of unarmed men awaiting the onslaught', presumably in reference to the stevedores, unarmed native and coloured non-combatants in the harbour area.[55] (He also attributed the lack of weapons and ammunition as the 'fatal factor' in his determination.[56])

Rommel, his signature British sand goggles atop his peaked cap, drove into the town of Tobruk just 24 hours after launching his assault. Surveying the damage with interest, he noted that 'practically every building of the dismal place was either flat or little more than a heap of rubble, mostly the result of our siege in 1941'.[57]

The longest day of the year had also been Klopper's longest. He notified Eighth Army headquarters of 'Situation shambles', and that he was 'doing the worst'.[58] *Parlementaires* were sent out at 6.30 a.m. under a white flag, to offer Tobruk's surrender. Soon afterwards German officers arrived at Klopper's headquarters to accept his surrender. Some 3 hours later, he met with Rommel on the *Via Balbia*, west of the town, to formally capitulate.

Whitehall received a most unfortunate appreciation from Auchinleck in the course of the day. Written on 19 June, it confirmed that the Tobruk garrison 'approximated to the force necessary to meet the expected scale of attack, and there were about ninety days' supplies and ammunition … We hope therefore that Tobruk should be able to hold until operations for relief are successfully completed.' As General John Kennedy afterwards narrated, 'This telegram was laid on my table simultaneously with another which reported the fall of Tobruk.'[59]

'What a night,' a German lieutenant in the 5th Panzer Regiment recorded in his diary:

> We assembled around the command tank and drank Scotch in the shimmer of innumerable fires … the red light flickered in faces, which were dirty and full of oil. Only our eyes continued to gleam … We had decided a battle; victory was in our hands now.[60]

Scattered Resistance

Rommel later talked with the bested fortress commander at his new headquarters in a former hotel. In his opinion, the reason for the abrupt capitulation was clear. Klopper lacked the 'necessary communications to organise a break out. It had all gone too quickly.'[61] Brigadier George Erskine, who was Gott's deputy, later interviewed a number of men captured at Tobruk. All concurred that by early afternoon on 21 June, Klopper was a 'beaten man with his head in his hands, bewailing that his "shell" had been broken ... his useless staff stood around, ineffective and inactive'.[62]

The decision to surrender shocked the garrison. Brigadier Cooper recalled how the blow was especially hard for those men along the coast and the western perimeter sector, though 'it was quite obvious to those in the know that the position was really hopeless';[63] it was with 'tear-filled eyes' that Captain De Jager of the Umvoti Mounted Rifles informed his men of the order to surrender.[64] Klopper, regardless of the facts, was the reason. The Reverend James Chutter observed that:

> The first to curse and denounce him were his own troops: his own Division. He has been accused of every military failing, from lack of courage to base treachery ... Human nature being what it is, blame for a catastrophe simply had to be passed on by every speaker, and it was freely and eagerly heaped upon the head of our General and his staff.[65]

Angry and disappointed, they felt that 'their fight had not developed. They had to leave their unattacked positions and march into captivity ... They had lost their honour – and not at their own hands.'[66]

For a seasoned British war correspondent, news of the surrender was:

> the bitterest moment I have known in the desert. At first it was purely a sentimental bitterness – a ridiculous, unwarrantable regret for a ruined, stinking, fly-blown town which had had nevertheless come to mean so much to us. But then

that was overtaken by a more immediate, human bitterness – a sick misery at this futile loss of so many men and so much material ...[67]

The 2nd Cameron Highlanders, and the 2/7th Gurkha Rifles, who had stubbornly resisted, were bypassed islands in a hostile ocean, gallantly resisting for a further 36 hours until the situation became hopeless and they surrendered. Some managed to escape. A miscellany of groups, however, including 199 officers and men of the Coldstream Guards plus 188 men from other units, slipped through the Axis cordon along the south-west perimeter to rejoin the retreating British columns.[68] Small bands of two or three men also escaped through the open desert, subsisting on the rusty water collected from the radiators of abandoned vehicles and scraps of food. One party reportedly captured an Italian tank, with crew and water reserve, using a broom handle as a weapon. Another group, escaping in a captured truck, were signalled by a group of Italians to halt, and they did so, hearts racing, until mines in their path were lifted and they were waved on.[69]

Within Tobruk, Rommel instructed Klopper that he and his fellow officers were responsible for order among the prisoners. They were also to organise their maintenance of captured stores. The South African officers were quick to assert their status – they were to be separated from the 'Blacks'. It was a wish Rommel denied. They were all soldiers, wearing the same uniform. They would to be housed in the same POW cage, the task assigned to the Italians. Rommel, whom Klopper later described as a 'tough, hard man', was particularly resentful about the demolitions carried out, threatening the South African general through an interpreter: 'I shall make you walk to Derna and you shall go short of water.'

Although the exact number of prisoners taken is unknown, the official British history concluded that some 19,000 British troops, 8,960 South African Europeans, South African Natives and 2,500 Indian troops – in total 32,220. While German losses for the assault, undoubtedly light, are unknown, total casualties since the beginning of fighting on 26 May were reported on 24 June as 3,360 men, representing some 15 per cent of their strength.[70]

An abundance of appropriated clothing and food was a godsend to the victorious Axis troops. Schmidt recalled:

> For a day or so we rejoiced in the blessings of the British Naafi [Navy, Army and Air Force Institutes]. It was a pleasure to snuffle round the field-kitchens, where pork sausages and potatoes, so long a rarity, were being fried. There was British beer to drink, and tinned South African pineapples for dessert.[71]

'Tobruk! It was a wonderful battle,' Rommel penned to his 'Dearest Lu'. A congratulatory Order of the Day to his men announced:

> Soldiers! The battle in the Marmarica has been crowned by your quick conquest of Tobruk. We have taken in all over 45,000 [*sic*] prisoners and destroyed more than 1,000 armoured fighting vehicles and nearly 400 guns. During the long struggle of the last four weeks, you have, through your incomparable courage and tenacity dealt the enemy blow upon blow … Now for the complete destruction of the enemy …[72]

Now he could follow in Napoleon's footsteps and rally his men onward to the Nile.

'Defeat is One Thing; Disgrace is Another'

'A painful feature of this melancholy scene was its suddenness.
The fall of Tobruk, with its garrison of about 25,000 men, in a
single day was utterly unexpected.'

— Winston Churchill

Winston Churchill was in Roosevelt's study in the White House
when a telegram arrived advising the 'unthinkable', 'Tobruk has
surrendered, with twenty-five thousand [*sic*] men taken prisoner.' It was news that Churchill, at first, could not believe, until
confirmation arrived in a second cable from the commander-
in-chief of naval forces in the Mediterranean, Admiral Sir Henry
Harwood.[1] 'Neither Winston nor I had contemplated such an
eventuality and it was a staggering blow,' General Alan Brooke
penned in his diary.[2] It was a bitter moment for Churchill:
'Defeat is one thing; disgrace is another.'[3]

Why Tobruk Fell

'I am ashamed,' Churchill confided to his personal physician. 'I cannot understand why Tobruk gave in. More than

30,009 of our men put their hands up.'[4] A spectacular military disaster and embarrassment for the Allies, just how did the 'unthinkable' – what Churchill deemed 'unexplained', and, it seemed, 'inexplicable' – happen?[5] Since the majority of General Klopper's garrison, including his senior officers, were taken prisoner, it took some time before accurate reports of the battle became available. In their absence, the first public reaction was one of stunned incomprehension. Baseless allegations spread of English-speaking German spies dressed as British officers having infiltrated Tobruk, of a fifth column and a massed German parachute drop. In a vacuum of accurate information, Rommel's masterful victory was seen by some wartime commentators as an 'abstruse subject', an event shrouded in 'contradictory evidence' and lingering obscurity.[6] The *Daily Mail* was blunt in its criticism, offering three possible explanations: 'First, our army was not good or strong enough; secondly, it was not rightly handled; thirdly, Rommel's genius out-generalled us.' From the victor's perspective, Lieutenant Alfred Berndt (aide to Rommel and protégé of Goebbels) believed that Rommel had 'outwitted the enemy' and that his success was derived from two reasons: 1. He personally made all reconnaissances and directed all battles; 2. He showed the greatest swiftness as soon as new possibilities of success arose. During the battle for Tobruk he changed his decisions no fewer than twelve times, driving his staff officers to the verge of madness.

Re-examining the fall of Tobruk today, we can see that it arose from a web of interlocking factors: the success of the 1941 siege, a succession of British leadership and tactical errors, and the challenge given to an ill-prepared, ad hoc garrison to withstand Rommel's most formidable assault during the entire North African Campaign.

What was Different in 1942?

In considering why Tobruk fell in 1942, we must remember that defending any stronghold – such as Kut, Bardia or Tobruk – against a sizeable enemy force is a task fraught with danger. 'It was inevitable that a determined attack would [sooner or later] breach a "ring fortress" with a perimeter of thirty-five miles, such as Tobruk,' former general Friedrich von Mellenthin explained in his post-war memoirs. 'The real test would be the enemy's arrangements for counter-attack …'[7] Tobruk was assailed in 1942 by a vastly superior German assault force, one that possessed significantly more tanks, aircraft, men, and intelligence than its predecessor in 1941. But other factors also played a part. Firstly, the British leaders – Churchill and most of the senior commanders in the field – erred in reversing the earlier consensus not to allow another siege. And secondly, Tobruk's defences had deteriorated significantly since the end of 1941. Let us examine these and other mitigating factors in more detail, beginning with the larger question of whether the defence of Tobruk was warranted in 1942.

Tobruk's Altered Role in British Planning

Holding Tobruk was not essential to the survival of the British Army in North Africa in June 1942. Major General John Kennedy, British director of military operation, noted in his diary on 16 June 1942 that Tobruk's altered status outweighed its military worth, that, 'The limelight had been on the place so much that its political and prestige value had now become very great.'[8] Auchinleck concurred. In a 1974 television interview, he declared that Tobruk, in 1942, 'had no strategic value at all'.[9] But how had Tobruk's *raison d'être* changed from when the siege was lifted only seven months earlier?

Firstly, Tobruk was no longer a solitary coastal stronghold, but a fortified 'pivot of manoeuvre' – one of a number of established Libyan strong points with which to 'break the teeth' of the enemy armour.[10] A 1942 inter-service agreement had also established Tobruk as the headquarters of the 88th Sub-Area, and the principal supply base of the Eighth Army. One of the army's primary sources of water, it was also an important forward base for the refitting of British tanks. Lambton Burn, a veteran naval officer from the 1941 siege, observed this transformation first-hand. He noted a different, more regimented atmosphere that, in his opinion, was 'not healthy', since the port – rather than fortress – had lost its 'splendid isolation'. New units arrived, bringing 'an avalanche of red tape, which put an end to the improvisation, the borrowing, the scrounging and the informal camaraderie-core of the old garrison's toughness and spirit'. In place of its once-formidable defences, Tobruk's primary value now rested on the docks and harbour installations, refrigerating plants and workshops, water distillation and pumping stations, in place of its fixed defences.[11]

The possibility of losing Tobruk had troubled Wavell and Lavarack in 1941 because of the vital stores that would fall into enemy hands.[12] This same predicament confronted Ritchie and Auchinleck in June 1942, though Tobruk was now an even larger prize in terms of its massive supply dumps of petrol, ammunition, transport and water. The roughly 100 tanks under repair in the workshops would be a jackpot for the Axis.[13] But whereas Tobruk in 1942 was different, and still important, it was not the essential redoubt that had withstood Rommel in 1941. It was, however, so very dear to the British premier's heart.

The Role of Winston Churchill

Churchill's doggedness, as we observed, was instrumental in shaping both the 1941 victory and 1942 catastrophe at

A Black South African soldier captured at Tobruk featured on the cover of *Die Wehrmacht*, 1 July 1942.

Tobruk.[14] Although not universally approved of in Whitehall, both decisions to hold Tobruk were at his behest, in the light of a rapid and unexpected Axis advance. At this point, it is prudent to recall the scale of British intervention in the Mediterranean – Churchill's largest single theatre on land to challenge the Axis, between the fall of France in 1940 and the Allied invasion of France in June 1944. Recalling the events of April and early May 1941, we saw how the British garrison at Tobruk had successfully thwarted several serious Axis attacks through a skilful co-ordination of defence, and a progression of errors committed by Rommel.

A legacy of this 'miraculous' stand was that by the end of the year, as noted above, the value of Tobruk's prestige had eclipsed its military worth. But in 1942, Churchill again needed a victory on land in the wake of the renewed German offensive in Russia, and Japan's string of conquests in the Far East. He disregarded a unanimous agreement by the commanders-in-chief in Cairo – *not* to allow Tobruk to become besieged again and to give it up should the desert tables turn again – by insisting on its defence. As Auchinleck summed up, the British leader was 'desperately searching after results, to keep the morale up in England'.[15] Tobruk had become a political issue; one 'that was bound to be a real difficulty for the Prime Minister,' noted Kennedy.[16]

In tandem with Rommel's push on Cairo, Churchill had travelled to Washington to discuss the direction of the war and the opening of a second front. Prior to his departure, Admiral Cunningham 'emphatically' condemned the possibility of a second siege, reminding the prime minister of the earlier unanimous agreement between the commanders-in-chief. Churchill, however, received the notion of abandoning Tobruk with scorn. Ignoring the decision of his senior commanders, he affirmed that 'it must be held'.[17] (Despite Cunningham's admission, controversy exists as to whether Churchill was actually informed of the opinion not to hold Tobruk.[18]) Regardless, the prime minister vigorously defended Britain's stand in his speech in House of Commons on 25 June, though he disingenuously attributed it to his commander-in-chief:

> If we had decided to evacuate the place, they [the critics] could have gone into action on the 'pusillanimous and cowardly scuttle from Tobruk', which would have been made quite a promising line of advance. But those who are responsible for carrying on the war have no such easy options open. They have to decide beforehand. The decision to hold Tobruk and the dispositions made for that purpose were taken by General Auchinleck ...[19]

It is pertinent to mention that prior to delivering his address, Churchill sent a draft of the speech to Sir Alan Brooke, CIGS, who suggested the following inclusion 'in fairness to Auchinleck, and in order to obviate any further allegation that your statement is not complete':

> When the possibility arose of having to withdraw from the Gazala positions, I [Churchill] and the C.G.S. expressed to General Auchinleck a strong hope that Tobruk would be held, but no order to this effect was ever sent from London.[20]

In deeming this passage unnecessary, Churchill distanced himself from any involvement in the disaster. Deceitfully, he later disavowed any knowledge of Operation Instruction No. 110 (Auchinleck's original January 1942 directive not to defend Tobruk, indeed any position west of the Egyptian Frontier) and the subsequent inter-service decision. In his post-war memoirs he recounted:

> At home we had no inkling that the evacuation of Tobruk had ever entered into the plan or thoughts of the commanders. It was certainly the Cabinet view that if the Eighth Army were beaten back, Tobruk should remain, as in the previous year, a thorn in the enemy's side.[21]

Leadership

As with all famous sieges and campaigns, the fall of Tobruk exposed the mettle and leadership competencies of the senior commanders involved. It also begs the question why such a thorny task was entrusted to such an inexperienced leadership group. The *Washington Post* ascribed Tobruk's fall to weaknesses in leadership and equipment: 'while there is nothing wrong with the British soldier, he lacks the leadership, organisation and mechanical aid which have so far accounted for Axis victories.' Turning to the beginning of the campaign the paper speculated that 'O'Connor was apparently the only man who could approach Rommel's genius'. We begin with General Hendrik Klopper, a relative unknown who, as one historian argues, never 'established his personal ascendancy'. [22] Assigned the daunting role of fortress commander, Klopper announced his appointment to his subordinate officers at a meeting on 15 June, only days before the Axis assault. He advised that Tobruk was to be held for a minimum of three months, though crucially finished the meeting without mention of a tactical plan. How was Tobruk to be defended? A second administrative meeting later in the day confirmed that the ammunition supply was adequate – a topic we will return to shortly.

Concerns regarding Klopper's suitability as commander immediately emerged. The American observer, Colonel Gooler, was eyewitness to the discordant working relationship between Klopper and his divisional staff and later reported on a 'decided lack of co-operation between the Divisional Commander, his Chief of Staff, and the heads of the various Staff Sections, in particular Operations and Intelligence'. Gooler presented a picture of a dysfunctional fortress headquarters, where:

> staff openly complained that General Klopper did not have the correct picture of the enemy situation or [realise] its serious

potentialities. And what was more serious, apparently did not trust his chiefs of sections. In my opinion he was not in touch with the situation and during the major portion of the 19th [June] to the best of my knowledge, neither he nor his Chief of Staff visited the Staff Sections ... although they were set up only a short distance from the Divisional Commander's CP [Command Post].[23]

Overwhelmed by the magnitude of the task before him, the relatively young and inexperienced fortress commander committed a succession of grave tactical errors. Suggestions from his subordinate officers were courteously received – and ignored. Criticism, for one, was levelled at the uncamouflaged transport vehicles that 'littered' the bastion, as well as the erroneous positioning of the 6th South African Infantry Brigade, which Klopper 'over imaginatively' placed on the coast, to guard against a possible seaborne attack, rather than committing it along the lengthy perimeter, where the enemy would more probably strike. As it eventuated, neither of the South African brigades participated in the fighting on 20 June; a plan to relieve the Indian Infantry with the 6th SA Infantry had been floated but never carried out.

Willison found Klopper's fortress dispositions 'anything but satisfactory'. Indeed, he became so anxious about the distribution of the armoured cars of the 7th SA Reconnaissance Battalion (twice the number of vehicles that were available in 1941) that he requested that they be placed under his personal command. Willison also condemned the placement of artillery as either too far forward or too far back, unlike Morshead's clever artillery positioning along the Pilastrino Ridge.[24]

Klopper's troop dispositions along the paramount southeast sector – where Rommel's infiltration would occur – also differed significantly from the previous year. Three battalions were in position along the perimeter line (behind which lay the vital communications hub of King's Cross, including the

El Adem road, which led directly into the town). Morshead, in stark contrast, had maintained only a single battalion in this sector, with another battalion available from the divisional reserve to form a second defensive line to protect the vital intersection. If necessary, a third battalion could move forward at short notice. Morshead was also insistent that essential infantry formations were not placed along the perimeter adjoining the precipitous Wadi es Zeitun, which he guarded lightly, using Army Service Corps personnel in an infantry role. Klopper, however, chose to position the formidable 2/7th Gurkhas here, at a segment of the perimeter quite unlikely to be attacked.[25]

A disparaging Springbok soldier who escaped capture suggested that General Dan H. Pienaar, commanding officer of the 1st SAI Division, was 'perhaps a more energetic and tactically skilful commander,' one 'who applied brilliantly traditional Boer strategy to modern warfare' and one who might have succeeded where Klopper – a relative novice – had failed.[26] And at one point in the fighting, a rumour even went round that Leslie Morshead was to be flown back into the fortress to rally its defence.[27]

We must appreciate, however, that the dearth of leadership experience extended well beyond Klopper.[28] Whereas Morshead's four veteran brigade commanders – Brigadiers G. Wootten, J. Murray, R. Tovell and A. Godfrey – had all served with distinction as infantry officers during the First World War, Klopper's headquarters staff were predominantly much younger, such as his Chief of Staff, Lieutenant Colonel Kriek, who was without higher staff training or operational experience. Two older and more experienced officers, though, were present to pass on details of the old 1941 defence scheme: Brigadier A.C. Willison (armour) and Brigadier L.F. Thompson (artillery). In yet another unfortunate decision, Klopper's request for the experienced Thompson to be appointed his deputy commander was quashed by Cairo upon news of the assault.[29]

Aggravating the senior operational inexperience was the apparently lax co-ordination between formations. Brigadier H.B. Latham, who was the commander of the 2nd Armoured Division's Support Group during the 1941 siege, for example, believed that neither Klopper nor his artillery commander, Colonel Richards, had ever visited the front line positions occupied by the 11th Indian Infantry Brigade.[30] Also, at no time in the course of the fighting did Brigadier Willison leave his dugout or directly influence the course of the fighting.[31]

The senior leadership void devastated the men in the front lines. Recalling the 'terrifying' attack, it is hardly surprising that a war correspondent with the South Africans condemned that, 'Worst of all was the fact that we did not know what was happening as there were no orders from our officers. Confusion reigned with fear and panic.'[32] An intelligence officer (4th SA Infantry Brigade) travelling on foot late in the afternoon to inform Brigadier Johnson of an order to send out a 'tank-hunting' force found him 'quite unperturbed … the HQ was having tea'.[33] A private in the 1st South African Police Brigade told of an order on the evening of 20 June for weapons to be handed in, only to have them reissued an hour later. In the absence of clear orders, and men walking off into the desert, he likened the men as 'sheep without a shepherd'.[34]

As prisoners of war, the men of the 2nd SAI Division – who had seen little combat since arriving in Egypt on 6 June 1941 – felt dishonoured. They had disgraced their nation. We saw earlier how the Australian 9th Division in April 1941 had been eager to emulate the feats of the 6th Division; so too was the 2nd SAI Division mindful of its sister division's record. Moreover, they felt shamed and loathed hearing 'themselves compared with the Australians who never surrendered Tobruk.'[35] Quick to denounce Klopper, his men poured scorn on him and questioned his decision to surrender. His reception at a POW camp in Derna shortly after his arrival revealed the prevailing mood:

The prisoners of war, especially those from the British forces, were in no mood to listen to someone whom they thought had betrayed them. They were in an angry and belligerent mood and, amid boos and hisses, Klopper did an about turn without saying a word.[36]

South African officers later imprisoned in the Italian Bari POW camp held what became known as the 'Bari Post Mortem'. Klopper and his divisional staff were, naturally, blamed for the debacle. Allowing for their expected chagrin in captivity, though, their evidence is still damning: Essential information had been withheld, and no plans existed for a possible break out (although orders had been received for such a contingency). Any mention of contingency planning, they recalled, had been met with the rebuff of being 'windy' (suggesting nervousness) and the sarcastic suggestion that, should they wish to evacuate, there was a hospital ship leaving from the harbour.[37] Equally, the SA Cape Town Highlanders had received an order that anyone leaving Tobruk would be 'classified as a deserter'.[38]

Esprit de Corp

Considering the succession of British defeats suffered at Rommel's hands since 24 May, Klopper had projected a misplaced sense of optimism. Downplaying the doubt expressed by some of his staff, he assured them that the nearby strongpoints at El Adem and Belhamed would hold, and was unrealistically confident that Tobruk could hold out for ninety days. In his last letter out of Tobruk to Major General F.H. Theron, dated 16 June, Klopper maintained this poise:

> Things are going very well indeed with us here, as spirits are very high, and I do not think morale could be better under

present circumstances. There is a general feeling of optimism, and I think there is every reason for it, although we expect to put up a strong fight. We are looking forward to a good stand, and we are supported by the very best of British troops.[39]

In truth, *esprit de corp* within Tobruk was flagging among the lower ranks. Rommel believed the 'bulk of the troops had already given us battle and were tired and dispirited'.[40] Several observers within the perimeter also detected a general feeling of despair among the front line troops. Only two months earlier, the South African censor had documented the struggle in the front lines, apparent from soldiers' correspondence home, of being 'tortured by dirt, dust, heat, thirst, cold, vermin and insects and bereft of all the freedom, individuality, amenities, associates and privileges of their normal lives', all of which 'would destroy all morale and courage, balance and sanity if not actively and constantly resisted'.[41]

Earlier in May, Crosswell Bowen, a US volunteer ambulance driver, noted several men with severe burns in the Tobruk hospital, allegedly due to an accident from spraying sand fleas when a cigarette was lit. But as a British medical officer explained to Bowen, 'It's more than burns they're suffering. It's a sickness of their soul. It comes from when they can't take life in the desert and won't ... Frankly I have never seen morale in the Western Desert as low as it is now.'

Australian newspaper correspondent Frank Clune noted a pessimistic, distrustful rumour circulating among some of the men prior to the battle, 'They will have surrounded us by the morrow, and we will surrender the place, as we have not enough to defend it.'[42] Fellow countryman and correspondent Alan Moorehead also found the mood of the defenders 'altogether different' from what he had witnessed the previous year. Likening the situation to new occupants of a strange house, he described the garrison as 'tired and hungry and embittered from their setbacks of the past five days'.[43] Yet it can be argued that the Australian 9th Division's withdrawal from the Benghazi Handicap into Tobruk in 1941 had placed it in much the same state, the troops likewise inheriting a deteriorating former Italian fortress that was far from impregnable.

Heightening the sense of foreboding in the days leading up to 20 June was the removal of troops, eighteen 3.7in heavy anti-aircraft guns – earmarked for an anti-tank role – and six US-made Grant tanks – surely a sign that higher authorities had precluded thoughts of another siege. Salvaged by the 2nd SAI Division, the six Grant tanks were regarded as a kind of divisional possession, their loss causing some heartburn.[44] The 'air of gloom' intensified inside the hospital following the evacuation of the nursing sisters.[45] Moorehead, moreover, observed that, 'It can scarcely have contributed to the morale of the defenders to see hundreds of lorries [filled with the troops of the 1st SAI Division] passing straight through the garrison and on to the east.'[46]

'As ever in the fog of battle,' the Reverend Chutter recounted, 'rumours were rife and repeated and distorted, according to the imaginative powers of the narrator.'[47] The 2,000 African Bantu people (of 2nd SAI Division), believers in witchcraft, or *tagati*, were demoralised by a Zulu witch doctor's forewarning that Mkizi (the Bantu term for *the Germans*) 'will come and take us all away'.[48] The native prophecy was apparently received as a joke by the rest of the SA Division, until a 'disastrous and insane' BBC broadcast – also received by Axis listeners – just prior to the assault, blithely announced that Tobruk was 'no longer of any strategic importance'.[49] Turning to his immediate circle, one soldier grumbled, 'That's our preliminary death notice'; another laconically remarked, 'they are softening up the British public for the shock that the fall of Tobruk may be to them.'[50] One of Klopper's last cables was allegedly to complain, 'I cannot carry on if the BBC is allowed to make these statements.'[51] A subsequent army memorandum in August 1942 concluded that there was a tendency among soldiers to regard such news broadcasts as 'an expression of the highest official opinion', when in actuality announcers had 'no official status'.[52] While the BBC was received loud and clear, communications inside Tobruk were erratic and unreliable at best. And little effort was given to solving the problem through liaison officers or the increased use of wireless networks. As we have seen, the absence of clear orders on the night of 20 June and next morning had impacted noticeably on morale.[53]

Lastly, British morale, particularly in the other ranks, was sapped by Rommel's escalating reputation as a masterful strategist. Unknown to the British defenders in early 1941, by the following year his eminence had grown substantially, through the publicity bestowed upon him by Allied politicians and the press alike. Churchill, for example, in speaking to the House of Commons in January 1942, paid tribute to Rommel as a 'daring and skilful opponent, and may I say across the havoc of war, a great general';[54] high praise indeed for Britain's foremost enemy commander at this point in the war. After he captured Tobruk, *Time* magazine rated him the 'best armoured-force general of World War II', and 'one of the great military commanders of modern times'.[55] For a time, British troops even used the term 'a Rommel' to describe an impressive feat.[56] Predictably, such complimentary exposure elevated Rommel to being the most recognised soldier in the Middle East, perhaps of the war. According to one observer, he was a 'general whose name, rightly or wrongly, was more of an admired household word among the Eighth Army than any held by our own'.[57] What we might call 'Rommel-envy' even prompted Field Marshal Sir Bernard Montgomery (of Alamein) to later hang a portrait of Germany's 'Desert Fox' in his caravan.

Sensitive to the menace posed by the Rommel 'phenomenon', Auchinleck later urged his officers not to be taken in by the cult of personality that had grown around their plucky adversary:

There exists a very real danger that our friend Rommel is becoming a kind of magician or bogey-man to our troops, who are talking far too much about him. He is no by no means a superman, although he is undoubtedly very energetic and able. Even if he were a superman, it would still be highly undesirable that our men should credit him with supernatural powers.

I wish you to dispel by all possible means the idea that Rommel represents something more than an ordinary German general. The important thing now is to see that we do not always talk of Rommel when we talk of the enemy in Libya. We must refer to 'the enemy' or 'the Germans' or 'the Axis powers' and not always keep harping on Rommel.[58]

But the message seems not to have reached Klopper's subordinates. A United Press correspondent scarcely exaggerated when he wrote after the fall of Tobruk that the root cause was a 'lack of aggressive spirit' among an officer cadre who 'looked on Rommel as a sort of bogey' and, mesmerised, 'let him make the first move'.[59] A memorandum on the 'morale of South African Troops', written in August 1942, raised a similar issue, 'It is interesting to compare the attitude towards General Rommel, who has been built up by propaganda into an imposing figure, and the attitude to General Auchinleck, where little has been done to make his personality familiar or impressive to his men.'[60] It may be said, then, that in many ways, the British were psychologically defeated before the battle had even commenced. As an article in the *British Medical Journal* (4 April 1942) detailed: morale, 'built by whatever means, is considered by the German leaders to be at least as important as weapons ...'[61]

'Fortress' Tobruk

In 1942, Whitehall, certain senior British commanders in the field, and the Allied press were collectively mistaken in believing that Tobruk's defences were in a state comparable to when the second siege was raised in late 1941. Churchill, Auchinleck, Ritchie and Gott all used the word *fortress* – a misplaced legacy of the previous year – to describe Tobruk in 1942. And as late as 20 June, Auchinleck reassured Whitehall that the 'defences were in good order'.[62]

In actual fact, Tobruk was a shadow of its former self – a neglected bastion whose walls had crumbled at the mercy of the elements, whose defences had been plundered and whose function had been relegated to more of a secondary role as an advance supply base. The progressive weakening of the minefields had started in November 1941, with large numbers of mines lifted in the south-eastern sector to assist the break out of General Scobie's garrison.[63] Sappers from the British 70th Division alone, assigned the task of rendering the fortress safe, lifted some 75,000 mines.[64] New Zealand troops, in accordance with Auchinleck's 'no siege' policy, also removed some 19,000 mines 'with full authority ... and in good conscience' for the fortification of the Gazala Line defences of El Adem.[65] South African Brigadier E.P. Hartshorn recalled after the war how units of the 1st SAI Division, among others, literally helped themselves to 'anything they needed from the Tobruk defences for the purpose of strengthening the Gazala Line. Mines, wire, steel pickets – anything that could be of use – were being removed in a spirit of "Help yourselves, boys, they won't be wanted here again".'[66] In marked contrast to Morshead's policy of defence in depth, Tobruk's inner minefields, perhaps able to stop the incautious at one time, were of no tactical value in 1942.[67]

From February 1942, new work toward strengthening Tobruk's defences was restricted to shoring up the western Medauuar sector and thwarting enemy raids by sea or air. As a consequence, the remainder of the perimeter defences were left to the elements, and certainly not maintained at a level capable of withstanding a renewed investment.[68] The first task facing Klopper's men was therefore to restore the run-down defences, particularly the minefields along the south-eastern perimeter. An enormous task, it was hampered by the absence of documents showing the exact location of existing fields, as well as ebbing morale.[69] An estimated 20,000 new mines were required to restore the minefields to a reasonable state, but only 4,000 were on hand. A thorough reconditioning would involve the colossal task of searching for and lifting individual mines, before remaking the fields. Many of the remaining mines, however, especially those of Egyptian pattern, had begun to decay after an extended period in the ground.[70] Disastrously, though, senior South African officers still believed that Tobruk's minefields, akin to Wavell's belief in a fictitious 'inner perimeter', represented a real obstacle. Klopped even explained to Lieutenant Colonel George E. Bastin (Assistant Quartermaster General) that he was basing his defence on the inner minefields localising an enemy intrusion.[71] As it stood, Tobruk's denuded inner minefields, perhaps able to stop the incautious, were of no tactical value in 1942.[72]

While the minefields had been stripped, a culpable lack of plans encumbered both the 201st Guards Brigade and the 32nd Army Tank Brigade in their primary role as the counter-attacking force. After the surrender of Tobruk, Major H.M. Sainthill, acting second-in-charge Coldstream Guards, explained:

> We had the greatest difficulty in getting anywhere at all because we had no maps of the minefields and we got what information we could from the South Africans. Brigade Commander helped us, but all he could do was send sappers to find the mines. There was such a mass of old wire lying about it was impossible to know what was what. The first information we got was when a truck was blown up.[73]

Issued with a trace of the minefields dating back to the 1941, the British tank brigade realised that the information supplied by the 2nd SAI Division was simply wrong, when enemy tanks were observed manoeuvring freely during their advance.[74] The Germans apparently believed that a secondary minefield stretched before the artillery inside the perimeter. Sappers using mine detectors were observed, at one point, testing for fields that the defenders knew nothing of.[75] Damning evidence from Lieutenant Colonel George E. Bastin (Assistant Quartermaster General) – who had been ordered out of Tobruk on a ship scurrying away from the battle, carrying 24,000 gallons of petrol – in the later Court of Enquiry later exposed Klopper's ignorance of 'gaps in the [mine] fields which tanks could go through'.[76] What is more, the fortress commander failed to comprehend that undefended minefields alone were no defence. According to Lieutenant D. Fyall (a sapper in 4th Field Company), all in Tobruk were influenced by 'that strange mystique the minefields exerted in those who feared them and failed to understand that undefended minefields in themselves were no defence'.[77] Britain's Court of Enquiry into the disaster (held in Cairo in August 1942) furthermore concluded that minefields not covered by fire, and which are insufficiently guarded, may offer a false sense of security to the point where it may aid the enemy more than defenders.[78]

If we look at reports from both sides, we see claims that Axis dive-bombing had been instrumental in clearing a path through the minefields.[79] Later experimentation by the Eighth Army, however, contradicted any 'chain reaction' method of mine clearance through bombing, verifying that bombing had little effect in exploding mines in situ, other than to render their lifting more difficult.[80] But the minefield, 'which did not prove any obstacle',[81] was not the only defensive defect. The boundary anti-tank ditch had also ceased to be an effective barrier. Current policy, when the 2nd SA Division arrived at Tobruk at the end of March 1942, dictated that it would be evacuated in case of a general withdrawal. Accordingly, one of the division's first tasks was to fill in two sections of the anti-tank ditch, dubbed the 'X', and 'Y' gaps, on the south-eastern perimeter, to assist vehicles in the event of a break out. Having already succumbed to months of neglect and the deleterious effects of the desert environment, by March 1942 the anti-tank ditch at the site of the 'X' gap required only a few shovels full of soil to completely fill it in. What remained of the ditch ahead of the Indian 2/5th Mahratta Light Infantry, who bore the brunt of Rommel's assault in the southeast sector of the perimeter, was now a nominal obstacle that 'would hardly have interfered with the progress of a garden roller'.[82] German prisoners later attested that the channel presented little difficulty in crossing. Wooden bridges specially constructed to cross the barrier were not required (though several featured heavily in propaganda photographs), and the depression was easily filled using empty fuel drums or rocks.[83]

Yet another problem for the defenders, as we have learned, was the design of the perimeter posts. As we have seen, the 'weak resistance' offered by the 2/5th Mahratta Light Infantry was attributed to the colossal Axis opening bombardment. The Axis onslaught, evocative of a Great War barrage, drove the Indian defenders below ground, into their concrete shelters – emplacements that we know afforded excellent protection, but were, as Morshead described, 'traps'.[84] Once driven below ground, the Indian infantry – in the same manner as the Italians before them – were rendered ineffective, and unable to bring their weapons to bear against the oncoming enemy troops.[85] However, before we rush to condemn their efforts, we also need to remember that while the commanding officer and staff of the 11th Indian Brigade were highly experienced, the 2/5th Mahrattas had suffered terrible casualties during the fighting of the previous winter, and the formation now contained many young and inexperienced replacements.[86]

Axis Aerial and Armoured Superiority

British fighter aircraft were noticeably absent above the battlefield on the morning of 20 June. Oblivious to the assault under way, Auchinleck nonetheless warned Ritchie that he was 'seriously alarmed' by the inability of the RAF to protect Tobruk. His army commander was henceforth to guard the forward landing grounds. Only two days earlier, however, the RAF's fighters were withdrawn from nearby Sidi Aziz because the Eighth Army could not guarantee their security. And only ten long-range RAF Hurricanes were available, operating from Egypt, although their effectiveness was limited to a radius of action of only several minutes. Even short-duration fighter sweeps over Tobruk, though, would have encouraged the troops on the ground and interfered with the uninterrupted, unescorted and unparalleled size of the Axis armada.[87] With information concerning the assault initially scarce, these much-needed fighters were diverted instead to escorting nine South African Air Force Douglas Boston bombers of No. 24 Squadron in their fruitless bombing of enemy forces along the eastern perimeter.[88]

The Luftwaffe and *Regia Aeronautica*, in stark contrast, played a pivotal role in the battle. Altogether, 580 sorties were flown on 20 June, equating to some three or four flights by every operational German aircraft, plus another 177 sorties by Italian machines. The Germans dropped more than 300 tons of bombs, the Italians around 65 tons.

'It cannot be too strongly emphasized', London's *Times* blasted, 'that apart from a blunder in generalship, the main reason for our reverse in Libya was the fact that once more we were outgunned.' Rommel, as we know, also wielded a far more formidable ground force than in 1941. His *Panzerarmee Afrika* was substantially larger, better equipped and more experienced than his original fledgling *Afrikakorps.* We saw how the 5th Panzer Regiment had first attacked Tobruk on 11 April 1941 with twenty-five Panzers, many of which were obsolete light tanks. His subsequent attack on 30 April was undertaken with eighty-one tanks, of which only half were medium and heavy models. On 20 June 1942, however, Rommel's armoured fist numbered 125 tanks, including more heavily armed and armoured recent models, in all out-numbering Klopper's operational armour by nearly two to one.[89] The tank strength of the 32nd Army Tank Brigade on 19 June was listed as fifty-four operational infantry tanks, Matildas and Valentines, plus a further twenty inside the workshops. All British tanks were positioned some distance from the perimeter and still only armed with the feeble 2-pounder gun.

Artillery: A 'Small Volume of Fire'

In recalling the decisive role played by British artillery in 1941, we must ask why then did artillery not feature more prominently in 1942. Similar to various failings we have so far examined, the cause was rooted in a multifarious mix of errors. The highly trained RHA Regiment was directed out of Tobruk on 16 June. 'Much would have been given for their presence ... on the day of the attack,'[90] Brigadier Johnson later remarked. Whereas Klopper possessed a similar field and medium artillery strength to 1941, most of the ammunition was stored in the main dumps rather than beside the guns.[91] Brigadier F.W. Cooper later criticised the poor co-ordination

of the artillery and the shortage of available ammunition.[92]
Rationed on the basis of a three-month siege, the daily allocation for the venerable 25-pounder gun, for example, was only
some 25 rounds.[93] Major P. Tower, a battery commander of
the 25th Field Regiment recalled: 'We had much difficulty in
getting permission to dump 200 rounds per gun and fired it all
on the 20th.'[94]

Although more anti-tank weapons were on hand than in
1941, including twenty-three new and relatively untried
6-pounder guns, no actual anti-tank regiment was present.[95]
And instead of building an impenetrable anti-tank screen, the
guns were widely spaced, up to ¾ mile apart along the perimeter. The arrangement might have stopped a broad assault, but
proved entirely inadequate against Rommel's concentrated
drive along a narrow front.[96] The Court of Enquiry judged the
defensive layout to be tactically outdated and requiring 'drastic
revision', especially with regard to anti-tank capability.[97] Major
Tower further painted a clear distinction between the operational capabilities between the 1941 and 1942 garrisons:

> It is clear from the records of the first siege that a highly devel-
> oped artillery force capable of concentrating all of its fire on
> any spot within the perimeter and any within range outside, at
> a moment's notice, was a great factor in defeating the German
> penetrations. Batteries and regiments of a similar artillery force
> were in Tobruk on June 20th 1942, and it had comparatively
> luxurious stocks of ammunition. The difference was that it had
> in no sense built into a tightly woven flexible fighting machine
> like its predecessor. The chain of command was vague, fire
> plans were complicated and obscure, and, above all, communi-
> cations were indifferent.[98]

According to Major P.G. Pope, Commander of the 25th
Field Regiment (positioned along the eastern perimeter),

forewarning of an attack against his sector was given, yet confusion arose when Richards (CRA) alerted him that Fortress Headquarters were unsure as to the *principal direction* of the German thrust. No additional artillery would be rushed forward until after this was known.[99] Like General Manella before him, Richards also believed that his artillery 'could effectively cope with attacks elsewhere on the perimeter'.[100]

Tardy in bringing fire to bear on the attackers, Tobruk's gunners also struggled to identify potential targets because of the dust cloud thrown up by the earlier bombardment and the use of coloured smoke. Not until 7.45 a.m. were all the regiment's batteries able bring down concentrated fire upon the area where the Germans had pierced the perimeter. It was more than an hour after the assault had begun.[101]

Absent too was the infamous 'bush artillery'. These notoriously unpredictable guns were again issued to the infantry in June 1942 – three to each battalion. Carefully sited during the preceding Gazala battles, however, the captured Italian guns were viewed with disdain and replaced by the new and unfamiliar spigot mortar on 17 June.[102] A heavy, low-velocity, short-range weapon (also known as a Blacker Bombard), the mortar had been hurriedly developed as a stopgap anti-tank weapon. Generally disliked, the anti-tank round fuses could be insensitive and fail to detonate, or alternatively expose the crews to a shower of metal fragments. Sighting was through the barrel, and only two rounds were allowed for familiarisation with this unknown weapon.[103] The success of the weapon in combat is dubious at best.

From the other side, Colonel Friedrich von Mellenthin noted the apparent lack of co-ordination between the various batteries, and, to his surprise the 'small volume of fire put down by the Tobruk artillery'.[104] Captured enemy sources also revealed the Germans' astonishment at the absence of counter-battery fire following their opening bombardment.[105]

History Repeated: A Failure to Effectively Counter-Attack

We saw earlier how General Petassi Manella had relinquished the initiative within his 'piecrust perimeter' by failing to counter-attack General Iven Mackay's assault eighteen months earlier.[106] In similar fashion, it was conceded from the British side that the 'lack of an early counter-attack [had] led to our failure to hold Tobruk'.[107] Reviewing the order of events, we see that it was not until 4.00 a.m. on the morning of 20 June that South African headquarters in Tobruk circulated a warning that an attack was expected, either in the east or at Ras el Medauuar in the west.[108] Roughly 2½ hours later, this warning reached the garrison's 32nd Army Tank Brigade – which raises the question of what might have occurred had this information been received earlier. Could the tanks of the 4th RTR have been positioned in 11th Indian Brigade area by dawn?[109] Certainly, Brigadier Anderson (11th Indian Brigade) held that if the divisional reserve had arrived an hour earlier, it would in all probability have closed the breach in the perimeter before the arrival of the enemy tanks.[110]

Three separate plans for counter-attacking in the eastern perimeter sector alone, using the Guards Brigade and the tanks of the 4th RTR, were circulated prior to the assault. These three plans, however, were all dependent upon the success of the British armour, although no rehearsal had been undertaken prior to the attack. As it happened, the Valentine and Matilda tanks crews, who had been 'standing to' since 7.00 a.m., did not reach the King's Cross intersection until 9.30 a.m..[111] Brigadier Anderson urgently needed the British tanks to stem the progress of the German infantry while the Guards infantry and their new 6-pounder anti-tank guns halted the enemy armour, which would allow the sappers to re-lay mines ahead of the enemy advance. But that didn't happen.

Conversing around 10.00 a.m. Lieutenant Colonel W. Reeves (commander of the 4th RTR) and Lieutenant Colonel Henry Foote (commander of the 7th RTR, ordered to take up position west of King's Cross) both agreed that the situation, though grave, was not desperate; the enemy penetration could be halted at the inner minefield. Foote subsequently reported that the situation was in hand to 11th Brigade Headquarters. This positive news was relayed by Brigadier Anderson to Fortress Headquarters, who issued a confident situation report around 12.00 p.m.

Despite Brigadier Willison's verbal order for co-operation between infantry and armour formations, Lieutenant Colonel W. Reeves (commander of the 4th RTR) neglected to contact either the Indian Brigade or the Coldstream Guards, seemingly concerned only with the movement of his own tanks – the closest armour to the German push. Reeves wasted valuable time journeying to the Tank Brigade headquarters to formally receive orders. As we observed earlier, his squadron of tanks did eventually arrive at King's Cross, but without the accompanying infantry needed to replace losses, guard the artillery batteries or hold any recovered ground.[112] Rather than unified action under a joint command, the two brigades of the counter-attacking force operated independently. Ignoring the principle of concentration, they were soon destroyed in piecemeal fashion.[113]

In a critical explanation as to why no definite counterattack plan was issued, one officer who managed to escape, Major J.R. Holden, pointed to the absence of a directive from division headquarters, the 'obvious lassitude' of Klopper, a lack of co-ordination with Colonel H. Richards' fire plan, no rehearsal, a failure by the headquarters of the 32nd Army Tank Brigade and the 201st Guards Brigade 'to press more strongly for orders and direction', and a failure by the two brigades to co-operate 'to the best of their ability'.[114] Here is yet more damning evidence of the failure to co-ordinate tactics and respond energetically and appropriately to shifts in the tide of the battle and the chronic misuse of armour that had doomed Tobruk since the beginning of the Gazala battles.[115]

Intelligence

The Eighth Army had amassed a wealth of intelligence prior to 20 June. Ultra decrypts had confirmed Rommel's intention to seize Tobruk, and his November 1941 plan for storming the fortress was in British hands – dropped by air to the fortress – and well known by many British staff officers. The Intelligence Directorate in Cairo, according to Major General Sir Francis de Guingand reasoned that the same plan would be adopted in 1942, though 'being forewarned didn't help us'.[116] Patrol reports by the 11th Indian Infantry Brigade added further weight as to where the main blow would strike, yet Klopper seems to have been more influenced by Ritchie, who had earlier suggested on 16 June that the enemy would stage a feint in the south-east before striking west at the Ras el Medauuar sector.

Rommel, on the other hand, was privy to the most remarkable intelligence – what he called the 'Good Source' – during the first half of 1942.[117] Unlike the dearth of intelligence available to him in early 1941, he received regular detailed appreciations of British dispositions in the Western Desert in June 1942 via the monitoring of British radio communications and the interception of detailed communiqués transmitted by the American military attaché in Cairo, Colonel Bonner F. Fellers. According to Rommel's former intelligence officer, Hans-Otto Behrendt, Fellers' diligent and detailed reporting to Washington was 'stupefying' in its 'openness' and spectacularly useful in the weeks after 26 May when Rommel punched through the Gazala Line and moved on Tobruk.[118] British spymaster (and supposed inspiration for the

James Bond spy character), Sir William Stephenson, even went so far as to suggest that 'the unadvertised tragedy' of Tobruk lay in the intelligence 'innocently' provided by Fellers' cables.[119]

Conclusion

To understand the capitulation of British-held Tobruk is to understand an embarrassment of factors merging in alignment. Like any major disaster, no single element comes to the fore; rather, a series of unfortunate elements unfolded in chorus. It begins with the agreed to 'no-siege' policy at the beginning of 1942 and the subsequent change of tack. We find damning evidence provided by those who evaded capture and in the official Court of Enquiry, regarding lapses in leadership, the inability of the garrison to counter-attack forcefully and the chronic misuse of armour – a limitation that had dogged the Eighth Army since the beginning of the Gazala battles.[120] Six months after its relief, Tobruk was at its weakest point under British tenure. Minefields in the area where Rommel's armour broke through proved ineffective, largely because they were practically non-existent.[121] The silted-up anti-tank ditch proved ineffectual, and the focused dive-bombing of the perimeters posts forced the Indian defending infantry underground, their morale crushed. Morale within the perimeter was also low; air support was non-existent. The garrison's artillery, having played such a fundamental role in 1941, lacked ammunition and the anti-tank guns were far too dispersed to provide a solid defensive barrier.

Major Tower believed that:

> The new 'defenders' of Tobruk were caught with their 'pants down'. They had very little time to put their defences in first class shape, they had few documents, such as mine charts, to

show them how their predecessors had done it, and, above all, their morale sagged considerably.[122]

In sum, we find all these factors deeply affecting a garrison hopelessly incapable of halting what the US War Department regarded as 'one of the outstanding instances of the closet co-operation between tanks, artillery and infantry in the whole [North Africa] campaign'.[123]

In the end, the official Court of Enquiry exonerated Klopper and attributed the disaster to the factors we have reviewed above:

> The eleventh-hour reversal of policy leading to the decision to hold the Fortress, regardless of the fact that Eighth Army was then in full retreat in the face of an enemy who had been uniformly successful and whose morale must in consequence have been high. It was impossible in the time available to make adequate preparations for the completely new role imposed upon the Garrison, which up to then had only been concerned with prevention of raids by land, air or sea.[124]

Klopper later escaped from an Italian POW camp at Sulmona in October 1943 after an eighteen-day trek over mountainous sheep trails. 'So, at last the full true story of those two tragic days in Tobruk will be told,' the *Daily Mail* questioned. 'There are a thousand things to be cleared up.' Churchill announced Klopper's flight to the House of Commons: 'Everyone will congratulate this gallant officer on his escape ... In due course I have no doubt the story of what happened at Tobruk in June 1942 will be reconstructed.' A 'returned soldier' – surely Klopper – later provided his version of the fall of Tobruk in the *Natal Mercury*:

> Many people still think that Tobruk fell without a fight. Tobruk fell because of a series of defeats and catastrophies

out in the desert long before the enemy columns pierced the perimeter. These defeats and catastrophies occurred because Rommel brilliantly exploited the limitations of our general defence strategy.[125]

In his post-war defence, Klopper similarly looked beyond the perimeter to senior British commanders who had insufficiently prepared the port's defences and then never undertaken the promised counter-attack. He argued in response to a despatch by Auchinleck, which we will examine, that responsibility for the fall of Tobruk resided with the decision-makers outside of the perimeter rather than the men within.[126]

Aftermath

'Tobruk was the key to Egypt; without that port Rommel
could not attack the Delta, with it he could.'

                – Lieutenant General Sir Francis Tucker

'The Fall of Tobruk reverberated round the world.'

                              – Winston Churchill

In July 1945, after the surrender of Nazi Germany, Churchill's
personal physician broached the subject of whether the fall of
Tobruk was the worst moment of the war for him. It was now
three years after the event, and in very different circumstances,
he replied immediately:

> Oh, no, it was painful like a boil, but it was not a cancer. I was
> miserable because thirty-three thousand men had laid down their
> arms; even now we don't know why. It was a muddle, but all war is
> a muddle. The two critical moments in the war, when everything
> was at stake, were the Battle of Britain and the submarine attack.[1]

In this interchange, the fall of Tobruk – a disaster Churchill
had been instrumental in causing – is relegated by the man

who had once so desperately sought victory there to a lesser setback; the man who had fought so hard for it was now discounting its importance. We have studied why the garrison laid down its arms, but the inference remains that Tobruk's importance in the war was minor in comparison to other turning points. True, Tobruk was not a key turning point of the war, such as Stalingrad, El Alamein or Midway. But the 'miraculous' 1941 stand was still a defining moment in Britain's war against Germany, before the Americans stepped in and began to share the honours. Britain's senior military leaders again turned to Tobruk during the darkest months of 1942, but with a catastrophic upshot that precipitated the fighting at El Alamein; a victory – occurring before Stalingrad – that heralded the beginning of the end of the Third Reich.

Upshot from the Fall of Tobruk

Rommel's greatest victory as General Franz Halder noted astutely, was 'of equally great value from the military and the political aspect'.[2] Its exceptional, far-reaching consequences would, ironically, also doom Axis fortunes in the Mediterranean. It was, at first, a shot in the arm for the Axis partners at a critical stage of the war. Possibly the most significant reaction came from Berlin. Hitler found the victory 'as great as it was inconceivable, and at the moment it comes as a real stroke of fortune for the German people'.[3] In gratitude, he immediately promoted 49-year-old Rommel to field marshal, Germany's youngest. This was 'like a dream', Rommel confided to his wife, though he added, 'I would rather he had given me one more division.'[4] Forgetting to change his epaulettes, Kesselring gave him his.

One of Rommel's subordinate officers was recuperating in a German hospital, 'glued to the radio' when news of Tobruk broke:

When things looked bad on the Russian front, with the encirclement at Stalingrad beginning to loom, Rommel's exploits in North Africa at last offered people a ray of hope again.[5]

Naturally, Goebbels seized upon the victory. With morale waning under the weight of the Allied bombing campaign, he coined the slogan: 'Our revenge for [the bombing of Cologne] is Tobruk.'[6] He mocked the British leadership, Churchill did not have a 'single general who has shown himself a real commander, on any current field of battle ... everyone a failure', and scoffed at the possibility of US intervention on a second front.[7] *Die Wehrmacht*, the German armed forces newspaper, trumpeted: 'Tobruk, the Verdun of the desert had fallen.'[8]

After nearly three years of war the German people were overjoyed by the good news from Africa. Swedish newspaper correspondent Arvid Fredborg (*Svenska Dagbladet*), based in Berlin, recorded how the 'unbelievable [had] occurred':

> Public spirits rose at once to a peak not experienced since the conclusion of the battle of France in 1940. Rommel was the man of the day to whom nothing seemed impossible. Perhaps we can win the war after all, everybody said, and gave themselves up to jubilation over a victory which they felt really was a victory.[9]

Lucie (Rommel's wife) wrote of a German populace 'full of just pride and admiration'; 'the entire people ... look up to you now that you have achieved the incredible feat of capturing Tobruk in such short time. I wonder what you felt like, entering Tobruk with your gallant men.'[10] Japan's ambassador in Berlin cabled Tokyo with news that the 'campaign has been a great victory surpassing expectations'.[11]

Tobruk was also a momentous victory for the Italians. Indeed, one of the reasons Kesselring had pressed for its capture was to elevate Italian prestige by reclaiming their former fortress. 'With the capture of TOBRUK a festering wound on Italian military honour had been closed', he later wrote.[12] Rommel's 1942 offensive also brought renewed hope to Mussolini, at a time when the Italians were becoming increasingly pessimistic about the Russian front and their partnership with Nazi Germany. Count Ciano believed that 'new developments' would now unfold.[13] A buoyant Mussolini flew to Libya with his prized white charger, in preparation for a ceremonious entry into the Nile Delta on the heels of the defeated Eighth Army.

But the fruits of victory were to quickly sour in Rome. Indignation arose over the delicate issue of Rommel's elevation and whether Generals Bastico and Cavallero should also have been promoted.[14] Mussolini also grew weary of Rommel's crowning association with Tobruk, his promotion and the sensitivity that it was a German victory, not an Italian one.[15] Regardless of its lesser role in the victory, planning commenced in Rome for the future governing of Egypt,[16] which Hitler had decided to place under Italian sovereignty.

Malta Spared

Thanks to Rommel, Malta had earned a reprieve. As Churchill later affirmed: the 'shattering and grievous loss of Tobruk' had spared Malta from the 'supreme trial'.[17] Earlier, on 28 April 1942 Mussolini and his staff had arrived by train at Klessheim Castle at Puch, near Salzburg, for a series of talks with Hitler and his generals regarding the direction of the war. Malta dominated the discussions. The Italians were keen to occupy the island as soon as possible whereas Hitler – swayed by Rommel and his 'almost hypnotic influence', according to Kesselring – was in favour of Tobruk.[18] It was agreed that Axis forces in Libya would seize Tobruk at the end of May. Malta would then be assaulted (Operation Hercules) after the full moon on 13 July.

On the evening of the Axis triumph at Tobruk, a letter penned by General Cavallero and signed by Mussolini was dispatched to Berlin. It called upon the Führer to 'consolidate the current results as quickly as possible', the centre of the strategic picture being Malta. A staunch advocate of the Malta project, Cavallero believed that a continued offensive into Egypt could provoke an Allied landing in Tunisia and threaten the rear of the Axis in North Africa. Rommel had also sent a message to Berlin, requesting permission to proceed to the Nile Delta. After ruminating on the subject for two days, Hitler responded in letter on 23 June:

> Duce, at this time, when historic events are in the offing, I would like to explain my thoughts as concisely as possible regarding a decision that may have a decisive impact on the course of the war. Destiny, Duce, has given us an opening that will never again become available in the same theatre of operations … The British Eighth Army is virtually destroyed.
>
> At Tobruk, with its practically intact harbour and piers, you have, Duce, an auxiliary base that is all the more important in that the British themselves have built a railroad all the way to Egypt. If we fail to pursue the remains of this British army now with the utmost effort of each soldier, we will follow a fate identical to that of the British when they lost the advantage very close to Tripoli because they diverted troops to Greece. Only this capital mistake of the British high command made our effort in reconquering Cyrenaica a success.
>
> If our forces do not march forward to the extreme limit, into the heart of Egypt, we will be faced with new, long-range American bombers able to reach Italy. At the same time, British and American forces can link together from all sides … This time, Egypt can, under certain conditions, be taken

from England. The consequences will have repercussions all over the world. Our own offensive, helped by the occupation of Sebastopol [in Crimea], will determine the fall of the entire eastern structure of the British Empire.[19]

From a 'deeply concerned heart', Hitler offered his advice, in effect an order, that operations into Egypt continue, for 'the goddess of fortune in battle comes to commanders only once, and he who fails to seize the opportunity will never be given a second chance'.[20] Mussolini's reply, which endorsed Hitler's appeal, stirred Comando Supremo to postpone the invasion of Malta until beginning of September and instead push on toward Cairo. Conceivably, not since the German intervention into Libya had an Axis decision of such magnitude affecting the war in the Middle East and Mediterranean been made; in effect the entire German–Italian Mediterranean policy had been placed at risk.[21] But while the tiny island stood proud, the British premier was faced with his greatest wartime challenge as leader.

No Confidence Motion Tabled Against Churchill

Trailing the Singapore disaster, Tobruk's capitulation represented a low point in the public's confidence in the war effort. The government's handling of the news was especially criticised. 'Tobruk's fall is a disaster,' London's *Daily Express* editorialised; many feared Egypt would follow suit. 'Our pen splutters rebelliously,' London's *Daily Herald* declared in a call for responsibility to be firmly fixed; 'it remembers writing these words after Norway, after Dunkirk, after Crete, after Hong Kong, after Malaya, and after the earlier Libyan reverses.' The UK Government's handling of the news was especially criticised; a readiness to listen to Lord Haw Haw was noted, with the public finding German news broadcasts more dependable than those of the BBC: 'We were told everything was all right at Tobruk, while the enemy were announcing its fall.'[22]

Spain's ambassador in London reported 'disillusioned public opinion, since it was expected that the resistance of the last campaign would be repeated'. 'Difficult moments' were imagined in light of Churchill's earlier optimism,[23] indeed the debacle became a rallying point for politicians opposed to his leadership. Political commentators predicted a 'first class political crisis' and his 'impending fall' as premier.[24] Not since Churchill had appeased the House of Commons over the earlier losses of Hong Kong, Malaya and Singapore had Britain been more unified in demanding a full explanation of recent defeats. Public reaction was noted at the polls with a 'sweeping overturn' in a lost by-election to an Independent at Maldon (Essex). In the Windsor by-election, another Independent candidate, Lieutenant W.D. Home was criticised for opportunism by using the defeat as campaigning capital, pledging 'no more Tobruks'.[25]

Tom Horabin, MP, expressed his reservations in a letter to London's *Times*:

> Our defeat at Tobruk has made an impression on people comparable with the [British] public feeling after the failure in Norway. There is now an almost universally-held opinion that the organisation of our war machinery is too loose and inadequate at the top. No confidence can be felt in the conduct of the war while these defects exist at the centre.[26]

Conservative Party politician (and personal friend of Churchill) Sir John Wardlaw-Milne tabled an embarrassing censure motion on 25 June. Calling for a Parliamentary debate in the central direction of the war, Wardlaw-Milne demanded to know who had been responsible for Tobruk's collapse, and who had earlier decided that it would again be held.

The debate began on 1 July. Wardlaw-Milne's speech included a proposal that the Duke of Gloucester (brother of George VI) should become commander-in-chief of the Army, an idea that saw the House erupt into insolent laughter. The next speaker, Admiral Sir Roger Keyes, whose son Geoffrey had tried to assassinate Rommel, took the approach that Churchill's advisers had let him down. In a stinging attack, socialist Aneurin Bevan criticised the prime minister's habit of winning debates but losing battles: 'The country is saying that he fights debates like the war and the war like debates.'

In his carefully worded response given on 2 July, Churchill skirted around the Libyan misfortune in what was described as a 'masterly' speech, though his personal victory on this occasion was also due to the ineptitude of his opponents. As one MP decided, 'He had a pretty simple job today because the censure motion was so stupidly framed. To vote for it was out of the question because if it had been carried it meant the fall of the Government in the middle of a great battle.' The debate closed with the no-confidence motion against Churchill rejected – 476 votes to twenty-five (with some forty conscious abstentions) – to the accompaniment of loud cheers. If Lord Beaverbrook (then minister of supply) is to be believed, Churchill actually emerged from the debate with his leadership strengthened. 'Good for you,' Roosevelt cabled.[27]

Soviet and US Reactions

As in London, the unexpected capitulation produced a shockwave in Washington and Moscow. In contrast to the Red Army's heroic stand at Sebastopol in Crimea, Stalin wasted no time in accusing the British of cowardice.[28] The Soviet ambassador in London, Ivan Maisky, received a frank explanation from the premier that the 'Germans wage war better than we do … especially tank wars'. Moreover, the British lacked the

'Russian spirit: die but don't surrender!' Maisky's opinion was blunt: Klopper should have been shot on the spot.[29]

The *New York Times* reported that Tobruk's fall draped Washington in a 'sober and realistic mood'.[30] Some observers in the nation's capital even saw the surrender of Tobruk as a blessing in disguise that promised to finally arouse America to the 'grim realities of the [British] military situation'.[31] Certain members of Congress also believed it would hasten the opening of a second front.[32]

Silence had followed the news of the disaster within Roosevelt's office. After several moments it was the president who spoke first: 'What can we do to help?' Only days earlier, the American Joint Chiefs of Staff had rejected Churchill's request for Major General George S. Patton, Jr. and the 2nd US Armoured Division to be shipped to Egypt on the grounds that they wished to confine US involvement in the Middle East to air units only. Now, in the aftermath of the Tobruk's collapse, General George C. Marshall was troubled by the situation unfolding in the Soviet Union and Egypt where Germany now 'threatened a complete collapse in the Middle East'.[33] To meet this threat he considerately offered 300 of the new M4 (Sherman) tanks and 100 M7 105mm self-propelled guns (known as the 'Priest' by the British), together with 150 maintenance personnel, aboard six of the fastest available ships. Originally earmarked for the partially trained US 1st Armoured Division, these tanks, manned by British crews, would play a vital part in crushing Rommel's army in the forthcoming battles at El Alamein.

Colonel Bonner Fellers (Rommel's 'Good Source') had long given the British little chance of defeating Rommel. Once more he proposed a large-scale US intervention in Egypt until the idea was stymied on 2 July with the understanding that the Middle East was an 'area of British responsibility' and that US forces were to restrict their activities to providing arms and co-operating with British forces by 'mutual agreement'.

The Desert Air Force, accordingly, was strengthened with American fighter aircraft and heavy and medium bombers originally intended for India, Australia, the Soviet Union and the Far East.[34] (An earlier outcome from the presence of US Consolidated B-24 Liberator bombers in Egypt was the diversion of the Halverson detachment, so-named after its commander Colonel Harry Halverson, to bomb the Ploesti oil refineries in Romania on 12 June 1942 to disrupt Hitler's oil supply. Although little actual damage was done, the raid was the first US air strike against a target in continental Europe, and a psychological lift for the Allies.)

Major General Lewis H. Brereton, commander of the US 10th Air Force in India, was ordered to take as many planes as possible to Egypt to assist the British in meeting the Axis emergency. Nine decrepit Boeing B-17 Flying Fortress bombers (described as 'near cripples') were duly located, and Brereton arrived in Cairo on 25 June, along with 225 assorted staff officers, pilots and mechanics. As early as 30 June, US heavy bombers were pounding Rommel's tenuous supply lines stretching back across the desert. The expeditious transfer of the US 10th Air Force bombers, their transports and crew, however, strained Sino-US military relations. Riled, the Chinese Nationalist Party leader (and Supreme Commander of the Chinese Theatre), Generalissimo Chiang Kai-Shek (together with his Empress May-ling) threatened to 'make other arrangements' with the Japanese, whom his forces were fighting, unless the order to transfer the bombers was rescinded.[35] It was the Chinese who suffered, May-ling argued, every time Britain was in difficult straits, 'and such being the case there is no need for China to continue in the war.' 'The Generalissimo wants a yes or no answer,' she continued, questioning 'whether the Allies consider this theatre necessary and will support it.'[36]

Roosevelt stepped in to quash the spat. A telegram to Chiang sketched the war in global terms with particular emphasis on

Rommel's advance. Unless the Axis was stopped, the Allied air routes to China and India would stop and the sea lanes to India would be disrupted. 'It is imperative that the Middle East be held,' the president finished.[37] (Beginning in July 1942, US military aid was airlifted to Chiang Kai-Shek and his army via an air route from India known as 'the Hump'.)

Torch

While the Middle East was indispensable to the Allies, so was the launch of a new front against Germany. General Sir Alan Brooke (CIGS) chronicled Churchill's time in Washington as picture of solidarity when news of the defeat was received:

> I always feel that the Tobruk episode in the President's study did a great deal towards laying the foundations of friend-ship and understanding built up during the war between the President and Marshall on the one hand and Churchill and myself on the other.[38]

But this picture of transatlantic camaraderie − if accurate on the subject of Tobruk − overlooks the strain on the rela-tionship developing over the issue of a second front and Churchill's use of the crisis to push for an invasion of North West Africa: Operation Gymnast, later renamed Torch.[39] The US War Department had earlier decided that a land attack against Germany should be launched as soon as pos-sible.[40] One plan, dubbed Operation Roundup, involved a slow build-up of men and materiel in Britain culminating in a massive cross-Channel attack to be launched in 1943. Another, Sledgehammer, drawn up to meet the contin-gency of a Russian collapse on the Eastern Front, called for a 'toe-hold' landing in France in September 1942, followed by a second, larger invasion later.[41] 'To defeat the Germans we must have overwhelming power,' Marshall had told a Combined Chiefs of Staff meeting on 20 June, 'and Northwest Europe was the only front on which this overwhelming superiority was logistically possible ...'[42] The premier's insistence on a landing in North Africa would, in effect, redirect the entire Anglo-American war effort away from north-west Europe. As relations between London and Washington sunk to their lowest point in the war, the US Joint Chiefs of Staff were even prepared to recommend that America's primary focus switch to fighting the Japanese in the Pacific.

Convinced that Sledgehammer was impractical, Roosevelt sided with Churchill on the North African invasion; and for the first time was at variance with his Chiefs of Staff.[43] On 15 July he announced that the nation's war effort against Germany would continue to be given priority. Through this resolve – one of the most profound edicts of the war – he determined that the Anglo-American alliance would continue to fight as a cohesive team.[44] But while Marshall and Brook deliberated on the merits of Torch, the president also needed to have US troops on the ground fighting the Germans before the polls opened for the next US mid-term elections in November 1942. In the event that the Republicans and the isolationists gained power, his Germany First strategy may well have been jeopardised.

Operation Torch, as agreed, would seize Vichy French North Africa and trap Rommel between US troops to the west and British troops in the east. A series of amphibious landings under Major General Dwight D. Eisenhower, involving mostly US troops (for political considerations), would take place on 8 November on Vichy-held French colonial territory near Casablanca on the Atlantic coast of Morocco, and on the Algerian coast near Algiers and Oran. This would be the first major Allied invasion of the war and, ultimately, the first major victory for the Allied coalition. Experience gained on the battlefield would prove invaluable in the forthcoming

Sicilian campaign and the Allied landings in Normandy in
June 1944.

South Africa's 'Dark Day'

In the Union of South Africa, the fall of Tobruk indicated more
tragedy than hope. Accusations of incompetence and cowardice erupted. The largest military reversal in South African
history, Tobruk dwarfed the earlier surrender by Boer General
Piet Cronjé and his 4,019-odd men in 1900, the carnage to
the South African 1st Brigade at Delville Wood in 1916 and
the loss of the South African 5th Brigade at Sidi Rezegh in
November 1941.[45] Roughly one third of the country's troops
in the field were now in captivity. Accusations of incompetence and cowardice flew. The disaster had the potential to
open a gapping rift within the Imperial alliance, remembering
just how unpopular the war was in certain quarters and the
simmering political unrest.[46]

General Jan Smuts bemoaned the Union's 'dark day'.[47]
Lord Harlech, Britain's high commissioner to South Africa,
recorded a 'grievous blow' to the Union's leader, who foresaw 'widespread political repercussions'.[48] The Portuguese,
for one, were apprehensive that the deteriorating political situation could even tempt Smuts to advance on their
African colonies.

Still in some ways, Tobruk served to stiffen the Union's
resolve to fight after losing its entire 2nd Division to Rommel.
Smuts, in his role as commander-in-chief, proclaimed that,
'South Africa can take it and South Africa will seek retri-
bution.'[49] A new recruiting drive was launched, aimed at
replacing the men captured at Tobruk, and producing 'an
even more formidable striking force'.[50] Some 5,000 men
volunteered within the first week. Only a few months afterwards, the Union's honour was restored during the fighting at

El Alamein.[51] Victory in Egypt also helped the Tobruk affair to recede from public attention.

Yet the surrender – under a South African general – remained a political sore point. A draft of a despatch written by Auchinleck, shortly after the event, was circulated between the War Office (WO) and the Dominions Office (DO) for comment. Churchill directed that publication begin only after the defeat of Germany, though a multitude of commentaries and revisions from Klopper, the WO and the DO pushed the deadline back several years. Auchinleck's version of events was not complimentary to Klopper, and that presented a problem for South African politics. The much-anticipated account finally appeared on 15 January 1948 in the *London Gazette*. Highlighting how the despatch failed to comprehensively explain Tobruk's swift demise, British papers (including London's *Times*) avoided pointing fingers at the Union or its general. An upset Klopper, nevertheless, maintained that he had 'tried for seven hours' to obtain permission to withdraw his forces and by the time this was agreed, Rommel had 'overrun our guns and cut off our transport'. In response to Klopper's request to be allowed to write his own detailed narrative, and the Union's High Commission asking London about an appropriate response, Smuts restated his support but also hinted that 'nothing further need be said'.[52]

A ripple from the fall washed over Ethiopia. Dissatisfied with the Anglo-Ethiopian Agreement of January 1942, which recognised Ethiopia's sovereignty but more closely resembled a British mandate, Emperor Haile Selassie (restored to power after the East African campaign) momentarily strengthened his relations with his country's Italian underground. Impressed with Rommel's victory – and the possibility of a march on Ethiopia to liberate his country from the hated British – Haile Selassie began negotiating a possible Italo-Ethiopian collaboration. El Alamein, however, was a watershed. Changing his tune and cutting relations with the Italians, he ordered the officials used to contact Rome be handed over to the British.[53]

Australia

'Of all the news from abroad this week,' Sydney's *Daily Telegraph* avowed, 'the most poignant to Australians was the lashing which Rommel's army gave the British Imperial Forces in Libya and the start of another siege of Tobruk.' Adelaide's *Advertiser* felt that the loss of Tobruk was a 'heavy blow to the Allied cause for reasons of sentiment and for many weightier reasons as well, the loss of this desert fortress is uncommonly painful.'

Although not understating the magnitude of the defeat, Prime Minister John Curtin singled out the 'carping criticism and fault finding' of Allied leaders in the Middle East from armchair critics instead commending the bravery and deeds of the men engaged in the fighting. Former Australian Prime Minister William M. 'Billy' Hughes was more outspoken:

> The news is very bad. I speak not only of the gravity of the situation but of imminence of the danger. We have got to be ready long before 1943 or 1944. All our hopes for tomorrow hang on how we prove ourselves now.

Hughes took aim at the official communiqués that:

> ladled out information like soothing syrup ... by emphasising minor successes they have created the impression that our forces, which actually have been driven slowly back, were on the crest of the wave. Every day people must be given their daily dope and told we are winning ... If they are not, they

won't sleep. Every retreat is a masterpiece of military strategy conceived by British genius, but now Tobruk has fallen and Rommel has captured Libya.

Whereas Army Minister Francis Forde called the defeat a 'serious blow' and appealed to 'Australians not to under-estimate its seriousness and the gravity of the situation', General Blamey (now commander in charge of Allied Land Forces in the South West Pacific) was more pragmatic, believing that 'events in Libya were given too much significance ... The position is not decisive.' But in one Digger's sardonic opinion, after being wounded and repatriated home from Tobruk, 'If the fleas, flies and scorpions treat them as rough as they did us, they will be glad to leave Tobruk.'

Reaction in Palestine and the Arab World

Scenes in Cairo following the surrender of Tobruk ranged from sheer panic in the European quarters to jubilation, a 'ver-itable Rommel-mania', particularly among the Arab youth, in expectation of Egypt's liberation by the 'great general'. RN warships departed Alexandria in haste for the Red Sea, while scores of sensitive documents were incinerated in Cairo on 1 July in a panicky disposal later dubbed 'Ash Wednesday'.[54] Half-charred papers marked TOP SECRET floating to earth became convenient cones for peanut vendors, while Europeans crowded into whatever transport was available and headed for the safety of Palestine.

German propaganda beamed to the Middle East via short-wave radio on 2 June – in Arabic – asked, 'Who of us Arabs has not been proud of Rommel? Who of us is not sympathis-ing with him?'[55] A declaration by the Grand Mufti, via Radio Berlin on 3 July, announced how:

The Glorious victory secured by the Axis troops in North Africa, has encouraged the Arabs and the whole East, and filled their hearts with admiration for Marshall Rommel's genius, and the bravery of the Axis soldiers. This is because the Arabs believe that the Axis Powers are fighting against a common enemy, namely the British and the Jews, and in order to remove the danger of communism spreading, following the aggression on Iran. These victories, general speaking, will have far reaching repercussions on Egypt ... and the collapse of the British mastery over the Mediterranean and the Red Sea ...[56]

Anwar Sadat, Nasser and their co-conspirators actively prepared an anti-British rebellion in Cairo. A plane carrying a message to Rommel promising support, however, was mistaken for a RAF aircraft and shot down.[57] Sadat later wrote that:

Egypt had been patient. We had suffered insult and provocation, and now we prepared to fight side by side with the Axis to hasten England's defeat ... We would carry out a military *coup d'état* in Cairo, overthrow the Wafd government under Nasha Pasha and put [former prime minister] Aly Maher back in power. The Egyptian Army would harry the British forces. We would join up with the Axis troops, and the fate of the British Empire would be sealed.[58]

(Sadat and several associates were subsequently arrested and imprisoned when Rommel was stopped at El Alamein.)

Yet the closer Rommel came to Cairo, the more the early pro-Axis sentiment purportedly began to wane. Miles Lampson, British ambassador to Egypt, cabled London that the 'appearance of the enemy at the doors of Egypt has caused a very general realisation of the unpleasantness of an Axis occupation, even amongst elements hitherto notoriously anti-British. Result has been a considerable turn of feeling in our favour.'[59]

Arab nationalist Khalil Sakakini recorded the mood of the Arabs in neighbouring Palestine, how everyone 'rejoiced when the British bastion at Tobruk fell to the Germans'. 'Not only the sons of Palestinian's rejoiced … but the whole Arab world, in Egypt and Palestine and Iraq and Syria and Lebanon, and not because they love the Germans, but because they dislike the English …'[60] The Jews became immediate targets. Surreptitious chalk markings appeared on their homes, later found to be property claims by opportunistic Arabs awaiting Rommel's arrival.[61] In response to the threat from Egypt, the Jewish National Council issued a statement called for all men living in Palestine between 17 and 45 years of age to report for service in the British Army, 'an imperative necessity, in order to drive back the enemy at our gate'. [62]

The threat from Egypt was real. Hitler planned to extend the Holocaust to the Middle East. *SS-Obersturmbannführer* Walter Rauff, the head of the design team responsible for the poison gas vans (in effect mobile gas chambers using vehicle exhaust fumes) arrived at Tobruk on 20 July. Hoping to receive the 'necessary instructions for the deployment' of his *Einsatzgruppe Aegypten*, it would appear that Rommel was absent, likely overseeing his troops at the front. Just over a week later Rauff's twenty-four man unit arrived in Athens in readiness for their murderous campaign against the Jews across Egypt and Palestine. The unit, however, was never deployed following the Axis defeat at El Alamein.[63]

The North African campaign is viewed today as an 'honourable' one, an almost gentlemanly conflict as opposed the far larger ideological struggles contested on European soil. Rommel even labelled the desert war *Krieg ohne Hass* (War Without Hate); however, few remember the labour camps – holding 2,500 Jews in Libya and 5,000 Jews in Tunisia – and the thousands of rural Tunisian Jews forced to wear the Star of David. Also forgotten are the reprisals and racial attacks against North African Jews, and the arrival of SS personnel in Tunisia in late 1942.[64]

Turkey, Afghanistan and Persia

Neutral Turkey's reaction was closely monitored by Whitehall. Would the disaster at Tobruk move the Turks to side with the Axis? From Istanbul, the Italian ambassador reported excitedly that the surrender had produced 'strong reactions in military and political circles', with some formerly pro-British Turks admitting to having reservations about Britain's fighting potential.[65] Likewise, the Japanese ambassador reported on 7 July that, 'Turkey was dismayed at the sudden change in the war situation, and seemed to be considerably agitated.' A shift of allegiance was anticipated.[66] Churchill perused these and other intercepted diplomatic signals with mounting trepidation. Yet the Turkish domino did not immediately fall. Although accepting a renewal of official Turco-German friendship, inducements of military and industrial materiel, and the offer of Greek islands, Turkey continued to entertain overtures from both sides before eventually joining the Allies and declaring war on Germany and Japan in February 1945.[67]

German agents operating in Afghanistan – a major centre of Nazi intelligence and subversive activities in the Orient – reported how the capture of Tobruk was regarded as the single most impressive Axis victory of the war to date. In July 1942, the deputy Afghan prime minister, Prince Muhammad Naim Khan, advised the German minister in Kabul that his neutral government was considering military co-operation with the Axis, an overture that dissipated once Axis fortunes began to plummet.[68]

The heads of the British War Office met at the beginning of August 1942 to consider a potential push by German forces from southern Russia into Iran, in concert with an

advance by Rommel through Egypt. It was estimated that
the Germans could conceivably reach the Aras River in
northern Persia by mid-October. To counter this renewed
threat, a new Persia and Iraq Command was set up under
General Sir H. Maitland Wilson. His primary tasks were to
safeguard the oil fields and installations of the two countries,
and safeguard the passage of American Lend Lease supplies to Russia from the Persian Gulf ports.[69] Meanwhile,
opposition to the Anglo-Russian occupation force inside
neighbouring Iran was reaching dangerous levels, with riots
in the streets.[70] Although the Persian government remained
formally pro-Western, a fifth column organised by German
agents flourished within the cabinet, the national parliament
and the senior ranks of the army.[71] A German invasion at
this time may well have succeeded. The only British troops
immediately available in Persia and Iraq in September 1942
were two Indian Divisions – both below establishment and
deficient in artillery, transport and signals – and an Indian
armoured brigade devoid of medium tanks. All were short
of transport. However, by November 1942, the course of the
fighting in Russia and the Allied offensive in North Africa
had rendered the Persian problem academic.

India and Japan

The fall of Tobruk caused immense damage to the prestige
of the Raj in India. Apprehension grew in New Delhi that
a victorious Germany would march across the Middle East
and strike across the North West frontier.[73] The crisis of the
British withdrawal into Egypt led to a fear of a convergence
of German and Japanese forces in the Indian Ocean. Among
those that believed the Allies would ultimately lose the war
was Mahatma Gandhi, the most influential figure in the Indian
Congress. Lord Privy Seal of the Churchill government,

Sir Stafford Cripps, had been sent to India with the offer of a new constitution in return for support for the war effort. Churchill had sanctioned this move in the context of a growing Japanese threat to India, but the negotiations with Gandhi and the Indian National Congress were overshadowed even more by events in the Western Desert. Gandhi, at least, seems to have read the very worst interpretation into the chain of British defeats culminating at Tobruk.

Later, he reportedly called the Cripps offer a 'post-dated cheque drawn on a failing bank'.[73] He meant the British Empire. Under Mahatma's inspiration, the Indian Congress rejected the Cripps offer and, on 14 July 1942, demanded that 'British rule in India must end immediately'. Three weeks later, the Congress launched the 'Quit India' movement, which developed rapidly into a violent insurrection that lasted the best part of a year. The Raj survived – but at great cost to its popularity and morale.[74]

In the meantime, all three Axis powers attempted to take advantage of the rising tide of anti-British sentiment in India. The fighting at and around Tobruk had yielded large numbers of Indian prisoners, who were now invited to break their allegiance and join the nationalistic Free India Movement led by the exiled Subhas Chandra Bose. By February 1943, Bose's German-sponsored Indian Legion had recruited more than 3,000 troops, although their subsequent service record in the service of the Reich was poor.[75]

In a gesture of pro-British support, Ibn Saud, the influential Saudi King and Muslim leader, sent his son, the Amir Mansur, to Montgomery's headquarters in Egypt to rally Muslim Indian soldiers serving in the Eighth Army and preparing to counter-attack Rommel.[76] This overture was especially important in light of the above-mentioned disobedience and non-co-operation campaign of the Indian Congress. Britain's precarious situation in North Africa or the Far East would have deteriorated further had Muslim

Indian troops rebelled in both theatres, even more so had Ibn Saud called upon the Muslim world to take up arms against Britain and its allies.

Hitler's thoughts also shifted to the Indian subcontinent. He briefly revived the grandiose scheme of German and Japanese pincers converging on India from the north and south – the so-called Plan Orient. Nazi Foreign Minister, Joachim von Ribbentrop, pressed Japan's ambassador Oshima on 9 July to attack the Soviet Far East with the reassurance that:

> … if we can succeed in eliminating Russia as the principal ally of England and the US, and can advance through the Caucasus to the south, while Rommel on the other side is pressing forward through Egypt into the Near East, then the war will have been won. In any case, in the last four weeks we have come closer to this goal than the German leadership, even in its greatest optimism, could ever have hoped to achieve.[77]

Berlin also requested that Tokyo attack Allied shipping movements in the Indian Ocean – ships bound for Egypt. The possibility that Rommel might reach the Suez Canal also inspired Japanese military leaders to fleetingly resurrect earlier plans for an amphibious landing in Ceylon (now Sri Lanka) backed up by naval operations in the Indian Ocean. The Japanese General Staff in Tokyo likewise weighed up the logistics of invading northeast India (Operation 21), before postponing the movement through of a number of factors, including poor supply lines and the inexorable US advance across the Pacific towards the Japanese Home Islands.[78]

Japanese editorials naturally condemned Britain's position: the *Yomiuri* declared that the Axis victories at Sebastopol and Tobruk would have great bearing on all European fronts, the latter rendering Britain's defence against the Axis advance 'impossible'. Tokyo also warned how the British sun was 'setting in the Middle East' with 'growing anti–British sentiment amongst the Egyptian people'.

Fortunately for the Allies, the tide was about to turn against the Axis in North Africa and British hegemony across Africa, the Middle East and India would remain in place for the remainder of the war.

The Lure of the Nile

'During the days to come, I shall call on you for one more great effort.'

— Erwin Rommel, 21 June 1942

'The loss of Egypt will be the *coup de grâce* for Great Britain.'
— Benito Mussolini

Rommel, in his *Papers*, reflected on his gamble to drive forward into Egypt, intent on:

> destroying the tattered remnants of the Eighth Army which had escaped from the Marmarica battles, plus its two fresh divisions … the British would [then] have nothing left in Egypt capable of opposing our advance to Alexandria and the Suez Canal.[1]

Four days after Tobruk's capitulation Auchinleck again assumed personal command of the shattered Eighth Army, this time from the luckless Ritchie. 'The danger of complete catastrophe,' he reflected afterwards, was 'too great for me to leave the responsibility with a subordinate already subjected for several weeks to extraordinary strain'.[2] Auchinleck also accepted full accountability for the Tobruk disaster, and had written to Alan Brooke in London, offering to vacate his post as commander-in-chief 'due to lack of success, absence of luck and all other things which affect the morale of an army'.[3]

When he (again) took over direct authority of the recoiling Eighth Army, Auchinleck immediately withdrew his forces back east towards Cairo, and – confronted with probably the most desperate situation of any senior British commander in the war – abandoned the idea of a stand at Mersa Matruh, instead favouring a new defensive front at El Alamein. In an effort to inspire the embattled Eighth Army, he dispatched a message on 30 June that Rommel 'thinks we are a broken army' and 'hopes to get to Egypt by bluff ... Show him where to get off.'[4] In an effort to increase the fight in the individual soldier and lessen the number of combatants listed as 'missing', he called (unsuccessfully) for the reintroduction of the death penalty in order to harden the resolve of his troops.[5]

On 3 August, Churchill flew to Egypt aboard a converted B-24 bomber to investigate and sort out the Middle East leadership situation personally. He had survived the no confidence motion, a close run thing, but a black cloud still lingered. News from the various theatres of combat against Hitler continued to stir despair. A British Arctic convoy carrying materiel to Russia, codenamed PQ-17, was annihilated by U-boats and Luftwaffe bombers in early July with only eleven out of the original thirty-seven merchant ships reaching their destination. On the Eastern Front, the *Wehrmacht* had overwhelmed the last resistance in Crimea, the city of Rostov fell on 27 July and the battle for Stalingrad was budding. In Egypt, another catastrophe was looming.

Having met with Auchinleck at Eighth Army headquarters, along with Air Marshals Tedder and Conningham, the premier embarked on what became known as the Cairo Purge. Auchinleck was axed as commander-in-chief Middle East and acting general officer commanding the Eighth Army on 8 August. General Harold Alexander, the officer responsible for saving the British rearguard at Dunkirk in 1940, was his successor, with 'Strafer' Gott given command of the Eighth Army. Tragically, Gott was killed before he could take up his post; his plane was shot down by a German fighter. Gott's replacement was Lieutenant General Bernard Montgomery. Similar to Rommel's arrival in Libya the year before, the influence of this new energetic commander and his 'no withdrawal' order was immediate.

Tobruk: More of a Millstone for Rommel

After perhaps the most spectacular succession of victories ever won against a British army, and despite vehement protests from Kesselring, Rome and the German Naval staff, Hitler approved Rommel's ambitious proposal to chase the retreating British forces into Egypt. 'I knew,' Rommel wrote in retrospect, 'that the fall of Tobruk and the collapse of the Eighth Army was the one moment in the African war when the road to Alexandria lay open and virtually undefended, and my staff and I would have been fools not to have gone all out to seize this unique opportunity.'[6] Tobruk was the windfall needed to keep his army marching on Cairo; the 'vast booty that had fallen to us', included 'ammunition, petrol, food and war material of all kinds'.[7]

Yet the prized town proved to be less of a prize and more of a millstone. The volume of captured stores, impressive as it was, was insufficient to propel Rommel's army far if regular shipments from Italy failed to arrive, a real danger in light of Malta's growing power. To their dismay, the Germans now discovered that the port had an unexpectedly small unloading capacity, far from what was required to ease their logistical crisis.[8] 'As a war harbour,' Siegfried Westphal (former staff officer to Rommel) later noted, 'Tobruk had only a very small unloading capacity, so that we were still chiefly dependent on Benghazi, indeed also on Tripoli.'[9] Westphal's post-war censure, however, ignored concerted efforts by the Italians to restore the port to working order and the fact that its capacity improved markedly under their management.[10]

Rommel's immediate advance into Egypt also continued to place immense strain upon those Italian resources. During August 1942, Tobruk was *the* primary Axis port in North Africa, receiving 10,931 tons of fuel, 248 vehicles and 4,379 tons of materiel.[11] Still, the Germans expected more, and Rommel – misguidedly – held that a five-fold increase in capacity was possible.[12] To guard this newly won prize – what Rommel called 'one of our most vulnerable points' – and protect its port, no matter how small, the Germans also assembled the strongest flak defence in the desert war to date, against heavy Allied bombing and mining of the harbour. In July, Tobruk was bombed thirty-three times, mostly at night, by RAF Wellingtons and the American B-24D heavy bombers of the newly established US Army Middle East Air Force. This was followed during August by another 1,600 sorties.[13] Tobruk town was targeted for its docks, tank workshops and related facilities. The British general hospital, boldly marked with the Red Cross, continued to function and care for the wounded of both sides – reminiscent of the 1941 siege. It, too, was hit.

Onward to Egypt

In the meantime, Rommel had cancelled the orders for rest days and harried the *Panzerarmee* to move off again; the British were in 'full retreat to the east' and should not be allowed time to 'get settled again'. The 'Gazala Gallop' resumed. Mersa Matruh fell on 29 June, along with another 8,000 British troops. On 1 July Rommel's vanguard reached El Alamein – the apex of his African adventure. The tiny Egyptian coastal town, just 70 miles west of Alexandria, is situated between the Mediterranean and the Qattara Depression – the natural

Western Desert obstacle that General Baron Leo Geyr von Schweppenburg predicted in 1937 would halt any advance from the west.

Yet Rommel remained confident. He would continue forward before the Eighth Army could dig in despite the perennial shortage of supplies and the sheer exhaustion of his Axis forces. Equipment-wise, Rommel's operational spearhead now numbered only fifty-five tanks, seventy-seven artillery pieces and sixty-five anti-tank guns. His 'mighty' *Afrikakorps*, was grossly understrength, its divisions numbering just over 2,000 active combatants.[14] Axis supply routes, meanwhile, were being annihilated at sea by the RAF and RN and on land by the newly formed special forces units – the Special Air Service (SAS) and the Long Range Desert Group (LRDG). In the end, he would not have the supplies, men and equipment needed to push forward against the strongest British force assembled in North Africa to date. In August alone, 254 tanks, 446 guns, 3,289 vehicles and 72,192 tons of stores were unloaded on to the busy Suez docks.

The subsequent battles fought at El Alamein marked a turning point of the North African campaign, and the first major irreversible German defeat of the war. Unable to push through the Allied line at Alam el Halfa (30 miles southeast of El Alamein) through a fatal combination of chronic fuel shortage, extensive minefields to negotiate and General Bernard Montgomery's devastating dominance in armour and air power, Rommel went on the defensive and prepared for a new British onslaught, much to Rome's annoyance. Hoping to resume the charge before the British, his precious supplies, especially fuel, were being lost at sea through a resurgent Malta. Unremitting attention by the Desert Air Force simultaneously decimated Axis supply lines emanating from Tripoli, Benghazi Tobruk, Bardia and Mersa Matruh.[15] In an audience before a pragmatic Duce on 24 September, a 'physically and morally shaken' Rommel was warned that, 'We have temporarily lost the battle in the Mediterranean,' that insufficient shipping was available and that a landing in North Africa by the US must be expected in 1943.[16] Regardless of the obstacles, Mussolini pressed Rommel to conquer Egypt before US troops arrived.

Rommel: 'We did not Intend to Repeat the Mistake ...'

General Bernard Montgomery's desert offensive erupted on the night of 23 October 1942 with a massive artillery barrage by 1,900 heavy guns. His well-trained force of 230,000 troops, comprising British, Australian, New Zealanders, Free French, Indian and South African troops faced a weary Axis army of some 50,000 Germans and 54,000 Italians. Montgomery's armoured superiority – 1,440 tanks to 540 – was matched in the air with 1,500 aircraft to 350. Despite the overwhelming disparity in men and machines, a week of fierce fighting developed. Rommel's attention was firmly fixed on overcoming the 9th Australian Division, his nemesis from 1941, but it was British armour that struck a decisive blow to his southern flank. It was a battle, Rommel observed, that:

> turned the tide of war against us and, in fact, probably represented the turning point of the whole vast struggle. The conditions under which my gallant troops entered the battle were so disheartening that there was practically no hope of our coming out of it victorious.[17]

Suffering crippling losses, Rommel ordered a general withdrawal on 2 November. The Axis leaders were blind to the circumstances and invited disaster. Hitler protested that:

> It would not be the first time in history that a strong will has triumphed over the bigger battalions. As to your troops, you can show them no other road than that to victory, or death.[18]

Mussolini was equally obstinate, advising Rommel to 'hold fast at the actual front at whatever the cost'.[19] Shocked, Rommel obeyed Hitler's instruction not to withdraw; the order was given for his battered formations to 'defend their present positions to the last'.[20] After twelve days of fighting, however, the situation was no longer tenable. The remnants of the Axis army were in full retreat; Hitler acquiesced and gave his consent to the retreat, 'given how the situation has developed …'[21] British figures, based on intelligence intercepts placed German casualties at 1,149 killed, 3,886 wounded and 8,050 captured; Italian losses stood at 971 dead, 933 wounded and 15,552 captured. The number of Axis prisoners had risen to 30,000 by 11 November.[22] For Churchill, the weight of recent criticism was lifted from his shoulders; his leadership would remain secure for the remainder of the war.

An Axis stand at Tobruk was now conceivable and the Italians were directed on 8 November to 'employ every means' necessary to prepare the fortress' defence, primarily along the south-eastern front.[23] The German quartermaster in Rome queried whether cranes were available at Tobruk or Benghasi capable of unloading the latest Mark VI Tiger tanks.[24] Rommel, however, elected to withdraw his Italo-German forces further west, on the basis that any stand would be tantamount to approving a new siege.[25] Elaborating later, he explained that Tobruk:

> now possessed only symbolic value. Militarily it could not be held in the situation at that time, without delivering up a large part of the Army to certain sacrifice. We did not intend to repeat the mistake which the British had made in 1942. Thus the enemy was able to occupy it, virtually without fighting, on the night of the [November] 12th, after its evacuation by the 90th Light Division.[26]

After a reconnaissance aircraft from No. 40 Squadron, SAAF, reported no sign of enemy activity, A Squadron of 4/6th South

African Armoured Car Regiment (fittingly) entered the town of Tobruk on the evening 12 November 1942 – 146 days after its fall. Retaken for the last time, twelve Germans fell prisoner and 10,000 tons of valuable supplies were commandeered. Several hundred native South Africans, in new uniforms pilfered from stores, waved to their liberators. Employed by the Germans as dockside labourers, they recounted their maltreatment, 'we helluva suffer', and told of their comrades killed in the Allied bombing.[27] Surveying the damage, a visiting US war correspondent recorded, 'The city was a shambles – an eery place of horrors with its sunken ships in the harbour and its buildings reduced to stunning battered rubble … a ruined shell of war – a name in history – with its wreckage the monuments of a graveyard for thousands of dead.'[28] Meanwhile, Rommel's battered formations continued to retire west, in one of the longest geographical retreats in the history of warfare.[29] The British, who were racing behind, finally entered the Libyan capital of Tripoli on 23 January 1943, liberating the Sanusi from thirty years of Italian oppression.

Sandwiched between the US–Anglo forces in French North Africa (who had landed on 8 November) and Montgomery's advance from the east, the Axis rushed a 250,000 German and Italian troops to Tunisia in a last-ditch effort to save their fading North African fortunes. But it was a case of too much too late. Had a fraction of this force been available to Rommel several months earlier, he may well have smashed Auchinleck's retreating army and reached the Nile Delta and the land beyond. Perhaps one of Mussolini's greatest mistakes – though at Germany's bidding – was dispatching some of the best Italian troops to Russia in July 1942. The ARMIR, *Armata Italiana in Russia* (Italian Army in Russia) and its 227,000 men, 16,700 vehicles and 960 guns would have been better used to stabilise growing partisan activity in the Balkans or to have participated in the attack on Egypt. As it happened, the miscellany of Axis forces, including two Panzer Armies, which finally capitulated in Tunisia on 13 May 1943, even outstripped Field Marshal Friedrich Paulus' German Sixth Army, which surrendered at Stalingrad three months earlier.

Mussolini's dream of a new African empire had collapsed and the Axis threat to the oilfields of the Middle East and British supply lines to Asia and Africa had ended. Allied troops invaded Sicily on the night of 9/10 July 1943, draining even more precious German resources from the Eastern Front. Sicily then became a springboard for an invasion of mainland Italy in the summer of 1943, spelling the demise of the Axis partnership. Mussolini was ousted from power on 25 July. His successor, Pietro Badoglio, signed an armistice with the Allies on 3 September. A month later on 13 October, Italy swapped sides and declared war on its former partner. Germany would continue to win battles in the remaining two years of the war in Europe, though the eventual outcome of an Allied victory was never seriously in doubt.

With the Third Reich in tatters, Hitler later reflected on his miscarried partnership while dictating his political testament in February 1945, 'When I pass judgment, objectively and without emotion, on events, I must admit that my unshakable friendship with the Duce and loyalty to the alliance may well held to have been an error on my part.'[30] *Reichsmarschall* Hermann Göring similarly condemned Germany's action in the Mediterranean, or lack thereof. When questioned after his capture in 1945 about Germany's greatest mistake of the war, replied, 'Not invading Spain and North Africa in 1940'.[31]

Postscript

The remote Libyan port of Tobruk was the centrepiece in the fighting across the Western Desert from its capture in January 1941 to its capitulation in June 1942. Unlike the pivotal battles fought at Stalingrad, El Alamein or Normandy, Tobruk is not generally associated with producing a key outcome in the war. Yet for a period in 1941, Tobruk was the focus of Churchill's struggle against the Axis on land. Sprung from obscurity, the fortress's slim fortune captured the world's attention and provided Churchill with a semblance of hope at a time when the march of Hitler's legions must have seemed unstoppable.

The war was never going to be won, or lost, in the Middle East. Yet the battle for Tobruk in 1942 – the nadir of the desert war – was one of Britain's worst military disasters, a fiasco that decided the fate of Malta and Egypt, rocked the very foundation of Churchill's premiership and laid bare the inadequacy of British command and combined armed tactics. It furthered the propaganda-assisted ascendancy of Rommel, soured relations within the British Commonwealth and consigned many of Britain's leading generals to posts in India. It revived the flagging hopes of the German people and fanned the flames of Arab unrest. A hefty knock to Britain's pride and military performance, it precipitated a turning point in Anglo-American relations, and a turning point in Allied intervention against Germany. It brought the latest US tanks to El Alamein that helped defeat the *Afrikakorps* and the Egyptian-based bombers that savaged Rommel's tenuous supply lines. And it culminated in the 'new experience' Churchill proudly announced to the House of Commons five months later. 'We have victory – a remarkable and definite victory ... Now this is not the end. It is not even the beginning of the end. But it is, perhaps, the end of the beginning.'[32]

Notes

Preface

1   Yindrich, *Fortress on Sand*, p. 157. Epilogue by Hans von Ravenstein.
2   National Archives (hereafter NA) CAB 106/384; Ministry of Information. *The 8th Army*, pp. 51–2.
3   Ministry of Information. *The 8th Army*, pp. 51–2.
4   Hartshorn, *Avenge Tobruk*. p. 112.
5   See Katz, *Sidi Rezegh and Tobruk*.

Chapter 1

1   Schweppenburg, *The Critical Years*, p. 139.
2   Askew, *Europe and Italy's Acquisition of Libya, 1911–1912*, p. 7.
3   Behrendt, *Rommel's Intelligence in the Desert Campaign 1941–1943*, p. 36. It was not until 1938 that a border was finally delineated between Libya and Egypt by treaty.

Chapter 2

1   Askew, *op. cit.*, p. 59.
2   Wright, *Libya*, p. 27.
3   *The Times*, 10 October 1911, p. 6; Beelher, *The history of the Italian–Turkish War*, p. 21.
4   *The Times*, 12 October 1911, p. 5.
5   Tittoni, *The Italo-Turkish War, 1911–12*, p. 100. See also Beelher, *op. cit.*, p. 54.

6   Kinross, *Atatürk*, pp. 47–51.

7   A page in aviation history was written the the next year when Italian Captain Monte achieved the 'distinction' of being the first airman wounded in combat while flying 'in the air with his machine'. Having spotted an Arab position from the air near Tobruk on 1 February 1912, Monte dropped several bombs before Turkish riflemen opened fire and wounded him. His observer, it was reported, landed the aeroplane safely. *Popular Mechanics*, April 1912, p. 499.

8   Herrmann, 'The paralysis of Italian Strategy in the Italian–Turkish War, 1911–1912', p. 332.

9   Bean, *Official History of Australia in the War of 1914–1918*, Vol. 5, p. 301.

10   Morshead believed his actions merited the Victoria Cross. Coombes, Morshead, p. 34.

11   Gilbert, *Churchill: A Life*, p. 320.

12   Ludwig, *Nine Etched from Life*, p. 321.

13   Evans-Pritchard, 'The Sanusi of Cyrenica', pp. 141–3.

14   Wright, *op. cit.*, p. 3.

15   Ciano, *The Ciano Diaries 1939–1943*, pp. 120–9.

16   Ciano, *op. cit.*, pp. 120–7.

Chapter 3

1   Ciano. *op. cit.*, p. 143.

2   Liddell Hart, *The Rommel Papers*, p. 73.

3   Ibid, p. 7.

4   Churchill, *Their Finest Hour*, p. 448.

5   Knox, *Mussolini Unleashed*, p. 12.

6   Ciano, *op. cit.*, p. 249.

7   Knox, *Mussolini Unleashed*, p. 43.

8   Gooch, *Mussolini and His Generals*, p. 492.

9   Long, *To Benghazi*, footnote 200.

10   Knox, *Common Destiny*, p. 157.

11   Liddell Hart, *op. cit.*, p. 91.

12   Knox, *Mussolini Unleashed*, p. 21.

13   Ibid, p. 264.

14   Eager to secure a slice of French territory before the campaign ended, he confided in his Chief of Staff, Pietro Badoglio that 'a few thousand dead' would help assure his place at the peace table. However, his

eleventh-hour offensive promptly stalled as a result of the French
Armée des Alpes' stubborn resistance and appalling weather.

Chapter 4

1 Raugh, *Wavell in the Middle East, 1939–1941*, p. 42.
2 Segré, *Italo Balbo, A Fascist Life*, p. 281.
3 Pitt, *The Crucible of War: Western Desert 1941*, p. 27.
4 Segré, *op. cit.*, p. 386.
5 Newsweek, 8 December 1940, p. 24.
6 AWM 52 8/2/26.
7 AWM 52 8/3/13.
8 Australian War Memorial (hereafter AWM) 52 8/2/26.
9 NA CAB 106/834 Western Desert: summary of the battle of
   Tobruk 1941, Jan; Keogh, *Middle East 1939–43*, p. 50.
10 AWM 52 8/3/13.
11 Cunningham, *A Sailor's Odyssey*, p. 267.
12 Segré, *op. cit.*, p. 387.
13 Ibid, p. 402.
14 Knox, *Mussolini Unleashed*, p. 160.
15 Ibid, p. 163.
16 Ciano, *op. cit.*, p. 291.
17 Hinsley, B*ritish Intelligence in the Second World War*, Vol. 1, pp. 215–6.
18 Raugh, *op. cit.*, 85.
19 Barnett, *The Desert Generals*, 29.
20 Ciano, *op. cit.*, 293.
21 Ciano, *op. cit.*, 296.
22 see Meskill, *Hitler and Japan: The Hollow Alliance*.
23 Warlimont. *Inside Hitler's Headquarters*, p. 109.
24 Young, *The Desert Fox*, p. 59.
25 Warlimont, *op. cit.*, p. 136.
26 Ciano, *op. cit.*, p. 300.
27 Burgwyn, *Mussolini Warlord*, p. 49.
28 Greene and Massignani. *Rommel's North African Campaign*, p. 43.

Chapter 5

1 Connell, *Wavell, Scholar and Soldier*, p. 273.
2 Eden, *The Reckoning*, p. 131.
3 Wavell believed that Churchill 'always disliked me personally' and,
   but for want of sufficient justification, chose not to replace him.
   See Connell, *op. cit.*, pp. 255–6.

4   Ibid, p. 265.

5   Connell, *op. cit.*, p. 277.

6   Wavell, *Speaking Generally*, p. 18.

7   Schreiber et al, *Germany and the Second World War*, Vol. 3, pp. 649–50.

8   Knox, *Mussolini Unleashed*, p. 76.

9   Ciano, *op. cit.*, p. 321.

10   Halder, *The Halder War Diary 1939–1942*, p. 294. These gull-winged aircraft with their spatted fixed wing undercarriage had been at the forefront of the European *Blitzkrieg*. Diving vertically to deliver their bombs, the psychological impact of their plunging attack was heightened by the addition of a wind-powered sirens mounted on their wheel covers.

11   Hawkins and Allen, ed, *The Oxford Encyclopedic English Dictionary*, p. 1349.

12   *Newsweek*, 22 September 1941, p. 25.

13   Barter, *The 2/2 Australian Infantry Battalion*, p. 109.

14   Ciano, *op. cit.*, p. 332.

15   Knox, *Mussolini Unleashed*, p. 256.

16   Chapman, *Iven G. Mackay Citizen and Soldier*, p. 196.

17   Wilmot, *Tobruk*, p. 3.

18   *The Times*, 18 January 1941, p. 3.

19   NA CAB 106/834 Western Desert: summary of the battle of Tobruk 1941 Jan; Maughan, *Tobruk and El Alamein*, p. 122

20   AWM 523/7/9 24th Aust. Inf. Bde. History of Activities at Tobruk, 1 Feb. to 25 Sep. 1941; Wilmot, *op. cit.*, pp. 3–6; Agar-Hamilton. *Crisis in the Desert*, p. 112.

21   NA CAB 106/834 Western Desert: summary of the battle of Tobruk 1941 Jan; Maughan, *op. cit.*, p. 122.

22   Ciano, *op. cit.*, p. 339.

23   Ciano, *op. cit.*, p. 336.

24   NA CAB 106/834 Western Desert: summary of the battle of Tobruk 1941 Jan; *The Times*, 25 January 1941, p. 4; *World War II German Military Studies*, Vol. 7, Part IV. *The OKW War Diary Series, Africa 1941*, MS # C-065f, p. 37.

25   Long, *op. cit.*, p. 215.

26   Wilmot, *op. cit.*, p. 10.

27   Barter, *op. cit.*, p. 121.

28   Chapman, *op. cit.*, footnote, 199; NA CAB 106/834 Western Desert: summary of the battle of Tobruk 1941 Jan.

29   Wilmot, *op. cit.*, p. 37.

30   Walker, *Australia in the War 1939–45*, p. 231.

31   Ciano, *op. cit.*, p. 339.

32   Thompson, *Forgotten Voices*, p. 26.

33   *The Times*, January 24, 1941, p. 4.

34   NA WO 201/345 Capture of Tobruk: Report by 13th Corps Commander.

35   Ibid.

36   Kennedy, *The Business of War*, pp. 90–1.

37   Barnett, *op. cit.*, p. 53. Quoted from General Micheal Creagh, commander of the 7th Armoured Division.

38   Raugh *op. cit.*, p. 118.

39   Ibid.

40   *Life*, 24 February 1941, p. 23.

41   Schreiber et al, *op. cit.*, p. 653.

42   Churchill, *The Grand Alliance*, p. 58.

43   Liddell Hart, *History of the Second World War*, p. 118.

44   Chapman, *op. cit.*, pp. 305–6.

Chapter 6

1   Liddell Hart, *op. cit.*, p. 87.

2   Trevor-Roper, ed., *Hitler's War Directives 1939–1945*, pp. 98–9.

3   Heckman, *Rommel's War in Africa*, p. 24.

4   Schmidt, *With Rommel in the Desert*, p. 16.

5   Behrendt, *op. cit.*, p. 14.

6   Maughan, *op. cit.*, p. 17.

7   Lewin, *The Chief*, p. 103.

8   AWM 54 523/7/19 Brief history of Tobruk, March to August 1941, Part 1; Connell, *op. cit.*, p. 385.

9   Pitt, *Crucible of War: Western Desert 1941*, p. 218.

10   Connell, *op. cit.*, p. 385.

11   AWM 54 523/7/19 Brief history of Tobruk, March to August 1941, Part 1.

12   Connell, *op. cit.*, p. 386.

13   Churchill, *The Grand Alliance*, p. 178.

14   Trevor-Roper, *op. cit.*, p. 108.

15   AWM 54 522/7/5 Summary of events, Defence in the Desert – The retreat; Hinsley, *op. cit.*, Vol. 1, p. 390.

16   Schreiber et al, *op. cit.*, pp. 673–4.

17   Liddell Hart, *op. cit.*, p. 107.

18   Ibid, p. 111.

19   AWM 54 522/7/5 Summary of events, Defence in the Desert –
     The retreat. (Written by Major Howard), p. 7. Schreiber et al, *op.
     cit.*, p. 678; de Guingand, *Generals at War*, p. 48.
20   Liddell Hart, *op. cit.*, p. 113.
21   Toppe et al., *Desert Warfare*, p. 11.
22   Ibid, pp. 59–60.
23   Churchill, *The Hinge of Fate*, p. 404.
24   Jentz, *Tank Combat in North Africa*, p. 44.
25   Tucker, *Approach to Battle*, p. 384.
26   Ibid, p. 128; von Mellinthin, *Panzer Battles*, p. 148.
27   Jentz, *op. cit.*, p. 42.
28   Schmidt, *op. cit.*, p. 34.
29   Reynolds, *Lord Lothian and Anglo-American Relations, 1939–1940*,
     p. 48.
30   Zimmerman, *Secret Exchange*, p. 169.
31   AWM 54 523/7/43 Chester Wilmot's papers, copies and original
     documents relating to the actions and activities of various units
     during the siege of Tobruk, April–September 1941, Narrative
     of operations in Cyrenaica during the period April 7–14 by
     Lieutenant General Sir John Lavarack, p. 5.
32   Eden, *op. cit.*, p. 277; Cunningham, *op. cit.*, pp. 338–9.
33   Churchill, *The Grand Alliance*, p. 183.
34   Liddell Hart, *History of the Second World War*, p. 179.
35   Day, *op. cit.*, p. 124.
36   Kennedy, *The Business of War*, pp. 90–1.
37   AWM 54, 523/7/43 Narrative of Operations in Cyrenaica During
     the Period April 7–14 by Lieutenant General Sir John Lavarack, 33;
     Maughan, *op. cit.*, p. 109.
38   AWM, EXDOC073 Wavell, Sir Archibald. Instructions to Maj.
     Gen. Laverack GOC 7th Division AIF to assume command of all
     troops in Cyrencaica and hold the enemy's advance at Tobruk.
39   AWM 3DRL 2632/ 18 Morshead Papers 1940 to 1944.
40   Maughan, *op. cit.*, pp. 117–8.
41   Churchill, *The Grand Alliance*, p. 184.
42   Connell, *op. cit.*, p. 404.
43   The horse-racing motif continued the next year, with the 1942
     withdrawal from the Gazala Line into Tobruk christened the
     'Gazala Gallop'. A wartime report recounted, 'It was a new expe-
     rience for the Australian soldier – running away from a fight.
     The infantry hated the idea, and didn't hesitate to say.' AWM 54

523/7/28 Brief History of the 9th Division, (Aust) in the Middle East 1941–1942.

44   Playfair, *History of the Second World War*, Vol. 2, p. 4. Third-line transport operated between rail/sea head and refilling points, second-line transport between refilling points and units, while first-line transport consisted of the vital fighting, technical and administrative vehicles that accompanied a unit.

45   AWM 54 523/7/43 Narrative of Operations in Cyrenaica During the Period April 7–14 by Lieutenant General Sir John Lavarack, p. 35.

46   AWM 3DRL 2632/18 Morshead Papers 1940 to 1944.

Chapter 7

1   AWM 54, 523/7/43 Narrative of operations in Cyrenaica during the period April 7–14 by Lieutenant General Sir John Lavarack, p. 34.

2   AWM 3DRL 2632/18 Morshead Papers 1940 to 1944.

3   AWM 523/7/9 24th Aust. Inf. Bde. History of Activities at Tobruk, 1 Feb. to 25 Sep. 1941, pp. 1–2.

4   Fitchett, 'The Siege of Tobruk'. *Infantry Journal* (April 1942), 45. Belfield, *Defy And Endure*, p. 5.

5   AWM 3DRL 2632/72 Morshead Papers 1940 to 1944, *Lecture on Tobruch*, pp. 14–5.

6   NA CAB 106/834 Western Desert: Summary of the Battle of Tobruk 1941 Jan; AWM 523/7/11 9th Aust Div Special Information Summary No. 1, dated August 23, 1941, Part II: Defensive Arrangements – Tobruch.

7   AWM 3DRL 2632/72 Morshead Papers 1940 to 1944, *Lecture on Tobruch*, pp. 14–5.

8   Fearnside, *Bayonets Abroad*, 88; AWM 54 (523/7/30) Personal papers of Brigadier A.H.L. Godfrey. AMW 523/7/4 2/28 Australian Infantry Battalion, History of the Battalion's activities in Tobruk, March to September 1941, p. 1.

9   AWM 523/7/41 9th Division report on operations Cyrenaica and Tobruk, 1941. Agar-Hamilton, *op. cit.*, p. 112.

10 Detwiler, *World War II German Military Studies*, Vol. 9, Part IV, *The Mediterranean Theatre, continued, War Diary Wehrmacht Operations Staff, Dec. 40–Mar. 1941*, MS # T-3 P1, p. 106.

11 AWM 523/7/11, 9th Australian Division, Special Information Summary No. 1, Part I: Brief History of Tobruch dated August 9, 1941.

12 AWM 523/7/41 9th Division Report on Operations Cyrenaica and Tobruk, 1941.

13 AWM 523/7/43, Chester Wilmot's Papers, Copies and Original Documents Relating to the Actions and Activities of Various Units During the Siege of Tobruk, April–September 1941, p. 23.

14 Masel, *The Second 28th*, p. 24.

15 Wilmot. *op. cit.*, p. 87.

16 AWM 523/7/27 Medical Aspects of the Siege of Tobruk, 1941.

17 Coombes, *op. cit.*, p. 105.

18 AWM 54 522/7/8 Main movements ordered and made Western Desert and Tobruk with chronology of AIF Units involved in operations – Libya and Tobruk (April–May 1941).

19 Maughan, *op. cit.*, p. 211.

20 AWM 54 523/7/43 Narrative of operations in Cyrenaica during the period April 7–14 by Lt-Gen Sir John Lavarack, p. 39.

21 Cull, *Hurricanes over Tobruk*, pp. 102–8.

22 AWM 523/7/30 Personal papers of Brigadier A.H.L. Godfrey.

23 Schmidt, *op. cit.*, p. 37.

24 Rommel was apparently sensitive to any criticism that he 'made a practice of gambling'. See footnote, Liddell Hart, *op. cit.*, p. 233.

25 Maughan, *op. cit.*, p. 113.

26 Behrendt, *op. cit.*, p. 76.

27 Reeder, *The Diary of a Rat*, p. 47.

28 Combat intelligence was a weak area in German doctrine. While *Truppenführung* (the German Army Manual for Unit Command) stressed the importance of intelligence in decision making, it also underscored the principle that uncertainty was the rule in combat. See Condell & Zabecki, *On the German Art of War*, p. 8.

29 AWM 52 8/3/13.

30 AWM, 3DRL2632/37 Morshead Papers 1940 to 1944, Translation of Captured German Documents.

31 Wilmot, *op. cit.*, pp. 94–5.

32 Jentz, *op. cit.*, p. 105.

33 Liddell Hart, *op. cit.*, pp. 116–22.

34 Jentz, *op. cit.*, p. 107.

35 Note that the spelling of this feature varies greatly in wartime and post-war literature, examples including: Midauuar, Ras Medawar, Ras al Mudawwarah, Ras el Mdauuar and Ras al Mudawwarah. The spelling adopted is that used in the Australian official history of Tobruk by Maughan: Ras el Medauuar.

36 Schmidt, *op. cit.*, p. 41.

37 Toppe, *op. cit.*, p. 68.

38 Jentz, *op. cit.*, 107; Wilmot. *op. cit.*, p. 96.

39 Liddell Hart, *op. cit.*, p. 123.

40 Connell, *op. cit.*, p. 408.

41 Warner, *Iraq and Syria 1941*, p. 119.

42 AWM 52 8/3/13.

43 Liddell Hart, *op. cit.*, p. 124.

44 AWM 52 8/3/13. Striech confrmed in an interview after the war that the 5th Panzer Regiment did not know that Tobruk was ringed by an anti-tank ditch.

45 AWM 52 8/3/13.

46 Maughan, *op. cit.*, p. 154.

47 Winter, *Stalag Australia*, p. 7.

48 AWM, 3DRL2632/37 Morshead Papers 1940 to 1944, Translation of Captured German Documents.

49 Churchill, *The Grand Alliance*, p. 186.

50 AWM 52 8/12/26.

51 Liddell Hart, *op. cit.*, p. 125.

52 AWM 523/7/4 2/28 Australian Infantry Battalion, History of the Battalion's activities in Tobruk, March to September 1941.

53 Liddell Hart, *op. cit.*, p. 125.

54 Schmidt, *op. cit.*, p. 44.

55 Day, *Menzies & Churchill at War*, p. 127.

56 AWM 52 8/3/13.

57 Liddell Hart, *op. cit.*, p. 126.

58 Wilmot, *op. cit.*, p. 118.

59 Maughan, *op. cit.*, p. 165.

60 AWM 523/7/11 9th Australian Division, Special Information Summary No. 1 – Information from March 1941–August 1941, Part 1: Brief History of Tobruk; AWM 523/7/29 Reports on 9th Division Operations in Cyrenaica by Lieutenant General Sir L.J. Morshead, March to October 1941. Parts 1, 7; AWM 523/7/27 Medical Aspects of the Siege of Tobruk, 1941.

61 Coombes, *op. cit.*, p. 113.

62 Churchill, *The Grand Alliance*, p. 190.

63 Halder, *op. cit.*, p. 365.

64 Taylor, *The Goebbels Diaries 1939–1941*, p. 339.

65 Liddell Hart. *op. cit.*, p. 127.

66   Wilmott, *op. cit.*, p. 119.

67   Mckenzie-Smith, *Tobruk's Easter Battle 1941*, p. 117.

68   Yindrich, *op. cit.*, p. 67.

Chapter 8

1   Liddell Hart. *op. cit.*, p. 128.

2   Schmidt, *op. cit.*, p. 48.

3   Wilmot , *op. cit.*, p. 123.

4   Ibid, p. 124.

5   Halder, *op. cit.*, p. 374.

6   Ibid. Ironically Paulus surrendered the entire German Sixth Army two years later at Stalingrad, having failed to order a break out due to his fear that the Führer would be offended.

7   Raugh, *op. cit.*, p. 199.

8   Ibid, p. 200.

9   Ibid, p. 201.

10   Churchill, *The Grand Alliance*, p. 219.

11   Wilson, *A Rat's Tale*, p. 19.

12   Liddell Hart, *op. cit.*, p. 131.

13   Churchill, *Blood, Toil, Tears, and Sweat*, p. 219.

14   Maughan, *op. cit.*, p. 222.

15   AWM 52 8/3/13.

16   Maughan, *op. cit.*, p. 194.

17   Liddell Hart, *op. cit.*, p. 132.

18   Ibid.

19   Ibid.

20   Serle, *The 2/24th Australian Infantry Battalion of the 9th Australian Division*, p. 72.

21   Ibid.

22   Wilmot, *op. cit.*, p. 131.

23   AWM 52 8/3/13.

24   Ibid.

25   Wilmot, *op. cit.*, p. 148.

26   Liddell Hart, *op. cit.*, pp. 132–3.

27   *The Times*, 29 May 1941, p. 4.

28   Hill, *Desert War*, p. 54.

29   Gunsburg, 'The Battle of Gembloux', pp. 97–140.

30   Yindrich, *op. cit.*, p. 8. Foreword by Major General H.L. Birks.

31   AWM 523/7/17 Notes on Tactics Employed in Operations at Tobruk in April 1941.

32   AWM 54 523/7/29 Reports on 9th Division Operations in Cyrenaica by Lieutenant General Sir L.J. Morshead, March to October 1941, Part 1, p. 6.

33   Wavell, *op. cit.*, p. 79.

34   'Sieges throughout history', *Newsweek* magazine noted in September 1941, 'have demonstrated that it is the spirit of the men rather than the material strength of their fortifications that has prolonged their defence. Perhaps in no type of warfare has the human element in war played such a part as within the confines of a garrison.' *Newsweek*, 22 September 1941, p. 25.

35   AWM, 3DRL2632/72 Morshead Papers 1940 to 1944, Lecture on Tobruch part 2, p. 34.

36   Combe, *The Second 43rd Australian Infantry Battalion 1940–1946*, p. 32.

37   Liddell Hart, *op. cit.*, p. 130.

38   Irving, *The Trail of the Fox*, p. 52.

39   Wilmot, *op. cit.*, p. 203. A US exchange officer in Germany from 1936 to 1938 attending the *Kriegsakademie* reported that his class received less than ten tactical problems out of seventy. No exercises involved position or trench warfare. See Condell & Zabecki, *op. cit.*, p. 13.

40   Maughan, *op. cit.*, p. 267.

41   NA CAB 106/834 Western Desert: summary of the battle of Tobruk 1941 Jan; *The Times*, 23 January 1941, p. 4.

42   AWM 54 522/7/8 Main Movements Ordered and Made Western Desert and Tobruk with Chronology of AIF Units Involved in Operations – Libya and Tobruk (April–May 1941).

43   Memo, Halifax [Earl, Ambassador the United States] to Franklin D. Roosevelt, April 17, 1941, Box 35, President's Secretary's File (PSF) Safe Files: State Dept., 1941, Franklin D. Roosevelt Library Digital Archives.

44   *The Sun*, 26 April 1941, p. 2.

45   Rosenthal, *Fortress on Sand*, pp. 38–9; *The Age*, 26 May 1941, p. 7.

46   AWM 54 523/7/29 Reports on 9th Division Operations in Cyrenaica by Lieutenant General Sir L.J. Morshead, March to October 1941, Parts 1, p. 10.

47   Fennell, *Combat and Morale in the North African Campaign*, p. 61.

48   AMW. *Lecky's letters: Saturday 26 April 1941*. See Devine, *The Rats of Tobruk*, p. 72: 'The main effect of bombing is psychological,

and is most marked on people who have not previously experienced it.'

49 Liddell Hart, *op. cit.*, p. 133.

50 *London Gazette*, 3 February 1948.

51 Ibid.

52 Wavell, *op. cit.*, p. 79.

53 Logistics was a major weak area in German military thinking at the time. Two out of twenty-three chapters in *Truppenführung (the German Army Manual for Unit Command)* covered logistics. Condell and Zabecki, *op. cit.*, pp. 8–9.

54 Greene and Massignani, *op. cit.*, p. 59.

55 Schreiber et al, *op. cit.*, p. 675.

56 Halder, *op. cit.*, p. 385.

57 *Truppenführung* (the German Army Manual for Unit Command) largely skipped over the political and strategic aspects of war. As a consequence, German officer schools did not produce graduates such as Dwight D. Eisinhowever or Alan F. Brooke. Field commanders, such as Rommel, conversely, had little comprehension of broader strategy. Condell and Zabecki, *op. cit.*, p. 9.

58 Liddell Hart, *op. cit.*, p. 97.

59 Ibid, p. 131.

60 Schmidt, *op. cit.*, p. 48.

61 von Mellenthin, *op. cit.*, p. 178.

62 Schmidt, *op. cit.*, p. 49.

63 Irving, *op. cit.*, p. 84.

64 Halder, *op. cit.*, p. 454.

65 Schmidt, *op. cit.*, p. 42. Success, however, casts a different light on proceedings, and Rommel's same conduct a year later was deemed partly responsible for his ultimate victory at Tobruk. In a radio broadcast to Germany, his then ADC recalled how: 'He personally made all his own reconnaissances and directed all his battles', and 'changed his decisions no less than twelve times, thus driving staff officers to the verge of madness'. *The Sun*, 26 June 1942, p. 16.

66 Schreiber et al, *op. cit.*, pp. 683–4.

67 Ibid, p. 693.

68 Mitcham, *Rommel's Greatest Victory*, p. 15. The 7th Panzer Division lost 20 per cent of its force in the six-week campaign: 682 men killed, 1,646 wounded and 266 missing.

69 Schraepler, *At Rommel's Side*, p. 89.

Chapter 9

1   *The Age*, 9 May 1941, p. 7.

2   Gilbert, *Winston S. Churchill*, Vol. 5, p. 1080.

3   Connell, *op. cit.*, p. 421.

4   Schreiber et al, *op. cit.*, p. 692.

5   Churchill, *The Grand Alliance*, p. 299.

6   Connell, *op. cit.*, p. 476.

7   Schreiber et al, *op. cit.*, p. 594.

8   Warner, *Iraq and Syria, 1941*, p. 127.

9   Satloff, *op. cit.*, pp. 84–5.

10 Sadat, *Revolt on the Nile*, p. 42.

11 Churchill, *The Grand Alliance*, p. 229.

12 Trevor-Roper, *op. cit.*, p. 122.

13 Rashid Ali Al-Gaylani spent the remainder of the war in Germany broadcasting propaganda to the Arab world.

14 Warner, *Iraq and Syria 1941*, p. 118.

15 Halder, *op. cit.*, p. 396. Diary entry for 30 May 1941.

16 Trevor-Roper, *op. cit.*, pp. 117–8.

17 Churchill, *The Grand Alliance*, p. 262. Interestingly, Joseph Goebbels was paying singular attention to the language of Churchill's speeches during this phase. For future reference, the Nazi propaganda minister made special note of the premier's vow: '… fight to the death for our defensive bases in Crete and Tobruk, as well as Egypt'. See Boelcke, *The Secret Conferences of Dr Goebbels October 1939–March 1943*, p. 160.

18 Churchill, *The Grand Alliance*, p. 289.

19 Kennedy, *op. cit.*, p. 119.

20 Raugh *op. cit.*, p. 218.

21 Churchill, *The Grand Alliance*, p. 290; Fergusson, *The Trumpet in the Hall*, p. 100.

22 Kimball, *Churchill and Roosevelt, The Complete Correspondence*, Vol. 1, pp. 204.

23 Churchill, *The Grand Alliance*, p. 298.

24 Ibid, p. 304.

25 Liddell Hart, *op. cit.*, p. 144.

26 Churchill, *The Grand Alliance*, p. 307.

27 Ibid, p. 308.

28 Murphy, *The Relief of Tobruk*, p. 9.

Chapter 10

1 A Spanish volunteer force of 17,692 men, known as the 'Blue Division', also fought in German uniform.
2 Trevor-Roper, *op. cit.*, pp. 131–2.
3 Churchill, *The Grand Alliance*, p. 309.
4 Ibid, p. 313.
5 Warner, *Auchinleck*, p. 80.
6 Wilson, *Eight Years Overseas 1939–1947*, p. 117.
7 Grehan and Mace, *Operations in North Africa and the Middle East 1939–1942*, ix.
8 Churchill, *The Grand Alliance*, p. 309.
9 Warner, *Auchinleck*, p. 86.
10 Murphy, *op. cit.*, p. 12.

Chapter 11

1 The Battle of Verdun was a ten-month struggle in 1916, between the French and German armies. What originally was a German offensive developed into one of the bloodiest engagements of the First World War, producing no strategic advantage for either side.
2 Johnston, *At the Frontline*, p. 131.
3 Ibid, p. 32.
4 Ibid, p. 24.
5 McKenzie-Smith, *op. cit.* p. 116.
6 Johnson, *op. cit.*, p. 43.
7 Hart, *The South Notts Hussars*, p. 150.
8 Fearnside, *Half to Remember*, p. 61.
9 Johnson, *op. cit.*, p. 42.
10 Devine, *op. cit.*, p. 57.
11 Johnson, *op. cit.*, p. 159.
12 Fletcher, *NX 20365*, p. 32.
13 Jacob, *A Traveller's War*, London 1944, pp. 50–1.
14 Devine, *op. cit.*, p. 71.
15 Devine, *op. cit.*, p. 64.
16 Yindrich, *op. cit.*, p. 160. Epilogue written by Hans von Ravenstein.
17 Wilmot, *op. cit.*, p. 124.
18 McKenzie-Smith, *op. cit.*, 116.
19 Ibid, p. 123.
20 Ibid, p. 116.
21 Devine, *op. cit.*, p. 74.

22 Burn, *op. cit.*, pp. 18–9.

23 Devine, *op. cit.*, p. 77.

24 AWM 523/7/41 9th Division Report on Operations Cyrenaica and Tobruk, 1941; Wilmot, *op. cit.*, p. 126.

25 Wilson, *A Rat's Tale*, p. 18.

26 Goodman, *A Hospital at War*, p. 86.

27 Austin, *Journey to Tobruk*, p. 138.

28 *The Age*, 6 June 1941, p. 6.

29 AWM 3DRL 2632/9 Morshead Papers 1940 to 1944.

30 *The Age*, 9 September 1941, p. 7.

31 *Newsweek*, Vol. 18, No. 23, 8 December 1941, p. 25.

32 Rosenthal, *op. cit.*, 46–47. In Australia, the fortress became a contemporary benchmark for courage, even moral conduct, with some extraordinary comparisons given. In September 1941, former Australian prime minister Robert Menzies commended the garrison's tenacious defence as no less than 'one of the greatest events of human history', adding that 'nothing short of the Tobruk standard will save you or will save me'. In his post-war memoirs, however, Menzies moderated his viewpoint to 'one of the noblest events in the war'. *The Age*, 5 July 1941, p. 10; *The Sun* 22 September 1941, p. 4; Menzies, *Afternoon Light: Some Memories of Men and Events*, p. 29.

33 Cunningham, *A Sailor's Odyssey*, p. 412.

34 Winton, *Cunningham*, 235; Maughan, *op. cit.*, p. 417.

35 Maughan, *op. cit.*, p. 417.

Chapter 12

1   Schreiber et al, *op. cit.*, p. 685.

2   Halder, *op. cit.*, pp. 530–4.

3   von Mellenthin, *op. cit.*, p. 68.

4   Maughan, *op. cit.*, p. 310.

5   Horner, *Blamey*, p. 235.

6   Ibid, p. 241.

7   Fergusson, *op. cit.*, p. 125.

8   Carver, *The Warlords*, p. 271.

9   Murphy, *op. cit.*, p. 79.

10 Crisp, *Brazen Chariots*, p. 94–5.

11 Providence was again on Rommel's side after his command vehicle broke down on the Egyptian side of the frontier. Rescued by Major General Alfred Gause, Rommel's new Chief of Staff, who,

by chance, had passed in his command car, the senior officers were unable to find an opening through the frontier wire, and spent an uneasy night in Egypt, surrounded by British troops.

12 Barnett, *op. cit.*, p. 137.
13 Murphy, *op. cit.*, p. 293.
14 Thompson, *op. cit.*, p. 106.
15 Kimball, *op. cit.*, p. 283.
16 Fischer, *Hitler and America*, p. 153.
17 Hamilton, *The Mantle of Command*, p. 307.
18 Yindrich, *Fortress Tobruk*, p. 213. Epilogue written by Hans von Ravenstein.
19 Johnston, *Australia at War*, p. 173.
20 *Life*, 16 June 1941, p. 30.

Chapter 13

1   Warlimont, *op. cit.*, pp. 226–7.
2   Weller, *Singapore is Silent*, p. 265.
3   Higgins, *Winston Churchill and the Second Front*, p. 67.
4   Kennedy, *op. cit.*, p. 245; Bryant, *The Turn Of The Tide*, pp. 340–1.
5   Liddell Hart, *op. cit.*, p. 328.
6   Ibid, p. 179.
7   Clifford, *Crusader*, p. 177.
8   Barr, *Pendulum of War*, p. 64.
9   von Mellethin, *op. cit.*, p. 110.
10 Horn, 'Narratives from North Africa', p. 96.
11 Eden, *op. cit.*, p. 384.
12 Moran, *Winston Churchill*, p. 63.
13 Barnett, *op. cit.*, p. 171.
14 Ibid, p. 124.
15 Mitcham, *op. cit.*, p. 55.
16 Johnston and Stanley. *Alamein*, p. 25.
17 Ibid, p. 25–6.
18 Tucker later wrote: 'His going was the latest of many misjudgments which had started to shake confidence in the leadership. We lost the wrong man. This serious and widely advertised change of command was to lead … to a British disaster only paralleled in World War II by that in Malaya.' Tucker, *op. cit.*, p. 81.
19 Brooke sacked Corbett advising: 'It's been decided to replace you'. An angry Corbett noted that 'one does not dismiss one's gardener without some explanation'. See Barr, *op. cit.*, p. 215.

20 Ibid, p. 242–3.
21 NA CAB 121 Telegram from C-in-C Middle East to the War Office, 7 March 1942.
22 Darr, *op. cit.*, p. 216.
23 Freudenberg, *Churchill and Australia*, p. 294.
24 Ibid, p. 424.
25 Kennedy, *op. cit.*, p. 242–3.
26 Barnett, *op. cit.*, p. 132.
27 Kennedy, *op. cit.*, p. 243.
28 Carver, *Tobruk*, p. 225.
29 Court of Enquiry on 'Operations in the Western Desert 27 May–2 July 1942' held by order of Middle East Command in August 1942, vol I, part III; NA CAB 106/718 Western Desert.
30 Piekalkiewicz, *Rommel and the Secret War in North Africa*, pp. 121–3; Agar-Hamilton, *op. cit.*, p. 17; NA HW 1/401 North Africa: German Requirement for Maps of Tobruk and of Fortifications and Essential Services as Far as Suez Canal.
31 Martin, *The Durban Light Infantry*, Vol. 2, p. 151.
32 Hartmann, *Panzers in the Sand*, Vol. 2, p. 23.
33 Aylett, *Surgeon at War 1939–1945*, pp. 183–4.
34 Tucker, *op. cit.*, p. 85.
35 Agar-Hamilton, *op. cit.*, p. 128.
36 Katz, 'The Greatest Military Reversal of South African Arms', p. 81.
37 Agar-Hamilton, *op. cit.*, 113; Rosenthal, *op. cit.*, p. 83.
38 NA WO 106/2238 A Fall of Tobruk; Court of Enquiry, Vol. I, Part III.
39 NA CAB 106/718 Western Desert: Studies on the Decision to Hold Tobruk and the Fall of El Adem 1942; Agar-Hamilton, *op. cit.*, p. 77.
40 NA WO 106/2238 A Fall of Tobruk; Court of Enquiry, Vol. I, Part III.
41 Lord Casey, *Personal Experience 1939–1946*, p. 107.
42 Court of Enquiry Volume I, Part III; NA CAB 106/718 Western Desert: Studies on the Decision to Hold Tobruk and the Fall of El Adem 1942, by Captain L.C.F. Turner.
43 Orpen and Martin, *Salute the Sappers*, p. 347.
44 Court of Enquiry, Vol. 2, pp. 52–4.
45 Churchill, *The Hinge of Fate*, p. 370.
46 Kennedy, *op. cit.*, p. 242.

47 NA WO 106/2238 A Fall of Tobruk; NA CAB 106/718 Western Desert: Studies on the Decision to Hold Tobruk and the Fall of El Adem 1942.

48 Statement by Lieutenant Colonel G. Bastin. Court of Enquiry, Vol. 2, Part V, p. 64 & p. 71; Agar-Hamilton, *op. cit.*, p. 105 & p. 117.

49 de Guingand, *Operation Victory*, p. 99.

50 Court of Enquiry, Vol. I, Part III.

51 Agar-Hamilton, *op. cit.*, p. 115.

52 Court of Enquiry, Vol. 1, Part III.

53 NA CAB 106/718 Western Desert: Studies on the Decision to Hold Tobruk and the Fall of El Adem 1942.

54 As Lt Col P. Tower noted in 1947, 'Once isolated, it was in fact invested. The experience of the November '41 battles was still pretty fresh in most people's memories.' CAB 44/421 Fall of Tobruk, June 1942.

55 Court of Enquiry, Vol. I, Part III. Author's Italics; Agar-Hamilton, *op. cit.*, p. 107.

56 NA WO 106 2238A.

57 Hinsley, *op. cit.*, Vol. 2, p. 385.

58 Rosenthal, *op. cit.*, p. 83.

59 Playfair, Vol. 3, pp. 263–4.

Chapter 14

1 Liddell Hart, *op. cit.*, p. 225.

2 *The Age*, 18 June 1942, p. 1.

3 Cadogan, *The Diaries of Sir Alexander Cadogan*, p. 458.

4 Liddell Hart, *op. cit.*, p. 225.

5 von Mellenthin, *op. cit.*, pp. 143–4; Liddell Hart *op. cit.*, p. 228; Agar-Hamilton, *op. cit.*, p. 155.

6 Agar-Hamilton, *op. cit.*, p. 150.

7 Orpen, *op. cit.*, p. 245.

8 NA CAB 44/421 Fall of Tobruk, June 1942.

9 Chutter, *Captivity Captive*, 27; Agar-Hamilton, *op. cit.*, p. 156.

10 See relevant discussion, Agar-Hamilton, *op. cit.*, pp. 156–8.

11 Orpen, *op. cit.*, 309; Agar-Hamilton, *op. cit.*, pp. 151–3.

12 Kesselring *The Memoirs of Field-Marshal Kesselring*, p. 127. NA CAB 44/421 Fall of Tobruk, June 1942.

13 Liddell Hart, *op. cit.*, p. 230.

14 Schmidt, *op. cit.*, p. 145.

15 Liddell Hart, *op. cit.*, p. 230.

16   Agar-Hamilton, *op. cit.*, p. 149 & pp. 158–9.

17   Ibid. p. 162. A 1943 study on the effect of enemy weapons on the
     morale of three hundred British soldiers wounded in North Africa
     found that the Stuka was the 'most disliked' weapon; moreover it
     was 'disliked to an extent out of all proportion to its real effective-
     ness'. Fennell, *op. cit.*, p. 61. A senior chaplain with the 2nd SAI
     Division afterwards described the terrifying effect of being dive-
     bombed. 'Down they whistled, always, it seemed to the anxious
     watching and prostrate observer, directly at him: then there was
     apparent a little curtsy in the bomb's flight – a strange illusion of
     tensed nerves – and it passed up and over to explode twelve or
     twenty-five feet away'. Chutter, *op. cit.*, p. 31.

18   Orpen and Martin, *op. cit.*, p. 357.

19   Carver, *Tobruk*, p. 252.

20   Agar-Hamilton, *op. cit.*, p. 162.

21   Mackenzie, *Eastern Epic*, p. 564.

22   Liddell Hart, *op. cit.*, p. 230.

23   Schmidt, *op. cit.*, p. 147.

24   Ibid.

25   Agar-Hamilton, *op. cit.*, p. 129.

26   Orpen, *op. cit.*, p. 314; NA CAB 44/421 Fall of Tobruk, June 1942.

27   Agar-Hamilton, *op. cit.*, pp. 163–4.

28   NA CAB 44/421 Fall of Tobruk, June 1942.

29   Chutter, *op. cit.*, p. 28.

30   Statement by Major H.M. Sainthill, Coldstream Guards. Court of
     Enquiry, Vol. 2, Part V, p. 159 & p. 229.

31   NA CAB 44/421 Fall of Tobruk, June 1942; Agar-Hamilton *op. cit.*,
     164–170; Orpen, *op. cit.*, p. 315.

32   Katz, 'The Greatest Military Reversal of South African Arms', p. 94.

33   Agar-Hamilton, *op. cit.*, p. 180.

34   Playfair, Vol. 3, p. 268.

35   Statement by Lt. Col. G. Bastin, 13th Corps. Court of Enquiry,
     Vol. 2, Part V, p. 72.

36   Martin, *op. cit.*, p. 162.

37   Ibid, p. 188.

38   Heckstall-Smith, *op. cit.*, p. 229.

39   Orpen and Martin, *op. cit.*, p. 190.

40   Heckstall-Smith, *Tobruk*. p. 229. Badly burnt blowing up the
     naval oil tanks when Tobruk surrendered, Harris was awarded the
     Distinguished Service Cross (DSC) for bravery.

41 Burn, *op. cit.*, pp. 41–3.

42 Barnett, *op. cit.*, p. 160.

43 Orpen, *op. cit.*, p. 316.

44 Cooper, *The Police Brigade*, p. 101.

45 Playfair, Vol. 3, p. 269.

46 Cooper, *op. cit.*, p. 101. The apparent dearth of ammunition was denied in 1946 by Captain D.G. Fannin, ex-intelligence officer, 4th Infantry Brigade: 'the only serious shortage of ammunition was in shells for the medium' artillery. Horn, *op. cit.*, p. 97.

47 NA CAB 44/421 Fall of Tobruk, June 1942.

48 Although Klopper had countermanded the orders to break out, it appears that Ritchie in fact radioed an order for a break out to occur, although it is unclear whether the garrison received it. NA CAB 44/421 Fall of Tobruk, June 1942.

49 Cooper, *op. cit.*, p. 102.

50 Court of Enquiry, Vol. 2, Part V, pp. 246–7.

51 Churchill, *The Hinge of Fate*, p. 376.

52 Katz, Sidi Rezegh and Tobruk, p. 140.

53 Heckstall-Smith, *op. cit.*, p. 240. Klopper was apparently never informed that Hayton's report was false.

54 *The Sun*, 29 June 1942, p. 2.

55 Stewart, 'The "Atomic Dispatch"', p. 80.

56 Horn, *op. cit.*, p. 97.

57 Liddell Hart, *op. cit.*, p. 231.

58 Maughan, *op. cit.*, p. 195.

59 Kennedy, *op. cit.*, p. 245.

60 Hartmann, *op. cit.*, p. 30.

61 Liddell Hart, *op. cit.*, p. 213.

62 Stewart, 'The "Atomic Dispatch"', p. 91.

63 Cooper, *op. cit.*, p. 103.

64 Horn, *op. cit.*, p. 101.

65 Chutter, *op. cit.*, p. 36–7.

66 Ibid, p. 41.

67 Clifford, *The Conquest of North Africa 1940–1943*, p. 309.

68 Playfair, Vol. 3, 273.

69 Hingston and Stevens, *op. cit.*, p. 213.

70 Ibid, p. 274.

71 Schmidt, *op. cit.*, p. 150.

72 Liddell Hart, *op. cit.*, p. 232.

Chapter 15

1   Gilbert, *Winston S. Churchill*, Vol. 7, p. 128.
2   Bryant, *op. cit.*, p. 408.
3   Churchill, *The Hinge of Fate*, p. 383.
4   Moran, *op. cit.*, p. 55.
5   Chuchill, *The Hinge of Fate*, p. 352.
6   Clifford, *op. cit.*, p. 304; Mackenzie, *op. cit.*, p. 561.
7   von Mellenthin, *op. cit.*, p. 146.
8   Kennedy, *op. cit.*, p. 242.
9   Warner, *Auchinleck*, p. 272.
10   Quoted from the 2nd South African Division War Diary, May
     1942. NA CAB 106/718 Western Desert: Studies on the Decision
     to Hold Tobruk and the Fall of El Adem 1942.
11   Burn, *op. cit.*, pp. 36–7.
12   AWM 54 523/7/43, Narrative of Operations in Cyrenaica during
     the Period April 7–14 by Lt Gen Sir John Lavarack, p. 5.
13   de Guingand, *Operation Victory*, p. 100; Court of Enquiry, Vol. 2,
     pp. 19–20 & p. 25; Agar-Hamilton, *op. cit.*, pp. 112–4.
14   Orpen, *op. cit.*, p. 324.
15   Warner, *Auchinleck*, p. 239.
16   Kennedy, *op. cit.*, p. 242.
17   Orpen, *op. cit.*, p. 170; Cunningham, *op. cit.*, pp. 464–5.
18   See Barnett, *op. cit.*, p. 156; Smyth, *Leadership in War 1939–1945*,
     p. 126; Pitt, *The Crucible of War: Auchinleck's Command*, p. 232.
19   Prime Minister Churchill Debate in the House Of Commons
     (and results of Vote of Censure), Parliamentary Debates, House of
     Commons Official Report July 2, 1942.
20   Kennedy, *op. cit.*, p. 245.
21   Churchill, *The Hinge of Fate*, p. 414.
22   Barnett, *op. cit.*, p. 159.
23   Agar-Hamilton, *op. cit.*, p. 137; Katz, 'The Greatest Military Reversal of
     South African Arms'. p. 89.
24   Agar-Hamilton, *op. cit.*, pp. 137–8.
25   Maughan, *op. cit.*, p. 536; Agar-Hamilton, *op. cit.*, p. 131.
26   Pollock, *Tobruk*, p. 71.
27   Moorehead, African *Trilogy: The North African Campaign 1940–43*,
     p. 385.
28   The 2nd SAI Division had been held in reserve during the
     Crusader offensive due to insufficient transport.
29   Court of Enquiry, Vol. 2, 29; Agar-Hamilton, *op. cit.*, p. 113 & p. 136.

30   NA CAB 106/570 Tobruk: Correspondence on the South African Historical Section's Narrative on the Fall of Tobruk 1942.

31   We should note that Willison's record during the preceding battles around Gazala, the Cauldron and Knightsbridge was questionable, and his appointment to command the tank brigade supporting the 2nd SAI Division, through the toss of a coin, was another tragic leadership decision. NA CAB 106/636 Tobruk: Report on the Defences of the Fortress 1942.

32   Rosmarin, *Inside Story*, p. 11.

33   Horn, *op. cit.*, p. 97.

34   Ibid.

35   Chutter, *op. cit.*, pp. 36–7.

36   Rosmarin, *op. cit.*, p. 17.

37   Martin, *op. cit.*, p. 161.

38   Horn, *op. cit.*, p. 98.

39   Agar-Hamilton, *op. cit.*, p. 129.

40   Liddell Hart, *op. cit.*, p. 229.

41   Fennell, *op. cit.*, p. 148.

42   Clune, *Tobruk to Turkey*, p. 109.

43   Moorehead, *op. cit.*, p. 346.

44   Agar-Hamilton, *op. cit.*, p. 128 & p. 135.

45   Aylett, *op. cit.*, p. 185.

46   Moorehead, *op. cit.*, p. 346.

47   Chutter, *op. cit.*, p. 28.

48   Ibid, pp. 16–7 & pp. 28–9.

49   Orpen and Martin, *op. cit.*, p. 356; Orpen, *op. cit.*, p. 309.

50   Chutter, *op. cit.*, p. 29.

51   Moorehead, *op. cit.*, p. 347.

52   Fennell, *op. cit.*, p. 155.

53   NA CAB 106/570 Tobruk: Correspondence on the South African Historical Section's Narrative on the Fall of Tobruk 1942.

54   Churchill, *The Hinge of Fate*, p. 67. Churchill stood by his commendation, writing in his memoirs, 'I do not regret or retract the tribute I paid to Rommel, unfashionable though it was judged'. see Churchill, *The Grand Alliance*, p. 177. The motif continued in British post-war biographical works by historians such Liddell Hart, Desmond Young and Ronald Lewin venerating Rommel's actions and tactical prowess.

55   *Time*, 13 July 1942, p. 22.

56   Liddell Hart, *The Other Side of the Hill*, p. 56.

57   Chutter, *op. cit.*, p. 42. A new word purportedly entered the German
      vernacular in the days after the fall of the fortress: "'Rommelin'
      meaning 'to go like hell'". *The Sun*, 24 June 1942, p. 2.

58   Keogh, *op. cit.*, pp. 246–7. As Keogh comments, throughout history,
      has a commander ever given an opponent a greater compliment?

59   *Newsweek*, 29 June 1942, pp. 21–2.

60   Fennell, *op. cit.*, p. 212.

61   Ibid, pp. 55–6.

62   *The Sun*, 2 July 1942, p. 16.

63   Agar-Hamilton, *op. cit.*, p. 114.

64   Orpen and Martin, *op. cit.*, p. 353; Court of Enquiry, Vol. 2, Part V,
      p. 50.

65   Agar-Hamilton, *op. cit.*, p. 141; Orpen and Martin, *op. cit.*, p. 351.

66   Hartshorn, *op. cit.*, p. 101.

67   Agar-Hamilton, *op. cit.*, pp. 131–3 & p. 141; Hingston and Stevens,
      The Tiger Kills, p. 210.

68   Court of Enquiry, Vol. 1, Part II, p. 18.

69   NA CAB 44/421 Fall of Tobruk, June 1942.

70   Agar-Hamilton, *op. cit.*, p. 131; Orpen and Martin, *op. cit.*, p. 355;
      Martin, *op. cit.*, pp. 163–4.

71   Agar-Hamilton, *op. cit.*, p. 141; Martin, *op. cit.*, p. 166.

72   Agar-Hamilton, *op. cit.*, pp. 131–3 & p. 141; Hingston and Stevens,
      The Tiger Kills, p. 210.

73   Court of Enquiry, Vol. 2, Part V, p. 158.

74   NA CAB 106/636 Tobruk: Report on the Defences of the Fortress
      1942. Major P. Pope, 25th Field Regiment, stated after the fall
      of Tobruk, that maps had been made available from the 2nd SA
      Division, who possessed records of the previous layout. Court of
      Enquiry, Vol. 1, Part II, p. 20 & p. 174.

75   NA CAB 106/636 Tobruk: Report on the Defences of the Fortress
      1942; Agar-Hamilton, *op. cit.*, pp. 167–8.

76   Statement by Lt. Col. G. Bastin, 13th Corps. Court of Enquiry,
      Vol. 2, Part V, p. 64.

77   Orpen and Martin, *op. cit.*, p. 355.

78   Court of Enquiry, Vol. 1, Part I, p. 5.

79   Agar-Hamilton, *op. cit.*, p. 161; Schmidt, *op. cit.*, p. 146.

80   Moorehead, *op. cit.*, p. 349; Agar-Hamilton, *op. cit.*, p. 161.

81   NA CAB 44/421 Fall of Tobruk, June 1942.

82   Mackenzie, *op. cit.*, p. 563; NA CAB 44/421 Fall of Tobruk, June
      1942.

83 NA WO 201/382 Fall of Tobruk: Through Enemy Eyes.

84 AWM 523/7/29 Reports on 9th Division Operations in Cyrenaica by Lieutenant General. Sir L.J. Morshead, March to October 1941. Parts 1, Lessons of the Campaign, p. 11.

85 von Mellenthin, *op. cit.*, pp. 145–6.

86 NA CAB 44/421 Fall of Tobruk, June 1942.

87 Agar-Hamilton, *op. cit.*, footnote, 203; Court of Enquiry, Vol. 2, Part V, p. 136.

88 Court of Enquiry, Vol. I, Part II, pp. 19–22; Court of Enquiry, Vol. 2, Part V, p. 191; Lord Casey, *op. cit.*, p. 108; Greene and Massignani, *op. cit.*, p. 164; Orpen, *op. cit.*, p. 316.

89 Maughan, *op. cit.*, p. 536; Agar-Hamilton, *op. cit.*, p. 166; von Mellenthin, *op. cit.*, p. 146.

90 Agar-Hamilton, *op. cit.*, p. 128.

91 Ibid, p. 134.

92 Cooper, *op. cit.*, p. 101.

93 Court of Enquiry, Vol. 2, Part V, p. 65.

94 Agar-Hamilton, *op. cit.*, p. 134.

95 Ibid. p. 135; NA CAB 44/421 Fall of Tobruk, June 1942; AWM 54 523/7/29 Reports on 9th Division Operations in Cyrenaica by Lt Gen. Sir L.J. Morshead, March to October 1941, Part 1, p. 10.

96 Mackenzie, *op. cit.*, p. 562; Martin, *op. cit.*, p. 171.

97 Court of Enquiry, Vol. I, Part II, pp. 23–4.

98 Agar-Hamilton *op. cit.*, p. 134.

99 Ibid, p. 170; Court of Enquiry, Vol. 2, Part V, p. 170.

100 Martin, *op. cit.*, pp. 164–5.

101 NA CAB 44/421 Fall of Tobruk, June 1942; Agar-Hamilton, *op. cit.*, p. 160.

102 Agar-Hamilton, *op. cit.*, p. 135.

103 A Gurkha officer described how, with the aid of the handbook, a spigot mortar was 'hurriedly unpacked and assembled' and brought into action on 20 June. 'The German tanks which approached us were just as afraid of the spigot bombs as we were of firing them … The bomb hits some unpredictable distance away, precipitates itself along the ground like a prehistoric monster, belching fire as it goes, until it finishes its career in an ear-shattering explosion. At least, that is the way they behaved for us. They scared off any tank that looked as though it wished to try conclusions with us.' Mackenzie, *op. cit.*, p. 566.

104 von Mellenthin, *op. cit.*, p. 146.

105 NA WO 201/382 Fall of Tobruk: Through Enemy Eyes.

106 NA CAB 106/834 Western Desert: Summary of the Battle of Tobruk 1941 Jan; Wilmot, *op. cit.*, p. 7.

107 Court of Enquiry, Vol. I, Part II, p. 174.

108 Mackenzie, *op. cit.*, p. 563.

109 NA CAB 106/636 Tobruk: Report on the Defences of the Fortress 1942.

110 Agar-Hamilton, *op. cit.*, p. 165.

111 Written statement by Major P.W.G. Pope, p. 25 Field Regt. Court of Enquiry, Vol. 2, Part V, pp. 230–1; Agar-Hamilton, *op. cit.*, p. 165; Orpen, *op. cit.*, p. 315.

112 Agar-Hamilton, *op. cit.*, pp. 164–9.

113 NA CAB 44/421. Fall of Tobruk, June 1942.

114 NA CAB 106/636 Tobruk: Report on the Defences of the Fortress 1942.

115 NA CAB 44/421 Fall of Tobruk, June 1942; Orpen, *op. cit.*, p. 315.

116 de Guingand, *Operation Victory*, p. 123.

117 Bennett, *Ultra and Mediterranean Strategy 1941–1945*, p. 359; Bierman, *Alamein*, pp. 126–9; Clayton and Craig, *End of the Beginning*, pp. 43–7.

118 Behrendt, *op. cit.*, p. 146, p. 166.

119 Stevenson, *A Man Called Intrepid*, p. 404.

120 NA CAB 44/421 Fall of Tobruk, June 1942; Orpen, *op. cit.*, p. 315.

121 NA CAB 44/421 Fall of Tobruk, June 1942.

122 Fennell, *op. cit.*, p. 202.

123 US War Department, The Libyan Campaign May 27 to July 27, 1942, p. 15.

124 Hartshorn, *op. cit.*, pp. 138–9. After Klopper escaped from an Italian POW camp in October 1943, Churchill announced to the House of Commons: 'Everyone will congratulate this gallant officer …'

125 *Natal Mercury*, 30 March 1944, p. 37.

126 Ibid, p. 81.

Chapter 16

1 Moran, *op. cit.*, p. 284.

2 Halder, *op. cit.*, p. 625.

3 Hitler, *Hitler's Table Talk 1941–1944*, p. 538.

4 Liddell Hart, *op. cit.*, footnote 232. Fliegerführer Afrika Otto Hoffman von Waldau was awarded the *Ritterkreuz* for the role of the Luftwaffe in the victory.

5   Von Luck, *Panzer Commander*, p. 82.

6   Boelcke, p. 246.

7   Hamilton, *op. cit.*, p. 306.

8   *Die Wehrmacht*, 1 July 1942.

9   Fredborg, *Behind the Steel Wall*, p. 121.

10 Irving, *op. cit.*, p. 171.

11 NA HW1/680/34/10.

12 Detwiler, *World War II German Military Studies*, Vol. 14, Part VI, The Mediterranean Theatre, continued, MS. # T-3 P1, The War in the Mediterranean Area, p. 47, p. 56.

13 Ciano, *op. cit.*, p. 501.

14 Ibid, p. 501.

15 Ibid, p. 502.

16 Ibid, p. 504.

17 Churchill, *The Hinge of Fate*, p. 420.

18 Kesselring, *op. cit.*, p. 124.

19 Corvaja. *Hitler and Mussolini*, pp. 204–5.

20 Ibid.

21 Orpen, *op. cit.*, p. 330; Agar-Hamilton, *op. cit.*, p. 237.

22 Doherty, *Nazi Wireless Propaganda*, p. 147.

23 NA HW 1/665 Spanish ambassador, London: British reaction to fall of Tobruk, June 22; Rommel's celebratory address to the troops.

24 *The Sun*, 24 June 1942, p. 2; Churchill, *The Hinge of Fate*, p. 386.

25 Fraser, Will, p. 58.

26 *The Argus*, 26 June 1942, p. 1.

27 Gilbert, *Winston S. Churchill*, Vol. 7, p. 140.

28 Overy, *Why the Allies Won*, p. 123.

29 Gorodetsky, *The Maisky Diaries*, p. 442.

30 *The New York Times*, 22 June 1942, p. 1.

31 *The Sun*, 23 June 1942, p. 2.

32 *The Daily Express*, 22 June 1942, p. 1.

33 Sherwood, *Roosevelt and Hopkins*, p. 592.

34 Orpen, *op. cit.*, pp. 327–8, p. 343; Butler and Schlesinger, Jr. *My Dear Mr. Stalin*, pp. 75–6.

35 McNeil, *America, Britain and Russia*, p. 189.

36 Pakkula, *The Last Empress*, p. 399.

37 Plating, *The Hump*, p. 89.

38 Alanbrooke, *War Diaries 1939–1945*, p. 269.

39 Moran, *op. cit.*, pp. 55–6 & p. 62.

40 Pogue, *George C. Marshall*, p. 304.

41 Ibid, p. 304, pp. 314–5; Morgan, *FDR: A Biography*, p. 637.

42 Casey, *Cautious Crusade*, p. 92.

43 McNeil, *America, Britain, & Russia*, p. 189.

44 According to Moran, Lewis Douglas (US Ambassador to the Court of St James 1947–1950) believed Roosevelt's decision to support Torch was the most important decision of the entire war. Moran, *op. cit.*, p. 62.

45 Katz, 'The Greatest Military Reversal of South African Arms', p. 71.

46 see Stewart, 'The Klopper Affair'.

47 Hancock, *Smuts*, p. 375.

48 WO 106/4946, 22 June 1942.

49 *The Times*, 23 June 1942, p. 3.

50 *Natal Mercury*, 29 June 1942, p. 7.

51 de Guingand, *Operation Victory*, p. 103.

52 Attempting to clear his name, Klopper authored a series of articles in the 1950 *Huisgenoot* magazine, while enjoying a successful post-war army career that culminated as commandant general, head of the Union Defence Forces (1956 to 1958). Significantly, none of the official South African histories were ever translated into Afrikaans despite the fact that over half the participants in the Union Defence Force were Afrikaners.

53 Sabacchi, 'Haile Selassie and the Italians 1941–1943', p. 36; Spencer, *Ethiopia at Bay*, p. 112.

54 Barr, *op. cit.*, p. 69.

55 Herf, *Nazi Propaganda for the Arab World*, p. 111.

56 Ibid, p. 123.

57 Cook, *The Struggle for Egypt*, p. 115.

58 Sadat, *op. cit.*, p. 48. Sadat's admiration for Rommel led to his establishing of a war museum at El Alamein in honour of the German Field Marshal. Cook, *op. cit.*, p. 321.

59 Motadel, *Islam and Nazi Germany's War*, p. 111.

60 Morris, *The Road to Jerusalem*, p. 56.

61 Mallman and Cüppers. *Nazi Palestine*, pp. 140–1.

62 Ibid, p. 149.

63 Ibid, pp. 117–8.

64 Satloff, *Among the Righteous*, p. 45.

65 NA HW 1/680 Italian Report from Istanbul on Reactions to Fall of Tobruk.

66 Denniston, *Churchill's Secret War*, p. 71.

67   Ibid, pp. 73–4.
68   Hauner, *op. cit.*, p. 516.
69   Rush, *Records of Iraq*, Vol. 9, p. 737; Hauner, *India in Axis Strategy*, p. 508.
70   Hauner, *op. cit.*, p. 508.
71   Rush, *op. cit.*, p. 742.
72   Hauner, *op. cit.*, p. 501.
73   Edwardes, *The Last Years of British India*, p. 79.
74   Quraishi, *The British Raj in India*, pp. 367–9, p. 382; Ahmad, *Indian Response to the Second World War*, p. 83; Hauner, *op. cit.*, pp. 471–4.
75   Ibid, pp. 580–7.
76   Kheirallah, *Arabia Reborn*, p. 254.
77   Mallman, 'Elimination of the Jewish National Home in Palestine', p. 14.
78   Hauner, *op. cit.*, pp. 499–505.

Chapter 17

1   Liddell Hart, *op. cit.*, p. 233.
2   Barnett, *op. cit.*, p. 171.
3   Connell, *op. cit.*, p. 609.
4   Fennell, *op. cit.*, p. 207.
5   Ibid, pp. 38–9.
6   Liddell Hart, *op. cit.*, p. 261.
7   Ibid, p. 233.
8   Toppe, *op. cit.*, p. 46.
9   Westphal, 'Notes on the Campaign in North Africa', p. 78.
10   Sadkovich, *The Italian Navy in World War II*, p. 271.
11   Ibid, p. 302.
12   Ibid, p. 287.
13   Ministry of Information, *R. A. F. Middle East*, p. 73–4.
14   Hauner, *op. cit.*, p. 494.
15   Operation Agreement was a costly British fiasco that took place at Tobruk on the night of 13 September 1942. Churchill, Field Marshal Sir Bernard Montgomery (of Alamein) and Admiral Cunningham all selectively ignored the event in their memoirs. The combined forces raid was intended to 'deal the enemy a damaging blow, one which might virtually knock him out of the African continent altogether by destroying the port, tank repair workshops and fuel storage'. A humiliating failure, the raid ended instead with some 600 British prisoners being taken, and ten gunboats and the destroyers *Zulu* and

Sikh and the *Coventry* being sunk. German and Italian losses were a
comparatively light: sixteen killed and fifty wounded.

16 Ciano, *op. cit.*, p. 525.
17 Liddell Hart, *op. cit.*, p. 302.
18 Burgwyn, *op. cit.*, p. 188.
19 Ibid.
20 Beckett, *Rommel: A Reappraisal*, p. 108.
21 Reuth, *Rommel: The End of the Legend*, p. 57.
22 Beckett, *op. cit.*, p. 109.
23 NA HW 1/1067/54/20.
24 NA HW1/1058.
25 Toppe, *op. cit.*, p. 50.
26 Liddell Hart, *op. cit.*, p. 350.
27 Gorrell and Gorrell. *Soldier of the Press*, p. 253.
28 Whitehead and Romeiser. *Combat Reporter*, p. 61.
29 Rosenthal, *op. cit.*, p. 98, p. 106; Westphal, 'Notes on the Campaign
    in North Africa', p. 79.
30 Schreiber et al, *op. cit.*, p. 186.
31 Strawson, *The Battle for North Africa*, p. 31. This is surely a remark-
    able statement given Hitler's colossal error in invading the Soviet
    Union in June 1941 – before having subdued Great Britain – and
    the consequences that flowed from his declaration of war on the
    United States later in the same year.
32 Gilbert, *Churchill: A Life*, p. 734.

Bibliography

A. Unpublished Sources

1. Official Records

Australia

Australian War Memorial (AWM), Canberra
52/3/13 2/13 Battalion War Diary
52 8/2/26
52 8/3/13
54 [The Siege of Tobruk – Reports]:

522/7/1 Notes on operations in Cyrenaica and Tobruk with particular reference to Armoured formations taking part, March–July 1941, by Maj. T.W. White.

522/7/5 Summary of events, Defence in the Desert – The retreat. (Written by Maj. Howard.)

522/7/7 The history of the 2/48 Battalion in Tobruk, March 1941.

522/7/8 Main movements ordered and made Western Desert and Tobruk with chronology of AIF Units involved in operations – Libya and Tobruk. (April–May 1941).

522/7/10 Report to HQ Africa Corps by Lt H.O. Behrendt on operations, 6–8 April 1941, during British withdrawal to Tobruk.

523/7/1 Notes on the transport for 9 Aust. Div. and Tobruk Fortress – Notes of the tactics employed in the action at Tobruk – Report on raids, morning 22 April 1941.

523/7/3 A history of the 2/32 Battalion during the Tobruk Campaign – Battle casualties, April 1941.

523/7/4 2/28 Australian Infantry Battalion, History of the Battalion's activities in Tobruk, March to September 1941.

523/7/6 Headquarters 26th Australian Infantry Brigade, Lessons from Tobruk, 1941.

523/7/7 Reports on action, 9th Australian Division – Tobruk 1941.

523/7/9 24th Aust. Inf. Bde. History of activities at Tobruk, Jan. to Sep. 1941.

523/7/11 9th Australian Division, Special Information Summary No. 1 – Information from March 1941–August 1941, Part 1 Brief History of Tobruk; Part 2 Defence Arrangements Tobruk; Part 3 Enemy DOB.

523/7/15 Tobruk Fortress – HQ Branch report. April to October 1941.

523/7/17 Notes on Tactics Employed in Operations at Tobruk in April 1941.

523/7/19 Brief history of Tobruk, March to August 1941.

523/7/24 9 Aust. Division Libya, 1941. Medical Services Tobruk Fortress, April–October. The medical history of the first six months of the siege.

523/7/27 Medical aspects of the siege of Tobruk, 1941.

523/7/28 Brief History of the 9th Division, (Aust) in the Middle East 1941–2.

523/7/29 Reports on 9th Division Operations in Cyrenaica by Lt Gen. Sir L.J. Morshead, March to October 1941. Parts 1, 2 & 4.

523/7/30 Personal papers of Brig. A.H.L. Godfrey.

523/7/33 The AA [anti-aircraft] defence of Tobruk Fortress, 1 April–10 October 1941.

523/7/37 2/1 Australian Pioneer Battalion, Brief report on enemy attack on 'Normie', 25/26 July – report on operations and conditions.

523/7/38 HQ Tobruk Fortress Intelligence Summaries and Sitrep Reports, 1941.

523/7/40 Chronology of AIF Units involved March to November 1941.

523/7/41 9th Division report on operations Cyrenaica and Tobruk, 1941. Engineers report on Tobruk Fortress – General state of defence on occupation by 9th Australian Division and attached troops.

523/7/43 Chester Wilmot's papers, copies and original documents relating to the actions and activities of various units during the siege of Tobruk, April–September 1941.

523/7/44 Narrative of 18th King Edward VII's own Cavalry during the period they were under command of 9th Australian Division, Tobruk 8 April 1941 to 26 August 1941.

United Kingdom

The National Archives, Kew, London

CAB 44/421 Fall of Tobruk, June 1942.

CAB 106/384 Tobruk: extract from a letter by Lt Col. Sir John Lavarack on Operations 1941 and 1942.

CAB 106/570 Tobruk: Correspondence on the South African Historical Section's narrative on the fall of Tobruk 1942.

CAB 106/620 Tobruk: correspondence between the Cabinet Office Historical Section and Field Marshal the Viscount Alanbrooke on the fall of Tobruk 1942, June.

CAB 106/636 Tobruk: report on the defences of the fortress 1942 June, by Maj. J.R. Holden; includes comments on the South African counter-attack.

CAB 106/718 Western Desert: studies on the decision to hold Tobruk and the fall of El Adem 1942, by Captain L.C.F. Turner, South African Historical Section.

CAB 106/812 Western Desert: notes on the siege of Tobruk 1941, by Lt Col. Loder Symonds; includes extracts from war diary of B.O. Battery, 1st Regiment Royal Horse Artillery.

CAB 106/834 Western Desert: summary of the battle of Tobruk 1941 Jan.

CAB 121 Telegram from C-in-C Middle East to the War Office, 7 March 1942.

HW 1/401 North Africa: German requirement for maps of Tobruk and of fortifications and essential services as far as Suez Canal.

HW 1/644 Turkish report Germans consider capture of Tobruk of utmost importance.

HW 1/665 Spanish ambassador, London: British reaction to fall of Tobruk, June 22; Rommel's celebratory address to the troops.

HW 1/680 Italian report from Istanbul on reactions to fall of Tobruk; Portuguese report from Ankara on reactions to the fall of Tobruk

June 26; Japanese report from Berlin summarising the war situation following the fall of Tobruk, June 26.

HW 1/898 North Africa: GAF measures against British landing at Tobruk.

HW 1/1058 Enquiry as to capacity of Tobruk harbour to land heavy tanks.

HW 1/1067/54/20

PREM 3/292/2 Enquiry into loss of Tobruk and Eighth Army retreat – with Principal Telegrams relating to Operations in Middle East 1942 May–June.

WO 106/2238A Fall of Tobruk.

WO 106/4946 22 June 1942

WO 201/345 Capture of Tobruk: Report by 13th Corps Commander.

WO 201/382 Fall of Tobruk: through enemy eyes.

WO 201/1980 Tobruk defences.

WO 201/2254 Appreciations of the situation by Commander of Tobruk Fortress and Gen. Rommel.

Imperial War Museum

Court of Enquiry on 'Operations in the Western Desert 27 May–2 July 1942' held by order of Middle East Command in August 1942.

United States of America

US Army Military History Institute, Carlisle, Pennsylvania

MS # D-045 The Role of Artillery in the Siege of Tobruk.

MS # D-213 The Siege of Tobruch.

MS # D-214 Advance Towards Tobruk by the Italian Division 'Brescia' April 1941.

2. Diaries and Manuscripts

Australia

AWM, Canberra

3DRL/3162 Papers of Capt. F. Hurley (Official Photographer 2 AIF).

AMW PR91/033 Desert memories as remembered by Sgt F.L. Carleton.

AWM PR91/190 20 Australian Infantry Brigade, Document describing a forthcoming cricket match at Tobruk on 30 July 1941, between 20 Aust. Infantry Brigade and 107 Royal Horse Artillery 3DRL 2632 Morshead Papers 1940 to 1944.

EXDOC073 Wavell, Sir Archibald. Instructions to Maj. Gen. Lavarack GOC 7th Division AIF to assume command of all troops in Cyrenaica and hold the enemy's advance at Tobruk.

Flak, J., Pages from a Life, *NSW, 2/4 Field Company, RAE.*

MSS1545 D Company 2/13th Battalion, 'From Tobruk to Scarlet Beach with 2/13th Aust. Infantry Battalion Teams'.

Paget, F.M., Tobruk to Tarakan, *2/28th Infantry Battalion.*

Perversi, F.G., Mirror of Time, *2/33nd Infantry Battalion.*

PR00667 Johnson, John Leslie. Three volumes of correspondence between Johnson and family.

Weston, R., *Nine Lives, 24th Anti-Tank Coy.*

3. Academic Theses

Barter, M.A. *The 2 /2 Australian Infantry Battalion: The History of a Group Experience.* Doctor of Philosophy, Australian National University. 1989.

Christie, H.R. *Fallen Eagles: The Italian 10th Army in the Opening Campaign in the Western Desert, June 1940–December 1940.* Master of Military Art And Science, Bloomsberg University, Pennsylvania, 1999.

Katz, D.B. *Sidi Rezegh and Tobruk: Two South African Military Disasters Revisited 1941–1942.* Master of Military Science (Military History), Stellenbosch University, 2014

B. Published Sources

1. Official Publications

Australia

Bean, C.E.W. *Official History of Australia in the War of 1914–1918,* Vol. V. (Canberra, 1937)

Keogh, E.G. *Middle East 1939–43.* Directorate of Military Training (Melbourne, 1959)

Long, G. *To Benghazi*, 2nd ed. (Canberra, 1986)

Maughan, B. *Tobruk and El Alamein*, 2nd ed. (Canberra, 1987)

Walker, A.S. *Australia in the War of 1939–1945: Army*, (Canberra, 1952)

——. *Middle East and Far East, Australia in the War of 1939–1945 Medical Series*. (Canberra, 1953)

United Kingdom

Hinsley, F.H. *British Intelligence in the Second World War: Its influence on Strategy and Operations*, Vol. I. (London, 1979)

——. *British Intelligence in the Second World War: Its Influence on Strategy and Operations*, Vol. II. (London, 1981)

Ministry of Information. *Destruction of an Army, The First Campaign in Libya: Sept. 1940–Feb. 1941*. (London, 1941)

Ministry of Information. *They Sought Out Rommel: A Diary of the Libyan Campaign*. (London, 1942)

——. Ministry of Information. *The 8th Army: September 1941 to January 1943*. (London, 1944)

——. *R.A.F. Middle East*. (London, 1945)

Playfair, I.S.O. et al. *History of the Second World War: The Mediterranean and Middle East*. Vol. II. (London, 1956)

——. *History of the Second World War: The Mediterranean and Middle East*, Vol. III. (London, 1960)

Richards, D., and H. St. G. Saunders. *Royal Air Force 1939–1945, Volume II: The Fight Avails*. (London, 1954)

Rush, A. de L. *Records of Iraq: 1914–1966, Vol. 9: 1941–1945*. (London, 2001)

Germany

Schreiber, G. et al. *Germany and the Second World War, Volume III: The Mediterranean, South-East Europe, and North Africa 1939–1941*. (Oxford, 1995)

Boog, H. et al. *Germany and the Second World War, Volume VI: The Global War*. (Oxford, 2001)

India

Bisheshwar, P., editor. *The North African Campaign 1940–43, Official History of the Indian Armed Forces in the Second World War 1939–45, Campaigns in the Western Theatre*, 'Combined Inter-Services Historical Section'. (Bombay, 1956)

Hingston, W.G and Stevens, G.R. *The Tiger Kills*. (Bombay, 1944)

New Zealand

Murphy, W.E. *The Relief of Tobruk*, Official History of New Zealand in the Second World War 1939–45. (Wellington, 1961)

South Africa

Agar-Hamilton, J.A.I., and L.C.F. Turner. *Crisis In The Desert*. (Cape Town, 1952)

Martin, A.C. *The Durban Light Infantry, Volume II: 1935 to 1960*. (Durban, 1969)

Orpen, N. *South African Forces World War II, Volume III: War in the Desert*. (Cape Town, 1971)

Orpen, N., and H.J. Martin. *South African Forces World War II, Volume VIII, Part 1: Salute the Sappers*. (Johannesburg, 1981)

South African Public Relations and Information Office. *South Africa at War*. (Washington D.C., 1943)

United States of America

US War Department, Military Intelligence Service. *German Methods of Warfare in the Libyan Desert*. Bulletin No. 20, July. (Washington D.C., 1942)

US War Department, Military Intelligence Service. *Artillery in the Desert*. Special Series No. 6, 25 November. (Washington D.C., 1942)

US War Department, Military Intelligence Service. *The Libyan Campaign May 27 to July 27, 1942*. Campaign Study No. 4, 18 January. (Washington D.C., 1943)

Newell, C.R., *Egypt–Libya: The US Army Campaigns of World War II*, (Defense Department, Army: Center of Military History, 1993)

Miller, W.A. *The 9th Australian Division Versus the Africa Corps: An Infantry Division Against Tanks – Tobruk, Libya, 1941*. (Kansas, 1986)

Toppe, A., et al. *Desert Warfare: German Experiences in World War II*, reprint. (Kansas, 1991)

2. Self-Published Diaries and Accounts

Fletcher, A. *NX 20365*

McGilivray, F.D. *One Man's War, Tobruk Diary 1941, Australia 1942–1943*

Rankin, K. *Top-Hats in Tobruk*

Wilson, H. *A Rat's Tale, Tobruk to Kokoda 1940–1945*

3. Newspapers and Magazines
Die Wehrmacht, 1 July 1942
Life
Newsweek
Time

Newspapers

Australia
Advertiser, 1941–2
The Age, 1941–2
The Argus, 1941–2
The Herald, 1942
The Sun, 1941–2

England
The Daily Express, 1942
The Daily Mail, 1941–2
The Times, 1911, 1941–2
Parade, Middle East Weekly, 1941

Japan
Yomiuri, 1942

South Africa
Natal Mercury, 1942
The Natal Daily News, 1942–3

United States of America
The New York Times, 1942
Chicago Daily Tribune, 1942
The Washington Post, 1942

4. Published Diaries, Memoirs and First-Hand Accounts by Participants
Alanbrooke, Lord. *War Diaries 1939–1945*. (London, 2001)
Aylett, S. *Surgeon at War 1939–45*. (London, 2015)
Badoglio, P. *Italy in the Second World War*. (London, 1948)

Boelcke, W.A., ed. *The Secret Conferences of Dr Goebbels October 1939–March 1943.* (London, 1967)

Brown, J.A. *Retreat to Victory.* (Johannesburg, 1991)

Burn, L. *Down Ramps: Saga of the Eighth Armada.* (London,1947)

Bryant, A. *The Turn of the Tide, Based on the War Diaries of Field Marshal Viscount Alanbrooke.* (London, 1957)

Cadogan, A. *The Diaries of Sir Alexander Cadogan, 1938–1945.* (London, 1971)

Casey, Lord. *Personal Experience 1939–1946.* (New York, 1962)

Churchill, W. *The Second World War, Volume 2: Their Finest Hour.* (Boston, 1949)

——. *The Second World War, Volume 3: The Grand Alliance.* (London, 1950)

——. *The Second World War, Volume 4: The Hinge of Fate.* (Boston, 1950)

Chutter, J.B. *Captivity Captive.* (London, 1954)

Ciano, G. *The Ciano Diaries 1939–1943.* Edited by Hugh Gibson. (New York, 1946)

Clifford, A.G. *Crusader: The Story of the 8th Army's Offensive.* (Libya, 1941) Reprint. (London, 1942)

Clifford, A.G. *The Conquest of North Africa 1940–1943.* (Boston, 1943)

Clune, F. *Tobruk to Turkey.* (Sydney, 1943)

Cooper, F.W. *The Police Brigade: 6 S.A. Infantry Brigade 1939–1945.* (Cape Town, 1972)

Crawford, K. *Report on North Africa.* (New York, 1943)

Crisp, R. *Brazen Chariots,* (New York, 1984)

Cunningham, A.B. *A Sailor's Odyssey.* (London, 1951)

de Guingand, F. *Operation Victory.* (London, 1960)

——. *Generals at War.* (London, 1964)

Devine, J. *The Rats of Tobruk.* (Sydney, 1943)

Dilks, D. ed. *The Diaries of Sir Alexander Cadogan 1938–1945.* (New York, 1971)

Dimbleby, R. *The Frontiers Are Green.* (London, 1943)

Eden, A. *The Reckoning: The Memoirs of Anthony Eden.* (Boston, 1965)

Fearnside, G.H. *Sojourn in Tobruk.* (Sydney, 1944)

——. *Half to Remember.* (Sydney, 1975)

Fergusson, B. *The Trumpet in the Hall.* (London, 1971)

Fredborg, A. *Behind the Steel Wall.* (Sydney, 1944)

Gorlitz, W., ed. *The Memoirs of Field-Marshal Keitel: Chief of the German High Command, 1938–1945.* (New York, 1966)

Gorodetsky, G., ed. *The Maisky Diaries: Red Ambassador to the Court of St James's, 1932–1943.* (New Haven, 2015)

Gorrell, H.T and Kenneth Gorrel. *Soldier of the Press: Covering the Front in Europe and North Africa, 1936–1943.* (Columbia, 2009)

Halder, F. et al., *The Halder War Diary 1939–1942* (California. Novato, 1988)

Hill, R., *Desert War.* (New York, 1942)

Hitler, A. *Hitler's Table Talk 1941–1944.* (London, 1988)

Jacob, A., *A Traveller's War,* (London, 1944)

Kennedy, J. *The Business of War.* (London, 1957)

Kesselring, A. *The Memoirs of Field-Marshal Kesselring.* (London, 1974)

Kippenberger, H.K. *Infantry Brigadier.* (Oxford, 1949)

Liddell Hart, B.H., ed. *The Rommel Papers.* (London, 1953)

——. *History of the Second World War.* (London, 1970)

——. *The German Generals Talk.* (New York, 1979)

——. *The Other Side of the Hill.* (London, 1983)

Menzies, R. *Afternoon Light: Some Memories of Men and Events.* (Melbourne, 1967)

Moran, Lord. *Winston Churchill: The Struggle For Survival 1940–1965*, ed. (London, 1968)

Neame, P. *Playing with Strife.* (London, 1947)

North, J., ed. *The Memoirs of Field Marshal Earl Alexander of Tunis 1940–1945.* (London, 1962)

Palmer, A.B. *The Pirate Of Tobruk: A Sailor's Life On The Seven Seas, 1916–1948.* (Maryland, 1994)

Pollock, N. *Tobruk: A Personal Account.* (Norfolk, 1992)

Rainer, P.W. *Pipeline To Battle.* (London, 1944)

Reeder, F.A. *The Diary of a Rat.* (Canberra, 1977)

Rosenthal, E. *Fortress on Sand.* (London, 1942)

Rosmarin, I. *Inside Story.* (Cape Town, 1999)

Sadat, A. *Revolt on the Nile.* (New York, 1957)

Schmidt, H.W. *With Rommel in the Desert.* (London, 1951)

Schraepler, H.A. *At Rommel's Side: The Lost Letters of Han Joachim Schraepler.* (London, 2009)

Schweppenburg, G. von. *The Critical Years.* (London, 1952)

Shaw, W.B K. *Long Range Desert Group.* (London, 1945)

Spencer, J.H. *Ethiopia at Bay: A Personal Account of the Haile Selassie Years.* (Los Angeles, 2006)

Taylor, F. ed. *The Goebbels Diaries 1939–1941.* (New York, 1993)

Tedder, Lord. *With Prejudice.* (London, 1966)

Thomas, R.T. *Born in Battle: Round the World Adventures of the 513th Bombardment Squadron.* (Philadelphia, 1944)

Thompson, D. *Captives To Freedom.* (London, 1955)

Tucker, F., *Approach to Battle.* (London, 1963)

Von Luck, H. *Panzer Commander.* (New York, 1989)

Von Mellenthin, F.W. *Panzer Battles.* (New York, 1956)

Wavell, A. *Generals and Generalship.* (New York, 1941)

——. *Speaking Generally, Broadcasts, Orders and Address in Times of War (1939–1943).* (London, 1946)

Warlimont, W. *Inside Hitler's Headquarters 1939–1945.* (London, 1964)

Whithead, D. and J.B. Romeiser. *Combat Reporter: Don Whitehead's World War II Diary and Memoirs.* (New York, 2006)

Wilmot, C. *Tobruk.* (Sydney, 1944)

Yindrich, J. *Fortress Tobruk.* (London, 1951)

5. Monographs

Aboul-Enein, Youssef H., and Basil H. Aboul-Enein, *The Secret War for the Middle East: The Influence of Axis and Allied Intelligence Operations During World War II.* (Annapolis, 2013)

Ahmad, M. *Indian Response to the Second World War.* (New Delhi, 1987)

Alexander, B. *How Hitler Could Have Won World War II: The Fatal Errors that Led to Nazi Defeat.* (New York, 2000)

Alhadeff, V. *South Africa in Two World Wars: A Newspaper History.* (Cape Town, 1979)

Askew, W.C. *Europe and Italy's Acquisition of Libya, 1911–1912.* (Durham [North Carolina], 1942)

Austin, L. *Journey to Tobruk: John Murray-Bushman, Soldier, Survivor.* (Sydney, 2009)

Austin, R.J. *Let Enemies Beware! 'Cavenat Hostes', The History of the 2/15th Battalion, 1940–45.* (Melbourne, 1995)

Badman, P. *North Africa 1940–1942, Australians at War.* (Sydney, 1988)

Balfour, M. *Propaganda in War 1939–1945.* (London, 1979)

Barclay, C.N. *Against Great Odds.* (London, 1955)

Barnett, C. *The Desert Generals.* (New York, 1961)

Barter, M. *Far Above Battle: The Experience and Memory of Australian Soldiers in War 1939–1945.* (Sydney, 1994)

Barr, N. *Pendulum of War: The Three Battles of El Alamein. (*London, 2005)

Beelher, W.H. *The History of the Italian–Turkish War, September 29, 1911, to October 18, 1912. (*Annapolis, 1913)

Behrendt, H-O. *Rommel's Intelligence in the Desert Campaign 1941–1943.* (London, 1985)

Belfield, E. *Defy And Endure: Great Sieges of Modern History.* (New York, 1967)

Bennett, R. *Ultra and Mediteranean Strategy 1941–1945.* (London, 1989)

——. *Intelligence Investigations: How Ultra Changed History.* (London, 1996)

Bierman, J., and C. Smith. *Alamein: War Without Hate.* (London, 2002)

Bingham, J.K.W., and W. Haupt. *North African Campaign 1940–1943.* (London, 1968)

Bosworth, R.J.B. *Mussolini.* (New York, 2002)

Bray, B., and M. Darlow. *Ibn Saud: The Desert Warrior Who Created the Kingdom of Saudi Arabia.* (New York, 2013)

Burgwyn, H.J. *Mussolini Warlord: Failed Dreams of Empire, 1940–1943.* (New York, 2013)

Butler, J.R.M. *History of the Second World War: Grand Strategy,* Vol. II. (London, 1957)

Butler, S., and A.M. Schlesinger, Jr. *My Dear Mr. Stalin: The Complete Correspondence between Franklin D. Roosevelt and Joseph V. Stalin.* (New Haven, 2005)

Carver, M. *Tobruk.* (London, 1964)

——. *Dilemmas of the Desert War: A New Look at the Libyan Campaign 1940–1942.* (London, 1986)

——. *The Warlords.* (Barnsley, 2005)

Casey, S. *Cautious Crusade: Franklin D. Roosevelt, American Public Opinion, and the War against Nazi Germany.* (Oxford, 2004)

Chapman, I. *Iven G. Mackay Citizen and Soldier.* (Melbourne, 1975)

Clayton, T., and P. Craig. *The End of the Beginning.* (London, 2002)

Combe, G. et al. *The Second 43rd Australian Infantry Battalion 1940–1946.* (Adelaide, 1972)

Connell, J. *Auchinleck: A Critical Biograph.* (London, 1959)

——. *Wavell, Scholar and Soldier.* (London, 1964)

Coombes, D. *Morshead: Hero of Tobruk and El Alamein.* (Melbourne, 2001)

Cook, S.A. *The Struggle for Egypt: From Nasser to Tahrir Square.* (Oxford, 2011)

Cooper, A. *Cairo in the War 1939–1945.* (London, 1995)

Corvaja, S. *Hitler and Mussolini: The Secret Meetings.* (New York, 2001)

Cowie, D. *The Campaigns of Wavell.* (London, 1942)

Cowles, V. *The Phantom Major: The Story of David Stirling and the S.A.S. Regiment.* (London, 1958)

Cull, B. *Hurricanes over Tobruk: The Pivotal Role of the Hurricane in the Defence of Tobruk, January–June 1941.* (London, 1999)

Day, D. *Menzies & Churchill at War.* (Sydney, 1986)

Denniston, R. *Churchill's Secret War: Diplomatic Decrypts, The Foreign Office and Turkey 1942–1944.* (Gloucestershire, 1999)

Detwiler, D. S., ed. *World War II German Military Studies*, Vol. 7, part IV, *The OKW War Diary Series*. (New York, 1979)

——. *World War II German Military Studies*, Vol. 9, part IV, *The Mediterranean Theatre, continued*. (New York, 1979)

——. *World War II German Military Studies*, Vol. 14, part VI, *The Mediterranean Theatre, continued*. (New York, 1979)

Doherty, M.A *Nazi Wireless Propaganda: Lord Haw – Haw and British Public Opinion in the Second World War Martin*. (Edinburgh, 2000)

Duffy, C. *Siege Warfare: The Fortresses in the Early Modern World 1494–1660*. (New York, 1996)

Edwardes, M. *The Last Years of British India*. (London, 1963)

Elliott, J.G. *A Roll of Honour. The Story of the Indian Army, 1939–1945*. (London, 1965)

Fearnside, G.H., ed. *Bayonets Abroad: A History of the 2/13th Battalion A.I.F. in the Second World War*. (Perth, 1993)

Fennell, J. *Combat and Morale in the North African Campaign: The 8th Army and the Path to El Alamein*. (Cambridge, 2013)

Fischer, K.P. *Hitler and America*. (Pennsylvania, 2011)

Fraser, D. *Knight's Cross, A Life of Field Marshal Erwin Rommel*. (New York, 1995)

——. *Will: A Portrait of William Douglas Home*. (London, 1995)

Freudenberg, G. *Churchill and Australia*. (Sydney, 2008)

Gilbert, M. *Winston S. Churchill*, Volume V, *1939–1941*. (London, 1983)

——. *Winston S. Churchill*, Volume VII, *1941–1945*. (London, 1986)

——. *Churchill: A Life*. (London, 2004)

Gooch, J. *Mussolini and His Generals: The Armed Forces and Fascist Foreign Policy, 1922–1940*. (Cambridge, 2008)

Goodman, R. *A Hospital at War: The 2/4 Australian General Hospital 1940–1945*. (Brisbane, 1983)

Greene, J., and A. Massignani. *Rommel's North African Campaign, September 1940–November 1942*. (Pennsylvania, 1994)

Grehan, J. and Mace, M. *Operations in North Africa and the Middle East 1939–1942: Tobruk, Crete, Syria and East Africa*. (Barnsley, 2015)

Guedalla, P. *Middle East 1940–1942, A Study in Airpower*. (London, 1944)

Graeme-Evans, A.L. *Of Storms and Rainbows, The Story of the Men of 2/12th Battalion A.I.F.*, Vol. I, *October 1939–March 1942*. (Hobart, 1989)

Hamilton, N., *The Mantle of Command: FDR at War, 1941–1942*. (Boston, 2014)

Hancock, W.K. *Smuts: The Fields of Force 1919–1950*. (London, 1968)

Hart, P. *The South Notts Hussars: The Western Desert, 1940–1942.* (Barnsley, 2011)

Hartmann, B. *Panzers in the Sand, Vol Two: 1942–45: The History of Panzer-Regiment 5.* (Mechanicsburg [Pennsylvania], 2011)

Hartshorn, E.P. *Avenge Tobruk.* (Cape Town, 1960)

Hauner, M. *India in Axis Strategy: Germany, Japan and Indian Nationalists in the Second World War.* (London, 1981)

Hawkins, J.M. and Allen, R. eds. *The Oxford Encyclopedic English Dictionary.* (Oxford, 1991)

Heckman, W. *Rommel's War in Africa.* (New York, 1981)

Heckstall-Smith, A. *Tobruk.* (London, 1959)

Herf, J. *Nazi Propaganda for the Arab World.* (New Haven, 2009)

Hetherington, J. *Blamey: The Biography of a Field-Marshal.* (Melbourne, 1954)

Higgins, T. *Winston Churchill and the Second Front.* (New York, 1957)

Horner, D. *High Command: Australia & Allied War Strategy 1939–1945.* (Sydney, 1982)

——. *Blamey.* (Sydney, 1998)

Howard, M. *Strategic Deception in the Second World War.* (London, 1990)

Hurewitz, J.C, editor. *The Middle East and North Africa in World Politics: A Documentary Record*, Second Edition, Revised and Enlarged; Vol. 2, *British-French Supremacy, 1914–1945.* (Yale University Press, 1979)

Irving, D. *The Trail of the Fox: The Life of Field-Marshal Erwin Rommel.* (Hertfordshire, 1977)

Jackson, W.G.F. *The Battle for North Africa 1940–1943.* (New York, 1975)

Jentz, T. *Tank Combat in North Africa, The Opening Rounds, Operations Sonnenblume, Brevity, Skorpion and Battleaxe February 1941–June 1941.* (Atglen, 1998)

Johnston, G.H. *Australia at War.* (Sydney, 1942)

Johnston, M. *At the Frontline: Experiences of Australian Soldiers in World War II.* (Melbourne, 1996)

——. *Fighting the Enemy: Australian Soldiers and Their Adversaries in World War II*, (Cambridge, 2000)

——. and P. Stanley. *Alamein.* (Melbourne, 2002)

Kheirallah, G. *Arabia Reborn.* (Albuquerque, 1952)

Kimball, *Churchill and Roosevelt, The Complete Correspondence*, Vol. 1, *Alliance Emerging October 1933–November 1942.* (Princeton, 1984)

Kinross, P. *Atatürk: The Rebirth of a Nation*, (London, 1971)

Knox, M. *Mussolini Unleashed 1939–1941*, ed. (Cambridge, 1999)

——. *Common Destiny: Dictatorship, Foreign Policy, and War in Fascist Italy and Nazi Germany.* (Cambridge, 2000)

Lebra, J. C. *The Indian National Army and Japan.* (Singapore, 2008)

Levine, A. J. *The War Against Rommel's Supply Lines 1942-1943.* (Westport, 1999)

Lewin, R. *Rommel as Military Commander.* (New York, 1968)

——. *The Chief.* (London, 1980)

Loewenheim, F. L. et al. *Roosevelt and Churchill: Their Secret Wartime Correspondence.* (New York, 1975)

Lord Kinross. *Atatürk: The Rebirth of a Nation.* (London, 1971)

Ludwig, E. *Nine Etched from Life.* (New York, 1934)

Mackenzie, C. *Eastern Epic.* (London, 1951)

Mallman, K-M, and M. Cüppers. *Nazi Palestine: The Plans for the Extermination of the Jews in Palestine.* (New York, 2010)

Masel, P. *The Second 28th: The Story of a Famous Battalion of the Ninth Division.* (Perth, 1961)

Mason, P. *A Matter of Honour: An Account of the Indian Army its Officers and Men.* (London, 1974)

Mckenzie-Smith, J.H.G. *Tobruk's Easter Battle 1941: The Forgotten Fifteenth's Date with Rommel's Champion.* (Brisbane, 2011)

McNeil, W.H. *America, Britain and Russia: Their Co-operation and Conflict 1941–1946.* (New York, 1970)

Meskill, J. *Hitler and Japan: The Hollow Alliance.* (New York, 1966)

Mitcham, S.W. Jr., *Rommel's Greatest Victory: The Desert Fox and the Fall of Tobruk, Spring 1942.* (Novato [California], 1998)

Moore, J.H. *Morshead.* (Sydney, 1976)

Moorehead, A. *Don't Blame the Generals.* (New York, 1943)

——. *African Trilogy: The North African Campaign* 1940–43. (London, 1965)

Morgan, T. *FDR: A Biography.* (London, 1986)

Morris, B. *The Road to Jerusalem: Glubb Pasha, Palestine and the Jews.* (London, 2003)

Motadel, D. *Islam and Nazi Germany's War.* (Harvard, 2014)

Naylor, P.C. *North Africa: A History from Antiquity to the Present.* (Texas, 2009)

Overy, R. *Why the Allies Won.* (London, 1995)

Pakkula, H. *The Last Empress: Madame Chiang Kai-Shek and the Birth of Modern China.* (London, 2010)

Piekalkiewicz, J. *Rommel and the Secret War in North Africa, 1941–1943.* (West Chester, 1992)

Pimlott, J., ed. *Rommel in His Own Words.* (London, 1994)

Pitt, B. *The Crucible of War:Western Desert 1941*. (London, 1980)

——. *The Crucible of War:Auchinleck's Command*. (London, 2001)

Plating, J.D. *The Hump:America's Strategy for Keeping China in World War II*. (Texas, 2011)

Pogue, F.C. *George C. Marshall: Ordeal and Hope 1939–1942*. (New York, 1966)

Quraishi, B. *The British Raj in India:An Historical Review*. (Oxford, 1995)

Raugh, H.E. *Wavell in the Middle East:A Study in Generalship*. (London, 1993)

Reynolds, D. *Lord Lothian and Anglo-American Relations, 1939–1940*. (Philadelphia, 2009)

Roy, K., ed. *The Indian Army in the Two World Wars*. (Leiden, 2012)

Satloff, R. *Among the Righteous: Lost Stories from the Holocaust's Long Reach into Arab Lands*. (New York, 2006)

Sadkovich, J.J. *The Italian Navy in World War II*. (Westport. 1994)

Segré, C.G. *Italo Balbo,A Fascist Life*. (Los Angeles, 1987)

Serle, R.P., ed. *The Second Twenty-Fourth Australian Infantry Battalion of the 9th Australian Division*. (Brisbane, 1963)

Sherwood, R.E. *Roosevelt and Hopkins:An Intimate History*. (New York, 1948)

Smyth, J. *Leadership in War 1939–1945:The Generals in Victory and Defeat*. (Melbourne, 1974)

Stevenson,W. *A Man Called Intrepid:The Secret War 1939–1945*. (London, 1984)

Strawson, J., *The Battle for North Africa*. (New York, 1969)

Taylor,A.J.P. *English History 1914–1945*. (Oxford, 1965)

——*Beaverbrook*. (London, 1972)

Thompson, J. *Forgotten Voices: Desert Victory*. (London, 2011)

Tittoni, R., translator. *The Italo-Turkish War, 1911–12*. (Kansas City, 1914)

Trevor-Roper, H.R., ed. *Hitler's War Directives 1939–1945*. (London, 1964)

Tute,W. *The North African War*. (Toronto, 1976)

Uys, I. *South African Military Who's Who 1452–1992*. (Capetown, 1992)

Van Creveld, M. *Hitler's Strategy 1940–1941:The Balkan Clue*. (Cambridge, 1973)

——*Supplying War: Logistics from Wallenstein to Patton*. (New York, 1980)

Various. *'What We Have … We Hold'. A History of the 2/17 Australian Infantry Battalion 1940–1945*. (Balgowlah [NSW])

Venkataramani, M.S. and B.K. Shrivastava. *Roosevelt, Gandhi, Churchill: America and the Last Phase of India's Freedom Struggle.* (New Delhi, 1983)

Verney, G.L. *The Desert Rats.* (London, 1957)

Von Taysen, A. *Tobruk 1941: Der Kampf in Nordafrika.* (Freiburg, 1976)

Warner, G. *Iraq and Syria 1941.* (New Jersey, 1979)

Warner, P. *Auchinleck. The Lonely Soldier.* (London, 1981)

Weal, J., *Junkers Ju 87: Stukageschwader of North Africa and the Mediterranean.* (London, 1998)

Weller, G. *Singapore is Silent.* (New York, 1943)

Winton, J. *Cunningham.* (London, 1998)

Wright, J. *Libya: A Modern History.* (London, 1981)

Young, D. *Rommel, The Desert Fox.* (New York, 1950)

Zimmerman, D. *Secret Exchange: The Tizard Mission and the Scientific War.* (Kingston [Ontario], 1996)

6. Journal articles

Collier, P. 'The Capture of Tripoli in 1941: Open Sesame or Tactical Folly?' *War & Society* 20, No. 1 (May 2002)

Condé, A.M. 'The Ordeal of Adjustment. Australian Psychiatric Casualties of the Second World War.' *War & Peace* 15, No. 2 (October 1997)

Cooper, E.L., and A.J.M. Sinclair. 'War Neuroses in Tobruk: A Report on 207 Patients from the Australian Imperial Force Units in Tobruk.' *The Medical Journal of Australia* (1 August 1942)

Evans-Pritchard, E.E. 'The Sanusi of Cyrenaica.' *Africa: Journal of the International African Institute* 15, No. 2 (April 1945)

Fitchett, I. 'The Siege of Tobruk.' *Infantry Journal* (April 1942)

Gunsburg, J.A. 'The Battle of Gembloux, 14–15 May 1940.' *The Journal of Military History* 64, No. 1 (January 2000)

Hauner, M. 'Afghanistan between the Great Powers, 1938–1945.' *International Journal of Middle East Studies* 14 (November 1982)

Herrmann, D.G. 'The paralysis of Italian Strategy in the Italian-Turkish War, 1911–1912.' *English Historical Review* 104, No. 411 (April 1989)

Horn, K. 'Narratives from North Africa: South African prisoner-of-war experience following the fall of Tobruk, June 1942.' *Historia* 56, No. 2, (November 2011)

Katz, D. 'The Greatest Military Reversal of South African Arms: The Fall of Tobruk 1942, an Avoidable Blunder or an Evitable Disaster?' *Journal for Contemporary History* (2012)

Mahncke, J. 'Tobruk 1942.' *The South African Journal of Military History* 7, No. 6 (December 1988)

Mohlamme, J.S. 'Soldiers Without Reward: Africans in South Africa's Wars.' *Military History Journal* (The South African Military History Society) Vol. 10, No. 1. (June 1995)

Paris, M. 'The First Air Wars – North Africa and the Balkans 1911–13,' *Journal of Contemporary History* 26, No. 1 (January 1991)

Robertson, K.M. 'The 2nd Field Company, R.E., 1940–2: From Desert to the Jungle.' *Journal of the Royal Engineers* (1954)

Robinson, J.R. 'The Rommel Myth.' *Military Review* LXXVII, No. 5 (September–October 1997)

——. 'The Rommel Myth-Continued.' Letters to the Editor. *Military Review* LXXVIII (September–November 1998)

Sadkovich, J. 'Understanding Defeat: Reappraising Italy's Role in World War II.' *Journal of Contemporary History* 24 (January 1989)

Sbacchi, A. 'Haile Selassie and the Italians 1941–43'. *African Studies Review* 22, No. 1 (April 1979)

Schmider, K. 'The Mediterranean in 1940–1941: Crossroads of Lost Opportunities.' *War & Society* 15, No. 2 (October 1997)

Sinclair, A.J.M. 'The Psychological Reactions of Soldiers.' *The Medical Journal of Australia* (1 August 1942)

"Stewart, A. '"The Klopper Affair": Anglo-South African Relations and the Surrender of the Tobruk Garrison.' Twentieth Century British History, 17, No. 4. (2006)

Stewart, A. 'The "Atomic Dispatch": Field Marshal Auchinleck, the Fall of the Tobruk Garrison and Post-War Anglo-South African Relations.' *South African Journal of Military Studies* 36, No. 1 (2008)

Van Creveld, M. 'Rommel's Supply Problem, 1941–42.' *Journal of the Royal United Services Institute for Defence Studies* 119, No. 3 (September 1974)

Weller, J.E. 'Tobruk 1941.' *Journal of the Royal Engineers* (1991)

Westphal, S. 'Notes on the Campaign in North Africa.' *Journal of the Royal United Service Institution* 105 (February 1960)

Wingate, R. 'Libya in the Last War: The Talbot Mission and the Agreements of 1917.' *Journal of the Royal African Society* 40, No. 159 (April 1941)

7. Internet Sources
Diary of Edmund Crawford Lecky. *Lecky's letters: Saturday 26 April 1941.* Australian War Memorial (AWM, 2011). www.awm.gov.au/blog/category/1941-tobruk/ (accessed 1 January 2014)

Matloff, M., and E.M. Snell. 'Strategic Planning for Coalition Warfare 1941–1942.' Washington D.C.: Center of Military History, United States Army, 1990. www.army.mil/cmh-pg/books/wwii/sp1941-42/index.htm (accessed 5 February 2014)

Memo, Halifax [Earl, Ambassador the United States] to Franklin D. Roosevelt, April 17, 1941, Box 35, President's Secretary's File (PSF) Safe Files: State Dept., 1941, Franklin D. Roosevelt Library Digital Archives, at http://docs.fdrlibrary.marist.edu/PSF/BOX35/T319Q02.HTML (accessed 23 November 2015)

Prime Minister Churchill. 'Debate In The House Of Commons (and results of Vote of Censure).' Parliamentary Debates, House of Commons Official Report July 2, 1942. http://ibiblio.org/pha/policy/1942/420702a.html (accessed 1 March 2013)

Index